Radio Shows

Radio Shows

Satsvarūpa dāsa Goswami

Persons interested in the subject matter of this book are invited to correspond with our secretary:

GN Press, Inc.
R.D. 1, Box 837-K
Port Royal, PA 17082

Printed in the United States of America
ISBN: 0-911233-60-1

GN Press gratefully acknowledges the BBT for the use of verses and purports from Śrīla Prabhupāda's books.

Library of Congress Cataloging-in-Publication Data

Gosvāmī, Satsvarūpa Dāsa
Radio Shows/Satsvarūpa dāsa Goswami.
p. cm.
ISBN 0-911233-60-1
1. International Society for Krishna Consciousness. I. Title.
BBL1285.84.g663 1995
294.5'512--dc20 95-12223
CIP

Author's Note

This is my private radio station. The red light is on over the door, warning, "Recording, Do Not Enter." It's 3:24 P.M. Time costs money. I had better get started.

I remember as a teenager listening to Jean Shepherd's radio shows. I was about seventeen when I started tuning into them. My sister, Madeline, who was two years older than me, made fun of my devotion to him. She painted an image of him speaking so close to the microphone that the microphone got wet as he slobbered his egoistic, self-centered intimacies over the airwaves. She thought he was just too *close*, too sticky. Of course, it didn't phase me and I went on listening as avidly as before.

Shepherd was a kind of religious experience for me. Listening to him was one of the first steps I took in breaking away from my parents' anti-intellectualism. My parents believed in working hard for the good things in life, and they didn't believe in wasting time on things unconnected to that end. They were first generation Americans and conformed to the "American way." The intellectuals, they thought, were somehow anti-American.

My parents had no real opinion about Jean Shepherd because they didn't listen to him. My mother preferred "The Make-Believe Ballroom" which played the top twenty-five pop hits from the 1940s and 50s. Shepherd's social commentary and underground humor were my own secret, and I listened to him from the privacy of my room.

Shepherd was attractive to youth. He would have us participate in his discussions by doing things like "hurling an invective." We would usually do this late at night. He would prime us to yell something at the people "out there," assuring us that no one would catch us because our invective would come over the radio. He would tell us to turn out the lights and put our radios on the windowsill. Then he would whisper, "Have you got it set up?" Suddenly he would yell, "It's not what you think it is! It's not what you think it is!" Then back to a whisper: "Okay, bring the radio in."

Shepherd spoke to the night people. We hurled our invectives at the day people—people like my parents who took the world for what it appeared to be. We were crying out, telling the world that their values and their work ethics were illusion. It's *all* illusion—your trying to be happy, your thinking that the world is secure with its buildings and jobs, its day people. "It's not what you think it is."

I would like to have a Kṛṣṇa conscious radio show modeled after that wonderful experience of my teenage years when I listened to a person who embodied the values I didn't dare live. I connected with those values through my radio. Jean Shepherd spoke to the insomniacs and frustrated youth just barely beginning to imagine a world outside their parents' purview. Can there be a Kṛṣṇa conscious version of that?

When I imagine my audience, I don't think of people who have never heard of Kṛṣṇa consciousness. Too much would have to be gone over before such people would be ready to hear what I really want to talk about, although as I say it, it's an intriguing idea, isn't it? Imagine being a close, underground friend to young high school kids, speaking to them about Kṛṣṇa over the radio and their parents not knowing they're listening. I wouldn't mind being able to do that.

I have the satisfying and life-saving task to speak in a Kṛṣṇa conscious way. Although I may talk about the same things any human being talks about, I see the world through the eyes of *śāstra*. And I know Śrīla Prabhupāda. That's the difference between me and Jean Shepherd. Jean Shepherd could not, of course, deliver the message of Godhead, so instead, he glorified trivia as if trying to elevate it to something important. He opened me up when I was a teenager, but he couldn't take me where I needed ultimately to go.

Back to my audience: I imagine someone cruising the dial—*bomp-bom-bom-bomp-ba-bom-bom . . .* then, "It looks like another snowstorm will be coming our way tonight. Two feet of snow expected. Now we'll switch to our Washington bureau . . . " Then he turns the dial and finds himself tuned into the Hare Kṛṣṇa station. In that split second, the devotee has to be saying something that will attract him. Different devotees approach this problem differently. I've heard that on the Spanish Fork radio station, they sometimes play lectures, but they also play New Age music. Other radio stations are straight Kṛṣṇa consciousness. Usually they try to capture the fickle listeners with lively discussions. I have different plans for my radio show.

—Satsvarūpa dāsa Goswami

1

Prabhupāda singing:

> *hare kṛṣṇa hare kṛṣṇa, kṛṣṇa kṛṣṇa hare hare*
> *hare rāma hare rāma, rāma rāma hare hare*

Writers sometimes do an exercise based on getting in touch with what actually makes them happy. They do it to get in touch with who they are as people and with their happy moments in a day. The exercise is to honestly admit where you found happiness, not where you were *supposed* to have found it.

I tried that exercise a few times, but I stopped after awhile. I think I stopped because I usually feel distant from experience. Here's an example. Last night we went on *harināma.* As we walked, I was conscious of my relief that the streets of Verona are so civilized. I could tell there would be no violence such as might happen on some American streets. In America, the air is filled with threat. Neither could these Veronese reach out and cut me with cruel comments; I don't speak Italian. Anyway, the Italians and I have different subtle makeups. Although Americans are so gross, so different from me, they have my number because I was born there and carry the same cultural understandings they do. Therefore, I was relieved that this *harināma* wasn't a heavy scene.

I couldn't really concentrate much on the meaning of being on *harināma.* I was mostly just functioning, walking behind the cart, looking at the wheel and seeing the rubber piece that was rubbing against the wheel. I also watched the children riding on the cart. There were two of them, both tiny. One of them looked completely spaced out. The other was alert and seemed to be enjoying himself. His enjoyment reminded me of an old man's enjoyment—just taking it easy and looking around. Then he got bored and wanted to be entertained in another way. Still, he was a little darling.

The back of the palanquin had a purple curtain. It had no walls, so the purple curtain was blowing in the breeze and looked beautiful. I thought of the people seeing the cape effect the curtain made and catching a glimpse of Gaura-Nitāi. I liked thinking about that, but mostly I wasn't deeply into the experience.

I liked the fact, too, that I didn't have a headache. I liked the fact that I could see I was going to make it through my promised hour of participation and that it wasn't going to be a big deal for me. I liked the fact that devotees weren't treating me special. I was just chanting, and in that nice protection that you have when devotees respect you but don't speak your language, I was able to be in my own world, functioning and contributing something simple.

Those are some of the elements of last night's happiness. I kept wondering, "Is it too cold? Should I put my knit hat on?" I was aware that I was functioning as "the mechanical man," who notices whether it's hot or cold, who walks on feet, who has a body with internal organs. I think, "So far, so good, as long as it lasts." I don't say these words, but I feel with those emotions.

There's one devotee here who has been in the hospital for forty days with a brain cyst. Another devotee from here died last year with a similar tumor. I hear these things and wonder when it's going to be my turn to get cancer or some terrible pain. When will it be my friend's turn? When is something really bad going to happen? I don't worry about it, but I am aware and I think, "So far, so good." This isn't an expression of anxiety, just an awareness that I am living on borrowed time. I should enjoy it while I can in a Kṛṣṇa conscious way, and even more than enjoy, I should produce. I should do something before I have to leave.

Recently, I was explaining to someone my desire to write. I expressed that one reason I write is that I have a strong desire to preserve the moment. Preserving the moment is part of the writer's life. The devotee I was speaking to didn't understand that desire at all. She said, "Why would anyone want to preserve the moment? Perhaps if a person has an elevated existence, then he would want to preserve it because it's so wonderful."

I don't want to preserve my life because my life is very wonderful, but I am surprised that this devotee didn't know the feeling. Maybe it's something only artists feel. Life is precious. Blood drips as it passes, drop by drop, through our veins. What about the passage of time through an hourglass? The beauty of it! Although we're removed from it, we know, in a sense, that this is all there is. Life is passing and then it will be gone. Life will be gone. Day after day, I bow down to Madhumaṅgala and he bows down to me. We don't say it, but it's another day taken off, then another and another. Our days are not unlimited. We have a small amount of time in this life and it's already coming to an end. Rather than lose, lose, lose,

āyur harati vai puṁsām
udyann astaṁ ca yann asau
tasyarte yat-kṣaṇo nīta
uttama-śloka-vārtayā

An artist wants to hold onto what happens between sunrise and sundown, and if he can write it down, it will be saved.

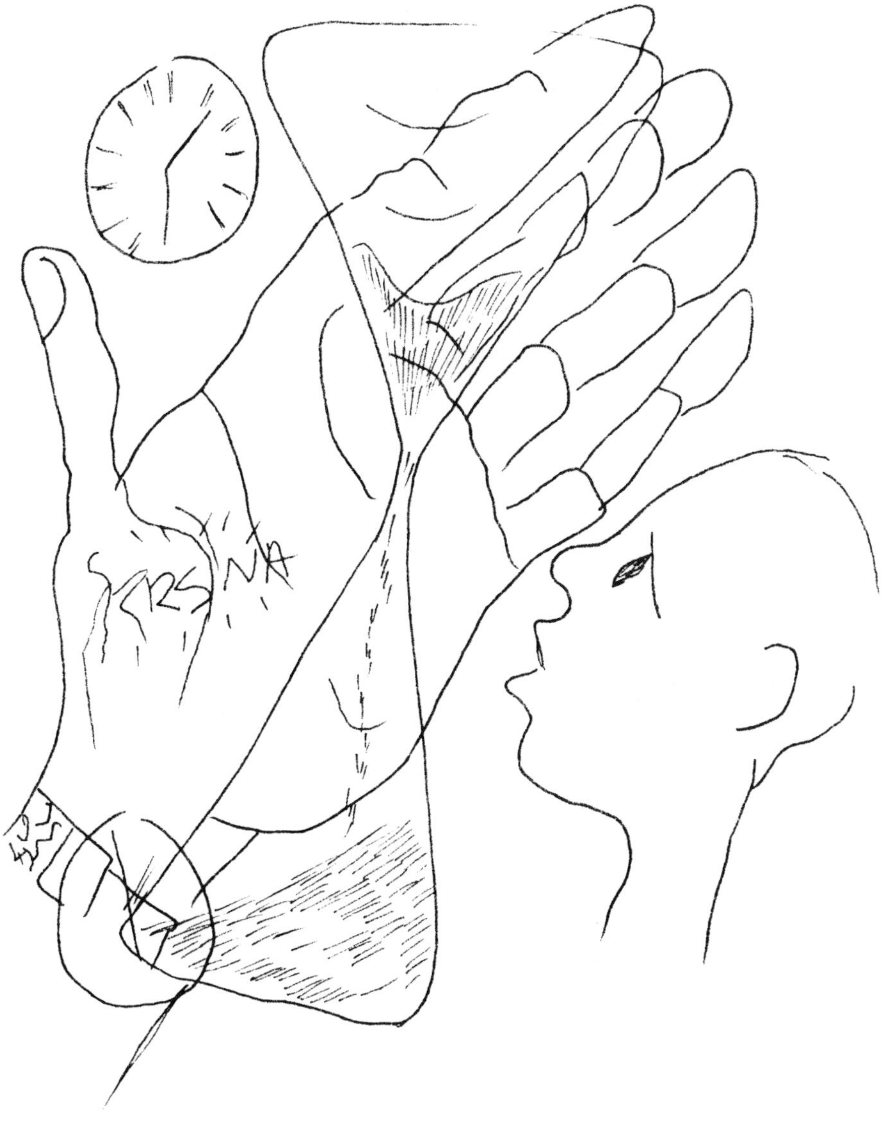

People call this a futile gesture because everything ultimately gets destroyed. An artist doesn't care. He is satisfied at having captured the moment and giving it to others. Doing this has even more meaning in Kṛṣṇa consciousness. There's something genuine about the Kṛṣṇa conscious desire to write something lasting and from which people, even hundreds of years later, can benefit. I don't think it's madness. It's an act so genuine that I don't even want to examine it in case I ruin it. It *could* become something egotistical, but that's what I mean by my desire to capture the moment. At least it makes me understand that life is not just trash or a series of trivial events. Although I can't feel it when I walk on the street with the *harināma* party, still, I know that even if I describe the mechanical level of existence, it will be meaningful. The essential Kṛṣṇa conscious impressions will be beautiful and worth saving.

I only wish the world's artists could all be Kṛṣṇa conscious, those who have that desire to hold onto life as it passes through their hands, knowing that they can't hold onto it, but who want to give it to the world anyway, as art. It is a gift. That gift is useless unless it helps people to strive for eternality, bliss, and knowledge. This has become the assumption of my writing life and the code I live by.

Prabhupāda singing:

hare kṛṣṇa hare kṛṣṇa, kṛṣṇa kṛṣṇa hare hare
hare rāma hare rāma, rāma rāma hare hare

2

Prabhupāda singing:

hare kṛṣṇa hare kṛṣṇa, kṛṣṇa kṛṣṇa hare hare
hare rāma hare rāma, rāma rāma hare hare

I have decided to have a "Vaiṣṇava studies" section on this show, where I can talk directly about Kṛṣṇa conscious scripture.

I'm going to use a notebook I've started. On the front I've written: "Quotes that arrest me, that make me want to remember them. Something to keep me going at as high an interest as possible in Prabhupāda's books. Don't neglect creative, prayerful reading. It's my link to Śrīla Prabhupāda as much as anything is." This notebook consists of quotes that I copied out while reading Prabhupāda's books.

Prayerful reading is something I reach out for but haven't attained. It means stopping and not letting the sentences go by quickly. It means trying to get closer to them and drawing from them.

And we can talk about prayer and utter spontaneous prayers. Let's keep a prayer-like quality on our minds.

The first quote comes from *Śrīmad Bhāgavatam,* Third Canto, Chapter 23. This is the chapter describing the marriage of Kardama Muni and Devahūti. These quotes almost all come from Śrīla Prabhupāda's purports. Here's the first one:

"By serving her devotee husband, Kardama Muni, Devahūti shared in his achievements. Similarly, a sincere disciple, simply by serving a bona fide spiritual master, can achieve all the mercy of the Lord and the spiritual master simultaneously" *(Bhāg.* 3.23.7).

I am attracted to statements about the exclusive shelter of the guru. They remind me to always take shelter of Prabhupāda. They also remind me to read his books and to serve him without interruption. We have to serve while we live. We're serving our senses or we're serving our boss. We're serving our art. If we can offer whatever we do as service under the guidance of a spiritual master, then we get mercy. The spiritual master gives us his mercy and then Kṛṣṇa blesses us. If ever I wonder whether Prabhupāda is pleased with me now, all I can do is hope. My whole life depends on his accepting my activities as service to him.

Somebody wrote me today saying he appreciated something I wrote in *From Imperfection, Purity Will Come About.* He said it's something that he's often thought, but he's never been so bold as to express it, even to his spiritual master. He was therefore encouraged that he found it publicly stated in my book. I don't have the book here (or his letter), but it had to do with wanting to place my whole person, *all* that I am, on the altar of sacrifice to my spiritual master.

Usually when we say we want to give everything to guru or Kṛṣṇa, we mean everything *he* wants, everything acceptable or credible. If we have money, we give him our money. We don't think of giving him the opposite of our money, or our poverty. If we have energy, we do something active for him. We run an errand or preach on his behalf. These are all good things.

We don't offer things that are not good. But what if there are many parts of ourselves that we put in the category of unacceptable? Do we go on performing devotional service through the few narrow pipelines left to us? What about the rest of us—the unacceptable parts, the monster, the garbage? Do we simply throw it away? Is it like toxic waste? We need to dump it, but as soon as someone finds out we have it, they say, "Don't dump that in our backyard. Don't pollute our farmland. Don't bury it here. Don't throw it in our oceans. Don't throw it in our rivers. Don't burn it in our air. Don't leave it in our forests." What do we do with it then?

I want to offer more of myself to Prabhupāda. I want to feel I have *really* surrendered. Although I said here that much of me is condemnable, within myself, subconsciously or intimately, I don't wholly believe that. I keep wanting to use those "condemnable" parts of myself in service. Unfortunately, they are not yet in the category of something considered acceptable.

For example, what about my desire to sometimes be frivolous? Can I be a clown for my spiritual master? Is there some way I can use that energy and make it spiritual? If I like to hum a popular tune—not whether I like to, but if such tunes force themselves into my mind—can I purify it and make it an innocent offering to my spiritual master? The self who I am, the memories I have, my relationship to the earth (which is temporary), my fears—what about all these things? My desire to offer that which makes up the self to Prabhupāda can be itself a kind of purification, and I hope he will accept it.

This radio show is another example. Can rambling talk, honest talk, which if monitored over certain stretches does not contain direct *kṛṣṇa-kathā,* be offered just because it's who I am, and because I basically want to be a devotee? Or does it have to be edited out? Even if it's edited out for public consumption, does that mean that Kṛṣṇa doesn't recognize it at all?

One answer to these questions is, "Yes, edit it out. Throw it away. Don't come to Kṛṣṇa with bleeding sores." I know that's part of the answer. You get it together, then you go to guru and Kṛṣṇa. I also tell people this.

A wife wrote to me, "I can't deal with my husband. He needs professional help for his psychiatric problems, but we thought maybe you could help him." But I can't help him. A spiritual guide teaches on the spiritual level. If you want to know about the Absolute Truth, you go to a spiritual guide. Don't go to him for lesser things that are troubling you. In the same way, when you really want to put your offering on the altar, you have to pray to Kṛṣṇa with the good things. Don't be asking for material benedictions or show Kṛṣṇa what a nonsense, obscene, doubtful person you are. You do have to work some of yourself out first. I know that.

But I am talking about something further, about converting the imperfection in yourself to Kṛṣṇa consciousness. In other words, something is done to the unacceptable parts of yourself before you offer them. Then the energy is used. You end up giving more than this stiff, straight-laced offering of a small part of yourself and omitting so much.

I think my kind and intelligent audience understands what I'm talking about and I don't want to belabor the point. Maybe like the devotee who wrote me, thanking me for expressing what was on his mind, this is on your mind too. We can both think about it some more and try to make more wholehearted offerings.

Prabhupāda singing:

> *hare kṛṣṇa hare kṛṣṇa, kṛṣṇa kṛṣṇa hare hare*
> *hare rāma hare rāma, rāma rāma hare hare*

Back to the quote book:

"In prison a prisoner is shackled by iron chains and iron bars. Similarly, a conditioned soul is shackled by the charming beauty of a woman, by her solitary embraces and talks of so-called love, and by the sweet words of his small children. Thus he forgets his real identity" *(Bhāg.* 3.30.8).

I wrote that down because it's such a knock-out. I remember the first time I read that statement. I was a *gṛhastha*. You can imagine how it hit me then, how it made me feel guilty to have my state exposed. Just for the pleasure of solitary embraces, you would shackle yourself like a prisoner in the material world and accept repeated birth and death.

It made me realize that the little fringe benefits the slaving *gṛhastha* gets are very costly. His wife speaks sweetly to him, saying things she never says to anybody else. Prabhupāda satirizes it—I heard him on a tape. The husband says, "You are my everything. Without you I cannot live." The wife says, "You are everything to me. I cannot live without you." Then he said, "A few days later they have disagreement and divorce."

Those words of love are sometimes cheating. As we hear in so many pop songs, cheating hearts and cheating words. Even the songs we hear proclaiming true love turn out to be lies in the end.

Part of the lie is hearing your children's sweet words. There's nothing wrong with that—nothing wrong with having a cute, effulgent child who says bright things, things that touch your heart, but they act as shackles because you think of the child and of your present place in that family and you don't work for spiritual life. That's the point.

Another one:

"He is in the heart of every living entity, but He can be realized only by a soul who is repentant" (*Bhāg.* 3.31.13, purport).

What can I say about that? Repentance. I wish I had it. Repentance is a philosophical mood. We should feel sorry we came to the material world. If we can feel the emotion of repentance, it means we feel with our real selves, the soul. We don't belong in this world. A repentant person hears talk of Kṛṣṇa and the spiritual world and feels left out. He feels millions of miles away from Kṛṣṇa. He understands that he is spirit soul and that he doesn't belong in the material world, yet because of his misuse of free will, he's so far away from home. How will he ever return? Repentance is painful.

It may take many, many lifetimes to recover our original nature of love of Kṛṣṇa by going through the process from *śraddhā* to *prema.* We feel sorry, "How did I get here? And why? I don't feel good about it. It's so hard here in Kali-yuga to even study a page, what to speak of having a day of intense devotional service and *kṛṣṇa-smaraṇam.* I'm just sorry I left the Lord in favor of this place." That's repentance.

Kṛṣṇa works to get us back, but we don't always like the way He works. I heard Prabhupāda saying today that Kṛṣṇa and His representatives are sometimes as soft as a rose and sometimes as hard as a thunderbolt. He was saying that if the Lord is hard on us, it's for our good, just like a parent may sometimes be strict with a child for the child's good. I thought to myself, "What does that mean?" We like it when someone is lenient with us, but often Kṛṣṇa is not lenient. He was strict with Arjuna: "Why are you acting like a non-Āryan? Don't take advantage of our friendship. Do your duty." At the end of the *Bhagavad-gītā,* Arjuna was grateful that Kṛṣṇa had been so strict with him and hadn't supported him in his desire not to fight. Kṛṣṇa was strict and in the end Arjuna was grateful. "Now my illusion is gone, Kṛṣṇa, due to Your mercy."

The mercy often comes in the form of Kṛṣṇa's strict or hard handling of us. When it comes like that, when we get dumped on in this material world or get knocked away from the solitary embraces and the children's sweet words, we may blame Kṛṣṇa. But we should understand that He's doing it only to break our attachment. Being lenient with us means leaving us here to rot.

Prabhupāda singing:

hare kṛṣṇa hare kṛṣṇa, kṛṣṇa kṛṣṇa hare hare
hare rāma hare rāma, rāma rāma hare hare

What made me happy today? It was a slow day, so I don't think of it so much in terms of happiness, but of getting work done. I answered a lot of letters. I have to admit that I was answering them to get through the mail, yet when I did surrender to the individual letters, I tried to be personal with the various devotees. I know it's a risk to admit I feel like getting the mail out of the way. Devotees might think I don't care for them. But it's not true. My next thought was that by getting through the letters, I would be able to go on to something else, like reading and writing, which appear to be *my* thing, but which are the reasons I am able to answer the mail at all. When I handled each letter, I thought of the person and said what I could. Then I moved on. I like it when someone I correspond with says to me, "It's nice to be with you. It's nice to hear from you. But it's even better to read your books and be with you in that way."

Anyway, the mail took up a good portion of the day. It's kind of a leftover day today after my week of giving morning and evening classes. Today I was left alone on the plea of my needing time to recover from dental work. It's an in-between period—in a few days I will be starting more dental surgery. I'll lose my front teeth and I'll probably be unable to speak even on this radio show.

Everyday pleasures for me are sense pleasures of the tongue. A nice breakfast, a nice lunch, the taste of the food on my tongue. What can I say? I like those things. I like the shower too, partly because it's good for me—the hot water, then the cold water. I know that I advocate living in the moment, but I don't do it so much.

I like how early this morning I read *Bhāgavatam* and felt like I was getting back into my regular routine. I also felt the satisfaction of writing a writing session early in the morning and getting back into that.

That's all for today.

3

Prabhupāda singing:

namo gaura-kiśorāya sākṣād-vairāgya-mūrtaye
vipralambha-rasāmbhode pādāmbujāya te namaḥ

I am Kṛṣṇa conscious by Prabhupāda's grace. I had a dream last night that I was an accomplice to a robbery and murder. Just before we were supposed to carry out the crime, by Prabhupāda's grace, we decided we didn't want to kill. Exactly what Prabhupāda's grace was wasn't clear in the dream, but when I think of it now, I realize how deeply he has influenced my life.

Sometimes we hear about planetary influences and how the planets are malefic or benefic in order to enforce our karma. The spiritual master's influence is causeless. Especially after he has left this world, and especially as his influence enters the dream world, although we feel his presence, we cannot define it. We're just grateful for it.

Later in that dream, we were listening to Prabhupāda on tape. He was talking about the importance of hearing from the spiritual master. This time he was present in his sound vibration.

I listen to Prabhupāda's lectures often. I hear and comprehend them, and to whatever degree I am capable, I appreciate them. Sometimes I fail to pay attention and thus fail to appreciate, but as long as I'm not offensive, exposing myself to the sun rays of his speech will have its effect.

akāmaḥ sarva-kāmo vā
mokṣa-kāma udāra-dhīḥ
tīvreṇa bhakti-yogena
yajeta puruṣaṁ param

Tīvreṇa. The powerful rays of the sun purify, so the powerful rays of *bhakti-yoga* and *guru-sevā*, hearing from the spiritual master, have their good effect, as much as any good planet gives benefic effects.

Prabhupāda singing:

namo bhaktivinodāya sac-cid-ānanda-nāmine
gaura-śakti-svarūpāya rūpānuga-varāya te

When I go into a room to stay on a visit and there's a mirror over the bureau, I cover it with a cloth. The reason I put a cloth over the mirror is that I don't want to see my face. I see enough of my face mentally when I write. I don't need to also have the visual image before me. I think of teachers like Bhaktisiddhānta Sarasvatī Ṭhākura who I heard never used a mirror even to put on *tilaka.* It's not that I avoid my face because I hate it; it's just that I've seen it enough.

Mirrors can enamor us to our faces. It sounds silly, because most of us will admit, especially as we grow older, that we're not that good-looking anymore. It's funny how it happens. I remember a segment in a movie where Bing Crosby looks at himself in the mirror. He talks to his reflection and at one point, makes fun of his looks. Bing Crosby's ears, like mine, stick out. He says something like, "My ears look like the two open doors of a taxi cab." Then he adds affectionately, "Well, stick around and I might give you a shave."

For me, the idea of speaking a monologue while watching myself speak is a bit too much. In the tradition of *sādhus* like Bhaktisiddhānta Sarasvatī Ṭhākura, I don't want the mirror around except when I need it. I already have enough internal mirrors.

Prabhupāda singing:

gaurāvirbhāva-bhūmes tvaṁ nirdeṣṭā saj-jana-priyaḥ
vaiṣṇava-sārvabhaumaḥ śrī-jagannāthāya te namaḥ

Now I'm turning to read from the quote book:

"The Lord is always seeking the opportunity to reclaim the fallen souls to His abode, the kingdom of God. . . . we can simply feel gratitude and pray to the Lord with folded hands" *(Bhāg.* 3.31.18, purport).

This is something I want to be reminded of. It's one reason that these quotes are here. These are deep points, good points, and I want them on my mind. This is a state of being I wish to achieve. Kṛṣṇa consciousness is not a collection of quotes that get taken out and looked at occasionally. It's constant, continual, unbroken acts and thoughts. *Ahaituky apratihatā, samādhi,* always being fixed in some kind of Kṛṣṇa consciousness. Here is the remembrance that Kṛṣṇa is always seeking the opportunity to reclaim the fallen souls and take them back to His abode.

Someone might say, "If God is all-powerful, why does He have to look for an opportunity to reclaim us?" The reason is that the all-powerful God has given us free will. He won't step over that. What's the meaning of a gift if someone gives it and then takes it back? With our free will, we are able to resist Kṛṣṇa and continue stubbornly trying to satisfy ourselves in the material world. With our free will, we will be able to suffer.

Sometimes our defenses become weak and we consider, "Why am I suffering? Why am I living my life based on false ego? If only I could surrender." At times like that, Kṛṣṇa steps forward to remind us and to facilitate our search for Him.

Devotees should be grateful that Kṛṣṇa has that attitude toward them. They should pray to Him, "Please, take me back. Please draw me to You. I may not be reciprocating with You due to my foolishness, but please take me anyway. Make me Yours again."

"When one is attracted by the transcendental beauty of Rādhā and Kṛṣṇa, he is no longer attracted by material feminine beauty. That is the special significance of Rādhā-Kṛṣṇa worship" *(Bhāg.* 3.31.38, purport).

Prabhupāda makes statements and then sometimes adds, "This is the essence of Kṛṣṇa consciousness," or, "This is the culmination of the teachings of the *Bhagavad-gītā,*" indicating that what he is saying is a *sūtra* to sum things up. We have heard so much about Rādhā and Kṛṣṇa worship, but what does it mean? From the viewpoint of the conditioned soul, Prabhupāda explains here that there is a beauty in Rādhā and Kṛṣṇa and it's the beauty of Their mutual love for one another, Their attraction for each other. This exists, you could say, in an objective sense. Anyone who sees Them can appreciate it. Even when we don't understand the inner workings of the *hlādinī-śakti,* we can recognize the sweetness of Rādhā and Kṛṣṇa. Although it appears to be connected to boy–girl relations, it has nothing to do with the material world. Rather, Rādhā and Kṛṣṇa's love is a cooling relief from material sexual passion, material dirtiness.

When we engage in sex, we try to take the position of Rādhā and Kṛṣṇa in a perverted way. That is dirty lust. All lust is removed by attraction to Rādhā and Kṛṣṇa. The reason we go after these perverted forms of sex pleasure is that we mistake a mirage for the real thing. We are pleasure-seeking at heart, and we think, "Ah, here it is. This woman [man] is great." Or, "I can enjoy in this way." But we don't actually find satisfaction there.

Rādhā and Kṛṣṇa are a great mystery. I have sometimes tried to understand Them according to *paramparā,* in terms of the highest goal of life. Then I realized I couldn't enter that understanding. But here, Prabhupāda says in a simple, concise way, what it is all about. It means finding the original attraction of the self. We find this original attraction by hearing of Their pastimes from authorized sources. If we understand how beautiful Śrīmatī Rādhārāṇī is, how Rādhā and Kṛṣṇa are decorated and served, how They are worshipped and thought of throughout the day, we will not be attracted to the opposite sex.

Prabhupāda singing:

vāñchā-kalpatarubhyaś ca kṛpā-sindhubhya eva ca
patitānāṁ pāvanebhyo vaiṣṇavebhyo namo namaḥ

namo mahā-vadānyāya kṛṣṇa-prema-pradāya te
kṛṣṇāya kṛṣṇa-caitanya-nāmne gaura-tviṣe namaḥ

From the sublime to the ridiculous, from the top to the bottom, the dirty mind and the pure mind, the duality which is my conditioned self in touch with the most sublime and liberated knowledge, the knowledge which brings fearlessness and at the same time, me being a fearful creature jumping at noises and mice, afraid someone will come, speculating and hearing the truth without speculation. Wanting to be pure, but dwelling in impure places—this is the duality that is me.

Being encouraged when I hear we should not associate with the nondevotees, yet I look for a nondevotee's book. Working against myself and my best interests. A devotee is happy, but I'm sad. A devotee is eternal, but I am disturbed by thoughts of death. A devotee is full of knowledge, but I don't know what will happen. A devotee is generous and friendly, but I want to keep my time to myself. I feel I can't give to others. This is a duality, my conditioned self.

The devotee always thinks of Kṛṣṇa in the center. Alas, I think of myself as the center. Yet I know I'm not. Stubborn, unredeemed, plagued by the uncontrolled mind, I have the best *sādhana* practices. I'm convinced of that.

I ran into an old acquaintance here. He's initiated, but his spiritual master gave up the practices of Kṛṣṇa consciousness. That, no doubt, contributed to his lack of faith, but actually, he always tended toward faithlessness and liked to speculate on other philosophies. He was always trying to determine whether they were as good as Kṛṣṇa consciousness. When I met him a few years ago, he was studying religions academically, trying to see how Kṛṣṇa consciousness could be explained by the university professors, and so on. He was also studying world religions from the interfaith point of view, where everything is smoothed out and you don't follow a particular path. He preferred dabbling in these things than chanting his rounds or hearing from Prabhupāda.

I remember one time he admitted to me that his lack of faith was all due to his painful reaction at the demise of his spiritual master. He said he didn't really want to be faithless. His wife is faithful to Prabhupāda.

I met him again this year in the hallway of the temple on my way to give a lecture. He was there as a Sunday guest. He came forward and in a friendly way, put his hand on my arm and said, "How are you?" I found out partly from him, and then later, in a distressed letter from his wife, that he has gone off the deep end in terms of his identity as a devotee and he wants instead to follow the path of impersonalism. Previously he may not have been getting up early to practice *sādhana*, but now he gets up early to read Rajneesh and to meditate. He also teaches *haṭha-yoga*. I was shocked to hear these things. It's one thing to hear that a devotee is burnt out on ISKCON's authorities and doesn't want to live in the temple. I'm sorry enough about that. Or to hear that someone is becoming materialistic. But to hear of someone becoming an impersonalist is so strange.

I thought about it. He had gone up to the top rungs of the ladder by Prabhupāda's grace. He was attached to a movement with *bhakti* as the goal. Now he's climbing down to consider that the soul will become one with the ultimate impersonal Soul.

Over the centuries, the Vaiṣṇavas have argued against the sanity of this proposition. I don't need to go into it here, but I happen to be reading Śrīla Prabhupāda's arguments with Dr. Radhakrishnan.

It's good for me to hear again and again that Kṛṣṇa is not an ordinary person, but the Supreme Personality of Godhead. The Brahman concept of oneness is Kṛṣṇa's bodily effulgence. Kṛṣṇa is all-powerful, inconceivably so. In His human-like form, He displays pastimes. His pure devotees don't think of Him in His impersonal Brahman feature. They don't even think of Him as Bhagavān. They just love Him for who He is—a cowherd boy in Vraja. Prabhupāda insists that we solidify our approach to Kṛṣṇa by being aware of His greatness. He doesn't want us ever to make the mistake of thinking of Kṛṣṇa as impersonal.

I want to hear this. I *need* to hear this. Maybe I have to defeat the Māyāvādī within myself. All these basic teachings are important. I am not a bumblebee stuck in the flower of *mādhurya-rasa*. I need the ABCs. The whole world thinks they are the body. To get on that nerve, on that point, and to face the world's ignorance, that's what I need. By being convinced of that ignorance and by being disgusted by it, feeling pity for whoever functions under that ignorance, especially with sex life and politics—I have to hurl my invective: "It's not what you think it is!"

These thoughts bring emotion—anger, disgust, compassion. If prematurely I spend all my energies collecting the nectar-dripping flowers of verses about the *gopīs'* jokes with Kṛṣṇa, then it seems like I won't be able to comprehend the philosophy necessary for a preacher. I'm at a stage in my Kṛṣṇa consciousness where it's good for me to hear the basics—good for me as a preacher and good for me as a practicing devotee.

This happened to me today; they gave me two sweets at lunch. I was starting on the first one—they were good too, made with coconut and crushed nuts—and as is usual for me when I eat, I was listening to Śrīla Prabhupāda lecture on tape. Prabhupāda said that there are six unfavorable things in devotional service: *atyāhāraḥ*—it seems I always get these tapes when I'm savoring my lunch—*don't eat too much.* Prabhupāda said to eat only enough to keep the body fit.

I needed to hear that. I'm not the body and I shouldn't live for sense gratification. I should develop my Kṛṣṇa consciousness. I should surrender to my spiritual master.

Recently, I was dipping into the lotus flowers of what Rādhā and Kṛṣṇa and the *gopīs* do. I was trying to understand the ultimate goal of Kṛṣṇa consciousness. Then I realized that Prabhupāda never taught us to focus exclusively on that. Therefore, I have withdrawn from it, but there's some part of me that wants to go back to it. Those desires remind me of the haunting feelings I had after being trained as a Catholic for so many years and then giving up the single-minded idea that Christ is the only savior. I felt guilty. The Christians say we'll go to hell because we don't accept Christ as the only way. They don't agree that we can accept Christ as one guru among many, one son among many sons. We have to accept him as the *only* way. That can nag at your conscience.

Some of our Indian friends go through similar trials. They contact ISKCON with its exclusive devotion to Kṛṣṇa and wonder whether they will be condemned by Lord Śiva if they give up *his* worship. These are emotional ties. Now I have an emotional tie that I should be hearing only *rāgānugā* topics. If I don't, I'm told that I'll never develop my *rasa* and I won't be able to reach that goal for many, many lifetimes.

My spiritual master didn't teach me that. I have concluded that I should study his books and the teachings he did give us, and that will lead me to the other.

These are some of my inner thoughts about wanting to hear basic teachings and to realize that they're good for me. If I do feel restless, there's always plenty of nectar available, even Rādhā-Kṛṣṇa nectar. Everything is there; Prabhupāda didn't withhold it. I should just keep taking in as much as I can. If Prabhupāda's emphasis happens to be on beginner's stuff, then I don't want to relativize it and think, "That was for the 1970s," or, "That's because his lectures were mostly public," or, "The devotees were so neophyte then. Now we're more advanced." Take it that he knew what he was giving as a long-term gift and that he felt the process of Kṛṣṇa consciousness is one where you give your heart to Kṛṣṇa. He can give us more knowledge and more direction Himself.

This is more a prayer than a radio show, but I don't mind if you hear this, even though you don't understand all the background to it. What good is the show if I don't speak from the heart in a way that I feel purified?

Prabhupāda singing:

> *pañca-tattvātmakaṁ kṛṣṇaṁ bhakta-rūpa-svarūpakam*
> *bhaktāvatāraṁ bhaktākyaṁ namāmi bhakta-śaktikam*

4

Prabhupāda singing:

> *pañca-tattvātmakaṁ kṛṣṇaṁ bhakta-rūpa-svarūpakam*
> *bhaktāvatāraṁ bhaktākyaṁ namāmi bhakta-śaktikam*

Haribol. It's Good Thursday (some people call it Maundy Thursday). Madhu was just out. He said there were so many people on the road that he couldn't even find a place to stop for a moment at the gas station island. People are enjoying the holiday. We're each part of it, even if we are apart from it. How can anyone have a purely original idea? We are each influenced by our race, our time, the people around us, what we are, what we've eaten, what's passed through us.

What *we* want is to be Kṛṣṇa conscious. I just read a statement by Prabhupāda about not meddling in the world's affairs: "Kṛṣṇa will take care of it. Everything is destined. You just take care of your business, which is to become Kṛṣṇa conscious and engage in Kṛṣṇa's service."

Prabhupāda's statement helps me answer a question Bhakta Massimo asked me. In *Renunciation Through Wisdom,* Prabhupāda quotes his spiritual master as saying that if a neophyte rings the bell once in the temple during the Deity's *ārati,* that does more good than thousands of welfare workers' building hospitals and trying to feed the poor. I love that statement. It's such a knockout, and it defies the common logic about how to help people. Bhakta Massimo asked, "How is this actually true? Who benefits from a devotee ringing a bell in the temple for the Deity unless he comes to the temple?"

At the time, I gave the best answer I could, but since then, I found more statements by Prabhupāda clarifying this point. I thought of that statement—I forget the Sanskrit—something like *jagat-tuṣṭe.* If Kṛṣṇa is satisfied, the universe is satisfied.

It reminded me of the story of how Durvāsā Muni approached the Pāṇḍavas with thousands of his followers demanding food. Durvāsā's intention was to embarrass the Pāṇḍavas because he knew that Draupadī had a benediction. As long as she hadn't yet taken her meal, any number of people could be fed from her cooking pots. Draupadī had already eaten that day. To save the Pāṇḍavas honor, Kṛṣṇa ate a morsel still sticking to the pot and all of Durvāsā's followers were satisfied. It's mysterious, but that's the way it works. Then I understood a little better today when I read Prabhupāda say that people's destinies are fixed. He was quoting from Prahlāda Mahārāja where he says that even if you have the best medical treatment, a man may still die. Even if you have the best ship, your ship may sink. Parents with all good intentions to raise their child may see their child go bad. These things are not within our control, and when people try to change destiny, they mess up. The best thing a person can do, or a nation, is to become Kṛṣṇa conscious. Prabhupāda admitted, however, that this is very difficult to understand.

Just like Bhakta Massimo, most people can't understand the relationship between Kṛṣṇa consciousness and destiny. But Prabhupāda makes it clear: when Kṛṣṇa is pleased, destiny can be changed. That's also true in a collective sense. In other words, the more devotees in the world, the better. If the devotees please Kṛṣṇa, He may save humanity from its otherwise horrible karma. Pleasing Kṛṣṇa is the only way things can be changed; karma cannot be changed in any other way.

This explanation defies the material concept of cause and effect. Therefore, these statements will not be accepted by atheists. But let's face it, we don't accept the atheists either. Just because they say that this is incredulous, superstitious, fantastic, that doesn't budge us from our understanding that everything happens by God's grace and not otherwise.

Prabhupāda singing:

he kṛṣṇa karuṇā-sindho dīna-bandho jagat-pate
gopeśa gopikā-kānta rādhā-kānta namo 'stu te

I want to speak this radio show every day, and if you'll come with me, we can be together. We'll run through the day doing our duties, then quiet down, put on the brakes, and stop to broadcast this show.

When I speak on the radio, it makes me want to remember things. I want to remember ISKCON, but sometimes I feel a block about telling those memories. To start with, I'd like to explore the resistance. Partly, the resistance comes because I have to become the protagonist in my memories. After all, they're my memories. But that's not always palatable because the memories inevitably include other people. One wants to be gentle and non-controversial, not defensive or offensive. Even if I don't defend myself and try to be objective, then I may have to discuss unpalatable times. That's the basis to my resistance. Inevitably, whatever I say will be one opinion with which anyone can disagree. Perhaps the quiet life I am seeking is not compatible with so many memories.

I was speaking earlier on this show how Kṛṣṇa will take care of us and we don't have to meddle. When I said that, I thought about my present life. Prabhupāda's statement is a justification why not to get involved in controversy. When people do get involved, they feel righteous. After all, we have to shape ISKCON and rectify it through different reforms. That's true. None of us can just sit by inertly while ISKCON is destroyed by internal or external attack. You can imagine if an ISKCON temple didn't lock its doors at night. Eventually, thieves would find out. Even the dogs would find out. The place would be overrun. We have to be upright and defend our temples and our movement. Pay the bills. Do the needful. I agree.

There are devotees who will do those things, and to some degree, we all must do them. But there is also a place for engaging ourselves in Kṛṣṇa's service without worrying about the world. The extreme activist is the person who never quits, even when he's contributed enough and it's time to let others take over. Prabhupāda gives the example of Gandhi. He worked so hard for *svarāj*, India's independence, and *svarāj* was achieved, but *still* he wanted to continue in politics. There would be no end to his activity. Prabhupāda said he should have retired and studied *Bhagavad-gītā*. That would have provided the best example to the human community. But no, he stayed in the political arena until he was shot.

When Prabhupāda invited me to take *sannyāsa*, that was a time (1972) when the newly formed GBC consisted entirely of *gṛhasthas*. Prabhupāda had a concept that *gṛhasthas* would manage the society and *sannyāsīs* would travel and preach. Then Prabhupāda indicated that perhaps the *gṛhasthas* were doing too much management, sitting behind their desks and not preaching. This was partly because he had been dissatisfied at an unauthorized meeting we had held in 1971 in New York. At that meeting, we had centralized power and created a new post, "Secretary of the GBC," which Atreya Ṛṣi would fill. His job was to keep us all informed of what was going on in all the zones. We also instituted other changes. Prabhupāda didn't like it. He saw that we were becoming too bureaucratic and he told us we should travel and preach. Then I believe as a follow-up, he gave *sannyāsa* to Tamal Krishna Mahārāja and Sudama Mahārāja and indicated that other GBC men could also take *sannyāsa*.

When I heard Prabhupāda's invitation, I asked, "What about me?" He said, "Yes, come on. When I arrive in Los Angeles, you can take along with others." There were quite a few going to take—Rūpānuga, Karandhara, Bali Mardan, Hṛdayānanda, and Puṣṭa Kṛṣṇa.

We were in the mood of giving up management. At that time, I was in charge of Dallas and worrying about the incense business. I wondered, "If I take *sannyāsa,* who will take care of the incense business so that the temple and the *gurukula* don't collapse and so that the very important project doesn't fail?"

Others assured me that it would go on. I had to take a leap of faith. As I did so, I entered the fire sacrifice arena knowing everything would be okay. Everything will go on with or without me. Prabhupāda quotes a Bengali saying, something like *rāja mari leo,* if the king dies, *rājya chali te thāke,* the kingdom will go on. Kṛṣṇa will take care of it. You just have do what's best for your Kṛṣṇa consciousness.

This can't be done irresponsibly. I was talking to a devotee about it and I gave the example of the way Madhu drives on the European highways. Drivers pass each other more often in Europe than in America. There are not as many lanes, so drivers tend to be more daring and creative. Madhu is always passing cars when he can. Our van is not that fast, but as soon as he sees an opportunity, he makes his move. If that opportunity weren't there and he went forward anyway, it would be a great folly. He might even crash. Similarly, in our Kṛṣṇa consciousness, we have to be alert. Take the opportunities that present themselves, and don't try to go forward when no opportunity presents itself. Our real self-interest is to please Kṛṣṇa, and that will also benefit others. Prabhupāda's point is that Kṛṣṇa conscious activities are the best activities for the material world; material efforts can't change anything. This point is difficult for people to understand. It's even more difficult to bring about. No politician can preach on this basis, what to speak of preaching it in what would be seen as a sectarian way. It isn't even accepted usually in terms of God consciousness, that God is in control and we should depend on Him. People don't want to hear it. Still, it's the way things actually work.

Prabhupāda singing:

he kṛṣṇa karuṇā-sindho dīna-bandho jagat-pate
gopeśa gopikā-kānta rādhā-kānta namo 'stu te

jayatāṁ suratau paṅgor mama manda-mater gatī
mat-sarvasva-padāmbhojau rādhā-madana-mohanau

What to do, what to do? Sitting in a room, the guest room of the Vicenza temple in Italy. Śrīla Prabhupāda is up from his post-lunch rest with his beadbag in his hand. The *mūrti* chants for many hours a day. I want to set up a dictaphone and book for him at 1 A.M. so he can do his translation work too. Sometimes he takes rest and sometimes he takes *prasādam.* I'm in such a rush sometimes that I don't make nice prayers when I offer him *prasādam.* Rather, I bow passionately at his feet without slowing down. Externally, my life may seem very slow to somebody else, but still I can't seem to slow down and say the prayers, can't slow down and say *gāyatrī.* I'm always moving from one thing to another. I even eat fast. But Prabhupāda is here and he gives me some sanity and a chance to feel close to him.

I'll be in this room for only one more day. Then we're moving on again. There's a picture of Prabhupāda here—that really wonderful one where he's wearing a rust-colored cable knit sweater. They used it for a Christmas marathon poster one year: "Prabhupāda wants you to go out and distribute books. Go out and get the mercy . . . " "If you really want to please me . . . " That was the line they used.

It looks like the picture was taken in an airport because he's sitting on a black, leather-looking chair. I wonder what city it is. But there he is, leaving his boys and girls in one place to go to them in another.

That's all you can see clearly. His garland—the gardenias and other flowers. His cane—the bamboo one, which means it's probably early 1970s. Dear Śrīla Prabhupāda. He's sitting straight, not cross-legged. *Paramahaṁsa parivrajakācārya,* looking pleased, smiling, but we can't see his teeth, the corners of his mouth turned down, compassion in his eyes. Our Śrīla Prabhupāda.

It's wonderful and it's right that in this movement everyone worships him and looks to him. I'm trying to do that by studying his words and trying to stay under his gaze.

Prabhupāda spoke in a lecture (1972 in Vṛndāvana) I heard today on the *śrama eva hi kevalam* verse. He said the most important thing is hearing. That means *kīrtana* hearing or *Bhagavad-gītā, Śrīmad-Bhāgavatam. Sthāne sthitāḥ śruti-gatāṁ tanu-vāṅ manobhir.* Then he said, "This is the purpose of Vṛndāvana. . . . As in Vṛndāvana, this place Vṛndāvana, there are so many people who are hearing about Kṛṣṇa, wherever you hear about Kṛṣṇa, that is Vṛndāvana." Vṛndāvana is not limited to a certain place, Vṛndāvana means wherever you can hear about Kṛṣṇa.

He then referred to that year's Janmāṣṭamī which he spent at New Vrindaban. There were hundreds of devotees there, he said, and it was as good as this Vṛndāvana. There was *tulasī,* there was *kīrtana,* he was speaking *bhāgavata-dharma.* "Of course, this Vṛndāvana in India is special. It is established. When Kṛṣṇa comes to this world, He comes here."

You know, hearing Prabhupāda speak is wonderful. He says things that he's always said before, but if you listen carefully, sometimes you get—what can I call it? Realization? New clarity? His words just click and you can't quite express that feeling that you get to someone else except with a certain force of conviction. Then your own clarity becomes expressed by it.

I really took heart from that lecture. It means that my traveling in the Western world can be as good as living in Vṛndāvana. It's a fact that when you go to Vṛndāvana, there are obstacles to Vṛndāvana consciousness and to Vṛndāvana *bhajana.* If for me, Vṛndāvana means a heavy emphasis on dealing with others, on the institutional program, on different opinions and socializing and ritual—then how is that Vṛndāvana? Vṛndāvana means chanting and hearing about Kṛṣṇa, and being in that mood as much as possible. I may be able to do that better somewhere else. Prabhupāda said that, even while in Vṛndāvana, lecturing at the Rādhā-Dāmodara temple. He didn't make a cult out of it—"Vṛndāvana only"—but said that Vṛndāvana is all over the world when we concentrate on hearing and chanting. I caught a glimpse of it when he said that and how we should aim for Vṛndāvana consciousness wherever we are.

Prabhupāda singing:

jayatāṁ suratau paṅgor mama manda-mater gatī
mat-sarvasva-padāmbhojau rādhā-madana-mohanau

All right, good-bye for today. I'm wishing you well and going on with my activities. This is like holding hands. I hope that it's not in a sticky way, but in a non-skin-disease way. It's not skin love, but a kind of love across the miles, sound vibration, pure *kṛṣṇa-kathā*—if not always pure, then at least wanting to be pure and being honest about that. We're living in our bodies, but we're not our bodies. We're the self within the body. When the body dies, it is automatically given up, although we don't give up the subtle body.

"What's the subtle body?" someone might ask. "Are you making it up? I don't see any subtle body."

Yes, there is a subtle body. There's a mind. You may not see it, but we all know there's a mind. Don't deny that, sir. And you have intelligence and a soul. But the soul is different. There's a mind, some intelligence, and there's the concept of being the body, false ego. These are the components of the subtle body. The gross body is given up at death—that's easy to see—but we don't give up the subtle body. The subtle body carries the soul, which is the real self, to the next body. This subtle body is what you become in the next life. It has a certain shape or attitude and karma imprinted on it. By understanding the science of self-realization—a science you don't know because you have no such technicians—we learn that karma means that the subtle body carries the soul to the next gross body.

The goal of life is to give up gross and subtle bodies and for the soul to attain its pure, original, spiritual position. That takes love of God, and that's what we're talking about. That's what we should be striving for whether we are sitting quietly together for a few minutes on a radio show or doing something else.

Anyway, right now I feel a little oppressed. I'm ready to bound out of here like a greyhound dog. Let me go, then, and let me come back another time to be with you in this mood, before all such meetings will come to an end. Hare Kṛṣṇa.

5

Prabhupāda singing:

> *jaya śrī-kṛṣṇa-caitanya prabhu nityānanda*
> *śrī-advaita gadādhara śrīvāsādi-gaura-bhakta-vṛnda*

Haribol. On the air. Last day here in the guest room. I think of Bhaktisiddhānta Sarasvatī Ṭhākura's saying, "We will leave tomorrow, if Kṛṣṇa desires." He would never definitely say that this was his last day somewhere and that he would be doing such and such tomorrow. I also try to remember that. I can make my plans, but I shouldn't engrave them in stone.

I plan to start a series of writing session notebooks in Brescia while we're stuck there for dental work. I could write with my indelible black pen on the cover of the first notebook tonight as a head start, but who knows? I may not arrive there despite my plans.

It's one thing to be tentative about something, to be aware that fate may not allow it. It's another thing to remember that Kṛṣṇa is in control. That's why things don't happen as man proposes—because God disposes.

That's the essence of Kṛṣṇa consciousness. *Smartavyaḥ satataṁ viṣṇur, vismartavyo na jātucit:* just remember Kṛṣṇa. All other rules and regulations serve that one.

I heard Prabhupāda talking about this and explaining his preaching in America. He was saying that he is just trying to attract people to Kṛṣṇa. He wanted them to chant Hare Kṛṣṇa and to engage in other acceptable activities. He said in India, there are devotees or transcendentalists who follow so many rules and regulations, but he didn't introduce them. He said, "I've introduced only one percent. Somebody says of me in America, 'Oh, Swamijī is so conservative. He has so many rules. You can't do this, you can't do that.' But I have only introduced one percent. I am not so interested in rules and regulations, but I am trying to follow Rūpa Gosvāmī's policy:

yena tena prakāreṇa manaḥ kṛṣṇe niveśayet
sarve vidhi-niṣedhā syur etayor eva kiṅkarāḥ

Just somehow attract people to Kṛṣṇa so they can think of Kṛṣṇa. Rules and regulations can come later."

"Always remember Kṛṣṇa" is the grand principle of Kṛṣṇa consciousness—to see that everything is controlled by Kṛṣṇa. *Samādhi* is not in a person's control. *Samādhi* is a sign that Kṛṣṇa is controlling the devotee. Therefore, the principle, "Always remember Kṛṣṇa" is both for the beginner and the accomplished devotee. Just somehow do something Kṛṣṇa conscious. Don't bother about the rules and what you are not able to do right now. Just chant [*singing*] Hare Kṛṣṇa Hare Kṛṣṇa, Kṛṣṇa Kṛṣṇa Hare Hare/ Hare Rāma Hare Rāma, Rāma Rāma Hare Hare. Anyone can start with that. That's the first step, and it's also the goal. That's what's so wonderful about Kṛṣṇa consciousness.

Prabhupāda was also talking about the *Bhagavad-gītā* as "ABCD," the beginning principles of spiritual life. *Śrīmad-Bhāgavatam,* he said, is a more advanced subject. Prabhupāda preached that ABCD throughout his life. We can too. As practicing devotees, we also profit from remembering the beginning.

We are not the body. Who has realized it? Who doesn't think of the self as the body? Who dares to neglect the body since it's just a covering? We can't expect the body to last forever. We're eternal. We are the life within the body, not the tongue. We're not the belly, the genitals. We're the self, and as the self, we're not satisfied by tongue-belly-genital action. As the self, we can tolerate cold or heat.

We're not the mind either. The mind seems to be more a friend of the body when it's under the sway of the senses. The body sends frantic messages to the mind and intelligence, "Woof! Woof! Please take care of me with all your intelligence and all your devotion. Please give me something to drink. Give me something to eat. I crave. I hurt. I feel pleasure." Like a child. Kids disturb us with their unabashed, frank attachment to their immediate feelings. Any little inconvenience or restriction can cause their uncontrolled minds and senses to leap into action.

There are people in this world who equate the uncontrolled mind and senses with primal man. They say that as we age, we move further and further away from who we really are. If you consider man to be a sensual being, then that may be true. As age encroaches, the senses weaken and we accept so many compromises and impositions on our natural will. Life seems to fade. We get further removed from our feelings because we think we are the body. The body doesn't lie. We have to surrender to it. This is the meaning of conditioning. The impositions we accept are rarely placed on us by spiritual realization. Instead, age teaches us to condition ourselves to others' reactions to us. We find out that if we act the way we really feel, people won't like us. Society dictates so many rules and regulations. We have to stifle our actual feelings to avoid improper behavior and punishment. No one thinks of that as odd. That's conditioning based on bodily consciousness.

I'm not attempting to explore this topic completely. I'm not a psychologist. I'm trying to steer this topic to Kṛṣṇa. The first step in spiritual life is to seriously approach a spiritual master. He will teach you to control the body and the mind and to uncover the soul. The child in his fresh, brash, body consciousness is not in contact with the soul. The child's consciousness is not more natural: "I *want*. I *don't* want." The natural state of the soul is to think of Kṛṣṇa, to meditate, like Lord Śiva, on the Supersoul. He was so lost to the outside world that he didn't notice Dakṣa entering the arena and everyone standing up in worship.

Getting back to so-called childlike, "natural" perfection: who would behave with the same indifference Lord Śiva displayed upon seeing Dakṣa enter that arena? Dakṣa had a fabulous bodily aura because he was the head of the Prajāpatis. Everyone, the *Bhāgavatam* verse tells us, stood up in deference. The child would be amazed and attracted. He would naturally offer respect. Lord Śiva, on the other hand, or any person absorbed in *samādhi*, didn't even notice. He was in the spiritual realm.

We may not be *avadhūtas*. Therefore, we may not be able to ignore the body. Thus we go through the motions of offering respect. But we shouldn't forget Kṛṣṇa. Remember the philosopher Rousseau who spoke about the noble savage? His noble savage wasn't religious per se. Religion is defined by *śāstra*. The noble savage was uncivilized and therefore free of the artificial values created by social institutions. The noble savage, according to Rousseau, was naturally good and therefore didn't need institutionalized religion. That is not what the devotee is aiming for. We want to be civilized by the *śāstras;* our nobility is in following Kṛṣṇa conscious rules and regulations. We don't want to be civilized in the way Mr. Payne was civilized, with his white cuffs and gold cufflinks, his artificial tan and his before-dinner cocktails. Civilization to a devotee means *Bhāgavatam* culture and sense control. Kṛṣṇa defines it:

śamo damas tapaḥ śaucaṁ
kṣāntir ārjavam eva ca
jñānaṁ vijñānam āstikyaṁ
brahma-karma svabhāva-jam

It means controlling the senses, practicing required austerities, and deepening spiritual life. It means being clean within and without. It means being simple, religious, knowledgeable, and realized. We want *that* kind of culture, not the urbane culture of E. B. White who knows exactly how to use the English language, who is not a boor, who tries to be decent to people, and who tolerates the inconveniences of modern society while at the same time takes advantage of them. Devotees are not interested in the liberal arts and sciences, or what has been passed down to us by the *jñānī* forefathers of the human race. That kind of civilization—of a civilized man without God consciousness—is *śrama eva hi kevalam.*

We didn't know all this until we met Śrīla Prabhupāda. We had an inkling that what passed as civilized was mostly bunk. We saw the establishment—the government and the military-industrial complex—and the mass of people out for money and sense gratification as phony, "square." We learned how to alter our consciousness with marijuana and LSD. We tried to free the language with Beat poetry and jazz. We were prepared to reject our parents' civilization and carve out our own civilization. Unfortunately, we were carving out yet another form of animalism.

Prabhupāda set up shop in the storefront and gave us real spiritual culture, real civilization. He taught us to chant Hare Kṛṣṇa Hare Kṛṣṇa, Kṛṣṇa Kṛṣṇa Hare Hare/ Hare Rāma Hare Rāma, Rāma Rāma Hare Hare. He wasn't dependent on furnishing or externals. There was no prerequisite to his teachings. He sat on a straw mat and without the advantage of a shared culture, gave us pure Kṛṣṇa consciousness.

yena tena prakāreṇa manaḥ kṛṣṇe niveśayet
sarve vidhi-niṣedhā syur etayor eva kiṅkarāḥ

Smartavyaḥ satataṁ viṣṇur, vismartavyo na jātucit: somehow or other, introduce Kṛṣṇa and give these people Kṛṣṇa consciousness. It's bound to work because Kṛṣṇa consciousness is not sectarian. It's not an artificial imposition on the mind. It's the original consciousness of the living entity. Just chant and this sound vibration will open the heart. Prabhupāda's daring and conviction still holds the Kṛṣṇa consciousness movement together. His teachings are the cutting edge.

Someone might argue, "Anyone could have done what Prabhupāda did. After all, Kṛṣṇa consciousness is universal." But no, it remains a puzzle why Westerners brought up in a materialistic, secular, Judeo-Christian world should accept Kṛṣṇa as God and take up Indian ways. Prabhupāda was empowered. That it has at all been planted in Western culture is because of Prabhupāda's insistence that it's not sectarian. He gave what's in the *śāstras;* Kṛṣṇa consciousness is for everyone. The hope that Kṛṣṇa consciousness could be taken up by people outside India seemed to have been something that would remain unrealized, esoteric. Prabhupāda changed all that.

I don't want to assume that I can go ahead of Śrīla Prabhupāda and say something better; I simply want to worship his example, remember his pastimes, and remember my own exchanges with him. I want to follow his order, because when you accept a guru, you agree that this person knows more than you do. If I follow Prabhupāda's instructions, I'll be dear to Kṛṣṇa.

Prabhupāda singing:

bhaja śrī-kṛṣṇa-caitanya prabhu nityānanda
śrī-advaita gadādhara śrīvāsādi-gaura-bhakta-vṛnda

Being here reminds me of sitting in a waiting room at a bus station or airport, or outside a dentist's office. I'm waiting. Some places have places for nonsmokers and places for smokers; some have magazines and even videos to keep you entertained while you wait. Other people go in and out. You look at your watch. If you're at the airport, flights take off and arrive. You look at your watch again, hoping there won't be a delay.

This room makes me think of waiting because there's something impersonal about it. It's like a motel room where many people have passed through. The facilities remain unchanged while people come and go. There's no way to know the history of such places. Who wants to know it anyway? Who would want to think of who was there before you and what they did in the room? Better that the cleaning women remove all traces of previous occupants. But sometimes we find a touch. They write something in the Gideon's Bible or leave a scar or stain that can't be removed.

Why am I saying this? I don't know. I'm just rapping while waiting in the ISKCON Vicenza guest house. There's a big wardrobe in here, a vase filled with dead flowers, a cloth over the mirror (which I'll take down just before we leave), and now cartons filled with our belongings, ready to be moved into the van. We're set for going tomorrow—if Kṛṣṇa desires.

Prabhupāda singing:

> *bhaja śrī-kṛṣṇa-caitanya prabhu nityānanda*
> *śrī-advaita gadādhara śrīvāsādi-gaura-bhakta-vṛnda*

I have been talking about half an hour, so good-bye.

6

Prabhupāda singing:

> *bhaja śrī-kṛṣṇa-caitanya prabhu nityānanda*
> *śrī-advaita gadādhara śrīvāsādi-gaura-bhakta-vṛnda*

Haribol. We're in a new location. I don't know the name of the town, but it's near Brescia. We'll probably be here for a couple of weeks because I have to make repeated visits to the dentist. On Tuesday, he removes my front teeth. I wonder if I'll be able to talk. I'm sure toothless men can talk, although they sound funny. When your front teeth are gone, you whistle when you talk. "All I want for Christmas is my two front teeth so I can wish you Merry Christmas."

As I speak, I can see the cloudy sky out the window. It's a nice, deep gray-blue. Right in front of the window, I see treetops (we're on the second floor) all in bud. The buds are closed, but I can tell they're almost ready to bloom. There's one tree that's already blooming. The blossoms look vaguely like reddish-pink *tulasī-mañjarīs,* and the leaves remind me of weeping willow leaves.

More about our location: this is an apartment building surrounded by other apartment buildings. I'm nervous about the noises. I am always waiting for *them.* The very word I use—*them*—those people who live in the other apartments, who make noises and who hear your noises, I'm waiting for them to crank up the Italian pop rock music (although I have to admit that Italian music isn't as bad as American music. Italian music has a silly bounce to it. I shouldn't feel menaced by it). I find myself waiting for chairs to scrape, walls to bang, and people to start shouting through the walls. Right now, it's relatively quiet.

I'm as nervous about the noises as I am about being heard. One thing I have to cure is the problem of the scraping chair. There are no rugs, and the floors are all tiled. The wooden chair in my room scrapes terribly. It disturbs me and I'm sure it can be heard all over the building. I mentioned it to Madhu. He suggested putting socks on the bottom of the chair's legs. He always has practical solutions for these kinds of problems.

Prabhupāda singing:

> *bhaja śrī-kṛṣṇa-caitanya prabhu nityānanda*
> *śrī-advaita gadādhara śrīvāsādi-gaura-bhakta-vṛnda*

On the desk—I was going to say "my desk"—even as I say it, I am aware of it. I don't claim ownership over anything here. This isn't my room. When you move around the way we do, it becomes obvious that the expression "my room" is only a convention of speech. My attachment for things is short-lived. Still, it's natural to want our own space, so we use the conventions.

So, looking over at my desk, I see a stack of Prabhupāda's books. The Fourth Canto is at the bottom. I read it early this morning. On top of that, Prabhupāda's *Bhāgavatam* lectures. On top of that, *Letters From Śrīla Prabhupāda,* which I read every day while sitting in front of my Prabhupāda *mūrti.* On top of the stack, with its binding falling apart, is *Renunciation Through Wisdom,* Śrīla Prabhupāda's Bengali essays from the '40s and '50s.

I haven't read today, except some *Bhāgavatam* early in the morning. What did I read? Something about Satī. Satī wanted to go to the *yajña* despite her husband's advice. She was followed by the different *bhūtas,* ghosts, hobgoblins, and other dedicated followers of Lord Śiva. It was impressive how they immediately followed without waiting for their master's order, knowing that their master wanted Satī to be protected. When Satī arrived at the sacrificial arena, her father ignored her.

I could really empathize with her, the description was so real. Only the women came forward to greet her. Prabhupāda said in his purport that women cannot cover their emotions artificially. These women were glad to see Satī, so they came forward and embraced her. They weren't interested in the disagreement between Dakṣa and Lord Śiva. After all, Satī was their daughter, cousin, sister, or friend.

Satī was hurt, however, by her father's neglect of her husband. She was so angry that she killed herself.

That's where I stopped reading, right in the middle of her calling Dakṣa an offender for not honoring Lord Śiva. This anger in her speech, we know, will build up to her renouncing her relationship with her father by giving up her body. Such a chaste wife. Why did she have to take such rash action?

Prabhupāda singing:

> *bhaja śrī-kṛṣṇa-caitanya prabhu nityānanda*
> *śrī-advaita gadādhara śrīvāsādi-gaura-bhakta-vṛnda*

This morning I gave the *Śrīmad-Bhāgavatam* class. What a wonderful event that is. What a great privilege to be in an ISKCON temple, to be what is called a senior devotee, to be listened to with respect. I told the devotees that they shouldn't take devotional service in ISKCON for granted. It's a wonderful opportunity. And here I was, having the most wonderful opportunity of all.

I spoke on a verse from the first chapter of the Sixth Canto about Ajāmila. I then turned to the eighth chapter of *Bhagavad-gītā* and spoke about remembering Kṛṣṇa at the time of death. I came up with a few original examples that stuck strictly to Prabhupāda's conclusions.

Then I recited the Hare Kṛṣṇa mantra aloud: Hare Kṛṣṇa Hare Kṛṣṇa, Kṛṣṇa Kṛṣṇa Hare Hare/ Hare Rāma Hare Rāma, Rāma Rāma Hare Hare. As in any ISKCON assembly, all the devotees joined in. Devotees don't sit silently while the Hare Kṛṣṇa mantra is vibrated, but they take the opportunity to chant it themselves. That's another nice feature of speaking to devotees: when we all chant together, you feel uplifted. Then you go on with your speech. We have to practice chanting throughout our lives if we want to remember Kṛṣṇa at the end.

I'll analyze my lecture. I made logical, clear, convincing arguments, but I also saw that there's a difference between good showmanship and personal realization. When you lecture, you're the arch-self, the one who sits on the *vyāsāsana.* You suddenly become a special representative of Śrīla Vyāsadeva and Śrīla Prabhupāda. When you step down from the *vyāsāsana,* you're back to ordinary you. I try to be human while I'm on the *vyāsāsana,* but I'm also aware of my arch-self.

At the end of my talk, I thanked the devotees for allowing Madhu and me to stay there. I congratulated them on all the varied and attractive dresses they have sewn for Gaura-Nitāi and encouraged them to work in harmony to maintain their big project. There I was, encouraging them to sacrifice and make the commitment. That was my arch-self. It's not hype, but I sort of rise to the occasion and think, "All right, I know there's a duality between this kind of ideal speech and the nitty-gritty of what's going on with me, but I won't neglect making this arch-statement because it ought to be said. Even if no one can live up to it, it ought to be said.

I've spoken these lectures enough to know when it's over. I always feel refreshed and even a little euphoric. It takes awhile to wear off.

Someone's knocking at the door. Since I have no engineers in the outer room to field such things—right now, Madhu and Dīna-dayārdra are out shopping—I'm alone in this apartment. I can't speak Italian. The knocking has stopped.

"Once upon a midnight dreary, while I wandered weak and weary, over many a quaint and curious volume of lore, there came a knocking, tipping-tapping knocking on my window. Only this was the wind and nothing more . . . Quoth the raven, 'Nevermore.'"

I'll get used to this new place with its new set of noises. We'll talk again tomorrow.

Prabhupāda singing:

> *bhaja śrī-kṛṣṇa-caitanya prabhu nityānanda*
> *śrī-advaita gadādhara śrīvāsādi-gaura-bhakta-vṛnda*

7

Prabhupāda singing:

> *bhaja śrī-kṛṣṇa-caitanya prabhu nityānanda*
> *śrī-advaita gadādhara śrīvāsādi-gaura-bhakta-vṛnda*

Haribol. Here we are to talk some more in Italy on a chilly Easter day while somebody hammers outside. Perhaps you can hear the hammering. This busy world. This busy world where we are all living and dying and where living mostly means trying to enjoy our senses. Prabhupāda and *Bhagavad-gītā* and the previous *ācāryas* analyze everything so clearly. That's why Prabhupāda gets angry: "And *still* the rascals don't accept it." Just one of his logical arguments should be enough for them to accept Kṛṣṇa consciousness, and when they don't accept it, it proves that they are *mūḍhas.* He gives examples to show that there's a universal controller. Wherever there's control, there must be a controller, a government. This material world—even this body—is subject to so many laws, yet the atheists *still* insist that there is no brain behind anything. What rascals they are!

Prabhupāda is the perfect theist. He doesn't belong to the 19th century or the 20th century or the 21st century; he's a timeless devotee sage. The atheists are timeless too. They have been with us in one form or another since the beginning of time. They are most prominent in Kali-yuga, blaspheming religion and preaching godlessness. What passes for religion in this age is a sorry spectacle. Prabhupāda is the educated theist of Vedic culture, the modern *parivrajakācārya paramahaṁsa* who speaks like a layman in language inescapably blunt and clear to us. And he calls them rascals for not accepting the obvious hints, conclusions, and analogies, and the direct statements of the Supreme Personality of Godhead in the scripture.

I accept Śrīla Prabhupāda as my spiritual master, so my business is to worship his words and pray to realize them, and to pray to be able to present them well to the innocent people. When something is stated in scripture, and when we accept *brahma-śabda* as the superior method for gaining knowledge, then everything will be revealed to us in the course of time. But for now, I simply pray to understand Prabhupāda rightly and to remove any obstacles to that understanding. I'm not testing him against my own intellect, trying to decide whether I shall accept him as a spiritual master or not. I have already accepted him, accepted the principle of guru, and surrendered my free will.

You could say that free will operates in such a way that at every moment you are asking yourself whether you still want to surrender to Kṛṣṇa and Kṛṣṇa's representative. However, a surrendered devotee gets beyond that wrangling. The Lord can count on his surrender and trust that he's interested in devotional service. I have already heard so many good instructions. Now I am praying to be able to act on them.

Prabhupāda singing:

hare kṛṣṇa hare kṛṣṇa, kṛṣṇa kṛṣṇa hare hare
hare rāma hare rāma, rāma rāma hare hare

Today I did my free-writing, writing practice, writing session. I plowed ahead, not knowing what would come next. I questioned the writing process, and in the back of my mind, I couldn't resist judging what I was writing, thinking, "This isn't very Kṛṣṇa conscious. There's no explicit *kṛṣṇa-kathā* here." But I was also aware that I was onto a vital subject, which was the questioning itself. When I looked at it later, it seemed like a Kṛṣṇa conscious, valid bit of writing, which means to me that if I really try, then I am performing *bhakti-yoga* in my writing. If I try to offer something to Kṛṣṇa, it doesn't matter what it is (as long as it's not forbidden), if it is offered with devotion. Otherwise, what is the basis on which Kṛṣṇa would think something was well done or not? It's not based on grammar or rhetoric, but on sincerity. Kṛṣṇa can see sincerity in the heart of any effort. His devotee can see it too, although others may not have that ability.

For someone like me who is making an offering and is not sure of its acceptance, perhaps there will be no relief from that uncertainty. It's probably not good to be too certain anyway. I've been listening to Prabhupāda on the 1968 tapes. Tamal Krishna asks Prabhupāda questions like, "I feel bad that my service isn't good. What about if your service isn't very good? How do you perfect your service?" Whenever the expression is made that a devotee doesn't think his service is good, Prabhupāda says, "That is your qualification. A pure devotee never thinks his service is nice." Then he gives the example of Lord Caitanya who said of Himself that He doesn't have a pinch of love for Kṛṣṇa.

"Oh, but You are crying."

"That crying is just a show so the people may think I am a devotee. But how could I be a devotee? I am living in the absence of Kṛṣṇa. If I really loved Kṛṣṇa, I would not be able to bear living while feeling separation from Him." Such intense pure love of God was expressed as not having any love of God. Prabhupāda gave that as an example, although it's not one we can follow.

I may not be able to get relief from my own uncertainty, but I should never doubt that the process of trying to make an offering is acceptable to Kṛṣṇa. I have no alternative but to keep trying. Whether I do it specifically by writing practice, well, that brings me back to the same question. I don't know the answer. I don't know if I'm doing the best thing, but I am trying to perfect it. I take it for granted that if Kṛṣṇa doesn't want me to do this, He'll take it away from me. Until then, I will write as well as I can and make the best use of my flawed offering.

Because I lack purity, I feel something lacking. I would like to not feel it—I would prefer to feel the symptoms of *sāttvika-bhāva.* But even that I don't know about. Those ecstasies are intense. They shake your body and mind.

I say this with a touch of irony because I don't have that problem. I am not disrupted by ecstasy. It's a moot point for me. Therefore, I have no choice but to perform my service without ecstasy. Secretly, I'm aware that I am in a good position to render service without ecstasy. That in itself is a kind of purity, although it's only a lower level of unmotivated service. That is, I don't get an ecstatic reward, but I continue to serve because it's my duty and because I am earnest about trying to please Kṛṣṇa.

What about the fact that I really like to be a writer and serve in this way? That's not necessarily harmful. Writing in devotional service is like having the snake's fangs removed. I could be poisoned by a desire for fame, but I do what I can to be detached from fame by not demanding that what I write be printed, by writing a lot and working at it.

If I happen to get a kind of satisfaction from it, that is something deep and private, a conviction that I have found my *bhajana.* I don't see satisfaction as bad. Everything is bad if it's misused, and anything is good if it's used properly.

Again, no relief from the uncertainty. That's all right, as long as the uncertainty isn't crippling. I have to push ahead and speak in ways that are bold for me. I have to disregard the inner critics and keep going, keep going, keep going.

Prabhupāda singing:

> *hare kṛṣṇa hare kṛṣṇa, kṛṣṇa kṛṣṇa hare hare*
> *hare rāma hare rāma, rāma rāma hare hare*

I imagine myself talking to someone about chanting. Even when you're with people who chant, you can feel like you're from two different planets. You appear close—you're from the same Kṛṣṇa conscious family, you're "soul brothers" because you both chant Hare Kṛṣṇa. You may assume you have similar experiences. You presume the other person struggles with the same things you struggle with—inattention, an uncontrolled mind, whatever else. Sometimes the other person even says things that make it sound like you share the same experiences.

But you can't be sure about that. What people say with their words and what it represents in terms of their feelings—you can't assume anything. For example, I have a man's body. What's it like to be a woman? Women and men are so different physically, mentally, and emotionally. What's it like even to be a big, very strong man? I'm not like that either. What's it like to suffer mentally? Someone says he has a headache; someone else says his back hurts. What does it mean? How does it feel?

This can get quite speculative, but the reason I bring it up is that I'm talking about personal experiences. I often assume others are relating to what I'm saying. If nothing else, I hope they find it interesting to hear another person express his feelings. The more we hear genuine expression instead of phony ones, we get both an idea of what other people are like and an insight into our own experiences. In fact, we can start to see in terms of others' viewpoints the way Śrīla Prabhupāda describes.

It's not that we have an inviolable, impenetrable fortress of the self that no one can enter. Some people say that individuality, life, and love are cheap. People sell them back and forth. I prefer to think that individuality is sacred. My individuality is sacred to me. Then to share that individuality with others while keeping the sense of it intact becomes a sacred act. That's why we worry whether another person is able to be sympathetic to our delicacies and personal details. And that's certainly true when we're talking about chanting.

I was going to say something about my own experience, and that is that I don't pay attention at all to the Hare Kṛṣṇa mantra. I can chant round after round and not once pay attention. By "pay attention" I don't mean thinking about Kṛṣṇa's individual qualities and meditating on them—I'm not even approaching that. I mean paying attention to the syllables of the *mahā-mantra*. It's a thirty-two syllable mantra and I don't fix my mind on it once.

What do I do? I think of other things. Then I notice that I'm thinking of other things. That's the first stage. Then, rarely, I stop the motion of those other thoughts and tell myself, "This isn't good. You thought about your travel plans for that whole round. You should stop this. You're chanting."

At that point, I may think of the words, but it's so outer and dry that it's only a flash (if I can poeticize a little), like those weak neons or Indian fluorescent bulbs. Many seconds after you switch them on, sometimes minutes later, they start to click on—click-click—then the light's on. My consciousness fixes on the holy name with that kind of weakness. Then it's gone again. I'm back to thinking of other things for another couple of rounds. I regard my chanting as good if at least I am basically alert and the rounds go at a good pace.

There, I've said it. I've confessed it. But I'm not proud of it. Unfortunately, I'm not remorseful enough to effect a change. I gave a talk a couple of weeks ago called "Positive Thinking for Neophytes." At the beginning I said I wasn't going to discuss repentance because I don't think most of us are at that stage. We talk about it and it sounds interesting, like talking about Christian mysticism, about monks in their cells performing unceasing prayer. An interesting concept. Or Buddhism (that's not quite as interesting), something that's not our own practice. Interesting in that sense. Distant.

For us, remorse is distant. It's something we really ought to get into, but we don't know how. Do we try to feel bad? We already know that devotees have many problems with feeling bad, feeling guilty, feeling depressed. If we advise them to feel bad about their chanting, that will lead to trouble. Therefore, in my talk I said we should think positively. Just be glad we're chanting sixteen rounds at all.

That's the level I'm at. I have a sense of satisfaction that although I don't get results, I chant my rounds. That's important, keeping the quota. If they don't improve, what can I say? What can I do? They don't improve.

Kṛṣṇa knows—Kṛṣṇa's well aware of our position. I don't want to compare Kṛṣṇa to a bureaucracy, but say you have some papers filed with a government office. You have called up a few times and you're in touch with the person who is handling your case. You know that he has your papers and he knows that you're waiting for his decision, so there's no need to bother him anymore.

Of course, Kṛṣṇa is not a bureaucrat. It's just a crude example to illustrate that I know that He knows I'm waiting. I know He wants me to go back to Godhead, and it's only time that separates us. Sometimes I wonder when it will happen, but it appears that everything is in Kṛṣṇa's hands. Still, Kṛṣṇa is waiting for me to do something more. I'm saying by my actions, "Kṛṣṇa, I don't think I *can* do more. If with my present activities You want to come and give me mercy or bring me to the next stage, I will be grateful. You know that. I don't have to sing it again and again (or write it again and again), although it sometimes helps me to do so. You know I want more Kṛṣṇa consciousness, and that's implicit in my attempts to chant Your name. As for changing my present state, I don't know how to do it."

Kṛṣṇa and I reciprocate like that with the holy name. Kṛṣṇa knows, but He wants to see more. He is waiting. I think (wishful thinking), "Wouldn't it be nice? I wish I could think of Kṛṣṇa during the day beyond my sixteen rounds. I'm such a—a what?—a hypocrite to recommend this to others when I give class. When we finish our sixteen rounds, we should not think that that's the end. We're not like a post office where all but one of the windows have signs on them: 'This Window Closed.' It's not that when we finish our sixteen rounds, we close the *japa* window for the day. Rather, we go on chanting." I give this example, but I don't do it myself. My own window closes, except for a slow and sweet "Hare Kṛṣṇa" here and there, a sincere Hare Kṛṣṇa. It's not so frequent; it's like a snail's Hare Kṛṣṇa at the end of the day when I'm walking into the bathroom or when I'm talking with a friend and I come to the end of a conversation and I feel a pang of having to part and get on with life. Hare Kṛṣṇa. Or I say it after hearing something that's a little tough to swallow. Hare Kṛṣṇa. Sometimes I even recite the whole mantra. Those mantras are dear, but it's not like the chanting is in my bloodstream or is part of the air I breathe. It's not coming constantly in dreams. (Sometimes it does come in dreams—painfully, slowly uttered to get me through some nightmare situation.)

Prabhupāda singing:

hare kṛṣṇa hare kṛṣṇa, kṛṣṇa kṛṣṇa hare hare
hare rāma hare rāma, rāma rāma hare hare

I was hoping for a lighter show today. I don't know if *you* think of this as heavy, but for me, these are serious topics. I'm in a serious mood these days, wanting to delve into where I'm at in the writing sessions. I'm on the quiet side as I spend these days near the dentist while he pulls out my teeth. Then I come back here and read and write and do this show. I wouldn't mind if a lighter topic presented itself. Maybe it's that it's Easter today and unseasonably cold and gray.

I remembered this morning how when I was a kid, I would get new clothes for Easter, sometimes a jacket and sometimes a whole new suit. My sister would get a new dress and my mother would certainly have a new hat. These would be lighter clothes, spring clothes, and in order to show them off to the congregation at the church, it would have to be warm.

I was thinking about that today when I saw how cold it was. I thought of the cheap suits I would wear (not so cheap, I guess, from my mother's point of view). Sometimes she would go with me on the bus to buy them at Garber Brothers Boys' and Men's Clothing store in Port Richmond. We also bought those crummy plaid, woolen shirts and what were considered the latest styles—or feeble attempts at style for the masses distributed through a store like Garber Brothers to Staten Island boys. Dear mother taking care of her son.

I heard Prabhupāda say that the relationship between parents and children in this world can be broken by the slightest provocation of sense gratification. He gave the example of Prahlāda and his father. Prahlāda's only fault was that he was Kṛṣṇa conscious, but his father completely rejected him. When there is some slight disruption of sense gratification, what seems to be a strong bond is completely snapped.

That happened to some of us, and we sometimes look back at those years, trying to piece together that past identity and see what it has to do with our present identity. Is it important or isn't it? Some devotees feel it is and others feel it's not. Certainly there's something in what we are now that comes from those formative years before we were devotees.

Easter is a day that has no meaning today for me in terms of social or religious behavior, family observance, or even theology. I do think that we are pleasing Jesus Christ by our activities. We are up early in the morning, chanting God's names, and Jesus will be pleased with us. We are obeying the commandments. In that sense, we're observing Easter better than the American method of chocolate eggs and jelly beans, colored eggs and Easter bunnies, or even walking as we did to Sunday Mass in our new clothes and sitting in the pews and hearing the sermon, then going home to our special meat-centered dinner, and never once discussing Christ or his resurrection—nothing. We're doing better now, but Easter Sunday is always a day that brings me back.

8

Prabhupāda singing:

hare kṛṣṇa hare kṛṣṇa, kṛṣṇa kṛṣṇa hare hare
hare rāma hare rāma, rāma rāma hare hare

Haribol. We read in Prabhupāda's books that perfection comes when we are ready to give up what we want to do and instead do what Kṛṣṇa wants us to do. Follow Arjuna's example. Arjuna had his own ideas about fighting in the battle, but he sacrificed them for Kṛṣṇa. Kṛṣṇa may require us to give up the thing we like most, which by now we have converted into a type of devotional service. We've come to the stage where we've given up sinful activities; we try not to do anything separate from Kṛṣṇa's instructions. Over time, we have developed a service and it has been authorized, as far as we know, by guru and Kṛṣṇa. The guru trains us to increase our devotion through our activities.

For me, that service is writing. I've been reading Prabhupāda's letters to me. He often said that he liked my writing. He encouraged me to go on with it. Others may be given a *prabhu-datta-deśa,* a place to serve. We try our best, but are aware that we still harbor attachment. We're not really ready to give our everything for Kṛṣṇa. We can still imagine scenarios where Kṛṣṇa and Prabhupāda ask us to do something that would be just too much for us. That means we're not pure devotees who only want to do what Kṛṣṇa wants us to do.

I'm not painting a flattering self-image. I remember one purport where Prabhupāda writes that there should be no instance where the disciple refuses the spiritual master. The disciple should always agree to serve however the guru requests him. I can imagine Prabhupāda asking me to become the temple president in ISKCON New Delhi. How could I realistically serve in that way? I hear myself saying, "I'll *try . . .*" but I already know that service runs against my conditioning and propensity.

As we grow older, we become less flexible. We need little amenities or considerations. Anyway, I won't worry about this right now. It becomes too self-defeating and speculative. Am I doing the right thing? Will the day come when Prabhupāda will ask me to do something else? Or maybe he won't ask me, he'll order me. How will I pass the test?

The value I see in at least discussing this is another way of admitting that I'm not yet fully surrendered. It makes me humble and thoughtful, and I try to work at the service I do have as best I can. It makes me clear whimsy from my heart, to be earnest and satisfied and hope Kṛṣṇa will help me improve.

Prabhupāda singing:

hare kṛṣṇa hare kṛṣṇa, kṛṣṇa kṛṣṇa hare hare
hare rāma hare rāma, rāma rāma hare hare

I'm a little embarrassed to come to the radio show while leading this retired, visiting-the-dentist life. When I'm alone like this, my concerns tend to be more self-oriented. I remember one Saturday morning Jean Shepherd show, he was talking about how he had traveled over to the radio studio that morning on his motor scooter. He described for us how he stopped for a red light, how he looked around, and what he saw. Then he told—it bordered on sentimentality but it was also nice—how he loved Manhattan life. He had such an exciting thing to talk about—watching Manhattan on his way to the radio studio, but here I am, a monk, right now living near a dentist so I can receive repeated treatment, and taking advantage of being unable to talk much and writing full-time. And what are my inner concerns? That I felt sleepy while I was reading? Who wants to hear that? That's the kind of statement someone puts in his diary. Even people who chance to read the diary ask, "Why's he always nagging himself?"

Anyway, this is my radio show. I'm not trying to get into the top ratings or asking the poll rating people how many people listen to my show at this time rather than what's on the other radio bands. This is just something I'm doing, sitting and looking at the clouds and talking.

Prabhupāda singing:

hare kṛṣṇa hare kṛṣṇa, kṛṣṇa kṛṣṇa hare hare
hare rāma hare rāma, rāma rāma hare hare

Dīna-dayārdra bought some potted plants. There's one (the flowers look like yellow marigolds) for Prabhupāda, he said. I accepted it. I watered it and it started to leak out the bottom, but the flowers are bright. He suggested I pick one every day and give it to Prabhupāda so that the flowers will last a week.

Then he said, "And here's one for you." The one for me has—I wouldn't call them roses, but they look a little bit like simple, pink roses. They're also sitting over there on the desk. A sweet gesture on his part. He bought them on Saturday, the day before Easter, maybe to do something Easter-like. And here we are with our flowers, the day after Easter.

It's cold out. I'm glad of that because it will keep people away from this resort area. I'm writing three times a day for an hour at a stretch. A writing session means coming to the page and emptying out my pockets. I'm building up to something. I'm not sure how usable it will be, but I have faith it will have value.

The only way for me to have faith in writing sessions is to consider them devotional service and acceptable to Kṛṣṇa. I was reading in Prabhupāda's book that a devotee may not immediately feel the results of his devotional service, but he performs it anyway with faith that it's doing good and that Kṛṣṇa is the protector. If we offer something to Kṛṣṇa, then we'll be satisfied. It's not *so* important that we feel something. It can be enough to feel dutiful and loving toward the spiritual master's order.

Now I'm writing in a way that I have developed, you could say, on my own. I have strong attachment to, and conviction about, it. It's a little bit unorthodox, but I have to pursue it anyway. To be out on such a limb, I have to have faith—not just faith in a mundane mind-revealing process of writing, but faith that the sincere offering will be accepted by Kṛṣṇa and will produce something wonderful as Prabhupāda asked us to do.

Although my "something wonderful" is not a helium balloon with the *mahā-mantra* emblazoned on it floating over the city of Bombay, or wonderfully sculpted Jagannātha Deities or a Jagannātha cart, or a big sum of money, it's still something the spiritual master can appreciate. I fear he may not appreciate it. He asks, "What are you doing?"

"Oh, I'm free-writing three times a day."

When he finally hears it out, he might wonder where this fits into the *saṅkīrtana* movement, but I can show him that it does fit in because it's *kīrtana* and *anartha-nivṛtti.*

I write whatever comes and try to purify it. In this way, I keep making myself more fit to be a serious devotee and trying to become pure. And the end result is good writing that strikes other devotee readers as authentic.

Sometimes I think about talking to Prabhupāda about my writing. If Prabhupāda asks me, it won't be necessary to go into all the intricacies of the professional vocation. Just tell him what it is. I'm writing about Kṛṣṇa and I'm writing about how I may improve in Kṛṣṇa consciousness so I can share it with other devotees. I'm writing instructions on how to practice Kṛṣṇa consciousness. I'm giving examples of how to overcome *anarthas* and ways to see Kṛṣṇa in whatever we do. Sometimes I read and write down the texts and express them in my own words. I encourage devotees that whatever service they do is also part of the *saṅkīrtana* movement. I try to avoid the too controversial and political issues that devotees talk about, and remind us that the most important thing is chanting and hearing.

When I describe my writing like that, it sounds positive. This is all I have to say if someone asks me to explain it, even my spiritual master.

Does that sound strange? It sounds like I'm withholding information from Śrīla Prabhupāda. But I'm not. I'm just saying that it's such an internal and technical thing, having to do with the nuts and bolts of my service. It might not even be appropriate to tell Prabhupāda all that, even though it's part of what I'm doing.

Let me think of an example. Say you were doing electrical work in the temple. The spiritual master asks, "What service are you doing?" You say, "I'm doing electrical work. Sometimes the devotees blow a fuse and I correct it, and in general, I see that all the wiring is in order." That's a very general description. If you started getting into all the technical details, it might not be appropriate. It may not even be appropriate if you started saying something like, "I'm not sure this is the service I want to do or if it is acceptable to you." You could raise some questions, but all I'm saying is that every last doubt that occurs to you about your service, or every description of what it is, does not need to be passed before the spiritual master. He wants to know results, the effect it has on others, the effect it has on you, and whether you have been instructed to do it by an authority.

Prabhupāda knows that my life is open to him because I'm writing before his eyes. What can I say? I'm shameless. I'm embarrassed sometimes at the nature of the work I do. But I'm drawn to it and I'm offering it.

One may say, "Well, why do you write something that is so liable to be doubtful, that is quirky, and so on, so full of yourself and the past?" The answer is that when I go to write what comes, that's what comes. That's who I am. I'd rather not be pretentious and take up my work as if it's something different than my inner feelings. That wouldn't make sense to me. My work *is* my inner feelings—learning how to express them.

Another way to say this is that I do a kind of writing that is constantly practicing writing. In this way, I keep in shape to do this service. Sometimes I take from that practice and share it with devotees so they can see that devotional service is not only an external process, but it's the actual thought process as we perform our work. A *sādhu* is not supposed to be private; his life is open. I try to write like that without any pretense.

To me, it's an exciting thought, and a positive one. I have some idea that it may be offensive. Will my spiritual master be able to understand what I'm writing and why? Will he tell me I'm only allowed to write expository essays if I want to write in devotional service? Sometimes I worry about that.

I expressed myself recently in a letter to our BTG editor-in-chief, Jayādvaita Mahārāja, who was saying how he prefers articles which are neutral and professional, that are researched and presented in a balanced way, rather than very personal, honest approaches. At least as they're done by the nondevotees, he finds them tiresome because so little comes out of it. That may not be exactly what he said, but it's close.

I responded, "Well, we're not going to get Kṛṣṇa consciousness from *any* nondevotee writer, whether he's a neutral writer who researches their articles for *The New York Times* or a poet who writes more his own deep experiences. But we can borrow from both of them and I hope that BTG magazine can represent both."

That's what I would want to say to Prabhupāda, that there are different ways to write, and this is the more—what should I say?—the more self-revealing method, to write very personally, but to offer it as a form of Kṛṣṇa conscious preaching. People mostly get the other kind of presentation, the formal, philosophical essay, although they are discovering that personal writing, even in terms of effective journalism, captures the audience better. Personal writing is a type of writing and it's the type I do.

I shouldn't have to have such a big lump in my throat when I try to speak about this. Partly that lump is there because I like it so much. I'm afraid it will be rejected, and I'm afraid I won't be able to accept the rejection. But I have to think more simply about it. It's a type of writing and it produces. I churn out all this practice writing and then carefully edit some sections to present to devotees. Devotees hardly know what it means to go through this churning process—they just read what I present and like it or don't.

So stay simple and get behind what you're doing. Otherwise, you'll spend a lot of your energy spinning your wheels, debating whether or not to write at all. There's the epigraph to the book called *Henry Miller on Writing.* I think I've quoted it before. He said, "I proved to my satisfaction that, like any other mortal, I too could write. But since I wasn't really meant to be a writer, all that was permitted me to give expression to was this business of writing and being a writer. In short, my own private struggles with this problem. My grief, in other words. Out of a lack I made my song very much as if a warrior challenged to mortal combat and having no weapons, must first forge them himself, and in the process, one that takes all his life, the purpose of his labors gets forgotten or sidetracked." To write about the life of a writer is something I often do.

This other point Miller makes is a little strange to me, that he feels he's not really a writer, so he can only *talk* about writing. I guess that means that since you can't really launch into a story or an essay, you always feel more at home talking about the writing itself, or your private struggles with the problem of being a writer. That shoe seems to fit me, at least as I'm talking today.

He says we are forging our own weapons. We're challenged. What are you doing? Are you a writer? Somehow you feel mortally challenged. It's a private challenge and you have to defend yourself. "Yes, I'm a writer. I'll show you that I'm a writer." Then you write about writing and you spend your whole life getting ready to be a writer or talking about being a writer, defending yourself and the way you want to write. You seem to forget what you were supposed to do.

There, dear friends, I've unburdened myself. I hope I haven't burdened you by talking about all this. Please don't feel burdened. We all have our struggles and I guess we want our struggles. At least I want to go on writing and to share with devotees this sincere attempt to serve Kṛṣṇa. I hope whatever struggles they have, I'll be able to match them and say, "I think I know a little bit of what you mean. I have undergone similar struggles. I face my struggles by sitting at the desk and writing. You do it in other ways. But life is a struggle as we try our best to serve Kṛṣṇa."

Prabhupāda singing:

hare kṛṣṇa hare kṛṣṇa, kṛṣṇa kṛṣṇa hare hare
hare rāma hare rāma, rāma rāma hare hare

9

Prabhupāda singing:

govinda jaya jaya, gopāla jaya jaya
rādhā-ramaṇa hari, govinda jaya jaya

Haribol. Today I finished reading *Renunciation Through Wisdom.* I also had my front teeth removed. Therefore, I will not be able to pronounce certain words properly, especially "fifth" and words like that. But I'll try my best.

Renunciation Through Wisdom was written in 1949, when Prabhupāda was a *gṛhastha*—early in his preaching career. It's a wonderful book and well translated. I marked different parts I particularly like and I want to read them aloud.

Prabhupāda writes about the three modes of nature and how we have to transcend them. As long as somebody is within these modes, he becomes proud and may even enter the religious field. That's also mentioned in the thirteenth chapter of *Bhagavad-gītā.* One should be prideless. The example of pride is the religionist. It's unfortunately one of the paths of life by which we may try to distinguish ourselves and want respect. Perhaps there's no feeling of grandiose pride to compare with what you can do when you think yourself the great religious master or an *avatāra.*

Even on a smaller scale, someone tries to see God through his own speculation and then considers himself an advanced devotee and everyone else inferior. Intoxicated by false ego, he will see his activities, which are motivated by passion, as divine.

In contrast to this, Prabhupāda writes, "One should constantly remember the Lord and pray to Him for mercy"—just the opposite of being confident that you know God or that you *are* God, and not accepting the mercy of guru, *śāstra,* and *sādhu.* We should always pray to Kṛṣṇa for mercy.

How wonderful that is! We hope again and again that it's something we can soon attain, but it's difficult to always pray to, or think of, Kṛṣṇa. It's hard to constantly beg for mercy. It's hard to be free of passionate activities even in the name of spiritual life, and always think of Kṛṣṇa. It's one thing to be under the mode of passion in material life, but then when you have a religious life and still you run under the mode of passion, then you've missed the point. The point is that one should constantly remember the Lord and pray to Him for mercy.

That doesn't mean you have to *only* pray for mercy; we're not *bhajanānandīs.* But while doing different things, we should never think we're doing them on our own, but ask Kṛṣṇa to please make them come out in a way that's pleasing to Him. If we forget to specifically ask Kṛṣṇa for help in that way, then what can we expect? We may think, "It's presumptuous to pray to Kṛṣṇa," but here Prabhupāda says, "Go ahead and do it. It's your constitutional position to think of Him as ordered by your spiritual master." By praying to Kṛṣṇa directly, we're not jumping over our spiritual master.

"Then the Lord, situated in the devotee's heart, responds to such a prayer and illumines his heart with knowledge, which dissipates the darkness of ignorance." Prabhupāda quotes Lord Caitanya:

tṛṇād api sunīcena
taror iva sahiṣṇunā
amāninā mānadena
kīrtanīyaḥ sadā hariḥ

He gives the translation and then says, "Often people do not understand the transcendental message of this verse. Although they are forced to act by the influence of the three modes, they make an artificial show of humility, pretending to be weak, lowly, and penniless beggars."

To understand that I am Brahman is one meaning of humility. Then, "The essence of this teaching is to understand that matter and spirit are diametrically opposed. When we are inspired by devotional service to the Lord, our original identity begins to manifest in us and ultimately brings us to God realization. The devotees work hard to induce people from the materialistic masses to take up devotional service, all the while trying not to disturb their minds. Such spiritual efforts are never to be confused with the mundane endeavors."

Again, the contrast between being in the mode of passion and being humble and favored by Kṛṣṇa. The devotee preacher is trying to preach so well, not to disturb people, but to somehow give them Kṛṣṇa consciousness. He may be quite active in organizing book production, Food for Life, or other ways to reach the public, but he does these activities while praying to Kṛṣṇa that they can be done nicely and that people will come. He prays that people will come to Kṛṣṇa consciousness. He begs Kṛṣṇa to allow him to be instrumental in this end.

Thus the devotee's attitude becomes fixed. He doesn't ask anything for himself. He has already received the mercy. Now he's taking that mercy seriously and even before he's perfect, he's giving it to others.

Sure, these are familiar themes, but that doesn't make them less rare, less wonderful. I don't think that by hearing Prabhupāda speak on them, I have realized them fully. But I do realize that this prayerful consciousness is not impossible. I can become humble. I can remember Kṛṣṇa. I can practice *tṛṇād api sunīcena.* And I can pray to Kṛṣṇa for success in preaching.

Now another sentence by Prabhupāda: "If we are inspired by our remembrance of the Lord and by His will, then we will never be misdirected. We will not be intimidated by the horrible hallucinations of this illusory material energy. By following the spiritual master's orders with single-minded determination, we will remain undeterred in executing the Lord's service and will make quick progress."

I liked this because I thought of the world and how we get overwhelmed by it. I just read one newspaper story and thought about a place in the world where there's war. I sometimes worry that the horrors of war will happen to me. I wonder whether I'm supposed to do something about that far-off place. I may even think about how material strife is unending and how I will be born into it again. These thoughts can be intimidating. But we're not meant to get caught up in that; we're meant to think of Kṛṣṇa. Then we'll see materialistic life as hallucination, a pleasant or unpleasant hallucination—it's not real. We're not meant to get entangled in the world, but to work in Kṛṣṇa consciousness. This isn't escapism in the negative sense. It's the real work of a human being. When we engage in Kṛṣṇa consciousness, we are assured of quick success.

I can just go on and on. There are so many good sections in the closing pages of this book. I'll do a few more.

Prabhupāda gives a quick, one-paragraph distinction between *vaidhi-bhakti* and *rāgānugā.* It's not a technical discussion; he just says that *vaidhi* is the stage of strict rules and regulations, and *rāgānugā* is spontaneous devotional service. In the spontaneous stage, the mood of surrender is the natural expression of the self. He says the more we follow, the easier our service will become. We will develop enthusiasm.

The Lord comes as bona fide spiritual masters. He Himself is guru. He's always there and He's always trying to help us.

"The sages say," Prabhupāda writes, "when we surrender to the Lord we will clearly see how He personally makes arrangements for us, even in small matters." That blew my mind because I really try to avoid thinking like that. When other people express it, I find it hard to take.

The other day, I complimented a devotee on the *capātis* he was cooking. He said, "Well, I'm really not doing this myself. I'm making a prayer before each one and someone else is actually helping." I thought, "How could he call upon God to help him make *capātis*?" Although the cooking was certainly a spiritual act, why would Kṛṣṇa be willing to improve the *capātis* if He weren't willing to improve the conditions in Bosnia or Russia or the United States in the ghettos? Then I read that passage. It seems that Kṛṣṇa *is* willing to directly help a humble devotee and He's not willing, on the other hand, to do what seems to be a more urgent, worthy cause like curing AIDS or stopping the big problems because no one is working on those problems in the right way. The people are getting more and more into *māyā* instead of asking for His shelter.

I saw this problem in a different way by reading that statement. I think I will always think like that now, remembering this quote. Why should I prevent Kṛṣṇa from acting in the world, or insist that He has to act in a certain way? I don't usually insist that Kṛṣṇa cure the big problems, but I don't dare imagine that He will act in an individual life. Hmm.

Next, Prabhupāda discusses how to study under guru, *śāstra*, and *sādhu*. We must denounce the Western mentality of defying spiritual tradition in scriptures. We should not raise too many doubts and questions. This is a nice reminder. The part about humility was mentioned earlier. I want to take it up practically. Don't keep raising doubts and wanting to debate issues which are impossible to resolve with logic. Accept the śāstric conclusion, the guru's conclusion. That's the way to gain knowledge. Stay away from philosophical debate based on logic.

I'll end here my appreciation of this book.

Prabhupāda singing:

govinda jaya jaya, gopāla jaya jaya
rādhā-ramaṇa hari, govinda jaya jaya

One little exercise on the lighter side is to try to get in touch with yourself so that you don't careen through the world under the mode of passion. You admit to yourself what really pleased you today, what you really had a feeling for aside from what you were supposed to have a feeling for. You scan your recent memory.

I know when I do this exercise, I always get embarrassed because I start thinking about the pleasure of eating. Eating makes me happy. It's usually more difficult to say that facing a writing session made me happy. Sometimes it feels more like despair, although usually by the end, I feel better.

Today I had a little extra time before going the dentist, so I wrote a little story. The theme repeated other themes I have written about, and it was very short, but it brought me satisfaction. There was play in it. I like those types of things.

When I was riding in the car on the way back from the dentist, I found a coat in the back seat and used it as a pillow. I was pleased to be able to find that and rest my head. A rest is always pleasing. You don't really notice it at the time, but it's pleasant to get a little rest when you need it and then come up again to serve Kṛṣṇa.

I guess little mental perceptions—trying to think of things to write and read—that brings me pleasure.

The sound of the rain. Getting things done. The resolve to go ahead with this kind of life. Sitting in a dentist's waiting room. And the dentist—I like the way he puts up with us and does the work for us and speaks to Madhu. Madhu's Italian is not so good, but mine is non-existent. Then when he's finally done with us, when he has not only done the work in my mouth, but made it clear when we can visit again, and when all of Madhu's questions are answered, he smiles, partly to signify that he's done with us, but also to show his good nature. He's doing such nice service for us and we're just receiving it, but he's good-natured about it and I like that. We devotees should also be like that. We should give people a little cheer in our lives as we go about our work.

We know that our work is tremendously beneficial for the souls of those with whom we work, but we shouldn't be dogmatic about that, or glum. People would see glumness as a contradiction to what we are preaching. Sometimes people complain about things like that, or they tell us we're too blunt, even to the point of being manipulative. Why do we expect people to do things our way (or for us) just because we are devotees? We sometimes respond to this complaint by saying that we're not sentimental, like Christians. We are doing good, so we don't need to accompany that with a smile and a pious face. But little gestures, when they're genuine, are important parts of exchanges. The main point is that we should be genuine. Genuine involves some effort, some awareness. If I ask a person how he feels, I shouldn't be absorbed in my own purposes, but smile and listen to him. That attentiveness touches people. Take the time to do it.

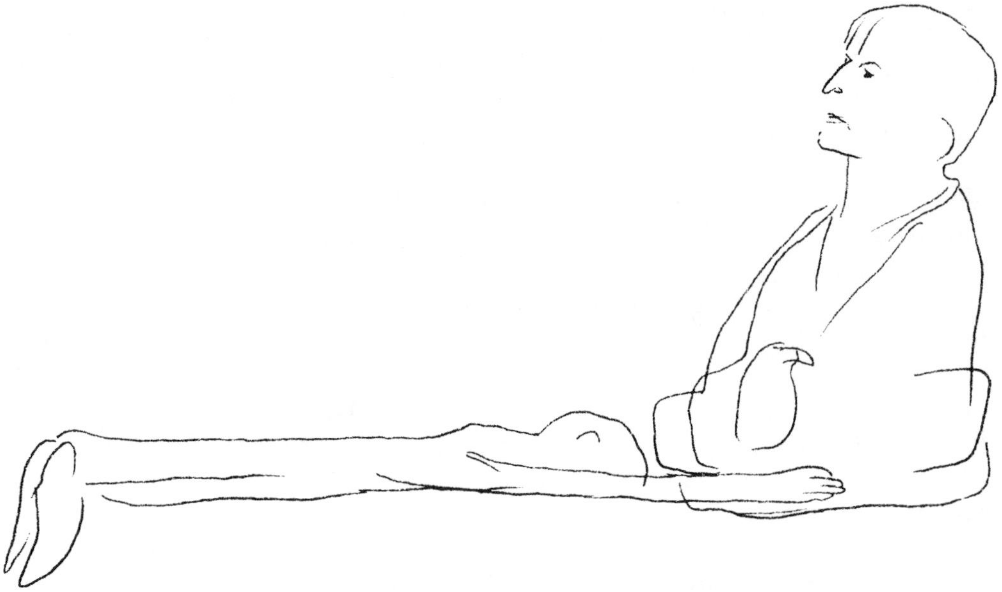

I don't generally feel any hoop-la happiness. It's raining today, so what do I expect? And I don't have my teeth. And my *dhotī* is too tight.

I don't have enough love for my Prabhupāda *mūrti.* I can't expect to be a blissful devotee, can I? Prabhupāda's book tells me that there's plenty to be assured about. He tells me that Kṛṣṇa is reciprocating with us even in little ways. Be thankful to Kṛṣṇa that when you think of the things you say you turn to—the hot *capātīs,* the rice and *dāl,* the sweet after the meal—rather than be embarrassed, remember that this happiness comes from Kṛṣṇa who wants me to have a nice taste in spiritual life, and He is willing to give it to me in whatever form I am able to receive it.

I'm not yet able to taste the *bhāva* of the holy name, but He sees that I want *some* satisfaction and that I have even heard that the cook is praying the *capātīs* will come out nice. Accept it. In fact, if I do, it becomes a first-class, spiritual reciprocation, eating *prasādam.* It's mainstream *bhakti.* Prabhupāda called it "kitchen-religion." *Prasādam* is not for sense gratification, but to be offered to Kṛṣṇa. In my case, I offer it to Prabhupāda and take the remnants as his mercy.

I heard Prabhupāda describing the way Kṛṣṇa eats. He said Kṛṣṇa doesn't eat the way we eat. When we get some fruit, we consume the whole piece. It all goes into the body. He made it sound so voracious.

But Kṛṣṇa is spiritual. All He has to do is hear our offering prayers and He accepts it. He leaves the fruit for us. He's so nice. To describe it really grossly, He's not like a garbage truck that takes in and grinds up everything. He's delicate. He takes what we offer as soon as we sincerely offer it. By the way, He won't take it unless we offer it. Then He leaves it for us to eat. He wants us to enjoy it.

I also heard today a famous inquiry by young Viṣṇujana in 1968. He said, "When we were making the offering, some of us looked up at the plate and we saw a rose-colored light vibrating, emanating just above the plate. Is that Kṛṣṇa taking?" Prabhupāda said, "Kṛṣṇa takes, but you can't expect to see how He takes. That's a very advanced stage. How can you know that He takes? Because in *Bhagavad-gītā* He says *patraṁ puṣpaṁ phalaṁ toyaṁ.* When devotion is offered with the offering, then I take. That is our evidence or proof." Good answer.

So, me lad, don't be afraid to enjoy *prasādam,* although you do it with some gusto that isn't exactly on the highest level. Increase the devotion of your offering to Kṛṣṇa and don't eat too much. Then use the energy you gain by eating to serve Kṛṣṇa. In that way, *prasādam* being a bright spot in your day is not a bad thing. Kṛṣṇa is merciful. He's making life easy—we can make progress by eating *prasādam* made from innocent foods—rice, *dāl, sabjī, capātīs—capātīs* that are prayed for to come out nicely.

Prabhupāda singing:

govinda jaya jaya, gopāla jaya jaya
rādhā-ramaṇa hari, govinda jaya jaya

10

Prabhupāda singing:

govinda jaya jaya, gopāla jaya jaya
rādhā-ramaṇa hari, govinda jaya jaya

Hare Kṛṣṇa. What were some happy moments? Happiness isn't always coming from the body. Sometimes it arises in the mind. As long as we are embodied, we will experience both happiness and distress. The *Bhagavad-gītā* tells us not to be enthusiastic about the happy moments or depressed about the unhappy moments because the happiness and distress simply follow each other. If we ride the waves of happiness, we'll also have to ride the waves of distress.

Body-centered happiness is extremely limited. I think about that whenever I try to enjoy something like a hot shower. The hot water is so pleasant, and to feel the chill removed, the warmth penetrating, is a deep, physical satisfaction. Then that's it. You can't take it any further. The body has been satiated to its limit. It's hard to describe, so I hope you know what I mean. Reaching that point is always a letdown. And as a devotee, I'm left to wonder why I invested so much of myself in this kind of limited, physical satisfaction. By then, I can already feel the inevitable downhill that inevitably follows any satiation. It's not real satisfaction.

I remember when my sister went to college and discovered the golden mean in her Greek philosophy class. She told me about it. You get excited by discovering ideas at college. You sometimes become so attracted to an idea that you decide to follow it. That's how it was with Madeline. The golden mean captured her enthusiasm; something in it vibrated with her own sentiments. She thought I would also benefit from following the golden mean. The golden mean is Aristotle's definition of the moderate middle ground between any two extremes.

"You really ought to take to this, Stevie. You always go too far one way or the other."

Looking back to what became of my sister, I realize now that the golden mean was her way to reconcile herself with middle-class American mediocrity. In her intellectualized way, she tried to climb above the middle class, but rationalized that kind of mediocrity where you never try to live out your dreams because they might lead you into excesses. Excess could turn you into a tragic failure.

All this is true. It can happen. Other philosophers, however, counseled differently. Nietszche, for example, said we should live dangerously. That was one of his mottoes. You have to take chances. We devotees who came to Kṛṣṇa consciousness certainly had to live dangerously and accept the risk of following our highest ideals for happiness, good association, God consciousness, and purity. We didn't only live the golden mean.

After you've entered the Kṛṣṇa conscious path, there is something similar to the golden mean that we have to follow to make advancement. Kṛṣṇa teaches, "Don't eat too much, don't eat too little. Don't sleep too much, don't sleep too little." Be balanced and moderate when you practice yoga.

Often in speaking the philosophy, we find ourselves doing what we call the balancing act. For example, we should be introspective, but we also have to be outgoing. We should be soft, we should be hard. We should be this, we should be that. Whenever a lecturer gives a class in which he stresses one side of things, someone in the audience will try to balance it. "Yes, but what about . . . ?" The balancing act goes on. It gets tedious. Are we here to balance everything into a perfectly neutral state rather than share our enthusiasm about something?

I'm rambling, I know. I started this talk by acknowledging the law of physical satiation. Before that, I spoke about trying to find my own small pleasures and mentioned that some of them come from the mind.

I felt pleasure today when I broke through in writing, by passing surface concerns to recognize my dedication for the kind of life I lead. I read a line this afternoon that supported what I was feeling. It's in the thirteenth chapter of *Bhagavad-gītā* where the items of knowledge are described. The verse says that one of the three items of knowledge is "aspiring to live in a solitary place; detachment from the general mass of people; accepting the importance of self-realization . . ." *Vivikta-deśa*, a solitary place. Prabhupāda writes, "Naturally when one is adapted to the spiritual way of life, he will not want to mix with materialistic men. That would go against his grain. One may test himself by seeing how far he is inclined to live in a solitary place, without unwanted association."

I liked the particular phrasing because when I started out writing this morning, I noted my own restlessness. I wanted to move on. I was pushing Madhu to get us out of here as fast as possible. I wanted to visit another temple. This present situation isn't something we scheduled. It had to happen because the dentist insisted that he needed me to come over a period of three weeks. Now that he has been working on me, I have had trouble speaking and I look odd without my teeth. Still, I was thinking to make a public temple appearance.

Then I thought, "Wait a minute, this is what I want. I'm doing well. I'm reading and writing. What am I afraid of?" This phrase is nice. "One may test himself by seeing how far he is inclined to live in a solitary place, without unwanted association." It's a test. Do you get restless when you are alone? Do you like it? Do you find it productive? If you have a favorable response toward *vivikta-deśa*, that's good. That shows you are advancing.

Prabhupāda writes, "Naturally a devotee has no taste for unnecessary sporting or cinema-going or enjoying some social function, because he understands that these are simply a waste of time."

Now, we will say, of course, that Prabhupāda is referring to materialistic association and that real solitude means living packed up with many devotees. Social functions in Kṛṣṇa consciousness are quite nice. When we find, however, that ISKCON social functions are not conducive to spiritual life, a devotee may want to avoid them and spend his time chanting and reading instead.

So that was a happy moment for me today, making the discovery that I did still have a taste for solitude and that there was no need to break out of it right now. It's a gift from Kṛṣṇa. If Kṛṣṇa thinks it's not good for me, He can take it away. But I have to use it as much as I can, showing Kṛṣṇa I'm grateful and that I can make good use of this *vivikta-deśa*.

Prabhupāda singing:

govinda jaya jaya, gopāla jaya jaya
rādhā-ramaṇa hari, govinda jaya jaya

The mountains are snow-topped here. It's raining where we are, but it's probably snowing on the peaks. I couldn't tell yesterday—it was so cloudy—but today with a brighter sky, I can see the jagged, snow-white peaks.

I heard Prabhupāda speaking recently about how experiencing love requires two people. Love has to be tangible and has to be tangibly shared with someone tangible. He illustrated his point by saying we can't love the sky. I've heard him say that before. It makes me uneasy because I titled a book, *Dear Sky*. He said that although the sky pervades a room, you can't relate to the sky, although you can relate to a desk in the same room. A desk is tangible. You can't love the sky.

I think you can love the sky, and Prabhupāda's words are not opposed to that. You can love the sky if you see it as an ever-changing, beautiful display of Kṛṣṇa's energy. The sky's color reminds you of Kṛṣṇa. As long as the sky doesn't remain neutral but is accepted in its connection with Kṛṣṇa, then there can be love. Prabhupāda was using love of the sky as an analogy for the neutral state of appreciation for God where there's not yet any love. You can't love God if you're overwhelmed by Him in a vague sense. You can only love God when His personality is evident. Prabhupāda said, "We want to love a boy or a girl, not the sky." It made me wonder, "Was I proposing we take up the very beginning of God consciousness, where you don't see God except vaguely?"

I would like to defend my *Dear Sky*. The title was, of course, designed to intrigue the reader. It's not a usual Kṛṣṇa conscious description. Devotees don't usually write letters to the sky. I originally planned to call that book *Dear Moon* because I remembered Prabhupāda said you can't love the sky and his tendency to compare the sky, the first of elements, to the earliest stage of God consciousness. "Dear Moon" was more tangible, but it also had connotations of being a materialistic heavenly planet. We went for "Dear Sky" because the book contained many appreciations of the changing Irish sky. The Wicklow sky is full of varieties. It also comes from a particular letter to the sky written over Santo Domingo one morning.

Prabhupāda also uses the ocean as an analogy for impersonal oneness, but he doesn't stop there. If you want to talk about the ocean, then find out what the ocean actually is. Enter into the ocean. Then you will see that it's not all one. There is a variety of aquatics, both large and small; there are plants and mammals and strange creatures. Similarly, the sky, although it may be used as an example for neutral oneness, has a variety of features. That's what I was noting in my book. Every morning, Kṛṣṇa, the Supreme Artist, would streak the sky with a new sunrise and then diffuse that color into the clouds. On one morning it might be as dark as somber music, with great piles of clouds and mist. There would be a lot of sky, then there would be very little sky. The clouds would move like big ships one day and the next the sky would be clear. Such variety! My "Dear Sky" wasn't just a meditation on the vast oneness of impersonal nature, but on the Lord's beautiful creation. Admittedly, I could be accused of loving a part of God's creation that speaks back to you only in intangible ways. Still, there's reciprocation.

A dawn sky seen from the Santo Domingo temple roof gave me hope. Dawn brings everything back to life, it seems. It illuminates variety. Dawn is cool and full of light. It's exhilarating. In that exhilaration, a devotee naturally turns to Kṛṣṇa in gratitude.

I think of it as a beginning stage, but one that's so tangible and so thrilling that even a dull soul can be touched. We are so covered over that we don't see Kṛṣṇa—not in the material world and not when we see the Deity. It takes us so long to appreciate the Deity. But the sky, it has so much power. From William Wordsworth: "My heart leaps up when I behold/A rainbow in the sky:/So was it when my life began;/So is it now I am a man/So be it when I shall grow old,/Or let me die!/The Child is father of the Man;/And I could wish my days to be/Bound each to each by natural piety. The heart does respond to the manifestations of awe-inspiring beauty of the sky.

There, I've confessed it. I'm a sky-lover.

Prabhupāda singing:

govinda jaya jaya, gopāla jaya jaya
rādhā-ramaṇa hari, govinda jaya jaya

What else? Prabhupāda is always with us. I hope Prabhupāda *mūrti* always stays with us. Madhumaṅgala wanted to make Prabhupāda an *āsana*. It was very nice. I didn't ask for it. The *āsana* was so that when we stop in the van, Prabhupāda can sit out on the desk. There's so little room in the van, so he has to share the same desk I use.

I thought it would be enough to put the two mats on the desk that he always sits on when I place him on an altar, but Madhu really wanted to make a small, wooden *vyāsāsana*. He has many duties, but he took time out one day, bought the materials, and worked on it. That night he expressed some frustration that it didn't turn out. The wood warped, so the nails didn't go in right. Prabhupāda never got that *vyāsāsana*, but I'm sure he liked Madhu's attempt.

Now I want to get a bookstand for Prabhupāda, and a miniature dictaphone similar to the one he used (he had a table model with a hand-held microphone). Then when I get up at midnight to read, I won't have to "ignore" Prabhupāda. I could place before him his dictaphone and book and he could start to translate. Then I can be reading *Bhāgavatam* while he's translating it. Anybody have a miniature dictaphone out there? Please let me know. I'll buy it off you or we can swap something for it.

I like to worship Prabhupāda without long rituals where you have to sing a *bhajana* and repeat each line two or three times and offer ten articles. I like my worship to be more personal and private. And I like it when it doesn't take all morning but leaves me time to go onto other services for Prabhupāda. Offering him a dictaphone would be like that, and offering incense and different garlands every day, different *cādars*, different hats. In the afternoon, I have been reading to him for ten minutes from his collection of letters. I love doing it. Otherwise, he becomes a statue or a piece of furniture if I keep walking by him or doing things "for him" without recognizing him.

In the evening, I've been reading his letters to me and speaking with Madhu about him and about ISKCON in those time periods. I think of Prabhupāda while I'm reading those letters, meditating on how he's hearing and reminiscing with me about those times. He is the central actor in the ISKCON drama, although he saw himself simply as the Lord's servant. I hope to increase my attachment to him and to be with him more. I don't need to think of Prabhupāda in any other form than as the elderly *sannyāsī* he appeared to be. That is not a lesser form of Prabhupāda; it's his liberated form how he appeared in this world and the form I can know and immediately serve. By this service, I will go on to other service. I don't have to imagine it now. This Prabhupāda—it would be foolish to jump over him as he appeared to me, the person to whom I can offer *cādars* and saffron clothes, a beadbag, and a dictaphone, that person in the picture next to Bhaktisiddhānta Sarasvatī Ṭhākura, who wrote to me and said, "Dear Satsvarūpa, I read your article in the college newspaper about the eclipse of the moon. It is very nice." I want to remember that person.

Prabhupāda singing:

govinda jaya jaya, gopāla jaya jaya
rādhā-ramaṇa hari, govinda jaya jaya

Govinda *jaya jaya,* we are worshipping that Supreme Person, Govinda, the supreme enjoyer. May Prabhupāda's descriptions of Kṛṣṇa lodge in our hearts. May we always read of them as if they were an interesting novel. May we always take time out to read all his books again and again and in that way be drawn into the descriptions of Kṛṣṇa—Kṛṣṇa who is in everyone's heart, who has hundreds and thousands of hands and arms, who is said to have no hands, but who has spiritual hands. The Māyāvādīs say He has no eyes, but He has spiritual eyes. May we know that great, great conception of Kṛṣṇa and also Prabhupāda's intimate conception of Kṛṣṇa as Arjuna's friend.

Prabhupāda says that Arjuna used to insult Kṛṣṇa in friendly talks, but later he accepted Kṛṣṇa as his guru. We can remember that Kṛṣṇa who played on the Battlefield of Kurukṣetra, whose original form is always in Vṛndāvana in the relationship of lover and beloved. All of Kṛṣṇa's qualities are described in Prabhupāda's books. Let's get attached to them and realize how supreme and important they are. Our spiritual master is giving us the knowledge that leads to devotional service. If we find it tedious or repetitious, it's our fault. We have to find the right ways and the right times to take it in and appreciate it and be touched by it. We're so covered over, so diseased. We're so forgetful and offensive. We have to pray, "Prabhupāda, please let me read your books. Bring me to Kṛṣṇa in your words, which you are repeating from the *sampradāya* in your own way. Let it enter me and let me be able to speak it."

Yes, let me remember Kṛṣṇa, that eternal, fresh Kṛṣṇa. *Advaitam acyutam anādim ananta-rūpam.* Śrīla Prabhupāda can deliver us to Him if we please him. *Yasya prasādād bhagavat-prasādo.* Kṛṣṇa is not dependent on the guru, but He insists that we come to Him only through the spiritual master's mercy. He's not my devotee who says he's My devotee, Kṛṣṇa says, but he who is a devotee of My devotee, that's My devotee.

Kṛṣṇa will reveal Himself to us when we please the guru. Kṛṣṇa and guru work together in an intimate bond to bring the *jīva* back to Godhead. It will be wonderful when those two persons become revealed to us by our service to them. Under the guru's order we chant Hare Kṛṣṇa mantra and Kṛṣṇa dances on our tongues. We go to the spiritual master and say, "O Gurudeva, I chanted Hare Kṛṣṇa as you ordered me and I have achieved some nice results. But I also have some doubts. Please explain this to me . . . " We should never think, "Now I know better than my guru," or, "He's an outmoded guru. I have another guru who is more important."

You know what I mean—this is the life I want and not the life of hesitation and fault-finding, or of thinking of the guru on a material level. Pray for it and work for it. Be happy in Prabhupāda's service and in reading his books. Fight, fight, fight the demons of doubt. Always stand like a good fighter—never resting and always ready for battle. Use the weapons that the guru has given. Fight boldly. Fight your own demons and fight the demons in the nondevotees. Don't indulge demons. Push them aside rudely as if they were puppets with ferocious faces or nightmares ready to be dissipated. Just push them the hell out of there and start representing Kṛṣṇa in all your words. Then you will feel exhilarated and happy in Kṛṣṇa consciousness. Prabhupāda assures you, and you can believe him because he is a great fighter. Appreciate what he has done and how he has led us forward to savor Kṛṣṇa consciousness through the practicing stage. That practicing stage includes preaching Kṛṣṇa consciousness.

I guess that's enough for today. Let me try to follow my own good advice.

Prabhupāda singing:

govinda jaya jaya, gopāla jaya jaya
rādhā-ramaṇa hari, govinda jaya jaya

11

Prabhupāda singing:

govinda jaya jaya, gopāla jaya jaya
rādhā-ramaṇa hari, govinda jaya jaya

Haribol. Your man here in Brescia, without teeth, sitting, tight-belted, looking out the window at the top of the *"tulasī"* tree, which is blooming its beautiful, pink-maroon blossoms against the dull, cool, spring sky.

I usually come to this session unrehearsed, although I tell myself it would be good if I could prepare some topics to talk about ahead of time. I did dash down a note on a Post-it before I came into the studio. It was about a moment that occurred this morning when I was at the dentist's office. I wrote: "All glories to Prabhupāda, John Franco said."

The moment was this. We had a very early appointment. John Franco is the dentist and he's also a devotee. I described him to someone recently as half Hare Kṛṣṇa and half Christian. He's had some experience associating with the devotees here and some of that experience has been, of course, permanent and profound for him, encouraging him to align himself as a devotee of Kṛṣṇa. He has pictures of Kṛṣṇa in his office and he plays, among other music, Kṛṣṇa Vision tapes. I don't know much about whether or not he practices *sādhana* or strictly follows the regulative principles, but I heard he was considering initiation at one point.

Unfortunately, he also has had some disappointments in the devotees' association. For example, last year he was quite sick with pneumonia. He said that while his Christian friends visited him, no devotees did. He felt disappointed by that and he began to build his disappointment into depression. Later, he admitted that his absorption in this became exaggerated because he has a tendency to get depressed when he's sick. But he said that this disregard is typical of ISKCON devotees and that they're not kind or caring. Maybe they write off sickness as "the body," or, "just your karma," whereas the Christians came through and saw it as part of their faith in Christ to go and see a sick brother.

Of course, when John Franco told us about this incident, we pointed out that neglecting our Godbrothers isn't our philosophy. On investigating, I also heard that some devotees did go see him. Still, this is how he felt.

He has been charitable to me and given me free dental treatments. He sees me early in the morning before his work day begins. We always greet each other, "Hare Kṛṣṇa." There's not much more I can say to him because I don't speak Italian. His talk with Madhu is 99% about the dental treatment.

He has always been genial, and I can see that he thinks of his treating me as devotional service. He's certainly not obliged to treat me for free. It's his offering. Anyway, I am aware of his strong Christian leanings. He went to Assisi on pilgrimage over the Easter weekend and he does that every year. This is all a lead-up to what happened.

We were in the dentist's office and somebody called. It happened to be a devotee who wanted to talk to me. When John Franco spoke to him in Italian on the phone, he said, "like Prabhupāda." I think he might have also used the word *homagio*, homage, obeisances.

The caller probably said *"homagio* Prabhupāda," obeisances to Prabhupāda. Then John Franco said the word "Prabhupāda." I was so touched by how he said it. I was so pleased. It made me think of this federation of people all over the world who greet each other, "All glories to Prabhupāda." They don't just say it, but they feel it. They're joined together by their recognition of Prabhupāda as an extraordinary, saintly person, an empowered pure devotee, and the spiritual master of us all.

nama oṁ viṣṇu-pādāya kṛṣṇa-preṣṭhāya bhū-tale
śrīmate bhaktivedānta-svāmin iti nāmine

namas te sārasvate deve gaura-vāṇī-pracāriṇe
nirviśeṣa-śūnyavādi-pāścātya-deśa-tāriṇe

"I offer my obeisances to His Divine Grace A. C. Bhaktivedanta Swami Prabhupāda, who is very dear to Kṛṣṇa on this earth, having taken shelter of the lotus feet of the transcendental Lord. My obeisances unto you, O spiritual master, servant of Bhaktisiddhānta Sarasvatī. You are so kindly teaching the message of Lord Caitanya and delivering these Western countries, which are filled with voidism and impersonalism."

That little incident created a happy moment for me this morning. I often take this simple bonding for granted, but to see the devotees touching each other in this faithful exchange of recognition of Prabhupāda and the mission of Lord Caitanya coming through Prabhupāda moved my heart.

I know there's a lot of sadness and disappointment about the fact that our coming together under Prabhupāda has also produced disappointment, schism, and so on, and that the different parties blame each other for this fact. It doesn't always seem possible that we find out how to cooperate and agree, but if we are really Prabhupāda's followers, we all look to him and individually, privately do our best to follow his instructions.

That's all I wanted to say. Maybe I said too much. All glories to Prabhupāda. Thank God there are people around the world who say those words and who thus establish the real basis of our devotional friendships.

Prabhupāda singing:

> *govinda jaya jaya, gopāla jaya jaya*
> *rādhā-ramaṇa hari, govinda jaya jaya*

Now I would like to tell you a story that relates to this radio show. It was Jean Shepherd who first told this story, actually, but I heard it for the first time only last year when it was printed in the introduction to a poetry book by the Pulitzer Prize-winning poet, Charles Simic. He said he was repeating a story he heard thirty years ago on Jean Shepherd's radio show. It's a story about a flute player.

There is a tribe of native Indians in the Amazon who have a practice of selecting the best flute player in their tribe. Every twenty years or so, they find an unexcelled flute player. They bring him to the forest and dig a deep pit. Then they put him at the bottom of the pit with enough food and water to last a couple of weeks. That's it. They leave him there with no way to get out. He's an offering to the gods.

What happens is that he's supposed to fast until death. Just before he loses all his strength, he is to play his best flute music for the gods. His villagers are not there to hear him; his music is meant for the gods alone, and in his final desperation, it is expected that his music will be at its best and most poignant.

Shepherd went on to say that the last time this had been done, an anthropologist hid himself in the jungle. When the flute player played his last music, the anthropologist recorded it.

Simic breaks into the story to say, "I don't know whether Shepherd was putting us on or not. He was not above doing such a thing to his audience of insomniacs. But when I heard it that night and Shepherd said, 'I have a copy of that tape. I'm now going to play it.' I was spooked. This is amazing. This is like the myth of Orpheus in the modern time."

Finally, in the wee hours of the morning, Simic says, "Shepherd put on the tape." It was an eerie experience, this rasping-for-last breath music coming from the person who was trying to make the best of the ultimately desperate circumstances he was in, playing this very lonely music.

Then Simic added that whether this story was made up or not didn't matter: he took it as a truth that we're each alone in our own pits, even if we are sitting in our apartments on the Lower East Side in New York City listening to that music on the radio. We're each alone.

I mentioned this story to a couple of devotees, especially those who are helping me and encouraging me in my writing. One of them said he didn't think the image fit me at all. "You're not in a pit alone playing for God. You're playing for the devotees. When I see you play your 'flute,' you're right there and the devotees can hear you."

But another devotee said, "I think this is a beautiful image and in a sense, you are like that. When you free-write, it's just for Kṛṣṇa. Fortunately, we get a hold of some of it and share it on your behalf with the devotees. But when you actually play, you play alone for Kṛṣṇa."

I'm not sure whether I fit into only one interpretation or the other, but I know that for me, there has to be some element of being in the pit. If I lost that, if I was sitting on the stage playing the flute—"Good evening, ladies and gentlemen. Thank you for attending tonight's concert and poetry-reading. I am now going to improvise right before your eyes. The first improvisation will be based on the popular, old, favorite song, 'My Gal Sal.' Then I'll play, 'My Funny Valentine.'"

I don't want to do that. Still, neither do I want to be sitting here talking meaninglessly, like Krapp, a lonely widower reminiscing about his own life, making tapes that nobody hears, and then realizing he's making his last tape and dying. That's a Beckett story. I don't like the image of a Beckett monologue, but something more cheerful and communicative, something more Vaiṣṇava that reaches past solitude to be shared with devotees. But if I am only playing for others, then what I want to say easily becomes compromised.

I'm trying to play a kind of trick—a seemingly impossible trick—to simultaneously stay in my pit and to talk to devotees, to speak *Entering the Life of Prayer* just for Kṛṣṇa, and at the same time, to share it.

Prabhupāda singing:

govinda jaya jaya, gopāla jaya jaya
rādhā-ramaṇa hari, govinda jaya jaya

12

Prabhupāda singing:

govinda jaya jaya, gopāla jaya jaya
rādhā-ramaṇa hari, govinda jaya jaya

Haribol. I want to continue the radio show despite the giant German shepherd next door (he's a floor above us) who guards that house. The house has a big fence around it, and the German shepherd is in the parking lot. Sometimes I can see his head and shoulders, and his pointy ears. He spends quite a few hours alone. I imagined him dying and how I would be glad for the peace—he barks so much it disturbs my sleep—but then I thought, "Why would I be glad if he died?" I would be sad if he were a devotee. Even though he's a dog, he works hard at what he's supposed to do. He's a creature, a spirit soul, with Supersoul in his heart as he guards that parking lot. What a bleak existence. He's alone a lot with almost nothing to do, completely exploited by his owners who, for only the price it takes to feed the guy, have a live security system.

He's always alert. He has his own strategy. He doesn't get too excited by passersby, although he might if someone came too close. Instead, he barks a few times, runs back and forth, and lets it go at that. The owners seem satisfied with his work. Anyway, he's finally quiet, so let's get on with our business.

Prabhupāda often thought of dogs as just the opposite of God—G-o-d, d-o-g. He said if you weren't interested in God, then you would immediately become plunged into the opposite—interest in dog. If you say you're God, that means you're dog. You could say that Prabhupāda's comparison is insulting to the dog. Dogs to Prabhupāda are the epitome of ungodliness. I once heard Prabhupāda say that if we show someone a book on how to care for dogs, then they will be quite interested, but if you show them a book about God, no one will be interested. "Just see their mentality."

Prabhupāda didn't use the God-dog imagery to be incredible or comical, but to point out the absurd state of degradation of godless people. Such is Kali-yuga.

Prabhupāda singing:

govinda jaya jaya, gopāla jaya jaya
rādhā-ramaṇa hari, govinda jaya jaya

I was sick yesterday. I had a headache—pain behind the eye—and didn't do my radio show. Didn't do my story-writing either. Didn't do anything. Just sat back and tried to tolerate. Took rest early. Then during the night I woke up a few times because of dreams and tried to see if the pain was still there. Even my dreams had some indirect connection to the pain. The material world is painful.

Although the pain is gone now, I lost my momentum. It's hard to start today, which is a shame because life is flowing by and I don't want to descend to the level where I don't appreciate my own activities and their inherent joy.

We should engage in activities that fit our natures. Then we should find joy in them, despite whatever difficulties we encounter. We should also take pleasure in dutifulness. When we lost that simplicity, we lost something precious. Then we have to fight to get it back.

What little I remember of before I was a devotee—here I go again, "before I was a *devotee*"—I mean, before I met Prabhupāda and aspired to become a devotee—what little I remember of the atheistic, existential writings of Sartre and Camus and their popularizers, is that man and life have no meaning. Therefore, the bravest and most worthy thing we can do in the face of such absurdity is to give it meaning: give your life value. Practice morality. Practice art. Love. Then die. There are theistic versions of Sartre's and Camus' value assignment, but I'm not articulate enough to express them. Kierkegaard's philosophy tries to express the theistic version. I used to understand them better than I do now. Although I'm exposing my ignorance, I'm bringing all this up to show that philosophers are aware of the importance of value.

I also remember an old, popular novel that was made into a movie, called *Something Of Value.* I saw it when I was quite young. It starred Rock Hudson and had to do with the Mau-Mau uprising in Africa. I remember coming home from that movie with a germ of an idea that you have to live for something. You have to find something important to yourself, give it value, and then that would infuse your life with meaning. Life has meaning. Everyone is seeking something of value.

We have the responsibility to assign value to whatever we have chosen. The perfect guru comes to us, the *śāstras* come to us, the Lord comes to us. They tell us what we should value above all else. They don't leave us groping in absurdity. They give us the nectar of immortality. What has value compared to that? What can possibly measure up to the supreme value of serving the all-attractive Supreme Personality of Godhead?

Although we are taught what to value by guru and Kṛṣṇa, we still have to voluntarily assign our own value to it. Otherwise—this may sound strange—it won't be valuable to us. Thus we see so many people not finding Kṛṣṇa consciousness valuable because they are unable to surrender. They don't willingly give their hearts.

Here is an example. In the beginning, we ask people to chant. Just try it for a week. When we say that, we're asking people to have faith, and on that faith to assign some value to the chanting. We want them to give themselves to the chanting long enough for the chanting to justify that faith.

We are not living in an absurd universe where we have to give everything to Kṛṣṇa and He gives nothing in return. We are not atheistic humanists who believe *only* in their self-assigned value. If we give to Kṛṣṇa, Kṛṣṇa will reciprocate with us. *Ye yatha māṁ prapadyante.* As a matter of fact, even if we don't give to Kṛṣṇa, Kṛṣṇa is giving to us. Therefore, if you want to have access to what's really valuable, to the nectar of immortality, to spiritual upliftment, to life behind the body and the daily doldrums, you have to give.

So, all this to explain how I deal with pain knocking me off the track of my usual activities. It happens to me too when I chant sixty-four rounds on an Ekādaśī simply because I don't do my normal activities. When I face them again, I have to ask myself whether I want to do them at all. The rest of the time I have a momentum, so I don't have to ask myself that question. One doesn't want to have to ask it and face the day with a heavy heart, or a big moral decision, "Do I want to be a devotee? Do I want to write stories? Do I want to do a radio show? Do I want to talk to people?" There's something to be said for momentum and the mechanical life. You don't have to start the engines up again, and sometimes you even get a glimpse of how fortunate it is to have a life filled with personally assigned value and which is meant for the ultimate good. Thank you, Śrīla Prabhupāda.

Prabhupāda singing:

govinda jaya jaya, gopāla jaya jaya
rādhā-ramaṇa hari, govinda jaya jaya

One of the worst things about being sick is the quality of my *japa*. Mine gets bad because I don't have enough energy to give to chanting when I'm in pain. I tend to excuse myself the way a lenient teacher excuses a student. The teacher sympathizes with the kid; he knows what it means to be sick, so he lets the kid off from school. I tell myself I don't have to eat, I don't have to read or write, I don't have to give all my energy to *japa*. It may be better for me to take a day of rest rather than to plow through the pain. Pain is a warning; it tells me I need to rest. Okay, I don't have to excuse myself when I offer shoddy *japa* to Kṛṣṇa: "Sorry, that's all I can do. I'm sick today." Is that right?

What is good chanting anyway? Is it so difficult to do? Is it only a matter of physical vigor and pronunciation?

After this radio show, I'll take a break, then write a story. I know what's facing me. The story is like a truck stuck in the mud. I'm going to have to push it. It has only been unattended for a day, but it still got stuck in inertia.

I sometimes imagine that I'm the father of five kids. They're rushing up to me, demanding and needing and complaining. After all, I've been away for a whole day. Their demands take on the voice of my inner critics and censors: "While you were gone, we considered that maybe your stories were so immature and artificial that there's no sense in continuing them. Also, you were so presumptuous to think that you could write improvisation and that it would have some worth. You shouldn't write this way. If you try, you'll definitely fail. You've set your sights too high." They scream at me.

"Stop!" I say. "I know what I have to do." Then I imagine myself climbing into a jeep with flaps on the sides instead of doors. I tell everyone to hang on and we all make the best of it. That's what happens.

I had a note to myself to occasionally try to remember myself listening to the Jean Shepherd radio show back in the 1950s. That may help me get into a rapport with you, my audience. I have one memory. I had my own radio, which I kept in my room. I had a bed with a headboard that had several shelves on either side. I kept the radio on one of those shelves so that I could lay down with my head on the pillow and listen late at night without disturbing anyone. Shepherd's program went late—until one or two in the morning. I usually had to shut the radio off by 11 if I was going to get up by 6 and make it to Brooklyn College in time for my first class. In those days, I communed with Shepherd. It didn't matter to me that his show was just a show and that it was being paid for by so many sponsors as he sat there, surrounded by technology, and broadcast from New York City. Although the show wasn't a private sharing between me and Shepherd, he managed to give it that quality. It was wonderful, actually, how he spoke to people's loneliness and how we would respond to him by finding hope. He seemed to be speaking on behalf of all lonely people because he seemed to be speaking out of his own loneliness.

That's what I meant earlier about my own attempt to live in the pit and yet communicate: the more you try to communicate and express something deep and sincere to people, the more it taxes your own integrity. Shepherd got around that problem. He spoke so privately, yet so publicly. I want to do that too.

Prabhupāda singing:

govinda jaya jaya, gopāla jaya jaya
rādhā-ramaṇa hari, govinda jaya jaya

13

Prabhupāda singing:

> *ceto-darpaṇa-mārjanaṁ bhava-mahā-dāvāgni-nirvāpaṇaṁ*
> *śreyaḥ-kairava-candrikā-vitaraṇaṁ vidyā-vadhū-jīvanam*

Haribol. This is a radio show for devotees. When devotees talk, they like to talk to devotees, although they also hold open classes for anyone interested. Devotees want to increase the number of devotees, so they risk the open talks. If people don't like it, it would be better if they left rather than disrupt the meeting. If they do try to disrupt the meeting, however, Kṛṣṇa would protect us.

Bhāgavatam narrations tell of extraordinary events. Modern scientists don't accept them—the Lord's direct participation in human, earthly events, His defiance of natural law by riding on Garuḍa's back, lifting huge mountains, leaping eighty-eight miles in a single bound. Even the demigods are mythological to the *asuras,* who prefer chance over intelligent direction. It's interesting how we who were born in the Western, materialistic camp could have come to accept *Śrīmad-Bhāgavatam.* That story is relived every time a Western-born man or woman comes to Kṛṣṇa consciousness.

I don't want to launch into this full force right now, but I am aware that there are some listeners out there who might not believe fully in Kṛṣṇa and His pastimes. Somebody is rotating the dial right now, looking for an "oldies but goodies" rock 'n' roll station or a sports broadcast, and he has stumbled onto this dial. He's stopping to listen for awhile. "What the heck is this? Are they stories?" Maybe he'll begin to wonder.

I have remnants of those questions. Still, I don't owe it to my waning demon to start a fight with him or to present another manifesto against his theories. I don't have to prove anything to him, but if every time I open the *Bhāgavatam* I have to go through that preamble, how will I be able to relish Kṛṣṇa's pastimes? I have come to accept what Jīva Gosvāmī calls "the inconceivable powers of the Supreme." Kṛṣṇa can do anything. I also have come to accept the *Śrīmad-Bhāgavatam* as a history of universal events, not just events that have taken place on earth. Therefore, the *Bhāgavatam* histories don't have to tally with the history we have learned in this world. I also accept that the *Bhāgavatam* will free me from the cycle of birth and death. We accept everything we know from authority, from hearing. Either we accept *śabda-brahma* or we accept scientist-*śabda*. It's either one or another. I am not over-awed by scientists, especially when I consider the long history of cheating and speculation and altering that has gone on in the name of science. The scientists are actually lacking in knowledge and in power. Therefore, even on the material level, the concept of a supreme, intelligent being, one who can give me protection from this world and beyond, is much more appealing to my sense of truth. And I am attracted to those saintly persons who practice renunciation and who develop devotion to the Supreme Person. I want to be one of them.

Spring is coming. Kṛṣṇa's in control. How can you get a better dose of Kṛṣṇa consciousness than by reading the *Śrīmad-Bhāgavatam*? The *Bhāgavatam* dispels the vagueness people attach to God and presents Him as He is.

People don't recognize the fact that they were born in a flash, and in another flash they're gone. They take their brief life spans as everything. What do they do with their time? They work to enjoy their senses and relieve their bodies from suffering, and they try to avoid decay and death. All that means struggle. People have to struggle whether they like it or not, or so they say. Thus they have made life difficult for everyone because it's a life arranged for maximum sense gratification at whatever expense. No one has a cool brain to consider how to reach the mode of pure goodness, how to hear about Kṛṣṇa, how to protect the soul and culture it. No, life is for sense gratification.

Whatever religion the different societies have been practicing has largely been spoiled by the drive for sense gratification. That drive is so powerful that it enters into the religious movements themselves. That fact doesn't in any way negate or tarnish real spiritual purposefulness; however, it's extremely difficult to get the purpose of spiritual life across to anyone, especially in this age.

Sometimes even the devotees are affected by the materialistic mentality and again succumb to this world. But we don't belong to this world; we belong to Kṛṣṇa and His spiritual world. Prabhupāda, therefore, drilled us over and over again on the basics: material life is wrong by its very nature. We are eternal spirit souls. The Personality of Godhead is the main person in existence. We should worship Him. He's our protector. We should take up our relationship with Him as the most important relationship in our lives. Follow the authorized process for approaching Him.

In this age, chanting Hare Kṛṣṇa and following the *bhakti* path will bring the best results, but if you follow some other *bhakti* process—*bhakti* in Christianity or Islam or whatever—then be serious. *Bhakti* is *bhakti.* Lord Caitanya's *bhakti* process is the most expert. Therefore, it has the most advantages, but *bhakti* is *bhakti*. Theism is theism. God is God. These are the basics: life is not meant for sense gratification or for seeking a temporary justice. We are not here due to some godless accident as the scientists would have us believe. The human form of life is very special. Don't waste it.

Prabhupāda singing:

ānandāmbudhi-vardhanaṁ prati-padaṁ pūrṇāmṛtāsvādanaṁ
sarvātma-snapanaṁ paraṁ vijayate śrī-kṛṣṇa-saṅkīrtanam

14

Prabhupāda singing:

> *ceto-darpaṇa-mārjanaṁ bhava-mahā-dāvāgni-nirvāpaṇaṁ*
> *śreyaḥ-kairava-candrikā-vitaraṇaṁ vidyā-vadhū-jīvanam*

Ceto-darpaṇa-mārjanaṁ. May the chanting of Hare Kṛṣṇa clean the dirt that's on the mirror of our minds. Although we don't chant with pure devotion and fixed attention, still, the chanting has its effect. We go on chanting whether we feel its effects or not, with faith that it will work. We'll be clear one day. We're already reaching, or in, the clearing stage, and even now, our sinful reactions have been burnt up by our attempt at chanting Hare Kṛṣṇa Hare Kṛṣṇa, Kṛṣṇa Kṛṣṇa Hare Hare/Hare Rāma Hare Rāma, Rāma Rāma Hare Hare.

I went to the dentist today. I won't tell you all the details, but my mouth is sore now that the anesthesia has worn off. You can never be completely comfortable in this body. You can never find just the right food. Usually, whatever your tongue likes messes up your digestion.

We can't blame God that He gave us faulty bodies. We have wonderful bodies actually, but they're delicate and prone to cancer and attacks from misuse. The material body is a network of paths leading to death. Anyway, it's our fault we've ended up in prison. We broke God's laws and we've been sentenced.

As the days pass, we also see a definite diminishing return on pleasure. Hopefully, though, old age will bring us a drop of wisdom. Pain helps, too, to teach us renunciation when we don't otherwise have the sense to take it up.

This morning I read about Dhruva Mahārāja. Dhruva practiced severe austerities, so Prabhupāda took the opportunity to discuss austerity in his purports. The first thing he did was make it clear that we cannot imitate Dhruva Mahārāja's severe austerities. Dhruva first ate only what he could find in the forest. Then he ate only some ill-tasting berry usually eaten by animals. Then he stopped eating altogether and fasted on a little water every few days. Then he slowed his breathing so that he took only one breath every few days. Finally, he slowed his breathing down so much that he was breathing only once every six months. We can't do anything that austere. At least we can become moderate in our habits of eating and sleeping, and we should accept only *kṛṣṇa-prasādam.*

Still, we may not be inclined to do even that. We might find ourselves always looking for sumptuous and palatable foods. My experience has been that Kṛṣṇa can take away our ability to chew. That sounds like such a basic function—to chew—but Kṛṣṇa can take it away. Then what will we do? Then it won't matter how hot and tasty the *capātīs* are.

Prabhupāda singing:

ānandāmbudhi-vardhanaṁ prati-padaṁ pūrṇāmṛtāsvādanaṁ
sarvātma-snapanaṁ paraṁ vijayate śrī-kṛṣṇa-saṅkīrtanam

Who are you, you who are listening to this show? None of us are exactly the same. We each have our own viewpoints and our own experiences. Strange, isn't it? All these lonely *jīvas* spread out, each doing their own thing. Even the people we intensely interrelate with all have their individuality. Kṛṣṇa is in everybody's heart, but nobody really looks that carefully at anybody else. We have to learn to be kinder to each other and more useful on this earth.

Prabhupāda taught us how to be non-envious and less self-centered. He wanted us to work beneficially for others as well as ourselves when he gave us Kṛṣṇa consciousness. Still, we're all different. We all want to improve ourselves, but not at the expense of others' peace. When self-improvement is practiced in mutual and respectful God consciousness, it becomes a beneficial, social act. We can see that practically by studying the lives of people like Jaḍa Bharata or even of Christian saints. They were so determined about their own spiritual advancement and they endured all sorts of difficulties and obstacles in order to reach their spiritual goals that their successes have become both inspirational and exemplary for everyone who comes after. In other words, their own spiritual advancement became their greatest act of charity to their fellow human beings.

Prabhupāda singing:

ānandāmbudhi-vardhanaṁ prati-padaṁ pūrṇāmṛtāsvādanaṁ
sarvātma-snapanaṁ paraṁ vijayate śrī-kṛṣṇa-saṅkīrtanam

I repeat, who are you, dear listeners? Are you safe in your own places? Are we sharing on a similar wavelength? I wish you the best. I hope we can all chant Hare Kṛṣṇa and know the Supreme Truth as Prabhupāda is teaching it. That aspiration in itself brings us together. Now I hope that we can all set a good example in our own ways to encourage the nondevotees to take to Kṛṣṇa consciousness.

Wow! That sounds like a real truism, or a platitude, or a dogmatic, do-gooder statement. But that's it. That's the Kṛṣṇa conscious message. It's bracing and optimistic. I feel the message, I preach it, and I believe in it. All I hope for is that I and the other devotees can attain the stage of being free of material misery even in this lifetime. Let us only be absorbed in serving Kṛṣṇa.

Kṛṣṇa's pure devotee is always thinking of Kṛṣṇa and how to serve Him; therefore, he is automatically protected by Him and free from fear, just as animals and babies are free from concern in their mother's protection. They simply rest in their constitutional dependency.

Prabhupāda singing:

ānandāmbudhi-vardhanaṁ prati-padaṁ pūrṇāmṛtāsvādanaṁ
sarvātma-snapanaṁ paraṁ vijayate śrī-kṛṣṇa-saṅkīrtanam

I'll say good-bye now. It was nice to speak about this wonderful vision given to us by Lord Caitanya. I hope whoever has been listening to this broadcast will take up this vision and find themselves detached from the pains inflicted by dentists and other persecutors in this material world. See you tomorrow under this pale-pink, dark-pink tree, which reminds me so much of *tulasī-mañjarīs* bending over like weeping willows and proclaiming Kṛṣṇa as the best artist.

Prabhupāda singing:

ānandāmbudhi-vardhanaṁ prati-padaṁ pūrṇāmṛtāsvādanaṁ
sarvātma-snapanaṁ paraṁ vijayate śrī-kṛṣṇa-saṅkīrtanam

15

Prabhupāda singing:

nāmnām akāri bahudhā nija-sarva-śaktis
tatrārpitā niyamitaḥ smaraṇe na kālaḥ
etādṛśī tava kṛpā bhagavan mamāpi
durdaivam īdṛśam ihājani nānurāgaḥ

Haribol. It's April 13 and not unlucky for us as long as we take shelter of Kṛṣṇa in His holy names. It's not unlucky. Quietly, methodically, practice Kṛṣṇa consciousness. Prabhupāda says don't be hasty. Come to the top stage. He says you can't get through the required stages without really passing through them. We preach *utsāha-niscarya dhairyat.* Be confident that it's happening. What more can we do but practice Kṛṣṇa consciousness and depend on Kṛṣṇa? Patience and enthusiasm are nice qualities. I like them when I see them.

We have limits. In one sense, it's human to admit our limits. We may have so many qualities. They may begin as subreligious principles, but if they end up devoid of thinking of Kṛṣṇa, they're roads that lead nowhere. It's especially wonderful when on the *bhakti* path one sees and hears about the brilliant goal ahead—direct service to Kṛṣṇa. Let's not be hasty and make wild claims how much we love Rādhā and Kṛṣṇa. We love Them, but we still have to go through the work of purification.

The qualities of patience and faith in the prosecution of duties is often referred to as the quality of a humble devotee. He's patient and faithful because he knows Kṛṣṇa is with him. How does he know? Guru and *śāstra* have told him so. Who are we? We may not know one way or another by realization, but we are faithful to the Kṛṣṇa conscious path. This is faith in what is yet to come about.

Śraddhā is the basis of every stage, even the most advanced stage. It's not dropped. Faith is present throughout our lives, even in the material sense. We have faith that we'll breath again, that the food we purchase hasn't been poisoned, that the house won't fall down on us, that the bank won't cheat us of our money. Life operates on faith.

A devotee, however, goes through these activities with his personal connection to Kṛṣṇa intact. He prays to remember that connection, to be grateful to pray constantly to please Kṛṣṇa, to realize he is just a tiny, dependent child.

We all need protection in this bewildering material world. The earth is insignificant in universal terms, yet Kṛṣṇa's material energy is just as bewildering to us here as on any larger planet. And it's just as full of fear as the *jīvas* become bewildered and act cruelly out of their lust and greed. Kṛṣṇa, we need Your shelter at every moment.

Nārāyaṇa-parāḥ sarve, na kutaścana bibyati. Prabhupāda teaches us that the pure devotees are not afraid to go anywhere because they always know that Kṛṣṇa is with them. That faith is a wonderful quality. To know that Kṛṣṇa will protect me. I may find myself in the darkest of forests, but I won't be alone. He is in my heart. Who will challenge that? "Is He in this pillar?"

The more desperate we become in our dependence on Kṛṣṇa and no one else, the more Kṛṣṇa reveals Himself. Conversely, the more weak-hearted we are, meaning the more attached to material possessions and security we are, then the more we can't know Kṛṣṇa. That's because we're telling Kṛṣṇa we don't need Him. "As long as I have my nice, warm socks, my apartment, and my bank balance, I can chant Your holy names, but I don't desperately need You. A man with such a comfortable arrangement as I have does not need to call on You, unless I need something else to add to my comfort."

I'm parroting now. This is a parrot radio show. Here in Italy, the neighbor has a parrot. The parrot repeats, *"Ciao, ciao,"* and something else whenever people walk by. I'm a parrot who can repeat long phrases. I want to represent my great teachers by my speech, and probably it doesn't matter so much how much I myself understand, as long as I accurately repeat their words.

I simply want to be an instrument. Does that sound ridiculous to you, creators of this civilized world? I also crave originality, like everyone else. Those who think that allegiance to their intellects is the ultimate honesty, the absolute truth—I'm sure this sounds strange to them. I'm trying for something more selfless. I'm trying for the parrot stage. The true parrot, of course, is not just the mechanical reciter, but one who adds sweetness to the message with his own beak, the *śuka.*

Prabhupāda singing:

nāmnām akāri bahudhā nija-sarva-śaktis
tatrārpitā niyamitaḥ smaraṇe na kālaḥ
etādṛśī tava kṛpā bhagavan mamāpi
durdaivam īdṛśam ihājani nānurāgaḥ

I was just thinking of the line of thoughts I've been expressing. A lot of it is argument against the kind of people, the skeptical agnostic; the people I went to college with. The kind of people I worked with after college. The kind of people I was in the Navy with. The kind of person I was.

On a radio show like this, I think of myself as mostly alone or speaking only to some devotee friends. I don't have to argue with *them.* Normally when I give a *Śrīmad-Bhāgavatam* class, I try to speak to the devotees and not argue against the skeptics. I try to speak about how we can get along with each other, how we can control our minds, and so on, devotee concerns.

Why, then, in this relaxed atmosphere, do I start sparring with these skeptics? One reason is because they are still so close to me. I'm still intimidated by them. I realize that meeting the opposition is preaching. These skeptical attitudes are the reason why the Kṛṣṇa consciousness movement is not more widespread. Therefore, I get in my jabs whenever I can. It's true that the skeptics aren't personified before me to receive my jabs, but the devotees will take them as jabs to their own skepticism and welcome them. Or if they're free from skepticism, they'll recognize the weapons they have to use to free others.

Prabhupāda hardly forgot those skeptics. He could certainly speak nectar only for the devotees, but he also knew that the rascals were so predominant that they had captured the prize of the material kingdom. He wanted to recapture it for Kṛṣṇa. He was a good soldier.

Prabhupāda singing:

nāmnām akāri bahudhā nija-sarva-śaktis
tatrārpitā niyamitaḥ smaraṇe na kālaḥ
etādṛśī tava kṛpā bhagavan mamāpi
durdaivam īdṛśam ihājani nānurāgaḥ

All right, I should say good-bye. I offer my obeisances, embrace the men, offer my *praṇāmas* to the ladies, and make *daṇḍavats* to all. I hope we can meet again and that I can loosen up and tell better stories, ones that are connected to Kṛṣṇa. I hope that we can all become Kṛṣṇa conscious, not hastily, but by very directly engaging ourselves in devotional service. Don't wait before becoming a devotee. We're already connected in *paramparā.* When will we become ripe mangoes for Kṛṣṇa to taste?

16

Prabhupāda singing:

vande 'ham śrī-guroḥ śrī-yuta-pada-kamalaṁ śrī-gurūn vaiṣṇavāṁś ca
śrī-rūpaṁ sāgrajātaṁ saha-gaṇa-raghunāthānvitaṁ taṁ sa-jīvam
sādvaitaṁ sāvadhūtaṁ parijana-sahitaṁ kṛṣṇa-caitanya-devaṁ
śrī-rādhā-kṛṣṇa-pādān saha-gaṇa-lalitā-śrī-viśākhānvitāṁś ca

It's a beautiful day. Do you see the clichéd image when I say that? Sunny. Warm. Verdant. But that's not what I mean. It's rainy and windy and beautiful. Even from where I sit on the second story of this house, I can see only a tiny bit of the world out the window. I see that *tulasī-mañjarī* treetop. It reminds me of the word *chartreuse*. I know it's not chartreuse—chartreuse is a clear, light yellow-green, isn't it? But try to imagine a pink version of chartreuse. That's what it's like. It's not a shocking pink, but something lighter, clearer—that's the color of this tree. At first I thought the tree was blooming even more fully than yesterday, but now I realize that the overcast sky has made it look intensely pink. The wind is tossing the heads of the weeping *"tulasī-mañjarīs."* I don't think you'll find a more striking—even disturbing and exciting—image of spring than this.

This tree makes me feel rootless. I'm not in America looking at North American lilacs or even a tree I can name. Since I'm always traveling, I don't get the privilege of being in tune with spring. I am always having to pick up spring from a car window as I drive by fields of rape flowers or European poppies. I wish I were in a country where I knew what spring meant, but still, I try to pick up spring wherever I can. Kṛṣṇa is the flower-bearing spring.

The sky is overcast. Of course, there are millions of kinds of overcast skies. This one is white and fleecy; no blue. Within that fleeciness, I can distinguish lumps of clouds. As I stretch my neck, I see a clear space just above the horizon. Beyond that on the horizon, I see snow-topped mountain crags.

How's that for an introduction of time and place? It's outrageous how evocative that tree waving it's *mañjarī* blossoms has become for me.

Prabhupāda singing:

nama oṁ viṣṇu-pādāya kṛṣṇa-preṣṭhāya bhū-tale
śrīmate bhaktisiddhānta sarasvatīti nāmine

I'm different this year than last year in that I don't have such a hankering to go to Vṛndāvana. Sound unhealthy? Maybe, but maybe not. I do want to get into *sādhana* and I want to write and distribute my writing as preaching. I don't want to waste time. I'm reading Prabhupāda's books more than I did last year, reading them exclusively, actually. Last year I read the six Gosvāmīs as we have them translated in ISKCON.

What about my weaker desire to go to Vṛndāvana? I just feel I should go for a purpose. I don't like to take my yearly trips to India for granted. It's fortunate that I had a sense of anxiousness, of desiring to touch the dust of Vṛndāvana and to stay there as long as possible. In Vṛndāvana, devotees have special access to Kṛṣṇa that doesn't seem available anywhere else. If that need to be in Vṛndāvana isn't present, but you still have a positive feeling for discovering Western places and becoming transcendental there, burrowing into Prabhupāda's books wherever you are, and then looking for another desk and chair at which to write, then you can go with that. Always remember Vṛndāvana, sometimes by going there and sometimes in separation.

Any kind of falsity, egging yourself on and pretending ecstasy isn't good. Most of us probably find that our desires, even our spiritual ones, ebb and flow. We're not yet permanently situated. What I really mean to say is don't judge others by your own mood. You may be in an ebb of feeling about how important it is for you to live in Vṛndāvana, and someone else is at a high tide of feeling.

This year I'm going to Māyāpur instead of Vṛndāvana. I don't have a great reason for doing that. It just seems to be a natural direction for me this year. Others seem to be doing it too.

I was thinking how I don't like to become overly influenced by others but like to follow my own resolution. But I want to dig what others are doing (like we used to say in the '60s). I want to go with it, appreciate that it's good for them, and then get on with my life. I know this isn't an entirely Vaiṣṇava philosophy, but we could all use a little of this "live and let live" attitude. We can hear what someone else is doing and say, "That's nice. I hope it's good for you." Then we can follow our current inspiration, absorbing what we're trying to learn while getting past the superfluous, cutting through dull matter, and hearing and chanting and serving Prabhupāda.

Prabhupāda singing:

śrī-vārṣabhānavī-devī-dayitāya kṛpābdhaye
kṛṣṇa-sambandha-vijñāna-dāyine prabhave namaḥ

mādhuryojjvala-premāḍhya-śrī-rūpānuga-bhaktida
śrī-gaura-karuṇā-śakti-vigrahāya namo 'stu te

I observed today before noon how there was such a pitch of activity in our apartment as the schedules ran tight and we had to move from one task to the next quickly with nimble fingers and intent faces. I was in my room worshipping Prabhupāda. I have rehearsed the *pūjā* many times in my mind, so it's easy for me to do one part of it after another—his bath, drying him off, putting on his clothes, then drying off the last specks of wetness on his face with a Q-tip. After that, preparing for my own oil massage and bath.

After having tended to him and glancing at my watch to make sure I'm not running late, I heard Madhu and Dīna-dayārdra going through the last phases of cooking lunch. This is the time Madhu always starts getting wild-eyed. He knows that Dīna-dayārdra, who is sixty-four years old, can't move as fast as he would like him to. Madhu tries not to push, but he can't quite control that. The two of them have a sweet relationship and they both know that this cooking tension is nothing to become disturbed about. Still, I heard the tense exchanges, Madhu saying, "No, no, not that, do this!" Then Dīna-dayārdra, "Yes, all right. Please excuse me. I'll try."

They're pounding the dough and getting it into the oven, then draining something, squeezing something else—there's a lot of action going on out there.

I'm taking Prabhupāda's bath water out of the room, and cleaning the copper *acamana* that holds his mustard oil, moving quickly out of the *pūjārī's* role into the bathroom role. I take a tape into the bathroom with me so I can hear Prabhupāda speaking.

I know these are little activities, but that doesn't make them less pleasing to Kṛṣṇa. Let's just hope, though, that wherever we are, we don't just spin our wheels in the name of "intense" devotional service.

Now it's afternoon and lunch has been served. Prabhupāda has already taken rest. It's almost 4 o'clock. The sky is getting darker. We'll be trying to push through with other projects before the day is over, but that pitch before lunch is always something memorable. I like the way the day's rhythms are varied. Kṛṣṇa is kind to give us those rhythms. I know He tastes variety in Goloka Vṛndāvana too.

Prabhupāda singing:

namas te gaura-vāṇī-śrī-mūrtaye dīna-tāriṇe
rūpānuga-viruddhāpasiddhānta-dhvānta-hāriṇe

I would like to believe in the saying that in creative enterprises, there's plenty more where that came from, and then spend lavishly. It's not that if I give out my best ideas, I'll be bankrupt. Conventional wisdom tells me I'll get more. Giving out creates momentum, so we shouldn't be stingy with the results of our creative endeavors.

Of course, that's different than the need to ration out energies, but there is a realm where you can tap into unlimited resources. *Ahaṁ brahmāsmi, tattvam-asi,* I'm spirit soul, the same as Kṛṣṇa. I can connect with Kṛṣṇa.

I was reading about Dhruva Mahārāja again in the *Bhāgavatam.* He attained such perfection that the Supreme Brahman appeared in his heart, and in quite a few incredible ways, Dhruva Mahārāja became the same as God. One example was that he became as heavy as God. When he put his toe on the earth, the earth rocked. Who can imagine that Kṛṣṇa became so much manifest in the body of this little boy?

Prabhupāda explains that when many passengers are flying in a plane, they assume the same speed as the plane, Or, you could say that they have the same force and velocity as the plane. They share in it. The unit energies share in the total energies.

Dhruva also stopped eating and held his breath. When he held his breath, the total breathing of the universe became choked up. This one boy had become like the universe itself. This shows that we are inherently capable of possessing a lot more energy that we think we have. It reminds me of how the scientists say that we use only 10% of our brain power. We're not very conscious.

Why do we settle for so much less? Dream and try to carry out those dreams. Be humble and patient, but don't be stingy.

Prabhupāda singing:

namo gaura-kiśorāya sākṣād-vairāgya-mūrtaye
vipralambha-rasāmbhode pādāmbujāya te namaḥ

namo bhaktivinodāya sac-cid-ānanda-nāmine
gaura-śakti-svarūpāya rūpānuga-varāya te

I read a nice statement in the notes in the back of the recently published edition of *Path of Perfection.* The editors give an introduction to ISKCON life after the reader has completed Prabhupāda's book about yoga. It's quite blunt, showing the connection of these lofty ideas and practices with the same Hare Kṛṣṇa movement known as ISKCON. But aside from the fact that it's somewhat brazen of them to do that (and I credit them for being so brazen, for having such a preaching spirit), there is one thing I noticed in their description about Prabhupāda. The writer says he was a genius in the way he was able to spread Kṛṣṇa consciousness.

> In *The Path of Perfection*, Śrīla Prabhupāda offers a brilliant summary of the methods of *bhakti-yoga*, revealing the universal applicability of this simple but all-inclusive form of yoga. He shows how even those who are entangled in the complexity and chaos of modern materialistic life can begin an uncomplicated practice which purifies the mind and puts one in touch with the Supreme Consciousness.
>
> This, perhaps, was Śrīla Prabhupāda's greatest contribution to our age. Śrīla Prabhupāda was an acknowledged master scholar of India's ancient spiritual culture and of its linguist foundation, the Sanskrit language. But he was not merely a textual scholar or a philosopher or theologian engaged in the manufacture of interesting philosophical or theological notions. He was a true spiritual genius who succeeded in bringing to life the efforts of India's universal spiritual wisdom in a form which is easy for twentieth century man to understand and practice.

Nice. The transforming quality of Prabhupāda—that he could make people devotees of Kṛṣṇa. He himself used to say, "So many editions of *Bhagavad-gītā* have been translated into English, but as a result, not one person has become a devotee of Kṛṣṇa. Now that we presented it as it is, so many people are taking to Kṛṣṇa consciousness."

Even the fact that so many schisms and splinter movements off ISKCON flourish to some degree is a credit to Prabhupāda. They are flourishing on his strength of having made something apparently foreign available to Westerners.

For myself, I like to think of Prabhupāda in a simple way. I don't feel the need to prove to myself that he was great. I just want to love him as the Vrajavāsīs love Kṛṣṇa. The Vrajavāsīs don't have to prove that Kṛṣṇa is God or that nobody else *but* Kṛṣṇa is God. They just love Him and want to be with Him forever. If Kṛṣṇa leaves them even for a moment, they simply think of Him and cry.

That's one way to think, but we also need the Rāmānujas and Mādhvas and their learned followers to prove Prabhupāda's exalted position to the world. And who's to tell us exactly how to develop our own relationship with Prabhupāda? Of course, we have to approach him in the standard way through inquiry and service, but there's also room for different attitudes, even within ourselves. Sometimes I like to take up that role where I prove Prabhupāda's uniqueness. Other times when that mood is preached in an official way and we are expected to beat the Centennial drum, for example, I think, "What are we trying to prove? Let's just love him and accept him as our guide."

Prabhupāda singing:

gaurāvirbhāva-bhūmes tvaṁ nirdeṣṭā saj-jana-priyaḥ
vaiṣṇava-sārvabhaumaḥ śrī-jagannāthāya te namaḥ

All right, that's all for today's show. I want to say good-bye and I hope that we'll do this again soon. In Kṛṣṇa consciousness, we get tested in different ways and at different times. Some of us seem to get a lucky break, a little padding, and some of us get everything stripped away and go through a lot of pain. There are different reasons for it. Some are weak, some are strong, but we're all parts and parcels of Kṛṣṇa. We should try to do our best to improve ourselves and not be unkind to others. Pray for that day when we and our colleagues in Kṛṣṇa consciousness will become mellowed and strong and Kṛṣṇa's mercy will be manifest in us. Then we'll all benefit. As one benefits, we'll all benefit because our hearts are charitable. Let's try for that.

Prabhupāda singing:

gaurāvirbhāva-bhūmes tvaṁ nirdeṣṭā saj-jana-priyaḥ
vaiṣṇava-sārvabhaumaḥ śrī-jagannāthāya te namaḥ

17

Prabhupāda singing:

> *gaurāvirbhāva-bhūmes tvaṁ nirdeṣṭā saj-jana-priyaḥ*
> *vaiṣṇava-sārvabhaumaḥ śrī-jagannāthāya te namaḥ*
>
> *vāñchā-kalpatarubhyaś ca kṛpā-sindhubhya eva ca*
> *patitānāṁ pāvanebhyo vaiṣṇavebhyo namo namaḥ*

I am proving to myself that I can speak any time by speaking today. One gets tired of oneself. Remember Samuel Johnson's remark to Boswell? "Sir, you have only two topics, yourself and myself, and I am sick of them both." Sometimes I hear myself saying something like, "Let us be charitable," and when I hear it later, I think, "Oh, who am I to so magnanimously advise everyone what to do?" It makes me feel uncharitable toward myself. Then, with somewhat sour feelings and also a desire to be truthful, I fall quiet. My mother used to say, "If you can't say anything nice, then don't say anything at all."

There are other reasons to be quiet: "Cat got your tongue?" My Uncle Jim used to say that to me. I remember when he used to call for my father, often he would ask to speak to me after. He would ask the usual questions—how I was or about school—or, "Don't you feel sorry for your fat old Uncle Jim?"

My responses were monosyllabic: "Yep." I said little else.

"How you doing in school? You doing all right?"

"Yep."

He called me Gary Cooper, the silent cowboy. What else could I say to my fat old uncle who was always cracking corny jokes and poking into my life?

"Yep."

"Cat got your tongue?"

There are reasons to be quiet, but if you have a radio show, then you can't be quiet. You have to talk about Kṛṣṇa, and that's the real definition of quiet, silent, *mauna. Mauna* is good for those who speak speculative nonsense and whose envy comes out, whose negativity comes out, whose doubts and confusion come out. They do better when they're quiet and listening to transcendental sound.

Speaking about Kṛṣṇa is better than quiet; it's real silence.

Prabhupāda singing:

> *namo mahā-vadānyāya kṛṣṇa-prema pradāya te*
> *kṛṣṇāya kṛṣṇa-caitanya-nāmne gaura-tviṣe namaḥ*

I can be quiet while I listen to that record of Prabhupāda singing his *kīrtana* in 1966. Baladeva said that Prabhupāda's vintage tapes are my Hare Kṛṣṇa love-song. Hearing those tapes is the way I can feel my own love for Kṛṣṇa and Prabhupāda, which may be contrary to the impressions I get when I chant and cannot pay attention to the sound. I *do* love chanting when I hear Prabhupāda singing and playing that drum, inducing us to go to the spiritual world. If I can sing with Prabhupāda, *something* will be evoked in my heart. We always think we don't have time to chant, although we seem to have time to talk and pile up sentences one after another. Do we think singing with Prabhupāda when he was introducing Kṛṣṇa consciousness in New York City is unproductive?

Yes, Prabhupāda started his movement at that same 26 Second Avenue that today is a lively preaching center in New York where you can walk off the streets and be with devotees in an atmosphere filled with the hopes of a new generation. It's right there in New York City, that transcendental oasis.

At the same time, I'm really talking about the 26 Second Avenue that exists only in my mind, only in my memory. It does exist.

When I hear him singing like that and I start to flash back a little on it, I wonder, "Prabhupāda, are you going to come back and do it again? Are you going to bring us to you again? You brought us out of such total forgetfulness that we can't even call it forgetfulness." Theoretically, we may say we had forgotten Kṛṣṇa, and that's true, but Prabhupāda woke us up.

Oh, I just remembered now that I had a dream. In this dream, I was telling someone that Prabhupāda said that in our past lives, some of us must have been Indians. I think in the dream I was talking to Gargamuni, or else he was present with others. As I said it, I broke down and began to cry, but I continued to describe what Prabhupāda had said, that some of us in our past lives were Indians and now have been born in this part of the world to continue the *saṅkīrtana* movement. In the dream, I felt ecstasy because Prabhupāda said that and I was to repeat it.

When the dream was over, a feeling flashed through me that I had cried but that I didn't have to. I had indulged in the tears. Then I thought, "If this happens again in my waking life, I'll be drier. I won't cry because I already indulged a tinge of desire to have a moment of ecstasy."

And the fact that it happened in a dream reinforced that it's even more unlikely I will allow it to happen in waking life. Anyway, I had forgotten that dream—it just popped up now. What I was talking about is how other memories of 26 Second Avenue are evoked when you hear Prabhupāda's early *kīrtanas* and you say, "Prabhupāda, will you come back for us?"

I am so firm in my other identity—when I was a young man who dressed all in black and who had broken away from his parents on Staten Island and had now lived for two years on his own on the Lower East Side. I wasn't doing so well actually, but I wouldn't have had it any other way. I didn't go home except to try to get some money and feel bad again.

Prabhupāda took me beyond that identity to a completely new consciousness. Talk about quantum leaps! I remember one devotee telling about his own change. He was a student at the University of Buffalo. He talked about his change from "buffalo to disciple." We were buffaloes, ignoramuses. Then we became disciples of the pure devotee of Kṛṣṇa.

If Prabhupāda would come back again, maybe I could make another quantum leap from *vaidhi-bhakti* practitioner to something more, from someone who has lost some of his daring and who is making an all-out effort to convince himself and Kṛṣṇa that he can go on writing and reading, chanting and hearing, developing his inner life, and who thinks that somehow this will do. I could be transformed into something more pleasing to Prabhupāda, or at least I could know what Prabhupāda wants. It's not that I have to change the nature of my activities. Prabhupāda might say, "This is good. Go on doing it. Now I'm going to show you the means to intensify it. You want to be an obscure prayer-maker? You want to be addicted to reading my books? That's good. You think that by doing this you will become a potent preacher of my message? All right, I'll allow you to do that service. You don't want to head up a temple? I understand. You don't want to be on the spot at a community and bear all the troubles, although I bear them for you? Then if you actually want to do what you say, this is how to do it and this is how to be blissful." Whatever it is, Prabhupāda can tell us. Or he might tell us something completely different. He might say, "Go back to Boston again," or, "Go to a new Boston and start up Kṛṣṇa consciousness. Do what I want. Be with me. Be like me." We could then help ourselves by depending on him again.

Prabhupāda singing:

he kṛṣṇa karuṇā-sindho dīna-bandho jagat-pate
gopeśa gopikā-kānta rādhā-kānta namo 'stu te

jayatāṁ suratau paṅgor mama manda-mater gatī
mat-sarvasva-padāmbhojau rādhā-madana-mohanau

dīvyad-vṛndāraṇya-kalpa-drumādhaḥ
śrīmad-ratnāgāra-siṁhāsana-sthau
śrīmad-rādhā-śrīla-govinda-devau
preṣṭhālībhiḥ sevyamānau smarāmi

Hare Kṛṣṇa. Excuse me, I'm sitting here daydreaming in my private way, thinking of things I'll do with my friend and disciple Baladeva when he comes in a few months. I forgot that I'm on the air on another overcast day, a rainy day. We have only two more days left before we continue our travels. We have a three-day drive to Spain ahead of us. I'm revved up to write along the way, writing into a story. It's a slightly veiled autobiographical fiction about a visiting *sannyāsī* and his *brahmacārī* assistant-companion, Narahari, and their sacred activities of trying to be Kṛṣṇa conscious. The story focuses on the fact that the visiting *sannyāsī* is a closet poet. I say closet because for different reasons, he can't bring his poem-writing into the ISKCON world. When he did try to discuss it recently, he was criticized. A Godbrother told him that a *sannyāsī* ought to do more than just write poetry. That helped put him in the closet. He's still writing poetry in there. We'll get to read some of his poems and hear about his trip as the story unfolds. We'll also hear about his inner bubbling of wanting to offer his services as a poet, but not finding how to interest his society in it. It's a hot, vital, potent theme.

I'm looking for ways to develop it into a story, but on the one hand, I'm not worried too much that I have to develop a big plot or a conflict. My main aim is to continue to express through mental vignettes the theme of the *sannyāsī's* feelings and thoughts about his writing, his exchanges with Narahari and others, and the mood of their travels.

Please stay tuned to that.

Hare Kṛṣṇa Hare Kṛṣṇa, Kṛṣṇa Kṛṣṇa Hare Hare/ Hare Rāma Hare Rāma, Rāma Rāma Hare Hare.

I'll tell you what I was thinking while the music was playing a little longer than usual—that I'm not able to speak very much about a period of my life in ISKCON, the nine-year period from approximately 1978 to 1987. Those were the years—I'll call them the guru-zonal-*ācārya* years—when only eleven persons could initiate in ISKCON, although a few people were added to that number near the end of that period.

But I want to be fearless on this show. Maybe since I'm growing older (and the incidents are too), I can talk about things that would be healing for me. But so far, I seem unable to discuss them. I think I need a more protected environment and not this radio show to try and explore why I am so reluctant to talk about those times.

I also want to be able to tell stories from before that: when I was an "ordinary" devotee, an ordinary *sannyāsī*—like when I was on the library party or doing college preaching before 1977. I ought to be able to tell some stories, but there's a certain inability or lack of verve there too. Why do it? I even wrote myself a note: "Some memories. Go ahead and tell an old ISKCON story. What about the fights or threats from the nondevotees when you were in Amherst or Atlanta?"

Telling them would uncork them for me. Some of them are wild stories about being afraid at night, about nondevotees coming to the temple and how the devotees responded. Details come to mind, but I don't know, I just can't work myself up to that sitting-around-the-fire-telling-stories mood—candid, confessional, funny, with mimicry, characterization, and the whole thing. I just can't bring myself to do it.

Here I am, collapsed back on the bed, with a pillow stuffed behind my back, fifty-five years old. This is my radio studio. I'm relaxed, and I want to talk. But when you say to me, "Look, you've had a rich life in ISKCON. Granted, ISKCON is insular according to worldly standards, but I'm sure you cultists have your own stories to tell. The press has told their version of some of the stories, smearing you, so why don't you tell *your* version of what it has been like to be a devotee? Tell the human side of the ISKCON story."

I do want to tell that story, but I seem to be stuck for some reason. I'm speaking, rather, in a low, confidential tone, which is about as far as I can get right now, just telling you that it's a gray day, that the tops of the "*tulasī* " trees are still today, and that they're wet and pink. A dark pink, like plumes hanging over, like weeping willows. As I look out, somehow I can't look right back into some rip-roaring ISKCON tale.

I hope I'm not putting you to sleep. I'm not putting myself to sleep, but I keep intoning in my relaxed, hypnotic mood. This is my reality right now. It's the kind of mood where you feel like chanting again and again: Hare Kṛṣṇa Hare Kṛṣṇa, Kṛṣṇa Kṛṣṇa Hare Hare, keeping close, like a doctor keeping his hand on the pulse, just listening to the pulse. I don't want to get worked up and tell a story; I just want to listen to the pulse. Pump, pump, pump, pump—keeping the count of the same things. That is, to read and tell you what I read about in *Bhagavad-gītā* and *Śrīmad-Bhāgavatam,* to tell you what I'm writing now, to tell you where we're going in a few days, to tell you what the sky is like *right now,* to tell you that I'm okay now, just to say hello, I'm here. No, I can't unwind to tell a story of something that happened over twenty years ago and embellish it just for the story's sake. In this limited time when we make our connection on this show, somehow I'm impelled to talk, to intone, to say Hare Kṛṣṇa, Hare Kṛṣṇa, and let it go at that.

Prabhupāda singing:

> *śrīmān rāsa-rasārambhī vaṁśī-vaṭa-taṭa-sthitaḥ*
> *karṣan veṇu-svanair gopīr gopīnāthaḥ śriye 'stu naḥ*

Now I'll make my little good-bye. When I was in the Navy, the officer in charge of our Public Information Office used to make fun of me because in the evening, I would want to say good night. I actually made a formal gesture out of it. I didn't like to simply walk out the door while they looked at their watches and thought, "Oh, I guess that's it. He won't be back." He used to say, "Are you going to kiss everyone good night?"

Saying good night is a sweet, human thing to do. I didn't want to give it up. I still like to do it—say good night to people—although nowadays I occasionally sneak out without getting too gooey at the end.

Namaste. All glories to Śrīla Prabhupāda. Thank you very much for listening.

Prabhupāda singing:

> *śrīmān rāsa-rasārambhī vaṁśī-vaṭa-taṭa-sthitaḥ*
> *karṣan veṇu-svanair gopīr gopīnāthaḥ śriye 'stu naḥ*

18

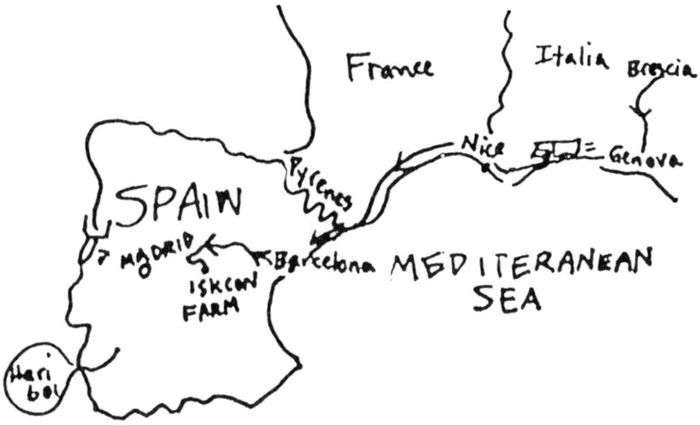

Prabhupāda singing:

> *hare kṛṣṇa hare kṛṣṇa, kṛṣṇa kṛṣṇa hare hare*
> *hare rāma hare rāma, rāma rāma hare hare*

Haribol. I haven't been on the air in over a week, mostly because I have been traveling and that was a good enough excuse not to do it. Now I'm in the temple and I'm about to leave here. I say excuse because it's hard to speak, to perform, and so I haven't done it.

When I arrived in Spain, I found that same *tulasī*-like tree just outside my window. One day Madhu came into the room. I opened the French doors—they're all windows really—and you have to pull them hard from both sides. Anyway, these doors overlook the property. I can see the hills and all the different trees that were planted for the aristocrats who used to live here. Among them, there's at least one or two of those *"tulasī"* trees. They're not very tall—I have to look down on them from this second floor window.

I pointed the trees out to Madhu and asked him if he could find out their names, even in Spanish. Then we can translate that into English. He made a note of it, but hasn't done it. Maybe it doesn't matter.

Later, when I was doing an initiation ceremony in the temple, I saw those same branches. I sat down before the pit made of bricks and mud, and lining the pit were branches from that tree. They have followed me (or I have followed them) from Italy to Spain.

We want to hold onto experiences, we want to record experiences. I don't know exactly why, and I don't know if it's a Kṛṣṇa conscious sentiment. I told you already how one devotee questioned me on that, saying, "Why do you say you want to hold on to the present and that you do it by writing? I can't identify with that feeling. Is it that when you have an advanced consciousness, you want to hold onto your worthy experiences?"

The question was put innocently, but I took it as an implied challenge, as if I'm claiming, "I'm in an exalted ecstasy." But I'm not claiming that. I told that devotee that all artists want to save their experiences. I identify with their desire. But I haven't really thought it out so much. Neither would I want to hear what the psychologists have to say about it. Probably they would think it's a futile attempt to be immortal. Artists are always grasping at immortality through their shared experiences.

Of course, in Kṛṣṇa consciousness, we try to accept everything. We don't just throw experience out, but save it by applying Kṛṣṇa consciousness to it. It's worth keeping a chronicle of a devotee's life, how he or she came to Kṛṣṇa consciousness, how they got out of the material well, how they strove to practice Kṛṣṇa consciousness. You could say that that chronicle, in all its details, is worth hearing. We save it in that sense—to share it with others.

Whether there is some subconscious or emotional motive in gropingly telling you that I saw this reddish-pinkish tree in Italy and now again in Spain, I don't know. I do know if I tell you, that detail won't go into oblivion.

I'm recording this show today in a rush. I hear the noises of devotees moving in and out of the rooms in this tower, and I know that Madhu may come in and interrupt my speaking. I'm always ready to accuse someone of violating my space and blame them for interrupting the evocation I was attempting to make. But I'm just alerting you, dear listeners, to the fact that I'm contending with noises and with the rush of events, and I'm trying as much as possible to incorporate all that into my song.

(I'd better keep talking because if I start playing background music, he'll probably think it's all right to come in. It's like when you're typing. People don't interrupt you, but when you're thinking, they think it's all right to interrupt. Or if you're reading. It's easy to interrupt a person who's reading. He doesn't seem to be *doing* anything you can't stop.)

That's another drive, to drop out of the interactions and demands of the day and to just read or write. Then someone comes in, "Am I interrupting you?" "No." What else can you say? You know you have to be interrupted sooner or later. You can't live forever on sabbatical from the galloping chariot of time. You can't just stay out of it by your absorption in other things.

Eternity, immortality is gained in a different way. It's gained by reaching the stage of Kṛṣṇa consciousness so that when you get interrupted by death, you go to Kṛṣṇa very specifically, very personally. That's what it is. It's not that by writing something you'll live forever. It's not like the primitive concept the Egyptians had that if they put all the right ingredients in the tomb, they could go to the next world. My written works are not going to carry me in themselves. They are not going to be something for me to read while I'm on my way. That journey only takes a moment, no matter where Kṛṣṇa arranges for me to go.

So what's the sense? If I have to go, then what's the sense of building up a big stock of writing? Is it for the people who are left behind? And how will that help me?

It will help me because it's a selfless offering. And I'm writing to help posterity. Posterity is a joke, actually. To the materialist, posterity means going to hell while his son takes his money or future generations live in his skyscraper. Posterity is useless to the materialist. But Cāṇakya Paṇḍita says if in this brief life you can do something to make yourself immortal, then you should do it. I think that means you should help others come to Kṛṣṇa consciousness, or you should act in such a way that you achieve pure Kṛṣṇa consciousness and you can go to Kṛṣṇa. That's immortality. The works that you leave behind are not immortal—they may last for some time and people may read them, but they're not immortal.

I sometimes speculate about it. I imagine how the value of my writings will increase after I leave this world. I have heard a couple of remarks like that. Once my Godbrother, Kuṇḍali, read some of *Journal & Poems*. He said, "I think these are good. This is the kind of thing that people are more interested to read when the author is dead." I heard that my Godbrother, Jayādvaita Mahārāja, was talking to one of my disciples. The disciple had been a little hurt that someone criticized the type of writing I do. He was trying to assure the disciple and said, "No, I think he's a good writer and this will be appreciated more after he is dead."

I can see the possibility of their value increasing, but that's irony. Imagine working hard at your art for your whole life and it not being of any use until you're gone. It makes me think of an artist like Van Gogh. Some people say he was mistreated by the world because they failed to appreciate him. He was driven to madness by that cruelty.

Now his paintings sell for millions of dollars, but what good is that to him? That's irony.

Of course, my situation is different because I am practicing Kṛṣṇa consciousness. If I am serving now by writing, and if my writing has a readership, and if that readership increases and the books do more Kṛṣṇa conscious preaching when I'm out of the way, then that's all right with me. That's like extra credit, like performing devotional service even after I leave. A *pūjārī* can only serve as long as his body is fit, but the books will continue to serve. Other things are like that too. If you build roads or temples, or dig wells, it lives on after you.

Your contribution may not be immortal—it will go on for a certain amount of time and then it will fall into disuse or disfavor or forgetfulness. The world may churn it under. Whole civilizations get lost, books get lost or are simply out of print—churned under.

We don't want to have undue anxiety about that. We shouldn't put such a high value on our works that our humility is compromised. We're not trying to live on in the form of our written words. That would be *māyā* for us. We are interested in preaching.

It's different, of course, for Śrīla Prabhupāda. Remember when he was ill in 1967? He decided to go back to India, perhaps to leave this world forever. From India he wrote in a letter to Hayagrīva, "I am very anxious about my publications, although I'm on the path of death. Even if I die, I want you to take care of them."

This is the preaching spirit. Prabhupāda so much wanted to preach that even after he left, he wanted to continue preaching, and that's how he would do it. He was determined. A pure devotee lives by his followers, so he gives them a mission to fulfill. Prabhupāda used to say, "I am an old man. I may die at any moment. But you continue this mission after I am gone." That's the preaching spirit.

That's another answer for the person who didn't understand why I would want to save my present experience. If I can write down what the life of a devotee is all about, then people can appreciate it. It's a form of preaching.

I'm speaking positively. Why not? Why be self-destructive all the time? Positively speaking, I sense the importance of Kṛṣṇa conscious life. Sure, it's possible to become contaminated and think myself great or to build a case for my worthiness. That would, of course, be foolishness: "All right, they don't appreciate me now, but after I'm gone and they study my books, they'll realize I was a wonderful person. Since it might go to my head now if they gave me the Nobel Prize for literature, they can give it to me after I'm dead and everything will be as it should be."

That's irony. What good will any of that do me? It's a ridiculous way to think. But it doesn't mean that I can't think humbly that a devotee's life—my life—is worthwhile. It's not so much the devotee's life, but the Kṛṣṇa consciousness that has value and should be recorded. Those other guys are recording their life experiences—what it's like to be a homosexual prostitute, how they became a millionaire, their memoirs as U.S. President. They're trying to make a claim to history, to have their human experience, no matter how ignoble, remembered. Anyway, I want to say that I have a real sense that life is worth living and I'm glad I had the sense to record it despite my worries that others may not understand. Let's all be aware of the value of life in Kṛṣṇa consciousness. Recording it is preaching, but it's not preachy. Raw experience is honest, real, and candid. It can help people.

Prabhupāda singing (Happening Album):

hare kṛṣṇa hare kṛṣṇa, kṛṣṇa kṛṣṇa hare hare
hare rāma hare rāma, rāma rāma hare hare

This '66 *kīrtana* is a good example of recording something worth saving. We have so many retrieval systems that we're embarrassed by our riches in this regard. We don't know which memory to read or which tape to hear. We don't have enough time to taste all the saved, valuable moments from the past. Otherwise, we would spend all our time savoring them and not living in the present. Everyone understands that, how we have to be able to turn off the tape at some point and go and apply what we have heard. Some of us record that application. Or we accept the moment: "Look at the beautiful green of those branches. A small bird just hopped among the leaves." It's a sparkling moment when the sun turns the tree light green. The little bird is so evanescent that he just sparkles and then is gone. He is the symbol of the present—here and gone. All you're left with is the empty branch.

This is spring. The bees are after the honey and the birds are after whatever they're after—eating, mating, sleeping, and defending. It's spring. Our present moment this spring day is that we are in Spain. We have completed our duties, had our headaches, played out our formal role as visiting *sannyāsī* and assistant with earnestness. I gave lectures, thought they were pretty good, but later thought them over and saw the shaky points. Still, I kept to Prabhupāda's message as his *śuka* and was satisfied with that.

We're going this afternoon. I was keeping a semi-fictional travel diary, writing a story about "the visiting *sannyāsī*" and his traveling companion, Narahari dāsa. I couldn't keep it up once I got here. I didn't do any writing here. Now as we're about to leave, I realize we have five days of travel coming up. I'm going to write a real travel diary—no fiction. That's my new idea. Kṛṣṇa gave me another idea. I hope to be able to do it without being obnoxious.

Hare Kṛṣṇa.

Prabhupāda singing (Happening album):

> *hare kṛṣṇa hare kṛṣṇa, kṛṣṇa kṛṣṇa hare hare*
> *hare rāma hare rāma, rāma rāma hare hare*

I hope we don't get jinxed. Two years in a row while leaving Spain, we got jinxed on the highway. The van broke down. It wasn't so bad, really, just inconvenient. We'll have to see what happens this time. I depend so much on Madhu's expert driving and the well-built mechanics of our Renault Master van, the engineering of the highways, the NATO forces to protect us, the U.S. dollar, nature's arrangements—dependent on so many things. They keep us going. So far so good.

This morning in the class, we talked, among other things, about madness and madmen. It was part of the verse. Jaḍa Bharata said to the king, "You are calling me a rascal and a madman, that I am so stupid that even if you punish me, I can't be cured." We talked about that, then about death. That's where I got shaky. I told a story about a devotee who had been hurt in a car accident. I don't want to get into the story right now, but I realized that to rush in and start telling someone's personal story without thinking it out well in advance and deciding whether it's a quirky story or whether it's really filled with good analogous material from the *Bhāgavatam,* is not good. Devotees were writing down what I said. I have to be responsible. Still, sometimes you have to drive into those uncharted areas and make the best of them, even if later you feel it wasn't the best. It's who you are. You're not a perfect *Bhāgavatam* speaker yet. You can think over what you said, but sometimes you have to go with your experiences and make the best of them.

Talking about the time of death and what we're going to do at the time of death—this is definitely something I don't want to be too chatty or too glib about.

I forget why I brought it up just now—oh, yes, I was talking about depending on all these different things. In the class, I said that we all hope to get some warning before we die so that we can go to Vṛndāvana and be surrounded by devotees chanting Hare Kṛṣṇa, but that may not happen. There may be time to be surrounded by devotees chanting Hare Kṛṣṇa, but that may not happen. There may be no warning, so we have to practice now.

When I give classes in Italy or Spain or France, there's always a translator. I like how having a translator gives me extra time, an extra moment to consider what I will say. Speaking of preparing for death, in a sense, every time you speak, you die. You're forced to say what you can. That's the best you can come up with. It just comes out and it can't wait, especially in a public talk. But when there's a translation, you get an extra moment to compose your thoughts and words. Then you see it come out neatly, shaped and satisfying, in a natural rhythm. When you're face to face with English-speaking people, it comes out more rapidly. You don't have that cushion.

It reminds me of making music, or of improvising. The sax player has half a moment somehow, by magic, to decide what to play before it comes out, but at other times, he just lets it out and everybody rides with it.

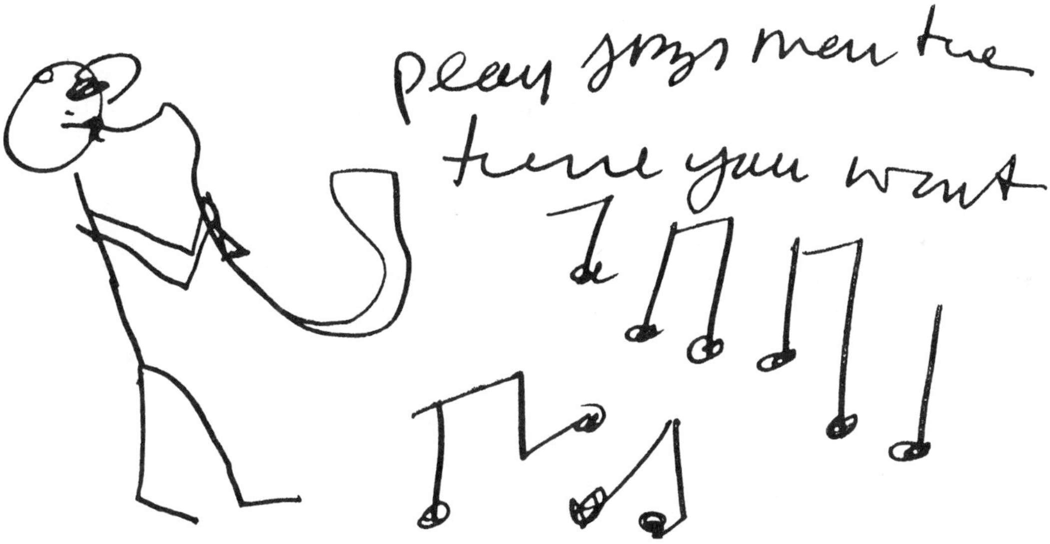

Similarly, you can prepare a lecture, but you still have to speak impromptu. You may have time to prepare for death like Mahārāja Parīkṣit, or you may have to go right away and say *haribol*, Kṛṣṇa. That's all the time you have. In any case, prepare, prepare, prepare.

How do you prepare? By saving the present moment, by writing as much as you can, by reading as much as you can, by building a preaching record so it doesn't look like a bad show, like you just petered out at the end, like you didn't do much. We don't want to indulge ourselves or make vain efforts to make ourselves immortal. Don't binge on reading or self-expression. We're not after our own enjoyment. Be selfless. We don't want to seem like this: "He made a mistake. He tried, but he didn't get the highest marks. He rationalized. He went out like that, not with a bang but a whimper. Not with a whimper but a croak. Not with a croak but a free-writing session while looking at a birch tree, while allowing himself to talk, while praying in the way that he could and looking forward to improved times as if he had so much time, as if he *has* so much time, looking forward to a rest and a walk outdoors." Already he's being interrupted. His heart is beating steadily, but his teeth are gone, his ability to digest is gone, his headaches are here, but he's going steady, making plans until the end.

I want Prabhupāda consciousness, like we all do in ISKCON. I know it's bigger than life. He is the *mūrti,* but he's bigger than the *mūrti's* presence. Got to find him in his books, in his devotees, in myself.

In the class, I gave the example of a devotee who was afraid when he was in the car accident. He called out, "Kṛṣṇa! Kṛṣṇa!" not so Kṛṣṇa would save him from the pain—he was pressed under the car—but he said later that he was afraid he was going to forget Kṛṣṇa. He said he was calling Kṛṣṇa to block out the pain so he could remember Kṛṣṇa. I said this was admirable, but a devotee in the class said, "Is this all we can expect? Or can we expect to be confident at the time of death?"

I said, "Yes, you're right. This isn't the highest form of Kṛṣṇa consciousness. The highest would be confidence." We're doing both. We're crying out to Kṛṣṇa, but at the same time, we want to do better than that. We want to be fearless. But we are afraid, and maybe that's another reason why we're stocking up and recording the present moment.

Now whether this is the best way to end my days or to live at present, I can't be perfectly sure, and Kṛṣṇa doesn't seem to want me to be perfectly sure. But I can love this and I can put my personal feeling into it. It feels right, and people are receiving it well. I'm going for it and assuming that Kṛṣṇa is so much concerned for me that He will take this away if it isn't right and give me something else.

Whatever happens, this kind of life that is given to us now ain't going to go on forever. So let's be quiet, take whatever limited doses we are capable of, and steadily offer our service, whatever it is. The perfection of life is to offer what we're doing to others. The per fection of reciprocation is when someone says, "Thank you. You really helped me," and they mean it. The sweetness comes when you recognize that that's Prabhupāda's kindness on you. Hare Kṛṣṇa.

Prabhupāda singing (Happening album):

hare kṛṣṇa hare kṛṣṇa, kṛṣṇa kṛṣṇa hare hare
hare rāma hare rāma, rāma rāma hare hare

19

Haribol. I'm starting another radio show. We're on the highway, parked at a P-stop above Bordeaux, France. As I speak, Madhumaṅgala is in the phone booth talking to America. We were jinxed again as we left Spain. The last two times we left Spain, our van broke down. This time something worse happened. Prabhupāda was not strapped in properly and he fell off the shelf. He broke his arm. Fortunately, Madhu had some very good glue and he glued Prabhupāda right away. He said he noticed that the arm was very thin there. I'm worried about it.

I didn't have so many feelings about it when it happened. We just dealt with it practically. I even said, "Well, if worse comes to worst, we'll just have to get a new *mūrti.*" Now my feelings are coming out. So much of my life centers around this Prabhupāda *mūrti.* I suppose the accident drove me to realize that even without the *mūrti* worship, I still have Prabhupāda's books. It also occurred to me that it's inevitable that this was going to happen sooner or later. Prabhupāda's arm was going to break or my arm is going to break. I think that realization was the source of my somewhat stoic or resigned attitude. It has been good while it lasted, but if it's taken away, what can I do? There's no point crying about it; I'll just do what has to be done. Eventually, I know I'll feel more the weight of what happened, but it still seems artificial, even theatrical, to make a big commotion over it.

Anyway, a whole day has passed and I still haven't bathed him, although I offered him *prasādam* and he looks all right. I just hope that the broken part isn't so thin that it will break again.

This is a sad discussion. We don't usually like to talk about things like broken *mūrtis.* It's unfortunate, inauspicious. We wish it didn't happen. But these things *do* happen, and they change the nature of life. We go on, and we don't unnecessarily detract from our lives because it's bad enough that something inauspicious has happened. We don't have to supply our own Greek chorus. We just go on, trying to be happy and to reduce our losses.

Prabhupāda singing (Happening album):

hare kṛṣṇa hare kṛṣṇa, kṛṣṇa kṛṣṇa hare hare
hare rāma hare rāma, rāma rāma hare hare

I would like to tell you a little bit about where I am. We're on the road on our way through France, and we've stopped at a rest stop. A few years ago, a devotee in France warned us not to park in secluded areas because there had been a rash of robberies—horrible-sounding tales where the thieves came and made holes in a parked van or camper, then pumped gas into the vehicle and killed the people sleeping inside. Then they robbed them.

I felt the devotee who told me that was a little irresponsible in the telling. I remember he brought it up during *prasādam*. He didn't give details, such as how many times it had happened or where it had happened, but told it like it was a commonplace event. It had its effect on us and when possible, we chose to sleep in areas that were more protected, like gas stations. We sacrificed our peace and quiet. That was too bad because France has many nice parks. They're parking areas, actually, but I call them parks because they are landscaped with trees and lawns. It's true, too, that no one stays in them overnight much, although they get quite busy during the day.

And that's just what I like about them—we have the place to ourselves. I especially appreciate this in the early mornings. Unfortunately, in the material world, peace is often accompanied by disaster. It's funny how we feel smug and secure in a group of *karmīs* when we're traveling—like taking shelter in a circle of covered wagons. Last night was like that. When I woke up in the morning, there were tractor trailers on all sides. It made me feel more secure than when we are alone. (It wasn't even noisy.)

Anyway, on the highway, I assumed Madhu would stop at a gas station like usual, but all of a sudden he said, "If you want, we can stop at this quiet place." It was coming right up. I usually like time to think these things over, but there was no time, so I agreed: "Okay, let's go. They seem safe." That was one of those pabulum remarks that we all tend to make, trying to assure ourselves without making any real investigation. "They seem safe." What did I mean by that? I don't know.

But here we are, and I'm feeling a little of that old nervousness. Still, I'm calculating that this isn't so bad. We're somewhat near the P-house. Would a thief really try to break in here? I can only hope he wouldn't. And of course, I hope Kṛṣṇa will protect us. That's on my mind, that no matter how much ease we feel, something will eventually go wrong. We'll get the Spanish jinx or the French invasion or the Irish screw up or the American clamp-down or the Italian disaster. These things happen anywhere. Of course, I have my list of BTG centers, so when the *gendarmes* come, I can say, *"Je ne peux pas parler français. Je suis Hare Kṛṣṇa.* Here are the addresses of our Hare Kṛṣṇa centers in your country." Maybe I'll have to hang around in some police station. Who knows how bad it can get? I try not to think about it.

The illusion, or even the external situation, is quite pleasant when you're traveling in a van. I have a little devotional atmosphere in the back—pictures on the walls, books, tapes, and privacy. The cooking is simple, but I appreciate the food more somehow. The privacy is certainly more complete. Even the little fears that something may happen may work in my favor; they make me read more seriously. For example, when I read a statement about how Kali-yuga is so bad that people should take Kṛṣṇa consciousness seriously and get out of the material world, I want to know what I can do to help.

Sometimes, when we're driving, I sit up front and chant. If I get drowsy, I spray my face with a spray bottle and that clears my mind. Then I think a step further than I usually do. Sometimes I can only get to a certain point in my thinking. There's something vague that stays around the edges. I can't go any further with it. But sometimes I'm blessed with clarity and I make progress.

What was I thinking about today? Something about my writing career and about reading. I was able to bring my internal discussion a step further. Usually, the discussion takes the form of asking myself more questions, existential questions like, "What do I want to do about it?" When those questions come up, it means I've progressed somewhat. It means I have accepted a certain decision. Instead of worrying about something, I'm ready to go on to the next step.

After this morning's moment of clarity, I prayed, "Kṛṣṇa, please tell me what to do and give me the strength to do it."

That same old prayer. I haven't been able to think of it lately. I don't even think of asking Kṛṣṇa for clarity and strength. Oh, yes, I'm the guy who writes that he doesn't get a taste for chanting and he has problems with inattention. Do I even experience that despair anymore?

What do we experience? We talk about what we experience—we may even advertise it—but we don't necessarily live what we talk about. That requires extra thought, clarity, and blessings.

Traveling definitely changes your point of view. These are some points. I hope to make some headway to settle with what I'm doing, to have the courage to continue it, or to do something new, if that's required.

Prabhupāda singing (Happening album):

hare kṛṣṇa hare kṛṣṇa, kṛṣṇa kṛṣṇa hare hare
hare rāma hare rāma, rāma rāma hare hare

Just outside my window, I can see a picnic table. There's an obese young woman sitting there. She's wearing a big, peach-colored T-shirt and black slacks. A younger girl, maybe her daughter, is sitting across from her. The big woman is drinking from a bottle and the daughter is eating a banana. A few hours ago at that same table, I saw a man eating a big sandwich. These are, you could say, the pitiful but dear activities of the human race. They've been going on for centuries in France and in every other place where human beings live.

I would take a walk myself, but it has become unseasonably warm all of a sudden. It was quite cold earlier today. We had to bundle up in coats and hats to stay warm. Now the sun is out and it's warmer. I could walk around without a hat and without my teeth, but I don't like people to see me and I don't like to see people. That's why I like to walk alone. But I think I will get out a bit.

Prabhupāda singing (Happening album):

hare kṛṣṇa hare kṛṣṇa, kṛṣṇa kṛṣṇa hare hare
hare rāma hare rāma, rāma rāma hare hare

Did you know that in former ages, the *brāhmaṇas* chanted mantras as a science? If they chanted every syllable exactly right, it would cause things to happen in the material world. It would be as good as striking a match or some more complicated material engineering feat. They could produce water from the earth or start a fire or even create soldiers. The mantras were powerful. That art is lost. Therefore, it is recommended that we chant the Hare Kṛṣṇa mantra. The nature of the Hare Kṛṣṇa mantra is that it doesn't have to be pronounced exactly right in order to be effective.

I just got a letter from an Irish *bhakta*. He said he notices that devotees, even older devotees, don't pronounce the *mahā-mantra* with all its syllables. He thinks he's made a big discovery and he now keeps noticing how different people chant. He even noticed one woman who he didn't think was chanting properly, and then the temple president. Now he's found another *bhakta* with whom he can discuss this problem. They both think it's a very serious problem.

In the first letter I ever got from him, this *bhakta* described this "major problem" we were having in our society. I told him to mind his own business. He might think people aren't chanting, but they might actually be chanting properly. And today I read that even if you don't pronounce the *mahā-mantra* perfectly, it still works.

Of course, I don't take it lightly. It's a fact that some people chant poorly. We all know the jokes: "Kṛṣ Kṛṣ, Rām Rām, Kṛṣ Kṛṣ, Rām Rām, dish dish, whisk whisk . . . " Still, we can just picture this *bhakta* focusing his attention in on the other devotees' sound vibration. "Aha! Another one. *He's* not chanting properly either. What will become of this movement? There's another one!" Prabhupāda said, "Oil your own machine." Better to attend to your own chanting than to investigate other people's chanting.

Then how to bring it up? It's a very touchy thing. Poor chanting can be discussed generally in lectures, but to think that you've suddenly discovered the source of ISKCON's ills by listening to other people's apparent mispronunciation of the mantra, or to think that you're going to change it, seems a waste of time and energy.

Prabhupāda singing (Happening album):

hare kṛṣṇa hare kṛṣṇa, kṛṣṇa kṛṣṇa hare hare
hare rāma hare rāma, rāma rāma hare hare

Curtains drawn, but slightly parted. Peeking out from the back of the van. Hearing the life of middle-class *bourgeois* motorists stopping to use the toilets and then drive on in their Citroens and Renaults and Peugeots, on to Paris, on to Nantes, away from Bordeaux. The little evergreen trees in spring, the picnickers, and this guy spying out the back of his van with American eyes and big bifocals. His radio show on the road. His precious words. His Prabhupāda overseeing all.

One devotee came to Prabhupāda (I read about it in Hari Śauri's diary) and said, "I can make millions of dollars by selling honey." The devotee wasn't wearing a shirt, and it was clear that he had taken off his *brāhmaṇa* thread. He asked Prabhupāda, "Can I have your permission to do this great service and engage the householders?" Prabhupāda mused, sat back, and then said, "What to do, what to do?" Hari Śauri doesn't interpret what Prabhupāda meant by that, but I could imagine Prabhupāda confronted by so many devotees with their proposals, one after another. All Prabhupāda said was, "Why aren't you wearing your *brāhmaṇa* thread?"

"Well, I'm not following the principles, Prabhupāda, so I thought it would be more honest not to wear it."

"No, you should wear it. Get a *brāhmaṇa* thread for him. What to do, what to do?"

Prabhupāda later wrote that devotee back and said, "I have thought about it and I think you ought to go ahead making money selling honey. Then give fifty percent of it to build a temple here." Prabhupāda is so intelligent.

What would he do with Satsvarūpa who broke the deity? What will I do with the Prabhupāda deity? What to do with Satsvarūpa? Prabhupāda sees me talking this show, roundabout talk. Why aren't you more direct?

Well, Prabhupāda, you see, I have to explore myself and I'm kind of an artist, you know? I'm making these different expressions of Kṛṣṇa consciousness. It's all the same, but I'm putting it in different bottles and people like it that way.

Oh, I see. What to do, what to do? And why aren't you managing any more on the GBC?

Well, Prabhupāda, I thought I wasn't doing it so well, you know?

I see. And how come you're not wearing your *dhotī* right now?

Oh, well, when we're on the road like this, you see, we have no facility for washing clothes.

Oh, what to do, what to do?

And when will you be a pure devotee? When will you do some substantial work? Why don't you finish the work?

Prabhupāda, I thought this was already substantial work.

I'm so insignificant in Prabhupāda's service. I was his servant for a while, but among other things, I was a poor financial manager. I couldn't keep good records. Prabhupāda joked about it later, how Satsvarūpa is "expert." Then I thought about so many devotees. Could Prabhupāda even think of me? I think of him and I *think* that he remembers me, even though so many of his other men are doing such important work. This is my line of work.

Please, Prabhupāda, I know you remember me. I know that you love me and that you do accept my service, but I want to do more. If it's to be in this line of work, then I'm willing to do it and engage in what it means to be an artist. I like to do it. You just please let me know what to do. Maybe for the time being, I will be absorbed in reading your books.

Hare Kṛṣṇa.

20

Prabhupāda singing (Happening album):

> *hare kṛṣṇa hare kṛṣṇa, kṛṣṇa kṛṣṇa hare hare*
> *hare rāma hare rāma, rāma rāma hare hare*

Haribol. I am speaking from the back of the van in a grassy field at a campground in northern France. I just read something Prabhupāda wrote about secrecy. The king kept his treasury secret, people didn't know his spying system, and even the citizens were entitled to some secrecy. That's still true today. Prabhupāda said that there's no harm in people keeping their savings secret.

Where I am in France is my secret today.

I was just outside. I felt dazed when I got out there, stretching my legs and breathing the fresh air. My legs felt wobbly. I wanted to get out of the van and clean the back windows, which are pretty dirty. I did that. My arms got black with dirt.

Then I was going to clean the mat I place outside the bathroom when suddenly a car drove up and an elderly man—I say elderly, but he was around my age—got out and started walking toward one of the caravans. The caravan was parked here when we arrived and looked unused. It's not really the season for camping, but this man just moved into the camper nearest us.

That's the thing about these kinds of places—all of a sudden, someone pulls up and steps into your privacy. You never know who's going to show up. I was walking toward him, he was walking toward me, and there was at least fifty feet between us. We didn't have any business together, so I didn't think of saying, "*Bonjour,*" or anything like that. I probably felt inhibited too because I don't speak French. If he had been an American, I might have cranked out a "How ya doin'?" People say different things according to where they live. Here, it's pretty standard—"*Bonjour,*" or in Italy, "*Bon journo.*" You can get away with that, anyway.

I like to have small and simple exchanges with people, but my main thought was that this guy probably thinks I'm a skin-head. He didn't look pleased when he saw me. He looked a little worried.

So neither of us said anything. He looked like a professor or something. Then I noticed as he came out of his car that he was carrying a long, thin loaf of French bread. What could be more typical? More innocuous? But don't think that loaf of bread in itself exonerates him. If I were a judge in the kingdom of God, I wouldn't let everybody in just because they had a loaf of French bread and looked innocent. He could be the most horrible guy.

Anyway, he's in his camper with the door open and I've come here to tell you about it. It seemed important.

Prabhupāda singing:

ānanda-cinmaya-sad-ujjvala-vigrahasya . . .

I was proud of myself for reading while traveling today. The last hour was the hardest because Madhu was doing what he calls his hyped-up driving maneuvers—tailgating, passing, driving the smaller roads off the *autoroute.* I read Hari Śauri's *Transcendental Diary* about Prabhupāda's last days in Hawaii in 1976. Reading it is like being there with Prabhupāda, how they drove him to the airport and how the temple president, Śukadeva, said, "Prabhupāda, I'll miss you." Prabhupāda returned the compliment, "I will miss you too. You were cooking so nicely."

That book isn't easy reading. You have to pay attention to all the lectures and conversations. Prabhupāda's unvarnished and heavy instructions make you think about yourself and question whether you are pleasing him. When you read about ISKCON in those days, that's heavy too. Still, it's definitely absorbing reading.

Reading, my thoughts drifting to my service or this microcosm of my whole devotional career.

When I looked up, it was quarter to twelve. I said *gāyatrī,* then asked Madhu about his plans. He said we would stop in half an hour.

"Where are we going to stop?"

"Well, this isn't an *autoroute,* so we'll have to stop for the night in a supermarket parking lot, unless we can find a gas station."

That didn't sound so great. "Well, if we see a sign for campers, we can stop there."

He said it was possible, but he really wanted to drive as far as possible. That happens to Madhu. He gets completely wrapped up in trying to drive as far as possible and then just stop anywhere for the night. I tend to have a little more nesting consciousness. I get nervous if we have to stay in a supermarket parking lot because you're not supposed to park there overnight. The lots are completely deserted after the stores close, and there you are. The police can come and ask, "What are you doing here? What's this water dripping out?"

Then I saw a sign for camping and told Madhu to pull over. He did it obediently, but even as he did so, he began arguing against it. He tried selling me some alternatives, which included only the vague possibility that if we pushed on, we might find another camping sign further on. But I didn't go for it. "We have a campground right here. We'll only have two more hours of driving tomorrow." Reluctantly, he drove to the campground. It turned out to be a nice place.

We're more relaxed now. We're not going to leave quite so early tomorrow. I read some *Bhāgavatam* about Mahārāja Pṛthu. The different purports led me to thinking about the GBC members when I was there and then one thing led to another and all these unpleasant memories began to float to the surface. I wrote some of them down.

This show, as you can probably hear, is a late-afternoon session from a guy who is glad to be alive, glad to be a devotee, and who very much wants to protect his privacy. I've heard that Jackie Onassis fiercely guarded her privacy. I don't know if I'm prepared to be fierce, but I do want a private life. The bubbling and simmering is not a bad thing as I try to decide what I should write, what I should do, how I should improve.

Prabhupāda singing, devotees responding:

jaya rādhā-mādhava kuñja-bihārī

then:

jaya oṁ viṣṇu-pāda paramahaṁsa . . .

Jaya, jaya, jaya Prabhupāda.

I had a good early morning. I wrote up a storm during my 12–1 A.M. writing session. I was aware that it wasn't just me; Kṛṣṇa was helping me, giving me intelligence. I was not only keeping to the writing session rules, but the session was churning other things as well. I would reach off the page and take notes, then put them in the out basket—different messages for Madhu about things I wanted to do. It was quite a generating session.

In the midst of it, I scribbled off a note listing topics I could speak on at the radio show. When I look at it now, I think, "What's this?!" One of them says, "Tell how your sister knew that you were hoping she would do something for you." I'm going to talk about that now, just to expose something in my character.

I have had a tendency in this lifetime to want to be served by others. It isn't something that came out when I gained seniority in ISKCON. ISKCON gave me the facility to be served that I never had in material life. I suppose it's a common desire. We can call it our deity complex or our false ego.

Some people are frank about their desire and they fulfill it through business and family. They dictate to others and others serve them. A classic example is the relationship between capitalist and worker.

I have never been a powerful, demanding kind of person. However, if somebody were willing, I would accept their service. At least that's how someone once explained it to me. That person said that it seemed like I would be willing to accept any surrender or service that a person wanted to give and I would even encourage it. In other words, a truly selfless person would take a strong stand against being served. I have heard devotees emphasize that this is real, saintly behavior. We have even heard descriptions how Indian *sādhus* are extremely careful about accepting service. They won't even allow anyone to open the door for them. They are always conscious that if they accept someone's service, they'll lose their independence, their *sādhu* nature, and their humility.

Another *sādhu* used to get up early in the morning before anyone else was up just so that no one would help him fetch buckets of water or milk his cow. *Sādhus* always resist that service. This is considered saintly behavior.

But I want to note something in my own character. I have always liked people to do me a favor or give me a gift. Sometimes, I even hankered for it. I remember my older sister, who was aware of my ways, always destroyed my hopes to get something special from her. I usually portray my sister as being cruel and as having a sharp, cynical wit. She always tried to puncture my balloon, not with the parental authority, but with the side-shots only an older sibling can give out.

Anyway, I remember one incident where I asked her to type a school paper for me. I was in high school and it was the first time I had to hand in my essay typed. I didn't know how to type, but my sister did. I remember really hoping she would agree, and she did, although she said she had her own homework to do.

Later I came back to see if she had done it. She read my mind, "You think I have done your typing, but I haven't. I didn't have time. I can see in your eyes that you were hoping I would do something nice for you, but I haven't." It hurt at the time—not so much that she didn't do the typing, but that she knew I was cherishing a hope that she had served me in this way.

I remember another incident like this. This one was a secret. My sister kept a sketchbook in which she wrote private things about her romances. Sometimes she wrote out their names and sometimes she drew pictures. I remember one thing in that notebook. There was a boy she had a crush on named Barry Corsen. He didn't like her though. When Barry showed a little interest in her and her hopes rose, but in the end, he made it clear that he wasn't interested. She cried a lot and felt rejected.

While the romance was still hopeful, she kept a jar filled with mementos of their relationship. I can't remember how, but I somehow found out about it. Although my sister could be cruel to me at times, I was also her confidant. Maybe she even told me about him.

Anyway, she had this jar, a "Barry" jar. One day, she was really crying, but she wouldn't talk about it, so when she wasn't around, I looked at her sketchbook. She had painted a little watercolor of her "Barry" jar, but in the picture, it was all smashed to pieces. That symbolized the end of the relationship.

What does that have to do with anything? The memory is vague and I'm groping, but it was something about her drawing in that sketchbook and her not letting me see it. Then she made a comment that I wanted to see what she was writing because I was hoping she had written something nice about me. I don't remember if that's what I was thinking, but it's true—I would have been pleased to know that she had had an affectionate thought about me.

My sister awakened a frustration or disappointment in me that although I wanted to be loved and even served, she wouldn't give me the satisfaction. I never spoke about my desire, but people close to me could see it in me.

People have pointed it out to me at other points in my life. Although I didn't canvass for servants, if one came along, I would allow him to serve me. I didn't try to stop people from serving me.

It seems strange that someone is willing to take such a masterly role with others, yet doesn't actively canvass. Rather, if someone doesn't approach me to render service, I myself take the serving role. I have a subordinate nature; I'm not a dominating person. I tend to be malleable and I don't usually expect so much of others. Still, in my heart, I have a willingness to be served.

These memories bring up something that is probably only natural, only human. Still, it's deep within me. If I want to become free of playing the role of the served, and instead become the servant, I have to go deep into myself and remove it. It's so subtle.

Prabhupāda singing (Happening album):

hare kṛṣṇa hare kṛṣṇa, kṛṣṇa kṛṣṇa hare hare
hare rāma hare rāma, rāma rāma hare hare

I'm stuck right now. I could talk about things I read in Hari Śauri's *Diary*. I could tell you about things I see out the newly cleaned window. The birds dip, make their bodies like rocks for a few minutes, then flap their wings again. I don't know their names. TV antennae on top of the campers. Freshly mowed grass already dying in little haystacks on top of the other grass. Hedges shorn. Spring. Business as usual.

Prabhupāda singing:

vande 'haṁ śrī-guroḥ śrī-yuta-pada-kamalaṁ śrī-gurūn vaiṣṇavāṁś ca
śrī-rūpaṁ sāgrajātaṁ saha-gaṇa-raghunāthānvitaṁ taṁ sa-jīvam
sādvaitaṁ sāvadhūtaṁ parijana-sahitaṁ kṛṣṇa-caitanya-devaṁ
śrī-rādhā-kṛṣṇa-pādān saha-gaṇa-lalitā-śrī-viśākhānvitāṁś ca

I'm thankful. I'm happy I took a shower today. I paid for it. I put the coin in the machine and the hot water came out. Now I have discovered that you can make it hot and then cold. The money lasted—a good shower—as long as anyone could want. When I came out of the shower, there was that guy. Oh, well, I guess I can't have the world to myself.

I've got enough things to keep me busy. I'm going to look at that essay I wrote called "The Inner Life of A Preacher." That will give me the conviction that this is a preaching business, to practice reading Prabhupāda's books.

Back to the *Diary*. Prabhupāda heard that Nitāi and Jagannātha weren't editing his books anymore. He wrote to them, "I heard you are not editing my books anymore. Then what are you doing with my books? You are not editing my books, so what is your engagement?" The implication of that sentence: "What are you doing with my books?" If you're not editing them, are you reading them? Are you speaking on them? I liked that. It's one thing not to edit them for some reason or other, although you should continue your service if you are an editor, but at least you should sell them or read them or somehow keep contact with the books. Don't become a rascal.

I'm reading them, Prabhupāda. I don't want to displease you. I'm reading. I'm your son, grown up a little, grown down a little, grown out a little, but I'm reading your books because I want to, not because somebody is pressuring me to. I'm reading them in a different way—in the same way, but in a different way also. Writing what comes as I read.

Damn it, I want to write more and not be confined. I want to discover more. By allowing myself to be free and confess and say what I feel, even when it's not good, that's how to reach good writing. It always has been. It's a way.

I want to read "The Inner Life of a Preacher" because I know it speaks about straight *sādhana* being as important as outward preaching and lecturing. That essay doesn't include everything the inner life means to me, which means engaging in creative and personal work. I rarely explore that area in public, but we all have a right to be persons and to express ourselves as such. I know there is a group of devotees, especially in America, who would like to hear that. Some of them are approaching this issue through psychology. They're trying to find out who they are and to understand the impact their experiences have had on them. I'm not against the psychological approach, but that's not exactly the approach I am taking. Neither am I necessarily advocating my approach to others. I don't advocate that devotees do free-writing sessions.

(Then what do I advocate? That they should read my sessions? That's the idea. Is it that I don't want people to write because I want to be the writer and I prefer them to be the readers?

No, I'm not saying that either. I wouldn't mind meeting another writer. I would read him if he wrote honestly. When John Young and I were teenagers, I liked to read what he wrote. We were friends. I commiserated with his hang-ups. He couldn't understand them and I couldn't understand them, so we laughed at them together. We were also both introverts. I wouldn't mind reading a devotee like that.)

Anyway, I want to write. I want inner life, and my inner life includes being a writer. I don't know what my message is when I write to people, and I don't know how they take it. They understand from it that they should practice *sādhana*, that they should chant and hear, but implicit in the inner life is the cultivation of self-honesty. Don't be lazy and don't deviate. I'm cultivating those qualities by trying to understand who I am and writing about it.

Okay, what does that say to others? Does that say that they should do that? How can you say it doesn't say that?

Well, my dear sub-self, since you want to talk with me about this, my answer is, and partly I expressed this in *Shack Notes*, that you can apply what I say about writing to your own life service. There should be honesty in your life. I am trying to be an honest *sannyāsī*. You can be an honest householder. It's the quality that is applicable, not necessarily the individual details, although if you want to write poetry, that's okay too.

As I'm speaking, I suddenly feel like an old drunk. I'm drinking water, one cup after another, and I think of "Krapp's Last Tape." I don't know if Krapp drank liquor, but I see myself alone like that man in the camper with his French bread. What can he be thinking? What do other people think about when they're alone?

I read in the *Bhāgavatam* today that Mahārāja Pṛthu was so impartial, he would punish his own son if he were guilty. If his enemy or enemy's son weren't guilty, he wouldn't punish him. Then I remembered how that verse was given to me one morning in Los Angeles when we had all gathered for emergency meetings. The purpose of our emergency GBC meetings was to judge and punish a wayward GBC man, or two wayward GBC men. It seemed unusual that the verse said that, that we who had come together shouldn't be an "old boys' club" but should be ready to punish our own man. We did it too.

It also made me think how I was there in that Los Angeles community (and at other communities), and as one of the top GBC gurus, I would be called upon to lecture to the devotees with political undertones, but appear as a more gentle, impartial kind of person.

I was definitely one of the boys—sometimes used as a tool by them so they could have such a "gentle" person represent them. Sometimes devotees have remarked to me that I disappointed them. They knew that that was my profile, or you could say my character, so why didn't I have the depth to see that it was a corrupt gang and then choose not to be part of some of the goings-on? Well, that was more integrity than I had at the time. Everything seemed to be so clearly what Prabhupāda wanted, that the GBC represented his will, and even if we made mistakes, our will should be impressed on others. We never saw it that the whole system should be changed or that the leaders were insincere or shouldn't be followed. But one by one, most of those leaders did fall.

I think I still haven't understood what that's done to my belief structure, to my personal self. I got off the GBC, but my shunning of participation in that sort of thing is quite thorough now and it has built up more over the years.

I'm willing to look at it, but I'm not willing to go back. I mean, I'm willing to concede that things are different now. Leadership isn't like that anymore. The leaders are definitely doing the best they can, and so on. But I don't want to be part of it. I don't want to be part of it.

While I was talking, I saw an animal. It might have been a cat—rust-colored—but it might have been a fox or a dog. Although I'm looking for it between the caravans, I can't see it anymore. Obviously it's taken my mind off what I was saying. Probably just as well. I don't really want to say more about it. Thinking of myself as that lecturer and how I was looked up to by most, always given some seat of honor and a choice time to speak. I didn't have the top manager's role, but was three or four back. Still, I was always at the most elite gatherings. Now, thank God, thank St. Francis, thank my Aunt Mary, *haribol*, and all that, I'm not in on that anymore. I'm here in a sweatshirt with a stretched neck that somebody gave me in Spain, nobody knows where, in some parking lot just off the highway, looking out the window for foxes and cats and dandelions and talking.

Prabhupāda singing:

vande 'haṁ śrī-guroḥ śrī-yuta-pada-kamalaṁ śrī-gurūn vaiṣṇavāṁś ca
śrī-rūpaṁ sāgrajātaṁ saha-gaṇa-raghunāthānvitaṁ taṁ sa-jīvam
sādvaitaṁ sāvadhūtaṁ parijana-sahitaṁ kṛṣṇa-caitanya-devaṁ
śrī-rādhā-kṛṣṇa-pādān saha-gaṇa-lalitā-śrī-viśākhānvitāṁś ca

Good-bye, good night. I hope to speak to you again, perhaps tomorrow. Tomorrow, we travel by ferry. Before this day is over, I hope to have more done. I hope you will get something done too, to fulfill your aspiration of what you want to do most in spiritual life. Be brave. I wish you the best. Thank you for listening to my meandering. I do hope that you will be blessed by Kṛṣṇa to do what you want to do to serve Him, to surrender to Him, and to get free of *māyā* and all the suffering of material life. We can do something about our own service and surrender and Kṛṣṇa will reciprocate. Don't be high-living and low-thinking. Don't live in a skyscraper like a roach and next life be born as a roach, but live plainly and think highly, think in terms of Kṛṣṇa and the soul.

21

Prabhupāda singing (Happening album):

hare kṛṣṇa hare kṛṣṇa, kṛṣṇa kṛṣṇa hare hare
hare rāma hare rāma, rāma rāma hare hare

Haribol. I see two lambs facing each other, forehead to forehead, and then butting each other in jest. Other new lambs join them and they run across the green field together until they reach another fence. It's raining today in this meadow, this secret meadow. A crow preens on a telephone wire. Seems like he was watching the lambs. The lambs haven't noticed the crow—they're too busy running and jumping. The crow sees them, though.

These animals and birds don't get the same chance humans do to eat much more than necessary. Humans mismanage our resources because of this. We make such a tremendous endeavor just so we don't have to sit in the rain. And for this we sacrifice our God consciousness. For this we end up with indigestion or sickness—full of complaints—while the sheep keep eating their allotted grass and the lambkins caper in the field. The sheep don't know they're doomed; we know it, but deny it.

Those who have Kṛṣṇa consciousness are very, very lucky.

brahmāṇḍa brahmite kona bhāgyavān jīva
guru-kṛṣṇa-prasāde pāya bhakti-latā-bīja

The *jīva* wanders life after life in the various species. If he is fortunate, he comes to the human form of life and then receives the mercy of guru and Kṛṣṇa. They germinate the seed of *bhakti* in his heart. *Bhakti* is special. Those who go by the names *"bhakta"* or *"bhaktin"* cannot really claim to feel spontaneous love. Still, they have become attracted to the pure devotee, sobered by knocks in material life, and serious enough to get Kṛṣṇa's mercy. They have turned themselves over to the *bhakti* practices, but how much do they really feel knowledge of Kṛṣṇa, love of Kṛṣṇa? Real *bhakti* is rare.

manuṣyāṇāṁ sahasreṣu
kaścid yatati siddhaye
yatatām api siddhānāṁ
kaścin māṁ vetti tattvataḥ

It's also rare to really want to give Kṛṣṇa consciousness to others. When a devotee, a practicing devotee, an aspiring devotee, lives in the *bhakti* camp but lacks these rare qualities, it's a little sad. Prabhupāda used to call them poor students.

You can see the spiritual poverty in the practitioners of any religion. You can't expect that most of them will reach whatever they call their pure stage. You can't even expect that most of them will be able to renounce the bodily platform. You see all degrees of that "poor student"—the militant, the fanatic, the political, and even the hypocrites.

Let's not speak of them, though, let's speak of ourselves. We're one of them. Somebody approaches you in the shopping market and asks, "How come you're so thin? Is it true that you think the angels are going to come and take you up to heaven by that piece of hair on the back of your head?"

"No, ma'am, I don't think so. I don't think a piece of hair is going to save me. I think I'll need more than that. And in fact, my hair is thinning out. I can't count on it. It will definitely take more than that." One light remark returned by another light remark. Where is inquiry? Where is real love? The rain comes down and you're indoors and it's cold indoors, but at least you're not a lamb or a crow.

Prabhupāda singing (Happening album):

hare kṛṣṇa hare kṛṣṇa, kṛṣṇa kṛṣṇa hare hare
hare rāma hare rāma, rāma rāma hare hare

Am I doing this radio show for myself or for an audience? And who is that audience? What is my relationship with them? Is it another duty? Do I feel good when I have done it for the day? So many things we have to do. We live in so many shadows that for most of us, dream-life is something we don't think important enough to recall, so we're out of practice at remembering our dreams. I have already learned that you can practice and recall dreams, and that you can go further with them—you can use them for a kind of psychotherapy. I don't seem able to keep that up though. I don't see the innate worth in it. Neither do I see much encouragement to do it from guru, Kṛṣṇa, and *sādhu*.

Prabhupāda said dreams are mental life. Just as we have a mental life while awake, similarly, we have a mental life when we're sleep. It's just that a wider range of impressions are combined. But that's all it is. We just have to make the best of it, as we would with any mental life.

Dreams come and go. They're a form of drowning. The memories drown if you don't recall them. They come to the surface and there's a brief moment where they ask to be saved. If you can, you take them. But it's such a brief moment, and we are indifferent rescuers.

I approach my dreams as a possible outlet for creativity. They come to me saying, "Here we are, full stories with so many characters, some known to you, some from your past, some juxtaposed into interesting combinations. Save us now . . . " and then they're gone. The indifferent rescuer thinks, "Well, I don't have much to do right now. Let me be magnanimous toward these dreams and write some of them down. Oh! It's too late, they're drowning. They have drowned."

We'll get other chances, but we remain indifferent, so our dreams remain in the world of dreams. We continue to will ourselves awake in the morning, "All right, if you don't get up now, you won't be able to sleep well at night." We're driven by practical, bodily regulation. We don't sleep late because we must get up and hear about Kṛṣṇa. We're simple, regulated beings. We get up and enter the cold room.

He thinks ahead to this radio show and another chance to read and write. Somehow the thrill and the quiet joy of the morning on a quiet day has progressed and now it's after lunch. Madhu cooked some extra Sunday preparations. When I went downstairs after eating, he said, "Have a happy . . . "—I forget the Irish words he used—but it meant "first of May." What does it mean? He said it's the first of May. The Irish have celebrated that long before Christianity came to Ireland.

All right, it's the first of May. It's also Sunday. I know it has been a good day, but as I say, it's a day in which I am feeling some of the lambs' sheer jumping spirit inside.

Now that I've had lunch, I feel quieter, more like the dumb feature of the lamb. You see them out there. One runs across the field, then suddenly stops. From the human's point of view, we can only guess that it ran out of steam. Or did some thought impel it to stop? Anyway, when it does that, that's when you see its real dumbness. What should it do now? Should it run to its mother and duck under her and tug and push and tug? Should it run some more? Should it butt heads with its friends?

Are we like that on this May 1 afternoon? I'm not out playing golf, not making a holy confession to the priest, not worrying about my girlfriend or wife or telephone, not having to put on a coat and go outside to see how the cows are doing, ugly, mean me and ugly them.

On the way here, we saw a cow or bull (I don't know which) in a little trailer just big enough to hold it. Its big head was sticking out like a Jekyll-headed human being, a giant, deformed human being with a head too big for him. It looked around, resigned, with its identification tag punctured in its ear. Its master was driving through the weekend town. Prabhupāda preaches, "Who is master of his body that he wants to enjoy his body and work so hard for his body? You have to consider who the body belongs to. Does your body belong to your boss? To your family? At least the body is a servant of its own senses. To whom does this body belong that you want to enjoy it? Better to find out whether it's your property to enjoy or not, because if the body doesn't belong to you, then it has to be used for the purposes of the owner, or else you'll get in trouble in the end."

The body belongs to God, who through His material nature created it to fit our karma. Let's use it for Him and be happy.

Rain, rain, tinkle, tinkle, then pouring sheets down, down. I hear the pebbly sound on the roof, sheets of rain, slanting rain, sound. Rain is sound, wet, cold, blind, falling everywhere on the grass and the backs of the sheep, on the bushes, turning the leaves greeny yellow. Down, down, gray sky. Hare Kṛṣṇa Hare Kṛṣṇa, Kṛṣṇa Kṛṣṇa Hare Hare/ Hare Rāma Hare Rāma, Rāma Rāma Hare Hare.

As I say, Sunday afternoon is a long way from Sunday morning, but it's all part of the same cycle of rhythms. It's an up and down cycle. The slough hits its bottom and starts to roll up. The peak tips its highmost and starts to curve down. Our rhythm is to remain in the Kṛṣṇa conscious groove whether the tide be high or ebbing. We want to avoid the groove of dull habit.

Prabhupāda singing (Happening album):

hare kṛṣṇa hare kṛṣṇa, kṛṣṇa kṛṣṇa hare hare
hare rāma hare rāma, rāma rāma hare hare

All right, let's close this one out. I'm making *daṇḍavats* and not allowing anything that comes into the mind to come out of the mouth. I offer a blessing to the listeners? "Dear friends, please chant the Hare Kṛṣṇa mantra." One devotee here vowed to chant sixteen rounds daily. Then he told me he had stopped chanting all his rounds. When he told a devotee that he wasn't chanting, the devotee asked him point-blank, "Why not?" He said he was so much taken by the directness of that question that he had no good answer. He decided he might as well chant. It's as simple as that. Once you accept Kṛṣṇa consciousness, there's no reason not to chant.

Now apply that same reasoning and go a step further. Since you're chanting sixteen rounds and you accept Kṛṣṇa, at least theoretically, and you have surrendered to your guru's guidance, as the man says, "Why don't you *chant* sixteen rounds?" Why don't you go for love of God? Why be mediocre? Ask yourselves that question. We can't claim that we haven't really dedicated ourselves to Kṛṣṇa consciousness. We have done that. We don't have anything else. Often we've grown older in Kṛṣṇa consciousness. It's not that we have a choice now to change religions. We should be grateful for our spiritual security. As Prabhupāda says, if you have government service, it's a good niche. You can't be easily fired. There's so much job security. Who quits a good job? There's no reason why you should be whimsical and say, "I did it, I quit. I don't have to be a slave to what I was doing." That would be foolishness. Why, then, don't we reach for the wonderful conclusions of Kṛṣṇa consciousness and not just stay with our sense of religious security? What's your answer to that?

"Oh, my answer is lethargy, slide and space, perfidy, loss, and counting on grace, nothin' better to do than to stew a brew in the mind and stretch and pause. And perfidy, perfidy, pause. Think it over and mull about, consider the doubts, don't act now. Whatever you do, don't forget to stew."

Like that man who is trying to decide whether he should get married. Well, I should get married, I know, but I don't know to whom. No need to make a decision now. But I really should, shouldn't I?

"Yes," we advise, "you definitely should. Now don't be shy. After all, it's a very personal thing, romance and all that, choosing a girl, and will she choose you? Maybe we can help. How about Bhaktin Sue?"

Together we mull it over and help him out and finally he goes somewhere to what we shall call a third world country, actually marries a girl, goes home without her, and she never hears from him again. Now how's that for acting without acting?

But you can't beat the laws of karma. You can't refuse to act and still act at the same time. What are you doing? We heard you got married and haven't gone back and called for her. Her father is disturbed. He wants a divorce. What kind of behavior is that? Please tell me, did you marry her and really think you shouldn't have?

He really can't say. He mulls it over. He wanted to go to Vṛndāvana and do *bhajana*. Sort it out and think of what's best, maybe someone else, or just go on the same, making money, helping the temple and all of that, but he's not getting any younger. Maybe you don't need to . . . naw, you ought to. That girl now, can't even remember her face. Just let it go. The years go by. Maybe he'll go back if nothing else comes up.

I don't want to expose anybody, but I'm telling you that although we may laugh at such an irresolute person, we're like that too in terms of our own surrender to Kṛṣṇa. He has appeared before us as *adhokṣaja* through the words of the pure devotee, Śrīla Prabhupāda: "Here I am. My name is Kṛṣṇa. I am all-attractive. I will appear in any form that attracts you. I come in all My incarnations just to satisfy My pure devotees. Do any service you want, but do it for Me. I'm willing to take any offering you make and see the best in it. But I do teach that the real conclusion is to surrender to Me. Come to Me and be happy. Renounce this world. I am the Supreme. Come on, give up the suffering of repeated birth and death. Accept the *bhakti* science. No, you can't expect to see it all, realize it all in a minute, as if that's your proof of God. You have to submit and take the time to work. What are you waiting for?"

I cannot speak for Kṛṣṇa. I come off sounding like a not-so-compassionate counselor in my imitation of God's voice: "Look, I know it's tough. But I can't make a better offer to you than this. Stop griping." At heart, you're really not satisfied and you say, "Well, I don't know. If there's a God, He ought to be better than that."

Yeah, you're right. God ought to be better than my imitation of Him as a disappointing, not-so-loving counselor who is part of the establishment, always admits limits on all sides, and seems to say, "Life is tough, isn't it? And that's the way it is. So you better grow up, buddy, and face it. And look, it really isn't so bad. If you can chant the holy names, it really isn't so bad. You understand? Now wake up and stop being such a fool. Why don't you wake up?"

O Kṛṣṇa, mostly You don't appear before me because You think, "This nonsense guy, he goes running and shouting everything that he hears (even things he doesn't hear from Me) and saying, 'This is what I learned today, this is what I found today.' It's all right that he wishes to do that on behalf of the human beings and take credit for it as a writer, but I don't know."

Again, I shouldn't imitate Kṛṣṇa, even to make fun of myself. My dear Lord Kṛṣṇa, without You, I am reduced to talking in circles while I am seeking you in all Your different manifestations. I wish that I could seek You in the right way.

Let's try in the direction of the *Śrīmad-Bhāgavatam.* All glories to Śrīla Prabhupāda.

Prabhupāda singing (Happening album):

> *hare kṛṣṇa hare kṛṣṇa, kṛṣṇa kṛṣṇa hare hare*
> *hare rāma hare rāma, rāma rāma hare hare*

22

Haribol. I asked yesterday whom the radio show is for—is it for myself or is it for an audience? Today I remembered the radio shows I did a few times with a few devotees in Boston. It was a student radio station and the student who ran it needed to fill up the time slots, so he invited us to do a few shows. They were *Kṛṣṇa* book shows, and we used to rehearse on our own before we went to the studio and performed.

I remember there was one lady—our *pūjārī*, I forget her name right now—and several men. We had a drum. We would rehearse briefly—our lines were improvised—and it was a lot of fun. We were all amateurs, including the man who produced it.

"At one time, when the earth was overburdened by military forces which were actually demons, the earth took the form of a cow and approached Lord Brahmā, her eyes full of tears, and said . . . " Then the girl would say, "Dear Lord Brahmā . . . " So it went. We used different voices for the various characters.

We did another show where I remember reciting the different ingredients for *yajña* from the Second Canto. I remember going back to the temple later and trying to find the radio band playing our show. It was faded, but we could hear it. We got some response too. Someone who had never heard of Kṛṣṇa consciousness heard the show and liked it very much.

Those shows were different from these because we were definitely conscious of our audience and were trying to preach Kṛṣṇa consciousness in an attractive way. I'm preaching here too—or at least I want to speak *kṛṣṇa-kathā;* talk about Kṛṣṇa, who appeared, Lord Kṛṣṇa, who is in our hearts, about Kṛṣṇa whose material energy makes a curtain separating us from Him. *Nāhaṁ prakāśaḥ sarvasya, yoga-māyā-samāvṛtaḥ/ mūḍho 'yaṁ nābhijānāti, loko mām ajam avyayam.* Only when we stop being foolish will that curtain be completely removed. That's what we're trying to do on this show, although we're progressing slowly and it's taking some work.

Bhagavad-gītā says it's easy. We can easily cross over the insurmountable *māyā* if we surrender to Kṛṣṇa. Whatever is difficult becomes easy for Kṛṣṇa's devotee.

"But it's not easy to be Your devotee."

Prabhupāda responds, "Why not? What is the difficulty? Is there anything in this *bhakti-yoga* that's not recreation? Put your counterargument that 'Swami, you say this is all recreation and very pleasant, but I find this item is not so pleasant.' Go ahead, put your argument." No one says anything. No one dares say, "It's dry, it's hard. We can't surrender. We don't know the way around. We can't work with the movement's leaders. It's too hard being identified as a Hare Kṛṣṇa devotee in public. We don't know how to live in this movement." No one dares because he would say, "Smash, smash." It's recreation—chanting, dancing—is dancing difficult? "You dance with us, chant Hare Kṛṣṇa, take *kṛṣṇa-prasādam.*"

Am I teasing you? Is this just a bluff and we still can't answer the questions? No, we all admit that it's hard because of our minds and our causeless unwillingness to surrender. Whatever appears to be a real obstacle—problems with others, problems that arise from circumstances beyond our control—it's a test. But no matter what they are, they don't prevent us from the direct, quick route of calling out to Kṛṣṇa: Hare Kṛṣṇa Hare Kṛṣṇa, Kṛṣṇa Kṛṣṇa Hare Hare/ Hare Rāma Hare Rāma, Rāma Rāma Hare Hare.

Another way to answer the question is to say that *bhakti-yoga* is easy. That statement means that *bhakti-yoga* is the only thing that's possible in this age for us. Everything else is impossible. Easy doesn't mean we can push the remote control button and *poof!* we're pure devotees. We have to work at it.

Prabhupāda singing (Happening album):

hare kṛṣṇa hare kṛṣṇa, kṛṣṇa kṛṣṇa hare hare
hare rāma hare rāma, rāma rāma hare hare

This is a nice radio studio. Out the window I see a small, gray bird with an orange breast. You can't call it a robin like we would in North America, but whatever its name, there it sits, twitching its tail in the strong breeze. A little further down, a larger bird, maybe a blackbird, sits on the stump of a tree branch. Then further off, hills and a mountain peak. There's snow-light clouds capping the mountains, reminding me of the analogy that my original Kṛṣṇa consciousness is covered.

I don't want to sulk about this or keep bringing it up, "Why am I covered? Oh, why?" Still, I want to face it because when I think of a radio show, I think that ideally I should come on the air and say, "Kṛṣṇa is so sweet. He wears a yellow *dhotī* and plays a flute. The sound of that flute bewilders all living entities, especially the *gopīs.* The *gopīs* run out from their homes to be with Kṛṣṇa." I can say those things, but where is my realization and spontaneity? There's a tangled underbrush of perversity that disables me and makes me want to talk about *that* instead of going to Kṛṣṇa. In fact, Prabhupāda warns us not to jump over and talk about advanced topics, although he doesn't say we have to go through every stage of *māyā* to get there. Go to *bhakti-yoga*. Go to the topics of *Bhagavad-gītā* and *Bhāgavatam* gradually.

Why don't I have a radio show like I did in Boston, with different voices? Once upon a time when the earth was overburdened with the demonic forces of kings, Bhūmi took the shape of a cow and went to the creator of this universe, Lord Brahmā, with tears in her eyes, just to attract the mercy of the creator-lord. She said how the earth and all the creatures were being so much harassed by Kaṁsa and his persecutions. It was a great burden for her.

Lord Brahmā took pity on the presiding deity of the earth, and together, along with all the other demigods, such as Lord Śiva, they went with Bhūmi to the Svetadvīpa planet, the spiritual planet within this universe. There is an ocean of milk called the *kṣīra* ocean. Brahmā and the demigods stopped at the shore of that ocean, which is as far as they are allowed to go. Within that ocean resides the gigantic form of Kṣīrodakśāyī Viṣṇu, who lies down on the bed of the Ananta serpent in the slumber called *yoga-nidra*, where He is served by Lakṣmī-devī. In meditation, Lord Brahmā chanted the Puruṣa-śukta prayers, hoping the Lord would hear his prayers and grant them all relief.

In silent meditation, Lord Brahmā received Kṣīrodakśāyī Viṣṇu's reply:

"My dear Lord Brahmā, please rest assured that what you have asked from Me has already come about. I am aware of the persecutions of King Kaṁsa and very soon I will appear in this world in My original form to vanquish this demon and enact many of My pastimes, pastimes that have never before been seen in their sweetness by the people of the earth. I shall appear in Mathurā-Vṛndāvana. Without delay, some of the demigods should now start appearing in those places of my pastimes and they will be My parents and elders."

Lord Brahmā then turned to the others and told them what the Lord had said. Everyone was relieved and went back to their places. Those who were designated took birth in the world as the elder members of the Surasena dynasty in Mathurā.

It's easy enough to do, isn't it? To hop and skip over yourself and your hang-ups, your immediate sense perceptions, and talk about Kṛṣṇa? Yes, it was fun, it is fun. I can almost smell the *dāl* and hear the drum beats. I'm back in the temple of those days seeing the smiles of the devotees. Still, I know that at sometime or other, I'm going to have to do some other talking. I can't just put one *Kṛṣṇa* book story to another and go through life that way, although someone could ask, "Why not?"

Kṛṣṇa book is there, the Tenth Canto, *dāsam-skanda,* but there are also other pastimes of the Lord and His incarnations in *Śrīmad-Bhāgavatam.* I'm reading the Fourth Canto right now, the section about Pṛthu Mahārāja leveling different areas of the earth.

Do you know that devotees today can do the same thing with bulldozers? When Prabhupāda was in New Vrindaban, he proposed that to Paramānanda. I think Paramānanda had said that he was always doubtful about how Pṛthu Mahārāja could break up mountains and level parts of the earth to increase agricultural production, but then when Prabhupāda asked him to do it and they did, he realized how something like that can be done.

Pṛthu Mahārāja, of course, leveled the land on a huge scale. He was empowered. Then Prabhupāda writes about being empowered. He says that anyone can, to some degree, become empowered by Kṛṣṇa if he tries to carry out Kṛṣṇa's order. He especially mentions preaching. Speaking in disciplic succession means taking up the Lord's order. Kṛṣṇa wants us to become guru and to spread Kṛṣṇa consciousness.

yāre dekha, tāre kaha 'kṛṣṇa'-upadeśa
āmāra ājñāya guru hañā tāra' ei deśa

kibā vipra, kibā nyāsī, śūdra kene naya
yei kṛṣṇa-tattva-vettā, sei 'guru' haya

Go ahead, tell everyone you meet about Kṛṣṇa. Become a devotee, a guru, and I'll be there. I'll back up your words. If we preach, we can experience the *paramparā* and what it means to be empowered. As we become more trustworthy, we can become more empowered.

The analogy given is of a fuse box and fuses. Each fuse has a certain voltage built into it. Some have more voltage and some less, but any fuse that is plugged fully into the fuse box can experience empowerment according to its capacity. If we just sit tight, as Prabhupāda says, meaning, we don't do anything particular in Kṛṣṇa consciousness, then where's the yoga? Kṛṣṇa consciousness isn't don't; it's do. Do serve Kṛṣṇa.

Mahārāja Pṛthu was a doer. He made many arrangements so that everyone could practice Kṛṣṇa consciousness and not be disturbed. He was a real king. We tend to get depressed by our governments. We tend to not want anything to do with the government. We won't read the newspaper—it's all *māyā* anyway—and it's a million miles away from our lives. Our only troubles are with other devotees or with our own senses or trying to make headway in the temple. Actually, the lack of facility and the impoverishment of temple life, the bad qualities of those we preach to or ourselves, is traceable to the bad government. Under good government, everything is auspicious. A good government can overcome all disadvantages, even weather and illness.

Have you ever had the experience of having your service fully facilitated, even down to attention to your personal needs? I'm sure you became cheerful when that happened, provided it wasn't based on a false economy and the person facilitating you actually understood your goals. Doesn't such an experience evoke gratitude? Well, that's how life should be under a government.

All the citizens are in their places. No one has exaggerated importance. No one is cheating. Mahārāja Pṛthu is mentioned as having made arrangements for agriculture. Then his prowess was challenged by a large-scale famine. People came to him, naturally expecting relief. They were all performing their *yajñas*, and grain comes from *yajña*.

annād bhavanti bhūtāni
parjanyād anna-sambhavaḥ
yajñād bhavati parjanyo
yajñaḥ karma-samudbhavaḥ

Where, then, is the grain?

Pṛthu went to the earth, that same Mother Bhūmi we just mentioned. Again, she took the form of a cow, this time not to cry tears and beg Lord Brahmā for help, but to protect herself. She saw that Pṛthu was angry and prepared to kill her. "Why are you withholding grains? I'm the king. People have to live. What's going on?"

She prayed to him first, "You are the Supreme Personality of Godhead. I take shelter of You. Don't kill me. I'm a woman." He said, "You may look like a female who expects protection, but anyone who is cruel and doesn't care for others deserves to be killed, even if she takes the form of a woman."

"No, don't misunderstand. I'm not being cruel. I'm not withholding. It's the fault of the demons. They take the grains and they exploit and cheat and neglect me. The demons are misusing the earth."

In modern times, we can see this same situation. People are finally waking up to ecological reforms and beginning to understand how the demons, for sense gratification, exploit and ruin the earth, throw poisons into the atmosphere, cut down the trees unnecessarily, and completely pollute everything. This was going on even in Mahārāja Pṛthu's day. Demons neglect the earth.

Mahārāja Pṛthu responded. Bhūmi said that *yajña* is not being performed. That was in the day when religious *yajña* could be performed, ceremonies that to us are too vague now. But we can understand that *yajña* should be performed to please the Lord. Then the earth will yield her bounty. When there is no *yajña*, the earth's inhabitants suffer scarcity. If they don't worship God and the demigods (of course, we don't worship the demigods separately), then there will be all kinds of calamity.

Therefore, in response to Bhūmi's request, Pṛthu arranged for *yajñas*. There were many different *yajñas* performed according to the desires of the persons performing them. Each party came forward with a calf to encourage Bhūmi in the form of a cow to give milk. The "milk" consisted of whatever produce the party wanted.

For example, the demigods came forward with a golden pot and Bṛhaspati as their calf. The earth gave them *soma* juice. The demons presented Prahlāda Mahārāja as their calf and caught beer and liquor in their iron pot.

Everyone got their desirables from the earth by *yajña*. Sometimes it's hard for us to understand why all these different parties had their material desires fulfilled, but we know that everything is done by the religious sanction of the king. He himself practiced and advocated worship of Lord Viṣṇu. In this age, the *yajña* to rescue the earth and inhabitants is *kalau tad dhari-kīrtanāt*, chanting Hare Kṛṣṇa.

I can tell one Kṛṣṇa conscious story after another on this radio show. I hope it's not too routine for you. At least it's a relief from the usual. But if you want to know, I'm sitting here on the edge of a meadow, looking out at the sheep who so seriously, busily eat grass all day. Their life is boring, it seems. Eat and eat and eat, with no time for anything else. We can sit and talk about Kṛṣṇa. That's the difference between me and the sheep and you and the sheep.

Prabhupāda singing (Happening album):

> *hare kṛṣṇa hare kṛṣṇa, kṛṣṇa kṛṣṇa hare hare*
> *hare rāma hare rāma, rāma rāma hare hare*

All right, I'll say good-bye. My desk is cluttered with books. I'm a little disappointed in myself for having drowsy patches today, which emphasize my opening remarks about feeling sorry that I'm not more Kṛṣṇa conscious and that I don't thrill to what I read and hear. I am not over-brimming with topics about Kṛṣṇa. This dissatisfaction came because I was disappointed with myself for being so drowsy.

Anyway, I won't bother to berate myself. I did have some good hours early in this morning, chanting, walking, talking, writing, and reading. Sometimes I have to plow through the drowsiness and get to the *Bhāgavatam*—that's my misfortune—but I'm not going to give up the attempt. I know good will come of it.

I wish the same for you. If I were to hear of your devotional activities, I would encourage you to go on, even if they seem mechanical. When Kṛṣṇa sees that you're trying, that you're doing things on time, and that you are concerned about your *pūjā* and your *sādhana*, then that itself is devotion. You are not devoid of devotion. We have no alternative but to work at improvement.

harer nāma harer nāma, harer nāmaiva kevalam
kalau nasty eva nasty eva, nasty eva gatir anyathā

Until tomorrow. Hare Kṛṣṇa.

23

Prabhupāda singing (Happening album):

> *hare kṛṣṇa hare kṛṣṇa, kṛṣṇa kṛṣṇa hare hare*
> *hare rāma hare rāma, rāma rāma hare hare*

Haribol. This morning I read in the *Bhāgavatam* how the king is responsible for his citizens. If he's a good king, he gets one sixth of their pious credits. If he is a bad king and taxes the citizens without giving them what they need, he receives one sixth of their impious credits.

In the purport, Prabhupāda writes that the same principle can be applied to parents and spiritual masters. If a spiritual master cannot direct his disciples to become free of sinful activities, he becomes responsible for their sinful acts.

I doubt this means if a spiritual master's disciples become sinful, he is automatically to blame. Otherwise, what about those disciples of Prabhupāda who have gone back to meat-eating? Or those who have become antagonistic to Kṛṣṇa consciousness? I don't know how many there are in that category. There are probably far more who have been disillusioned with practicing Kṛṣṇa consciousness, or who are unable to practice actively.

I think the real point is that Prabhupāda gave them all direction. He supplied the society and the books and he awakened in us the understanding that we're meant to practice Kṛṣṇa consciousness in this lifetime. No one can say that Prabhupāda didn't guide us sufficiently. No one can say that we simply served him, but that we didn't get anything in return. That's not true.

I'm bringing this point up to question myself. What have I done, (or, what am I doing?) to direct devotees? It's something I have to consider.

I don't want to defend myself on the air; I'm raising it as a point I have to consider. The main thing is that I shouldn't misdirect anyone. We think of "gurus" who are cheaters—outright cheaters—who take money or who exploit their women disciples. Then there's another category of those who have a general inability to lead others. They often can't even lead themselves. Even though they work in the mission, they finally flop. They get credit, I suppose, for having done good work, but in the end, they are a great disappointment. They can cause a lifelong crack in a disciple's faith. Therefore, seeing how fallible we are, I try to take care of myself.

I read in Hari Śauri's *Diary* about Prabhupāda talking about the spiritual master. Professor O'Connell from Toronto asked Prabhupāda if a woman could become a guru. Prabhupāda said yes, there are examples, although it's rare. Not so many. He said, "Actually, one who has attained the perfection, she can become guru, but man or woman, unless one has attained the perfection, *yei kṛṣṇa-tattva-vettā, sei 'guru' haya* . . . The qualification of guru is that he must be fully cognizant of the science of Kṛṣṇa. Then he or she can become guru."

Sometimes Prabhupāda says it's easy to become guru because you simply have to repeat what Kṛṣṇa says. Kṛṣṇa is the supreme teacher and guru. Anyone can represent Kṛṣṇa. *Kibā vipra, kiba nyāsī, śūdra kene naya/ yei kṛṣṇa-tattva-vettā, sei 'guru' haya* . . . Anyone from any social condition can be a guru. All they have to do is tell everyone they meet about Kṛṣṇa.

That phrase sounds so permissive. *Yei kṛṣṇa-tattva-vettā, sei 'guru' haya.* If you know the science of Kṛṣṇa, *sei 'guru' haya,* you can be guru. This time, however, Prabhupāda emphasized that becoming guru means becoming fully cognizant of the science of Kṛṣṇa. Becoming guru is a perfection, not a beginner's state.

I don't know if I can fully face up to all the implications of that statement, as we try to take Prabhupāda's guidance. On the other hand, we have to have compassion. People have a crying need to take direction. We want to respond to that. We want to present Śrīla Prabhupāda's instructions. That's the preaching mood.

Anyway, this is enough food for thought for many talks, more than I can talk my way out of right now. My first business is to become fit. First, *ācārya prabhu jīvera śikhaya:* set the example, then preach. Preaching is a matter of communication. What's more important, communication, or the state of what you're communicating? The truth of the communication, the depth of it, the purity of it, the non-hypocritical nature of it—communication is the order you give or the form of teachings, and it has to carry the potency of deep, personal realization.

I count on devotees being able to accept the form of communication I do give, which is, I hope, effective, open, personal, and non-bluffing. That is, my personal writing coming in book form. Then, for better or for worse, as they say, in sickness or in health, in happiness or distress, we can deepen our relationship. Let us prosecute it together and go with it as far as we can.

Prabhupāda singing (Happening album):

hare kṛṣṇa hare kṛṣṇa, kṛṣṇa kṛṣṇa hare hare
hare rāma hare rāma, rāma rāma hare hare

I'm coming to the end of Hari Śauri's second volume. There are moments when it's hard to take. That is, you see how Prabhupāda preaches and you wonder, "How can I possibly measure up?" There was so much stress on book distribution and the ISKCON temple, the uncompromising, bold preaching to smash the materialists who are actually demons in different guises. I don't disagree with any of this, but I don't know how I can measure up. The feeling of Prabhupāda's strong presence, how we didn't dare confront him with compromise. We didn't even allow ourselves to *look* at any compromise that might exist in our hearts. Because Prabhupāda would smash compromise, we didn't dare.

Now things have changed. Prabhupāda is not here to write us a letter about our various services, so we go on with what we're doing. ISKCON has also changed in so many ways. This creates—what shall I say?—a tension in me when I read about those times. It's a strength of the *Diary* that Prabhupāda's so present. Professor Hopkins says the great strength of the *Diary* is that it lets us into Prabhupāda's immediate presence. He writes, "Prabhupāda was a truly remarkable man who was willing to let Kṛṣṇa use him for his own purposes until his own mortal frame was used up." Naturally, we want to respond to him, to help him and serve him and be like him, but we just can't imitate him. We can't carry a cane like Prabhupāda carried and just because we get toothaches and don't go to the dentist, it doesn't mean we are as detached from our bodies as Śrīla Prabhupāda was. Can we keep lecturing with our faces swelled up, as Prabhupāda did on his American tour? Even if we can keep lecturing, we're still not able to imitate his spiritual realization. Prabhupāda showed such power when he smashed the atheists and Māyāvādīs. His followers can also preach boldly, but we again cannot imitate him. The audience won't applaud us the way they applauded Prabhupāda when he called them cats and dogs. Prabhupāda was so self-realized that he could be sweet and strong at the same time.

I'm saying all this, expressing my feelings, but not with an aim to solve all contradictions. It's not that I have all the answers. Basically, I just wanted to tell you what I experienced while I was reading the *Diary*. Nobody can solve another's internal contradictions and I for one would hesitate to accept another's easy solution. For example, some people say that Prabhupāda was a strong presence when he was here, and that that same presence is there in his books and tapes. Does that mean, then, that right now in 1994, Prabhupāda's presence and orders are exactly the same as they were in 1974? Is hearing from or about Prabhupāda like playing an old movie over and over—nothing ever changes?

"Hey, there's Satsvarūpa. He looks about thirty-six years old. He's wearing that rust-colored sweater he always used to wear. And there's Jagadīśa, there's Viśvakarma. There's that man who was a Catholic priest who had just become a devotee. They're all asking Prabhupāda questions and he's smashing their doubts and encouraging the Toronto temple leaders in their preaching." Everything is so different now.

I can almost hear Prabhupāda ask, "What is different? What is that difference?" Then I approximate Prabhupāda's answer and say with conviction that this is exactly what Prabhupāda said, so this is the way we answer it now. Still, Prabhupāda is a person. That recording of his voice in 1976 is his separated energy. It's not *exactly* him now. He might very well say something different. He was always full of surprises. We could never be certain what he would say was right or what, according to his judgment of time and circumstance, he would say was wrong. What he did then was perfect and right, but what exact lessons or applications it has in the present is not always so easily discerned. We can't simply adjust whatever he said according to our own judgment and claim that we're following Prabhupāda despite what he said. But neither can it be done by taking a transcript of a lecture or conversation and blindly using it to answer all problems that arise now.

We have to work at understanding Prabhupāda's guidance. We have to purify ourselves, we have to cooperate, and in some cases, come up with a consensus about what Prabhupāda wants. We'll do that by giving a heavy emphasis, certainly, on what he actually said in those years. And that means thoroughly studying his teachings, not just pulling out isolated quotes. It is true that whatever he said in the '60s and '70s and in his conversations and letters was applied to individual circumstances. Become a Prabhupāda scholar and humbly try to represent him as you teach Kṛṣṇa consciousness.

What is it we want? To fear his displeasure, to have enough love and determination to do whatever he wanted and to be corrected by him.

That's another aspect, isn't it? We so willingly accepted Prabhupāda correction, but how is that present now? Someone might say that Prabhupāda's correction is present through his followers—any group of them, any older one—but unfortunately, we've lost some of our faith in that regard. His leaders have sometimes misrepresented Kṛṣṇa consciousness or have even fallen down. ISKCON leadership is regrouping and reforming, but still not satisfying everyone.

If there is a lack of faith in the leadership—and we can't always escape that—then we may be left to face our Kṛṣṇa consciousness and our service to Prabhupāda out of our own conviction. We have to give a strong emphasis to that. We want to serve him and also have to admit that we are individuals with individual needs. It may be that without his being here to immediately smash our ideas, we allow some weakness to come out. But we don't ignore that weakness. We face it in his service. If possible, we immediately banish it; if not, we try to make it a strength. But we serve Kṛṣṇa, even if we have to serve in a different way than we did when he was here.

Prabhupāda singing (Happening album):

hare kṛṣṇa hare kṛṣṇa, kṛṣṇa kṛṣṇa hare hare
hare rāma hare rāma, rāma rāma hare hare

Hare Kṛṣṇa. I'll say good-bye now. I was reluctant to begin the show today, but I don't want to be like that. Better I do the best I can. Doing this radio show every day takes effort, so I pray to Kṛṣṇa that something good can come from it. I'm not a rabbit, I'm not a sheep, I'm not green grass or the sky. I'm *gopī-bhartuḥ pada-kamalayor dāsa-dāsānudāsaḥ*. I'm just a person who wants to serve Kṛṣṇa, who has somehow taken on different assignments from my spiritual master, including the assignment to guide others. With that service comes a lot of recrimination if I don't do it right, if I take service and don't return service, if I'm not humble to those who are humble with me. Guiding others is just another way to serve others.

It should be with fear and trembling that I recognize and accept someone's approaching me. Please, Kṛṣṇa, don't let me reciprocate impurely. Don't let me take this service as a vehicle for my sense gratification, but as a Vaiṣṇava duty. As Prabhupāda writes in one purport, the disciple is not the provider of material facilities. Guru-disciple or parent-child—these relationships are for exchanging service. It may be a service where I appear to be superior and the disciple subordinate, but at heart, there should be a clear understanding of my duty.

That's all for now. All glories to Śrīla Prabhupāda.

24

Haribol. This is going to be a no-frills radio show. No music today. I'm starting early because I want to go out on a bicycle ride around the countryside. We're looking for Kṛṣṇa wherever we go.

Someone may ask, "Are you really looking for Kṛṣṇa, or are you just tagging that on to what else you are doing?"

That's quite a cynical question. If you want to know why I'm going bike-riding, I'll tell you. I'm going out to exercise this body to keep it fit for Kṛṣṇa. A sign that it's not an indulgence is that we will be watching our time and taking a notebook out with us. Halfway through, I plan to stop and write.

But really, why do you create a duality between anything I do and Kṛṣṇa consciousness? That's unfair of you. It's unfair of you to say that my dedication is merely official. Give me a break. What devotee goes out to look at women? Ha! Imagine an old guy like me doing something like that. Neither do we go out like materialistic old-timers to look for other kinds of fun—butterfly-chasing or pub-hopping. Neither are we dedicated poets and writers who go out to exercise to stimulate their circulation so they'll be able to sit down and write that poem that they were hoping to write today. Give me a break. Why would anyone think I won't use my time and energy in Kṛṣṇa's service?

All this to explain why I'm in a hurry to get this show off the ground and into the air.

I wish I were something that I'm not yet—a pure devotee. Prabhupāda knows we're trying for that. It's nice when we hear him acknowledge that we're still striving for pure devotion, but what we are doing constitutes the beginnings of devotional service. He spoke so optimistically.

I heard him speak about that today. Devotees were asking him questions after a 1969 lecture in Los Angeles. He said that they shouldn't imitate Raghunātha dāsa Gosvāmī. He said that each Gosvāmī set a unique example that cannot be imitated. We have to go forward from where we are now and try our best. We go forward by following the rules and regulations. He was also praising preaching as the best service we can do for Kṛṣṇa. He said that the *yogī* satisfies himself in a lonely place, but the devotee thinks that if this mantra has power—and he sees that it has power for himself—then let me distribute it. When a devotee preaches, even against opposition, then

Kṛṣṇa is pleased. Kṛṣṇa's intention is that everyone should chant the holy name. Everyone should get out of this material world and go back to Godhead.

Those words ring in my ears and have stayed in my heart. I don't want to forget them. In one sense, I used to live up to them even more than I do now, or so it seems. Some of the brazenness of preaching work which is exciting when you are young is difficult for me now—to run out in my sneakers and stop someone in their tracks. Even if they didn't stop, we used to run beside them, begging them to take a look at our magazine and give a donation. I just don't have it in me to do that anymore. But there are many other types of preaching that I like to do—gathering together with congregational members, telling them about Kṛṣṇa, and answering their questions. That's just as important. Anyway, if we want to please Kṛṣṇa, preaching is the best method.

Why do we feel encouraged to hear Prabhupāda acknowledge our actual position? It's natural. We know we're not pure devotees, but we don't want to be discouraged by that fact and we don't want anyone to hold us back. The pure devotee says, "I know you're not pure and it's all right. Kṛṣṇa knows it too. Don't worry about it. Just go ahead in your practices and you'll get better. Kṛṣṇa will help you." That's encouraging.

Prabhupāda also spoke about patience and enthusiasm, which he said are two components of determination. Enthusiasm is a gift. It flows through your blood. It gives you energy. Enthusiastic people have verve, life, a desire to practice Kṛṣṇa consciousness. I have enthusiasm for my writing and publishing work. I work at it—I get up early to work at it. I put all the assets of my reading and hearing into it. I'm enthusiastic.

Prabhupāda often defines determination as the sparrow who tried to empty the ocean to recover her eggs. It was an impossible task, but she wouldn't give up. Determination is also a gift. You work against the odds, but you keep trying.

He also gave the example of Gandhi. It's the second lecture in a row, in fact, where he discussed Gandhi's determination to drive the British out of India. Previously, he said that the strength of determination came from celibacy. In the next lecture he said, "Just consider the situation. Here was Gandhi fighting against a powerful British empire, and what was his weapon? Nonviolence. He thought, 'If they fight me, I won't fight back at all.' Just consider the odds." In fact, he said, the British laughed. "Look at this Gandhi. Who does he think he is to fight the British empire with nonviolence?" But Gandhi was determined. Therefore, he successfully defeated the whole British empire because after they lost India, they lost all their holdings in the Far East. That is the result of determination.

I think there's an English saying, "Determination breaks iron." In the example of the sparrow, Garuḍa came and helped her recover her eggs. Therefore, we need determination, but patience that we probably won't immediately attain pure devotion. We'll have to keep working at it little by little. It will come eventually. For now, be enthusiastic, but don't be unreasonable. Don't demand immediate victory.

About the preachers, Prabhupāda said, "Sometimes they are defeated. Sometimes someone is more interested. Sometimes they are told to stop. But they keep their determination, one way or another, one way or another."

I should be determined that if I can't go out on the street to distribute books, but I still want to preach, then somehow or other I will find a way to preach effectively. I'll reach people. I'll help people who are already devotees, nurse them, tend to them, serve them, preach, help people—not just sit idly by myself.

When Prabhupāda said a devotee doesn't sit idly, I thought, "I don't want to sit idly either. I sit on a pillow, I sit at a desk, I seem to be alone, but I'm engaged in preaching. I'm making something." Talk about warriors. What about the man in his studio or laboratory? He works day and night to devise a secret weapon. Isn't he a fighter?

He's always thinking, "If I can make a smart bomb, I can wipe out my enemy's whole army and the soldiers won't have to die on our side. We'll have a quick victory. Just see how this bomb will go down into their chimneys. Ha ha! It will seek them out wherever they try to flee. It will seek them out by heat, by intelligence, by computerized message. Now I have to make a tangible plan. Costly it will be, but not impossibly costly. We'll make the ultimate smart bomb."

Such a person is a fiendishly aggressive warrior. You can't say he's less of a warrior than a frightened recruit or even a veteran soldier with a rifle on the field. The foot soldiers face the most immediate danger; therefore, they receive the most praise. All of those *saṅkīrtana* preachers face the immediate danger. But that doesn't lessen the contribution of the guys who make the smart bombs.

I'm not a big scientist or preacher or strategist, but I think, and try to carry out a plan, of preaching to the best people, the devotees, through their trials, in their travails. Even if I go on a bike ride, I'm thinking, "Maybe while I'm out there, we'll be streaming along, tears coming from our eyes from the vigor, and an inspiration will come how to serve Kṛṣṇa and the devotees."

I don't like to waste time. For me, it gets down to particulars—how I spend the hours of the day. We each have our own cycles. Sometimes we feel alive and sometimes we're tired. As we examine our cycles over a twenty-four-hour period, we become more familiar with them and that helps us stop wasting time. Time is such a rare commodity.

Why should we be so stupid as to day after day, year after year, keep trying to do something at a time of the day when we're really not capable of doing it? For example, I find that late morning, after the strenuous early morning excitement of my personal *sādhana* and after breakfast, I'm tired. I take rest. When I wake up, it's the beginning of a new cycle. It's one of the weakest points in my day, but it's not a time for sleep. It's time to get up and do something else and build up again toward the peak that comes just before lunch.

So seeing that weak point, I don't try to do something very meditative or mentally demanding. It just doesn't work for me. On the other hand, there are things I can do that completely overcome my drowsiness.

Each of us can do this—go through our days and find all the weak spots. By learning our limits, we can plan our strategy and not waste time. The tendencies may come at different times. Like sleep, there's a low tendency to over-sleep. You know when it's coming. There may be a time for lust. There may be a place for anger. You avoid the places, the persons, and the times that get you into trouble and do the things that you are capable of doing without being ashamed of them.

You might have some idea that you would like to read Prabhupāda's books five hours a day. As you work on it and work on it, you never seem to accomplish it. If you ignore that fact and continue on as if you are accomplishing it, that's a waste of time. It's better to admit that you can only read his books two hours a day and then fill your time with other worthy projects.

The Christian monks have had centuries to work out this problem. The Catholics actually have different orders or rules that people can join according to their interests and natures. It can be said that those orders accommodate the various psycho-physical natures. Few people would be capable of staying in a cell all day to pray and study scripture. Therefore, most Catholic rules advocate a certain amount of physical work to keep the monks honest and religious and meditating on God.

We can apply a similar process to ourselves. Better to do what's possible for us rather than plan for what is impossible. We are not Haridāsa Ṭhākura or Raghunātha dāsa Gosvāmī. Haridāsa chanted for twenty-two hours a day at Benapol. Raghunātha dāsa Gosvāmī slept so little that I doubt any one of us could imitate him. Better we do what we can. Prabhupāda was expert at teaching us to do that.

And we may also change over time. Our physical powers may diminish. The *saṅkīrtana* book distributor finds that his legs hurt or his back aches and he just can't stand up all day long anymore. He still goes out, but for fewer hours. The rest of the time he engages himself in some other *saṅkīrtana* activity. Similarly, as you age, other powers increase. We're often able to concentrate for longer periods of time and the passion in our blood diminishes. Therefore, we may have to manage our time differently.

Devotees imagine that they have twenty-four hours at their disposal and then plan against their lower natures to fill up those hours with as much nectar as possible. But they have to fight for the time which is being stolen, not only by our own natures, but by the world. Imagine those who have to work, giving huge blocks of time—eight hours, ten hours—to an employer. Then they have to deal with their priorities. *Sādhana* comes first. That's what deserves our vital energy.

All right, speaking of time, I've run out of it. Our Raleighs are waiting and I'm eager to go while there's still some life in this old frame to pedal up and down the lanes and finally arrive at my writing spot. See you tomorrow. Hare Kṛṣṇa.

25

Prabhupāda singing (Happening album):

hare kṛṣṇa hare kṛṣṇa, kṛṣṇa kṛṣṇa hare hare
hare rāma hare rāma, rāma rāma hare hare

Haribol. Let me tell you how my writing is going. It's coming out with a double-barrel, triple-barrel, quadruple-barrel, quintuple-barrel, sextuple-barrel expression of whatever is passing through me. For example, I was just talking about Hari Śauri's *Diary*. Well, you'll find references to the *Diary* in the story that I'm writing and in the writing sessions, and you may find me quoting from it in other things. Right now, I'm doing writing sessions, reading sessions, a walk in which I speak prayers and read aloud, poems, story chapters, and a reading and recording of *Here Is Śrīla Prabhupāda.*

Originally, I was trying to keep each writing form in an airtight compartment. I wanted each to have its own point of view. To some degree that's natural; they all have their individual moods and differences. But I've stopped worrying about redundancy, and neither am I going to be embarrassed about the smallness of events in my life. It's nice. I like it. Of course, I'm not going to be foolish and think that what I say is of great moment: "Well, folks, Madhumaṅgala has not returned yet from shopping, but Nanda dāsa and I are going out on our bikes."

I can say that—I did say it—and I can write it into the story. I don't think I can't write about it in the story because I just said it on the radio show. In each form and in each instance, I am looking for a genuine humility about my life. People tell me sometimes that it's not humble to keep a diary or to write in the first person. That's nonsense. Humility depends on something else. You can write and be humble or you can not write and be proud. You can try to build yourself a good reputation by writing a lot in a diary or you can build a reputation by withholding the truth. Humility is something different. You can publish a lot about your life and still be humble. It's the quality, the attitude, that counts.

Therefore, if you do tell little things from your life, you have to be aware that you're not very great, yet this delicate texture, like the layer of skin covering your body, is so precious, yet so delicate. The whole life itself, the way your heart beats, the way the soul is present, the way you are trying to advance in spiritual life, trying to surrender, death's approach, the whole delicate texture of a *jīva's* life is the subject matter of autobiography, of this kind of expression. It's something to be honored. You're drinking from the chalice of life itself made up of all these little atoms.

I remember—please pardon the unwholesome reference—taking LSD and having I guess what you would call a hallucination. Life was made up of very beautiful atoms. Not the scientist's atoms—who knows what they are?—but I saw stretched before me air and life itself, as the skin of life. Within it, I could see what looked like tiny, multicolored snowflakes. It was such an aesthetic treat to see this. It was something a person is not usually privileged to see. Whatever it was—concocted as it might have been by me—was presented to me by some minor god as a reward for something I desired to see. It made me see life as precious. When I was on that trip, life wasn't tawdry or cheap. It wasn't for enjoying sex and power. Instead, this texture of the very smallest aspects of existence, those diamond-like atoms joined one another and made life beautiful.

As I said, please pardon the unwholesome reference. I'm not exalting LSD or suggesting that anybody should take it, but life is precious and it doesn't require a big adventure to see that. If you want to understand the preciousness, then be quiet and listen to the wind. There's so much wonder in the universe's functions. With wind-listening quietness, if you can read *Śrīmad-Bhāgavatam*, then you'll see the many wonderful things, spiritual things, not just the aesthetic physical elements. You'll see Kṛṣṇa. Your vision will then be as pure as water, as clear as good air, and millions of times more than you could expect from attending to nature. Kṛṣṇa will reveal Himself to you.

That's not a trip, unless you want to call the Absolute Truth the ultimate trip. It's a trip from which you never come down. Prabhupāda chuckled and accepted our language in those days. "Stay high forever." No more coming down. Yes, he said, this is what this is. In your perverted way, you are seeking something that will keep you high forever. You want to drop out of material reality. Well, this is it. This is the Absolute Truth. You are trying to reach the spiritual world by chemical derangement, but you cannot get these things unfairly. First deserve, then desire to be with Kṛṣṇa.

Life is like that and I can write about it. Drop by drop, blood flows in the veins. Not only blood, but the stool moving down through the intestines, urine in the bladder, the pain of being a person, the foolishness of it—blood, sweat, and tears. I want to capture it and write about it as honestly as I can. And I want to see it all as part of the spiritual journey. Whatever a person experiences as he tries to be a devotee, that's part of the spiritual journey.

That has been my contention. I go forward with it. Sometimes I hold back and say, "Wait a minute, this is *māyā,*" but the fool will persist in his folly and become wise. Everything is holy because Kṛṣṇa is behind everything: *sarvaṁ khalv idaṁ brahma.* That doesn't mean we should embrace the tiger or smoke *gañja,* because after all, it's all Kṛṣṇa. No, there are serious and specific restrictions placed on human beings.

Then what do we mean when we say that everything is Kṛṣṇa? Well, it's true that even nefarious activities take place within Kṛṣṇa's energy, but it's His prison-house energy rather than His free energy. Prabhupāda likes to use that example. The prisoner is still under the government, but he's being punished.

We should stay within the sattvic area as much as we can. When we see traces of our past criminality or the seeds of material desire, we don't indulge in them. Now, here is another contention of mine: we can mention those desires and then pass through them. We can admit the desires and render them powerless. That's all I'm saying. By making those admittances, we can purify ourselves. We don't indulge in them, but we acknowledge them to dissipate them.

And it doesn't mean we always have to mention them. It would be weird if we started listing off every trauma we've even suffered. We really want to forget those things once and for all. I wrote about that in my essay, "Blessed Forgetfulness." When I was a kid, I used to be afraid that if I thought too much about my breathing, I would have to breath consciously. I would lose the unconscious facility to do it. That's an interesting hang-up. I don't even want to think about it now. It's like the hang-up of thinking about ghosts and their coming around. Some things are better left unconscious because we really can't deal with them in the conscious state.

We don't want total consciousness. We want some things to run autonomously. Autonomous—the heart beats and blood circulates. Don't become conscious of every damn thing. At the same time—I don't know exactly what I'm saying—let's have more consciousness. Let's raise our consciousness up to the point of danger. Let's dedicate ourselves to more total expression of Kṛṣṇa consciousness.

Therefore, we probably all contain a self-preserving critic. We can't banish him completely because he's there to preserve us. In a devotee's case, it's the Kṛṣṇa conscious conscience who says, "I'm on your side. You should write a total expression of your day and your life, but be careful that it doesn't get into too much."

Natalie Goldberg says that when you're in a restaurant and you're writing about a fly, it's good to get into some detail, but don't marry the fly. Don't tell everything that you ate for lunch on every single day, but tell us, sometimes, what the rabbits are doing, what the sheep are doing, what the grass is doing, and how today, after asking Nanda dāsa to pick flowers for Prabhupāda, waiting for him to do so, then not seeing them come, you went out yourself with your little pair of scissors and cut some little bell-shaped flowers. Now there are two vases filled with them on Prabhupāda's desk.

Prabhupāda singing (Happening album):

> *hare kṛṣṇa hare kṛṣṇa, kṛṣṇa kṛṣṇa hare hare*
> *hare rāma hare rāma, rāma rāma hare hare*

Now I'll make my good-bye speech and then go out with—I was going to say with Hari Śauri. Hari Śauri can come with us too, but I'll go out with Nanda dāsa on our bikes. I'll have to lead the way. I don't know exactly how to get there, but we'll go to a place where I can sit down and write for twenty minutes from a different side of things, the story.

"Orange marmalade" is what Alice saw written on the label of a bottle as she descended down, down, down into the rabbit hole. She was glad to reach out and take it, but was disappointed to see that there was no marmalade in it. As she continued to float down, down, she returned the jar to one of the shelves that were lined along the inner wall of the rabbit hole's downward passage.

Yes, I was looking at that book recently. Lewis Carroll really chats with his readers. He doesn't take any responsibility morally or spiritually, except to take them through impossible adventures. He builds such a confidential relationship, in a sense, with his readers. He and his readers enjoy such a rapport as he invites them on this trip beyond the pale of society. At the same time, his story retains a complete familiarity with the mores and habits of 19th century England. He doesn't question anyone's identity; he just takes them on a voyage through the wonderland of his imagination.

I don't know what lessons the book holds, but in the name of research, I have looked at a few pages. I'd like to capture that rapport with my readers too.

I want to write peacefully, with that reverence for life, that simple and quietly intense reverence for this life that Kṛṣṇa has put us into. I am grateful for the rope of Prabhupāda's mercy. I want to try and express it all. I want to express my gratitude at being able to rise early in the morning to write.

When the devotees wanted to move out of the temple in New York, they asked if they should beautify it first. Prabhupāda said yes, you should beautify it even if you are only going to be there briefly. Our business is to beautify things that are given to us in Kṛṣṇa's service.

Prabhupāda singing (Happening album):

hare kṛṣṇa hare kṛṣṇa, kṛṣṇa kṛṣṇa hare hare
hare rāma hare rāma, rāma rāma hare hare

26

Prabhupāda singing (Happening album):

> *hare kṛṣṇa hare kṛṣṇa, kṛṣṇa kṛṣṇa hare hare*
> *hare rāma hare rāma, rāma rāma hare hare*

Haribol. A bird's sitting on a bumpy branch. Now it's flown off. A smaller, bluish bird does the same on a higher branch. I see a rabbit playing between the trees and a white butterfly fluttering through the field. The breeze is moving the tops of the brush, the dwarf trees, the weeds, and the bramble that separates one farmer's pasture from another. The mountains are immovable and reflect shadows from the clouds. I can see the houses in the foreground of those mountains, their roofs thatched on securely. They look like toys from here. I offer my obeisances to you, to whom I am speaking, and try to begin a short afternoon show.

I thought I would speak about Prabhupāda and what I am listening to on the tapes. Right now I'm listening to the tapes from Prabhupāda's May 1970 *Īśopaniṣad* lectures. They're different than other lectures. For example, each lecture is quite short. There's almost three on a side. And Prabhupāda sticks to the verse. He reads the verse aloud himself—that's unusual in itself—and follows the text closely. He also covers more than one verse per class.

There are other things I notice on the tapes. For example, it's Los Angeles, 1970, and Gargamuni is the temple president. He seems so senior to the devotees there. He was one of Prabhupāda's first disciples, and he's an intimate. The fifty or sixty devotees here all regard him as something special.

On these tapes, Prabhupāda repeatedly says Gargamuni's name: "As I was saying to Gargamuni last night," or, "Gargamuni and I, when we were walking through Venice Boulevard, such and such happened to us."

Another thing I notice is a trace of what ISKCON was like in those days. I went to ISKCON Los Angeles in 1970 and I remember, for example, the tension between the neighbors and the devotees. This died down after some time, especially as the temple got bigger. But around 1970, it was tense. I remember that there was even a gang fight on the temple lawn one night. Prabhupāda refers to this unfriendliness in one of his lectures. He said he was taking his walk on Venice Boulevard. Gargamuni gave someone a card, inviting them to the temple. The person immediately threw it away. Prabhupāda noticed it, of course, and cited it in his lecture as an example of how people are simply not interested in Kṛṣṇa consciousness. They think it's crazy.

Then he mentioned that he was talking to Gargamuni. Gargamuni told him that someone said, "Why do you have so much money? You have all these cars and fifty or sixty people living together." They didn't think it was nice that the Kṛṣṇa consciousness movement had such a drive to make money. Of course, Prabhupāda related that incident many times and said that the neighbors were envious.

Anyway, that's the background, but the real point, of course, is to hear the pure philosophy. We all like to hear Prabhupāda preach and understand the context in which he spoke. That's what Hari Śauri is offering in his diary. He applies layer after layer of data and background, and then layer after layer of transcript and lecture. He wants to give Prabhupāda's teachings in the context of the time in which he said them.

Often when I talk about Prabhupāda—I especially see it in a book like *Here Is Śrīla Prabhupāda*—I talk about the obstacles to appreciating him. I don't know if devotees appreciate that kind of approach, always talking about problems. It can border on blasphemy or offense. I know if somebody were always telling me why he had a problem relating to me, I wouldn't appreciate it so much. One disciple has written to me several times, "You know, I didn't pick you as my spiritual master. It was during the times when these things were decided for us by our authorities."

If somebody says, "You know, you're a junior. It's hard for me to see you as my spiritual master because you are from a Western background, and compared to Prabhupāda who appeared so recently, who are you? I tend to see him as my spiritual master and you as a brother." These are things my disciples might see as obstacles in relating to me. Fair enough. Obstacles will be there for everybody. It's not wrong to have them, but we hope they can be overcome. To the person who says he has trouble relating to me because he didn't choose me as his spiritual master, I say, "Well, if you want me to be your spiritual master, why don't you choose me now?"

Problems can be overcome, but you have to face them. If all you hear is the rash of problems, then it's more unhealthy or unpleasant. Get rid of doubt. When you accept a spiritual master, that means you don't doubt him. You examine him and he examines you. Then you surrender and whatever he says, you try to understand and accept his way over your way. If you can't surrender to his way over your way, then how is he your spiritual master? How can he point out your faults if you object to his methods?

Whenever any doubts come up in me, I tolerate them and go on listening to Prabhupāda. It reminds me of how when we are driving on the highways, the windshield inevitably gets dirty with the marks of bugs who have been blown against it. What can we do except stop and wipe it off time and time again? Similarly, I keep listening to clean up those spots.

These *Īśopaniṣad* lectures are nice. Another series I have listened to often is Prabhupāda in New Vrindaban (1969) lecturing on Nārada's instructions to Vyāsa. The acoustics are good on those tapes.

Does that sound strange, that part of my reason for liking a tape is that the acoustics are nice? But it's part of listening. I find it harder to listen when Prabhupāda's voice is loud and public, such as when he's speaking to a large group over a big sound system. There's a lack of intimacy there. His voice is so loud and I can almost see him up on the podium with the people down below. That's all right, but I like it when it's more intimate.

These New Vrindaban tapes are well-recorded. Prabhupāda was lecturing inside that small building that was there during New Vrindaban's primitive era. And the Los Angeles ones are also nice because even though there are a few hundred people in the audience, they recorded him so well that Prabhupāda seems relaxed.

Another thing I like about the '69 series is that Prabhupāda talks about literature. I always sit up and hear him when he says, "Don't write nonsense literature. We don't want nonsense. We just want one page of something that's Kṛṣṇa conscious." Then he talks about Vyāsadeva's fault of not writing about Kṛṣṇa.

I hope you like to listen to Prabhupāda.

Prabhupāda singing (Happening album):

> *hare kṛṣṇa hare kṛṣṇa, kṛṣṇa kṛṣṇa hare hare*
> *hare rāma hare rāma, rāma rāma hare hare*

Prabhupāda is incredible the way he talks. I can't always remember the details of the individual lectures, but I'll be eating and then suddenly, bang! He says something, and that's the Absolute Truth. It's so stark, so complete, that it wipes out all falsity. It's such a contrast to ordinary thinking. He's often speaking the basics of Kṛṣṇa conscious philosophy—that we're spirit souls, not these bodies, that we're going to die, and that we should become Kṛṣṇa conscious as soon as possible. We're meant to love Kṛṣṇa. He's the Supreme Person. These are the basics for Prabhupāda. When he says things like this, it can have such a tremendous effect if we tune into it. He smashes through our barriers.

I was listening to one *Īśopaniṣad* talk the other day and I realized that sentence after sentence, he was hitting on astoundingly true precepts. These were so important for me to hear and so eloquently stated, and he didn't let up. At that point, I thought, "What does it matter whether he sounds too formal or too distant or that it's not a perfect recording? It's incredible how he's piling up sentence after sentence of such truth like this." Truth to live by—I can live by each sentence.

It occurred to me that Prabhupāda is like that, he gives himself. Of course, I thought of myself by comparison. I can't do that. I talk about things leading up to Kṛṣṇa consciousness, or I talk about my inability to practice Kṛṣṇa consciousness, inability to flow with *kṛṣṇa-kathā.* I feel awkward. I feel artificial. I feel too preachy. I can't do what Prabhupāda does, although when I give a lecture, my lecture is similar to his lecture in the sense that there's very little small talk. Not like this radio show.

I also try to structure a lecture as Prabhupāda does—it lasts twenty-five minutes and I try to cover the points in the purport. I see myself as a faithful lecturer because I try to stay on the point. Lecturing is a genre too.

My lectures tend to be simple, to stick to the purport, have Prabhupāda stories in them and are applied devotional service to contemporary devotees. I don't discuss ISKCON controversy, but the same pure philosophy Prabhupāda presents. I don't speak on books other than Prabhupāda's. I can't talk like that when I'm not giving a lecture. That's the difference.

Prabhupāda can speak like that all the time. When he lectures, he seems so much in his element and conveys that strongly to his audience.

Unfortunately, it's difficult for me to sustain complete receptivity. I listen anyway. It takes attention and a lot of sympathy to put yourself as a quiet member of the audience, especially twenty or twenty-five years after it was spoken, and to listen to a subject you are externally familiar with.

Better to listen and sometimes lose attention than not to listen at all, though. What else am I going to do? I have to become Kṛṣṇa conscious. Here he is, speaking the perfect knowledge, hoping I'll take to Kṛṣṇa consciousness. I have no choice but to respond by hearing.

Another point about the strength of his presentation and how it's easy to miss it. I rarely sit down and say, "For the next thirty minutes, I'm going to sit here and twiddle my thumbs while I listen to a lecture." I don't think I can do that. I always listen while I'm doing something else, but that something else contributes to the hearing. I'm usually attentive when I'm eating.

They are two functions. It's not that I eat absorbed only in the hearing. I eat absorbed in the eating, but very much absorbed in the listening at the same time. Eating and listening go together well for me. In fact, I often end up with tapes where Prabhupāda is telling me not to eat too much when I'm honoring lunch *prasādam.*

Okay, I should say good-bye now. I have to go out on my bicycle ride. I hope this wasn't too inconsequential, talking about lecturing. This is not a commercial radio show, so I shouldn't worry. And if you don't like this show, there'll be another one. If you don't like any of these shows, then don't listen.

The wind is whistling and the road is calling. Yesterday I came back exhausted, but I'm going to go out again anyway. I'm facing a crossroads in my writing, and bike-riding helps me think about it. Anyway, thank you for listening. Hare Kṛṣṇa.

Prabhupāda singing (Happening album):

hare kṛṣṇa hare kṛṣṇa, kṛṣṇa kṛṣṇa hare hare
hare rāma hare rāma, rāma rāma hare hare

27

Prabhupāda singing (Happening album):

> *hare kṛṣṇa hare kṛṣṇa, kṛṣṇa kṛṣṇa hare hare*
> *hare rāma hare rāma, rāma rāma hare hare*

Hare Kṛṣṇa. I wrote myself a note before coming to the radio show today: "How can I be more Kṛṣṇa consciousness and a better servant of Śrīla Prabhupāda? How can I express it, or help it by this expression?"

Well, that's a big question. How can I be more Kṛṣṇa conscious? It's almost innocent of the inquirer to put forward such a question and think that I'm going to answer it. It's like when people ask me questions based on the fact that they are limited living entities, but they assume that I have far greater access to the answer than they do. I don't, though.

(As I speak, I feel breathless as I look out the window at a huge bird out on the branch. I'd say by the size of it that it is a hawk, but I can make out the familiar markings of the ravens—all gray, black wings, a black head—he's a big one!)

All right, let me accept my question as earnest and answer it earnestly, although it humbles me, since I can't really confer instant Kṛṣṇa consciousness upon the questioner by my reply.

First, I have to analyze what my mentality was in even writing such a question down. I think it expresses a hope that the radio show would be vaulted up to a high level of discussion. Maybe I was trying to ensure that we wouldn't talk about things that were details for insiders, Satsvarūpa lore, but would be universal, substantial, and very personal. How can *I* be more Kṛṣṇa conscious?

Inevitably, I think of Prabhupāda handling this kind of question. He would usually say something standard and then drive it home. Or he might reply with unusual directness. For example, there was a question and answer session at New Vrindaban during the *Bhāgavata-dharma* discourses. A man asked, "If Kṛṣṇa wants us to be with Him, why does He make *māyā* so strong?" Prabhupāda replied, "Because your will is not strong." That answer was disarming and unusual. It makes the devotees laugh and exclaim it's truth when they hear the answer.

The more usual question, "How can I become more Kṛṣṇa conscious?" might be answered like this: "Go on applying yourself to the process. Follow the rules and regulations. Avoid sinful activities. Chant Hare Kṛṣṇa. The more you do this and serve the devotees, the more Kṛṣṇa conscious you will become." That answer calls for faith and full conviction in the effectiveness of the Kṛṣṇa conscious process. That answer perhaps tells the inquirer nothing he doesn't already know, but if the inquirer hears with submission, his spiritual master can jump-start his enthusiasm to practice Kṛṣṇa consciousness.

How can I become Kṛṣṇa conscious? It's a daydream question with a fantastic answer. But we keep at it anyway, practicing and practicing, and we become more Kṛṣṇa conscious.

As I recall ways that Prabhupāda might answer such a question, I say things like that too. You want to put Kṛṣṇa on your mind? Then *man-manā bhava mad-bhakto, mad-yājī māṁ namaskuru.* You say you want to be more Kṛṣṇa conscious? Do you know what it is to be Kṛṣṇa conscious? What is your definition of Kṛṣṇa consciousness? Kṛṣṇa defines surrender as always thinking of Him, bowing down and worshipping Him, and always serving His devotees. Think only of Kṛṣṇa and Kṛṣṇa's service. That is Kṛṣṇa consciousness. When you are practicing that, then you can speak of becoming *more* Kṛṣṇa conscious. More Kṛṣṇa conscious means less materially conscious. All that should be left in life is Kṛṣṇa's service. Your mind should be absorbed in it. More Kṛṣṇa conscious, less *māyā* conscious. Less consciousness of eating, sleeping, mating, and defending. More spiritual taste overwhelming the other taste.

I read a nice description by Prabhupāda that although desire cannot be stopped, it has to be changed to spiritual desire. Such happy, full, spiritual desires don't stop our desires; they transform their nature. He gave the analogy of a flowing river. In this analogy, the river represents material desire. When a flood occurs, the ocean overwhelms the river and what we really have is the ocean instead of the river. The ocean is spiritual desire. When we become overwhelmed with spiritual desire, the act of desiring doesn't stop, but its nature is changed.

I can be more Kṛṣṇa conscious by wanting to be more Kṛṣṇa conscious, by praying for it, and by strongly desiring it.

What do you want? You can have whatever you want if you try for it. What does Christ say? To those who knock, it shall be opened. For those who ask, it shall be given. Are you asking for more Kṛṣṇa consciousness? Are you ready to pay the price?

If you ask, "How can I become more Kṛṣṇa conscious?" I can say, "No problem, you buy pure love of Kṛṣṇa from the seller of Kṛṣṇa consciousness. That's how you get more of it. Do you have the price? Then buy more." The price is simply your desire to have it. That's another answer. How to become more Kṛṣṇa conscious? By paying the price. By going for it. By having greed.

That answers the second part of the question, which was how can I become a better servant of Prabhupāda. Find out what he wants you to do, then do it, and then try to improve it. What service does Prabhupāda accept? What does it mean to be the servant? It means to be initiated by him or in *paramparā* from him, you could say, and to take his orders and carry them out. That's how you become his servant. That's all you have to do, no matter where you are in the world. Take up his instructions. Make him your spiritual master. Hear from him as your teacher. Accept what he says and does. Do what he says to do. Associate with his other servants. It's open to everyone.

There's that remark a devotee made who later became Bhakti-cāru Swami. "I love you, Prabhupāda," he said, and he felt such emotion while serving Prabhupāda. Prabhupāda answered, "Then you should love those who are serving me." You will become a better servant, certainly.

It's open to you. Behind the question shouldn't be the hint that you're already a good servant. You're already working on it so hard that you can't think of any way to improve. How could you become a better servant? Is it even possible? If that's the question, you should know that you have a long way to go before you become good, better, or best.

Now your question also addresses how to express all this and how to help your advancement by expression. For me, Kṛṣṇa conscious service has a lot to do with my writing expression. I could give *Śrīmad-Bhāgavatam* lectures, and that is certainly an expression of Kṛṣṇa consciousness. I do give lectures. But I want my writing to help me be a better devotee of Kṛṣṇa. If the writing doesn't do that, if it doesn't purify me, if it doesn't please the devotees (and therefore please Kṛṣṇa), then it is *śrama eva hi kevalam.* It won't be good no matter what else it has. It can be a good story with good characterization, a vivid, honest, a boy-he's-really-got-voice story, but if it doesn't make the reader more Kṛṣṇa conscious or at least offer him the opportunity to improve, then what good is that expression?

My inquiry is, how can expression help me? The answer to this very question is being attempted on this radio show today. Kṛṣṇa says we should always hear about Him and always chant His names. When we get on the radio, we should do just that.

I often thought like that when I would see devotees or even myself given an opportunity to preach on a TV or radio broadcast. Often, we're placed on a panel with others. I remember being on such a panel in Dallas. The topic was something like, "How do you think religions can get along better?" Or, "What is your message to the people?" The panel consisted of representatives from a variety of religions. The moderator finally turned to me and asked, "What do you think?" What could I do but go with it and try it, perhaps out-expressing what others had already said, or emphasizing a basic tenet Prabhupāda would want the people of the world to hear? On such shows, you usually have about two minutes to speak. What can you say in two minutes? What would you say to those people who are about to die? You would send out the most urgent broadcast.

I often think that if we were to take a random clip from Prabhupāda's hundreds of hours of lectures and say, "Okay, this will be his message to the world," it would be full of the vibration of Kṛṣṇa conscious truth. People can hear it and be nourished by it. We have to express ourselves like that too.

Do I do that on this radio show? I have to admit that sometimes I am covering ground that's only implicitly Kṛṣṇa conscious. It's my spade work so that I can become more honestly Kṛṣṇa conscious. I don't want to wait too long or dwell too long on sub-religious principles. Let me deliver the nectar as soon as possible.

Prabhupāda singing (Happening album):

hare kṛṣṇa hare kṛṣṇa, kṛṣṇa kṛṣṇa hare hare
hare rāma hare rāma, rāma rāma hare hare

At the risk of stealing and scooping local news from my other means of expression—my other writing projects—I can tell you that today is Sunday, and although Madhumaṅgala is fasting, he made some Sunday sweets—a kind of biscuit to go along with a carob pudding. After offering this to Prabhupāda—I didn't see what it was that I was offering—I was pleasantly surprised when Nanda brought it in. Otherwise, the Sunday lunch was spare—one *sabjī*, a thin *dāl*, rice, and a couple of pieces of bread. By spare I mean not fancy, just good, simple *prasādam*.

I thought of what I had just been reading in O'Crohan's *The Island Man*. So much of his life on the tiny Blaskett Island, which he lived in such extreme poverty, was taken up with eating and trying to get enough to eat. When a ship wrecked on the rocks, it became a great occasion. One ship wrecked with a full hold of wheat. He said it kept them alive. Otherwise they would have died during the famine.

Aside from such crises, the normal food was simple. Unfortunately, it was fish. When people have very little, filling their bellies is the main principle. It reminds me of how my mother used to pick at me for picking at my meals. She said I should be grateful that I was getting a good meal without any struggle. If I were starving like so many other people in the world . . . I couldn't really think of those starving people, but I did feel guilty, which is what she really wanted me to feel. Having her talk to me like that didn't increase my appetite, but it made me feel that I was a bad person. The evidence was my not having a good appetite and the desire to eat at her table in a world where such privileges were rare.

That was part of my parents' propaganda—that I was privileged to have such good parents. It's naive and transparently manipulative. I shouldn't even take advantage of it now by making sarcastic remarks about it. They used that argument to overwhelm any opposition to their authority I might raise. Anyway, I can relieve myself of that memory by making a little joke now. And the joke is partly at my own expense because it was I who was befuddled by such an argument.

My father also sought to befuddle me when I wondered why we had to eat animals. Perhaps I had heard a rumor that some people didn't eat animals. He said, "Well, if we didn't eat them, they would overpopulate the earth." That sounded reasonable at the time.

But their main propaganda was that they were such good parents. So many children in this world suffer through broken homes, and you don't want to hear about all the nasty things parents do to their children, or how unqualified they can be or how they can't provide them with their needs. I should count my blessings, I was told. Not only have you avoided having terrible parents, but you have first-class parents. You're so lucky you can't even measure your fortune. Therefore, *you should be grateful.* You should be grateful. And out of gratitude, you should cheerfully do what we say in whatever way we think you should do it. You should be a model in every way, based on our desires for what we want you to be. Get it, O privileged one? Yeah, I got as much of it as I could swallow.

I remember the odious vegetables that were put on my plate—especially the beets—vegetables that if you were forced to eat them, you might even vomit. That wasn't any excuse though, because you had to live up to your privileged position. I managed to get my fill and get away.

Why am I talking about my parents? I don't remember how I got onto this. I know I was saying earlier that our expression should be Kṛṣṇa conscious and not wasting time, but I may not always be able to do that. (Excuse me. I'm having trouble with my voice—my voice isn't nice, my thought content isn't nice, and I'm not Kṛṣṇa conscious enough. But I still try to talk. What a wonder.)

Prabhupāda singing (Happening album):

> *hare kṛṣṇa hare kṛṣṇa, kṛṣṇa kṛṣṇa hare hare*
> *hare rāma hare rāma, rāma rāma hare hare*

When I hear the chorus from the 1966 "Happening" album, I think of it washing out the sins of those boys and a few girls who were up to their necks in the New York City counterculture. Not only counterculture, but square culture. Square culture we had been raised in and rebelled from. Now on top of it, we had the corrupt film or icing of trying to be young hippies. So much nonsense we picked up from others—our leaders—Timothy Leary, Allen Ginsberg. We were such confused people. Then suddenly, "Hare Kṛṣṇa, Hare Kṛṣṇa"—Prabhupāda's beating on his one-headed drum led us out of all of it. All that sin getting washed out. Hare Kṛṣṇa is a washing song, a cleansing song.

It's a different kind of cleansing because it produces tears. Those tears clean the body and soul and mind. And whether we know it or not, the chanting can take us out of the material world if we just keep with it. It's not like any other singing. It seems to be ordinary, but that's because we don't understand what liberation is. Liberation doesn't mean that suddenly your body is immune from birth, death, disease, and old age, or that you suddenly sprout two extra arms. It means that instead of doing things for yourself, you do them for Kṛṣṇa under the spiritual master's direction.

In our case, we found ourselves chanting just a few blocks away, in Tompkins Square Park, to the thud of several conga drums and the strummed chords of a folk guitar. We would normally have been chanting political slogans, but we were chanting the Hare Kṛṣṇa mantra with the Swami. It was a washing, cleansing.

What I was just talking about, the years of being with my parents and their manipulating me at the dinner table—it's not that I'm the hero and they are the villains. I was a baby villain and they were grown-up, befuddled villains. Who's right and who's wrong? Everyone's entangled with each other and entangled with the modes. Junior is being asked to eat his meat in Great Kills, Staten Island, while everywhere else, there's something similar going on according to the different wrinkles and configurations of the modes of the world of names.

That's still going on, but when we chant Hare Kṛṣṇa, it begins to go away. It loses its hold. We can cry at it or smile at it, but it goes away. Let it go. And chant.

Prabhupāda singing (Happening album):

hare kṛṣṇa hare kṛṣṇa, kṛṣṇa kṛṣṇa hare hare
hare rāma hare rāma, rāma rāma hare hare

It's almost time for me to say good-bye. It's a little early, perhaps, but I want to get out on the bicycle. It's not so early in the day—it's almost three-thirty—so I want to get out, then come back and write decisively later in the afternoon. Going on the bike ride is becoming a kind of hypnosis for me, especially when I go to a certain spot and write for twenty or twenty-five minutes before turning back.

Starting today when I come back, I'm going to give considerable time to reading about Prabhupāda in Hari Śauri's *Diary*. After that I'll do some free-writing and try to churn some nectar, to get the story out. I am committed to writing this story, but I don't know what it's going to be like. Therefore, I beg the blessings of my radio listeners and the blessings of Kṛṣṇa to do my service. I just wish that I could do it nicely so that I am not wasting my time and so that I can be a better servant of Kṛṣṇa and Prabhupāda. It would be nice if everyone could do that and become fixed up. Then the world would get the benefit of so many fixed-up devotees who would work together to overcome ignorance and usher in the era of *bhāgavata-dharma.* At least we can usher in the happy days of *bhāgavata-dharma* in our own lives. Why not?

Prabhupāda singing (Happening album):

hare kṛṣṇa hare kṛṣṇa, kṛṣṇa kṛṣṇa hare hare
hare rāma hare rāma, rāma rāma hare hare

28

Prabhupāda singing (Happening album):

> *hare kṛṣṇa hare kṛṣṇa, kṛṣṇa kṛṣṇa hare hare*
> *hare rāma hare rāma, rāma rāma hare hare*

Haribol. It's a blustery Monday afternoon. I don't have anything prepared. I wrote down one note, but sometimes I write myself a note to cue me on some subject and then when I go to discuss it, I don't feel like it. One thing I wanted to do was to talk about my earlier life and link it to Kṛṣṇa consciousness. Then I thought, "That's all right for Spalding Gray to do, or even Jean Shepherd, but it just doesn't appeal to me right now." After all, we're supposed to be *Bhāgavata* speakers. Of course, the great *Bhāgavata* speaker, Śrīla Prabhupāda, spoke about his personal life on some rare occasions, and we all loved to hear it. But what was his life? It was all about his struggles to come to America to preach and how in his childhood, his father was a pure devotee of Kṛṣṇa and rang the *ārati* bell while Prabhupāda slept. Prabhupāda woke up to see Rādhā and Kṛṣṇa. Sometimes Prabhupāda even told snippets from his household life—how he traveled by train and met the medical men for his business, or how his little son was walking with him on the street and asked, "Father, why is the moon going with us?" It is all part of the favorable impressions we have of Śrīla Prabhupāda and his divine life, which we don't even hesitate to call *līlā.* Naturally, I'm hesitant to talk about my life, although I admit that when I finally do pull out some memory, like painfully pulling a tooth, I feel some relief from it.

There's also that area I am reluctant to dip into, which could be more efficacious in a direct way—the memories of my life as a devotee. I had one memory flash that I was returning to Boston in 1968, just after Śrīla Prabhupāda married me to my wife in the storefront at 26 Second Avenue. My wife and I were carrying a big box filled with paraphernalia for the Boston temple. It was quite a job to move this cardboard box because it was so bulky. We were going to the bus station, I guess, and it was evening, indoors, in some kind of terminal setting. From a distance, a New York City policeman, who was standing and watching us with some other policemen, called out something to us. He was entirely friendly. He said something like, "I know you guys! How you doin'? Hare Kṛṣṇa, huh?"

I remembered that incident with fondness today and remembered how even at the time, it was so warming. We were hungry for praise and recognition, and we also carried the fresh conviction that it was beneficial for people to favor devotees or to say Hare Kṛṣṇa. Prabhupāda says seriously that this is a fact. If someone thinks, "These are nice people," then he gets spiritual benefit. Just imagine this policeman and all the things he does all day long, which from a civic point of view, means risking his life to uphold the law and order. He doesn't get much credit for his sacrifice. He doesn't get *any* credit toward *mokṣa* or transcendentalism. The policeman is also asked to indulge in things that are not pious, and his life is always on the edge of violence. Still, here was this policeman making a gesture of friendship toward the devotees. The other policemen didn't make it too, only that one. We weren't even so well known then. We had only been preaching in the city for a couple of years.

It pleased me at the time and it pleases me to remember it now. I don't want to remember, on the other hand, all the hoots and hollers, the threats and attacks, that came from the demons. In that case also, however, Śrīla Prabhupāda assured us that their attacks were normal. It wasn't something to be bewildered about. If you want to know whether you are practicing Kṛṣṇa consciousness, you can gauge it by how vehement the opposition is. There are some people who are favorable to us, and some people against us. Each gets his or her results.

We have to be steady. We can enjoy the happy times and endure the unhappy times, but always within ourselves, we have to allow these events to add to the conviction that we want to be devotees in the Hare Kṛṣṇa movement. I fully accepted that at the time, and I want to be a devotee even more than that now—more than I am now. I'll take whatever results come.

Prabhupāda singing (Happening album):

> *hare kṛṣṇa hare kṛṣṇa, kṛṣṇa kṛṣṇa hare hare*
> *hare rāma hare rāma, rāma rāma hare hare*

Just today I heard Prabhupāda speaking a short farewell to the devotees in 1970 in Los Angeles as he was about to go to Japan to see to the printing of his books. Then he was to go on to India where he wished to establish some temples if he could. That was his program as he announced it to the devotees. He spoke quietly—his speech was moving, personal, and humble. It also sounded momentous. Like so many momentous events, we really couldn't grasp what was about to happen. We heard Prabhupāda with awe, yet we had our own misgivings because he was leaving America due to his dissatisfaction with the behavior of some of his leaders.

He said nothing about that in his talk, but he did say that he was an old man and that they might not see him again. That was heavy. He didn't lighten that statement for us either. He didn't tell us that of course, it was his intention to come back. He just said, "I'm an old man, and in case you don't see me again . . . " Prabhupāda was always willing and ready to leave if that's what Kṛṣṇa wanted.

Then he left for the airport. Just before he left, he told the devotees that if they didn't see him again, they should follow his instructions and keep up the program they were following. He said he had tried his best to train them. It was thrilling for me to hear Prabhupāda say openly that he had trained us—the Deity worship, the performance of *saṅkīrtana*, the book distribution—everything he had taught us should be continued.

I also thought it was moving—I can't think of the word I'm reaching for—but he was asking so much from the devotees after such a short amount of association. Some devotees had been there less than a year in Los Angeles, yet he was asking them to dedicate their whole lives to following his order. He was asking them to be Hare Kṛṣṇa devotees.

I am linking up this memory with the little memory about the cop in New York City because they both lead me to think about lifelong dedication to ISKCON. Here was Prabhupāda saying, "I may not come back, but you should definitely keep up with this." He was satisfied that he had done enough and that we should go on with it. Prabhupāda's assumption that we were so dedicated might have taken us by surprise. Although he expected so much, he had already given us so much. Prabhupāda said the devotees in the Hare Kṛṣṇa movement are very, very intelligent. He quoted *Caitanya-caritāmṛta* that anyone who takes to Kṛṣṇa consciousness is intelligent. He gave us that credit. He did give us enough to hold on to, enough to push on, even though it's hard to work together in a group. Prabhupāda wasn't asking only for individual practice, but for living together in a community. At that time, we gave up careers and normal nuclear family life in order to live together and serve together. Fortunately, Watseka Avenue has continued.

These are some memories of ISKCON and myself, a tiny member of ISKCON. We want to stay in this context despite so many changes, and then be able to say to Prabhupāda at the end, "I did my best. I didn't leave your movement. I wasn't such a brave soldier on your behalf, but I stuck to your lotus feet."

Prabhupāda singing (Happening album):

hare kṛṣṇa hare kṛṣṇa, kṛṣṇa kṛṣṇa hare hare
hare rāma hare rāma, rāma rāma hare hare

Will we all come back again? All the old devotees, as we die off one by one like American Civil War veterans, will we come back and join this movement again, stripped of our honors as seniors, and have to be the most green newcomers, growing up in the suburbs or the city, black or white, born in a family of nondevotees? Will we have to become interested in Kṛṣṇa consciousness all over again and then struggle to give up our sinful habits? Or can we follow the model that because we have been devotees, yet didn't perfect ourselves, we will be born in modern-day Vaiṣṇava families with a head start in Kṛṣṇa consciousness? Will we still have to vomit and cry and catch the measles? Will we have to go to *gurukula,* become teenagers, and wonder if we really want to practice Kṛṣṇa consciousness despite the many discrepancies we see in our elders? What's ahead? If we knew, would it change us now?

I heard Prabhupāda quote a Cāṇakya *śloka* and it hit me like a hammer. He said that a *karmī* should think he will live forever, but an aspiring transcendentalist should think he will die very soon. It's a shorter version of the anecdote of the saintly person who blessed four different people in four different ways. If the *karmī* thinks he's going to die, how will he be enthusiastic to carry out his plans by working? And that's his *māyā*. He consumes all his energy in working hard to make money.

nidrayā hriyate naktaṁ
vyavāyena ca vā vayaḥ
divā cārthehayā rājan
kuṭumba-bharaṇena vā

"The lifetime of such a envious householder is passed at night either in sleeping or in sex indulgence, and in the daytime either in making money or maintaining family members" *(Bhāg.* 2.1.3).

When he gets money, he spends it on his *kuṭumba,* his family. He enjoys sex and then falls asleep. Where is the time for self-realization?

When Prabhupāda recited that *śloka*, I thought, "This is an order from all the *ācāryas* not to become wrapped up in what most Americans think is the essential duty for a human being, something that nobody can expect to get out of except by cheating, stealing, being eccentric, or being born wealthy. To get out of the 9–5 grind. To *not* have a job, to *not* live like everyone else with a wife and kids and to spend your time and money buying things and having sex." Prabhupāda and the *ācāryas* condemn this way of life. "Where is the time for self-realization?"

It made me appreciate, also, that I have escaped the rat race in this life. I suffered a few bruises in my early years, especially when I was in the Navy, but Prabhupāda's mercy kept me away from the 9–5 grind. What if I had to be born again? Could I keep my resolution *not* to get a job? If I didn't have a job, how would I live? Still, I have to heed the *ācāryas'* advice. If I have to come back—and I'm sure that I will—I want to at least pray at the end that I can remember Kṛṣṇa. Let me be with the devotees. If I have the instinct that I don't want to live like everyone else, but want to save my time for self-realization, that's good.

Speaking of coming back, who knows what it's going to be like? I might come back during the post-nuclear holocaust and no one will be working at a job anyway. It could be a horrible scenario as the material world moves forward into Kali-yuga. Usually, human society repeats itself, so as the *karmīs* try to reestablish their civilization, a transcendentalist can remain detached, fixed in his conviction that the main duty to is worship God, to pray to God.

Whatever happens to us, we'll have to accept as karma given out by the Supreme. It is due us. This understanding is a background to Kṛṣṇa consciousness because many devotees have come to Kṛṣṇa consciousness, not already poised and detached, looking for God, but in the midst of their attachments. Everything in their lives became auspicious when they contacted the Hare Kṛṣṇa mantra and the devotees.

Perhaps we don't have to anticipate our next lives. We can pray only to remember Kṛṣṇa and to be allowed back in His association as soon as possible. Everything will be worked out in Kṛṣṇa's association.

Prabhupāda singing (Happening album):

hare kṛṣṇa hare kṛṣṇa, kṛṣṇa kṛṣṇa hare hare
hare rāma hare rāma, rāma rāma hare hare

On the same tape that Prabhupāda spoke his 1970 farewell address, there is an unannounced snippet of a lecture recorded over an echo-y kind of sound system. Prabhupāda was speaking to an American audience of that time, no doubt, and he was saying, "We don't insist that you have to join with us and live as a devotee, following all these rules. We just ask you to chant Hare Kṛṣṇa." It was a public, permissive invitation. The basic point is the chanting. Such a novel and interesting idea, to take up mantra chanting. You didn't have to do anything else in the name of being a Hare Kṛṣṇa person; simply chant.

He explained that the mantra consists of three words, but they are adjusted to form a sixteen-word mantra. Then he recited it very slowly: Hare—Kṛṣṇa—Hare—Kṛṣṇa. At that time, the devotees didn't follow him in unison as they began to do later. You hear his voice alone: Kṛṣṇa—Kṛṣṇa—Hare—Hare. Hare—Rāma—Hare—Rāma—Rāma—Rāma—Hare—Hare. There it is, the *jagad-guru* of the holy name has given them *harināma-dīkṣā,* if they will accept it.

That's the answer to the earlier discussion—how to pray at the time of death. We have to take up the chanting in earnest and have attachment for it at the time of death. As Cāṇakya Paṇḍita says, if you are an aspiring transcendentalist, then be ready for death. Mahārāja Parīkṣit was already a devotee. If you are talking about getting ready for the next life, he was prepared. He was born in a family of great devotees. He was executing intense duties as emperor on behalf of those devotees and the Lord. When he heard that he would die in seven days, he thought, "Let me put everything else aside and hear only about Kṛṣṇa." When he went to the riverbank to die, the sages gave different opinions about what he should do, but when Śukadeva appeared, everyone bowed to his conclusion. Mahārāja Parīkṣit said in effect, "I will do whatever Śukadeva says. My dear Śukadeva Gosvāmī, what is the best thing a man can do especially one who is about to die?" As soon as he heard Mahārāja Parīkṣit's question, Śukadeva said:

varīyān eṣa te praśnaḥ
kṛto loka-hitaṁ nṛpa
ātmavit-sammataḥ puṁsāṁ
śrotavyādiṣu yaḥ paraḥ

Your question is glorious. You want to hear about Kṛṣṇa.

Getting ready means becoming attached to the holy name and desiring to hear about Kṛṣṇa in this life. If you are filled with that, it will continue in the next life.

Okay, I've used up my time. Talking to myself and talking to you is what makes this radio show happen.

I just want to mention one thing about something I said today. I said that little by little, as I pull my memories out as a dentist would pull teeth, I get some relief. But there is one part of the metaphor that isn't relevant. When you pull teeth, at a certain point, there are none left. Then you have to get false teeth. I don't like the allusion to falsity replacing something true or the idea of a limited number of memories. Memories are unlimited. Perhaps I should compare pulling them out of me to pulling weeds. Anyway, if I compare it to pulling teeth, please understand that it's a crude image and not to be applied all the way across.

I'm willing to come to the dental office and chat about Kṛṣṇa in this condition, right in the midst of surgery. I'm afraid that it may not be Kṛṣṇa conscious, but I'm not afraid of the pain. I don't like pain, and I'm afraid of the pain of not being a devotee, not doing what a devotee should do, not speaking what a devotee should speak on the temple *vyāsāsana*. This radio show is a special kind of meeting/ talk. It's a little sloppy. Dental activity is not public activity. Nobody sees you being afraid or sees the blood and drool coming out of your mouth. Only the dentist witnesses it and he's trained to deal with it.

In a sense, this isn't always going to be a public show. I think we have that mutual understanding. For example, in pulling that tooth about the New York City cop, I had to remember that I was just married, something I don't like to think about. I'm glad I remembered that story, though. It's like being in the dentist's office, and right in the midst of the pain and the blood and being humiliated in the chair as your teeth are extracted, you sigh with relief and laugh a genuine laugh. Then you say something Kṛṣṇa conscious, and somehow it's all meaningful.

Prabhupāda singing (Happening album):

hare kṛṣṇa hare kṛṣṇa, kṛṣṇa kṛṣṇa hare hare
hare rāma hare rāma, rāma rāma hare hare

29

Prabhupāda singing (Happening album):

hare kṛṣṇa hare kṛṣṇa, kṛṣṇa kṛṣṇa hare hare
hare rāma hare rāma, rāma rāma hare hare

Haribol. I heard Prabhupāda say today, "That same story—not story, it is fact." He told it as a story, or a history, an *itihāsa*, a *Purāṇa*. He refers to historical incidents, but the *ācāryas* tell them as interesting stories. What is it when a man like Tom, one of the Great Blaskett Islanders who was known as a storyteller, tells in his stories but histories of the old people? They are facts. Someone recounts them. We hear them again and put ourselves there.

Today I heard Prabhupāda tell the story of the *brāhmaṇa* in South India who was told by his Guru Mahārāja to read the entire *Bhagavad-gītā*, every day, although he was illiterate. I already knew all the details, but I heard it again with interest. We're trained to hear these things over and over.

I don't want to invent stories about my youth. That would disturb someone. One devotee's mother complained to me that she read something I wrote about drinking beer. She thought this might mislead the ISKCON youths. I have to be careful, but I still want to tell those stories. Just give me a little time to get some confidence that I can do it.

Prabhupāda singing (Happening album):

hare kṛṣṇa hare kṛṣṇa, kṛṣṇa kṛṣṇa hare hare
hare rāma hare rāma, rāma rāma hare hare

In a lot of the stories we tell from our pre-Kṛṣṇa consciousness, the moral will be at the end—how unhappy we were, how lost we were, and how we were bound to more suffering. Our blindness:

oṁ ajñāna-timirāndhasya jñānāñjana-śalākaya
cakṣur unmīlitaṁ yena tasmai śrī-gurave namaḥ

Just see, we were standing in darkness with our eyes shut, but our spiritual master has come. Or, as Prahlāda said, I was falling into a pit of snakes like the way of the demons, but my guru has come. So many of the stories will be like that, whether they tell of painful times or times of reckless enjoyment. That will be the moral to many of our stories.

Here we are today, Thursday, engaged in our own activities and writing about Kṛṣṇa. Writing about why we can't write better about Kṛṣṇa. We're just making this poor offering at the feet of our spiritual master and the devotees, wishing we could be better persons, more heroic, confident in our Kṛṣṇa conscious place.

I heard Prabhupāda say that the difference between *viddhi-mārga* and *rāga-mārga* is that in *viddhi-mārga,* you do something on the spiritual master's order, and in *rāga-mārga,* there's no question of order. You act out of bliss and spontaneous feeling. You are attached to serving Kṛṣṇa. You think of Him even without outward reminders.

I found that interesting, to think of the difference between the two being based on the spiritual master's order. In *rāga-mārga,* it's not that you disobey his orders, but you don't have to wait for his orders. The first stage implies that if you weren't ordered to think of Kṛṣṇa, you probably wouldn't do it. You would take a neutral attitude toward service. But because you have somehow placed your trust in your spiritual master to teach you and to tell you what to do, you accept his training. He gave the example of an Indian child marriage where before love, the husband and wife are brought together. Eventually, it turns to natural love and no one has to bring the couple together by formal arrangement anymore. That's *rāga-mārga.*

Then I thought, "Hey, I have spontaneity for writing. My spiritual master doesn't have to order me to do this service. I find pleasure in it." This is a stage that perhaps many of us are in, where we feel inclination for a particular kind of service and a way to be in Kṛṣṇa consciousness. Now we are trained up so rigidly—and it's good that we have been—but so much so that we're afraid to do anything unless we have that direct order from our spiritual master (or his representative, the temple president or GBC). In the past, anyone who acted independently was in *māyā.* "Independence" was a word that described a bad state of mind. Don't be independent. Be dependent and follow. Be a follower. We don't know whether this new-found enthusiasm is part of that badness or whether it's us moving in the direction of *rāga-mārga.* We don't assume our spontaneity is full-blown *rāgānugā-bhakti,* but we accept it in a simple way, as Prabhupāda did.

Prabhupāda expected us to come to the stage where we wanted to get up in the morning and go to *maṅgala-ārati.* He expected us to form attachments to the Rādhā-Kṛṣṇa Deities, to ring the bells, and to speak to Them in prayer.

I like to write for Kṛṣṇa. When we actually like to serve Kṛṣṇa in a particular way, I think we should be encouraged to do it bit by bit, learning how to do it, without being independent in a bad sense. Until we reach this stage, our devotional service won't be pleasing to Kṛṣṇa. Yet if we go ahead prematurely, we can ruin what progress we've made. Devotional service is like the razor's edge.

O Lord, please engage us in Your service. Let us come safely to the spontaneous stage. Let the symptoms of our joyful service show to us and others that this is actually *bhakti* and not nonsense. O Lord, give us the courage to overcome lethargy and hesitation. We don't want to remain mediocre, wishy-washy devotees and defend ourselves by quoting *śāstras* and policy and saying that this is the only way to perform devotional service. We don't want to be that kind of *niyamāgraha* fellow who follows rules and regulations but doesn't know the goal. The goal is to love You. We are training to reach that goal in *viddhi-mārga.*

Prabhupāda singing (Happening album):

> *hare kṛṣṇa hare kṛṣṇa, kṛṣṇa kṛṣṇa hare hare*
> *hare rāma hare rāma, rāma rāma hare hare*

Somebody wants to know, when are we going to fly? When is it going to become more exciting? When are we going to have fun? Why does everything seem like preparation now? Talk about the meal without the meal coming. When is "it" going to happen? When will we see Kṛṣṇa and dance with Kṛṣṇa?

We say, "It *is* happening, Prabhu. You are already flying compared to what you were doing ten years ago. As for further flying, just wait. Be patient. It's coming. As you surrender more, 'it' will happen more.

"Prabhu, do you know what 'it' is? It is pleasing Kṛṣṇa, not pleasing yourself. It means when you finally give up your ambition to become an achiever and enjoyer in this world and you start to perceive Kṛṣṇa as the center of the universe. Let's give up all our material ambitions, even the ones we carry out in the name of *bhakti.* Let's give up our attempts to enjoy ourselves and please Kṛṣṇa. When we actually enter into a work attitude like that, then we will see Kṛṣṇa and He will become the *puruṣa* for us, the most important person in our lives. Then we will be very, very fortunate. But if 'it' to us means bliss for the self, we could be making another mistake."

I think I'll end today's rather somber, non-daring talk—talk about talk rather than talk itself. But that's who I am. A lot of me is entangled. I'm a conservative fellow who analyzes his own ropes and who speaks to fellow bound inmates about our bound condition. I try to bring about patience and hope, but I haven't done the actual untying yet. I suppose there's a place for that too and that's my place for now. If it's a fact that I have a tendency to speak and someone will listen, then I shouldn't waste his time and involve him in illusion, but tell him, "My dear friend, we are now bound up still in these knots of *guṇas.* Our hearts are attached to this world and our bodies are bound up in the modes of nature. Then let us think about Kṛṣṇa, Gadāgraja, and by thinking of Him, we will become happy and free. Chant: Hare Kṛṣṇa Hare Kṛṣṇa, Kṛṣṇa Kṛṣṇa Hare Hare/ Hare Rāma Hare Rāma, Rāma Rāma Hare Hare. Tell each other stories about Kṛṣṇa. Talk about the science of *bhakti.* Pass the time in this way. Let us devise ways, even within our limits, to serve Kṛṣṇa. Think of cooking for Kṛṣṇa's pleasure, writing something for His pleasure, doing something for His pleasure. Let's think like that, you and I. Let's think like that and chant Hare Kṛṣṇa."

That's advice for being bound; if you are unbound, you call out, "Throw off your ropes. Let's go to the spiritual world and serve Kṛṣṇa." In any case, pleasing Kṛṣṇa is the goal, and hearing about Kṛṣṇa is the way to that goal.

So you can understand why I'm hesitant to talk about a time when I was completely covered by *māyā*. You can understand my sorrow and inadequacy in not being able to give you more direct nectar full of joy and attraction to Kṛṣṇa. But we have to be who we are, follow what Prabhupāda says and do good to each other in Kṛṣṇa consciousness.

I won't mislead you, but I hope we can get together again tomorrow, or soon, for *kṛṣṇa-kathā* and the *kathā* of serving Him.

30

Prabhupāda and the devotees chanting Hare Kṛṣṇa kīrtana

Haribol. I have a few topics to discuss today. I went out into the van and out of curiosity, brought back two tiny paperbacks I have (both Shambala Pocket Classics), *The Way of the Pilgrim* and *Walden.* I read the first few pages of each.

There are a few books—nondevotee books—which an ISKCON devotee picks up at different times in his or her spiritual life. They have some substance to them and they affect us in different ways. Usually, they become a temporary interest, leaving us with a favorable impression, but don't amount to a deviation.

Nowadays, if I hear of a devotee reading a book like *The Way of the Pilgrim* and taking it seriously, or reading the autobiography of Thérèse of Lisieux, I don't feel alarmed. But I have to admit that I get a little condescending, "Oh, yes, he's going through that now. I went through that." I'm surprised that I'm looking at it again.

I was thinking about both of these books. One attraction is they corroborate Kṛṣṇa consciousness, at least partially. Another is that for some reason, we look to our countrymen or to those outside our movement, our *sampradāya,* to give us support. After all, we are resisting all the libraries, all the opinions and scholarship, and we know we don't have to rely on anybody else for guidance, but if we can get some corroboration, we like it. It's reassuring. Prabhupāda liked it if somebody offered support or showed their similarity with what he was teaching.

Then my other point is that these books are revolutionary, meaning, so different from their own contemporaries, their own *karmī* neighbors and religionists. In other words, they have come a long way out of the ordinary and have attained a rare status, whether it's nearly yoga or some kind of advanced sentiment even in *bhakti.* We are assured in Kṛṣṇa consciousness that we have really separated ourselves from the flock. Therefore, out of so many books and interests, we sometimes look at them.

Even in the opening pages of *Walden,* we see Thoreau's skill with language, his telling remarks, and his strong criticism of his countrymen back then, before the American Civil War in the 1840s. In his opening piece, he says that there are greater austerities than even what the *brāhmaṇas* of India perform (he calls them *brāhmaṇas,* but he is referring to *yogīs* and severe renunciates). The austerities his neighbors perform, however, are much greater than that and he doesn't know why they do them. People work like slaves day and night and they have no energy left to be decent human beings toward each other or themselves or to question the higher purpose of life. They waste their lives accumulating money and working like asses. His condemnation of the *karmī* mentality is very strong and it resembles Prabhupāda's preaching.

I remember when I first heard Prabhupāda preach on this point. It was revolutionary to me because my parents were *karmīs* and I was about to become one too. The American work ethic was impressed upon me since I was a child. Here was Prabhupāda saying that only fools think that work and its results have anything to do with the goal of life. Thoreau says the same thing, and then he spells out at least one practical alternative to having a big farm and working like an ass. (In his time, working hard usually meant on farms.) How does someone who wants to get out of the *karmī* mentality survive? Thoreau insists that you don't have to sell your soul and give your life away like that. He preaches simple living and dependence on God.

Here is an immortal line: "The mass of men lead lives of quiet desperation." They don't even know what they're missing. They don't know it's a mistake.

> The better part of the man is soon ploughed into the soil for compost. By a seeming fate, commonly called necessity, they are employed, as it says in an old book, laying up treasures which moth and rust will corrupt and thieves break through and steal. It is a fool's life, as they will find when they get to the end of it, if not before. . . . Most men, even in this comparatively free country, through mere ignorance and mistake, are so occupied with the factitious cares and superfluously coarse labors of life, that its finer fruits cannot be plucked by them. Their fingers from excessive toil, are too clumsy and tremble too much for that. Actually, the laboring man has not leisure for a true integrity day by day; he cannot afford to sustain the manliest relations to men; his labor would be depreciated in the market. He has no time to be anything but a machine. How can he remember well his ignorance—which his growth requires,—who has so often to use his knowledge?

The Way Of the Pilgrim discusses religion directly. This is closer to our own experience as devotees. I remember how the first time I read it, a Godbrother had also just read it. Since it mentions the *Philokalia* as an important book for prayer, ISKCON devotees sometimes look at that too. My Godbrother was doing that. *The Way of the Pilgrim* is a thrilling story. It opens by telling the story of a man who is already religious. He attends a sermon and hears a quote from St. Paul in the Bible that you should pray unceasingly. He decides he wants to do this, so he goes from person to person, trying to find out how to pray constantly. Suspense builds because no one knows. Everyone gives him different advice. Finally, someone introduces him to a *staretz,* or spiritual director, and under his guidance, the pilgrim begins chanting the Jesus prayer.

Chanting the Jesus prayer is the Christian version of chanting Hare Kṛṣṇa. Usually, what happens to an ISKCON devotee who reads this is not that they start chanting the Jesus prayer, but they immediately see the relevance of these instructions to chanting Hare Kṛṣṇa *japa.* It touches their souls. They think that they too would like to chant constantly. It has that kind of influence.

About ten years ago when I read *The Way of the Pilgrim* for the first time, I spoke about it with Ravīndra-svarūpa Prabhu. He said, "Yes, it does seem to enliven you spiritually when you read it." He made an interesting point establishing this in Kṛṣṇa consciousness, and that is that in this Christian tradition in which this pilgrim comes, there is a sole dependence on prayer, and among prayers, the Jesus prayer. The life of someone who is very serious, who separates himself from his religionists as much as Thoreau separated himself from his fellow *karmīs,* includes the desire to pray constantly. That's attractive to many devotees. Ravīndra-svarūpa said, though, that in addition to chanting, we also have many other things to do and that those things share an equal status with the chanting. For example, we worship the Deity and honor *prasādam,* hear the scriptures and engage in preaching. He emphasized that we have more spiritual food for the senses and a variety of activities to help us renounce the sensual world rather than just clinging to prayer, which is the more desperate and difficult thing to do.

That tempered my way of seeing it, the idea that I was going to chant constantly. It made me feel that the method *The Way of The Pilgrim* represents is too distant from what we are as devotees to have a deep influence. Instead, it becomes an excitement or a fad. Not that the pilgrim is faddish—he is quite serious about his prayer, and so were the desert fathers and the Greek and Russian Orthodox monks who practiced it before him. For an ISKCON devotee to take it up, though, it usually becomes a fad. We can't follow up with it. I went as far as reading all the books I could find of the *Philokalia* and the different monks who teach prayer there, but they teach that you should live in a cell, in solitude, and bring prayer down from the intellect to the mind to the heart. I read it, but I never really translated it into practice. We're chanting Hare Kṛṣṇa and we already know what to do. Still, *The Way of the Pilgrim* was both beneficial and supportive to read.

My time is running out for today. I should get ready for my bike ride while the sky is holding up. See you tomorrow. All glories to Prabhupāda.

Prabhupāda and the devotees chanting Hare Kṛṣṇa kīrtana

31

Prabhupāda and the devotees chanting Hare Kṛṣṇa kīrtana

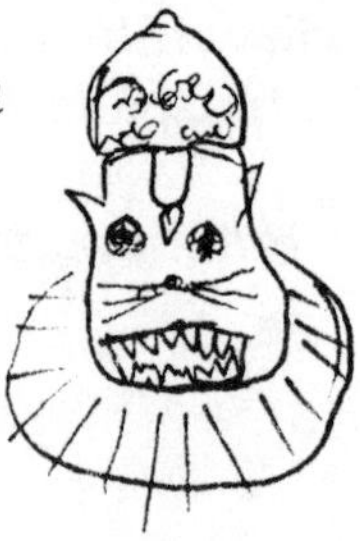

Haribol. I haven't spoken on this radio show in awhile. I'm glad to get back to it.

I arrived in Rāḍha-deśa, Belgium, and today is the appearance day of Lord Nṛsiṁhadeva. This is also the anniversary of my *sannyāsa* initiation.

I got initiated into the *sannyāsa* order in L.A. We didn't use what we called the sanctuary (now the temple room) for the fire sacrifice, but there was another room, a smaller temple room, and four of us were initiated. I'm not going to describe all my memories of that day, but I sure am grateful Prabhupāda gave me *sannyāsa.* It always sounds hollow when you say things like that—"I'm grateful"—but it's true: Prabhupāda saved me.

It's not a small thing to be pulled out of marriage after only a few years. Most people have to live through at least twenty years of marriage, and they are as sincere or more sincere than I am, and often more detached. But marriage is heavy because once you take those vows, you have to live through it for many years, and if it breaks up, there's usually something shameful and failed about it. In many cases, leaving a marriage doesn't necessarily give you more facility, but Prabhupāda took me out after only a few years. My marriage was a kind of ISKCON hobby marriage. I am grateful to him and have felt a lot more energy to serve Kṛṣṇa since taking *sannyāsa.*

I do remember walking on the beach with Prabhupāda the day after the initiation. We still have those wonderful black and white photos that were taken: Prabhupāda, his head held high, wearing a Swami hat, and us surrounding him. I remember it was cool out and we were all cold. I didn't wear a sweater because I was a *sannyāsī* now and ready to be renounced. I didn't really know what renunciation meant for a *sannyāsī,* whether it would require a lot of physical austerity or boldness in preaching. I didn't know whether I could measure up to whatever it was. Nowadays, it has become more complicated and involved than simply preaching and traveling, but at the time, that was our essential understanding.

I still remember how Śrīla Prabhupāda emphasized preaching as the real meaning of *sannyāsa.* Preaching for me has become not selling a book, but writing a book; not knocking on someone's door, but knocking on the door of their heart through different genres. That's how I "preach, preach, preach." I hope that Prabhupāda will accept this form of preaching I have developed.

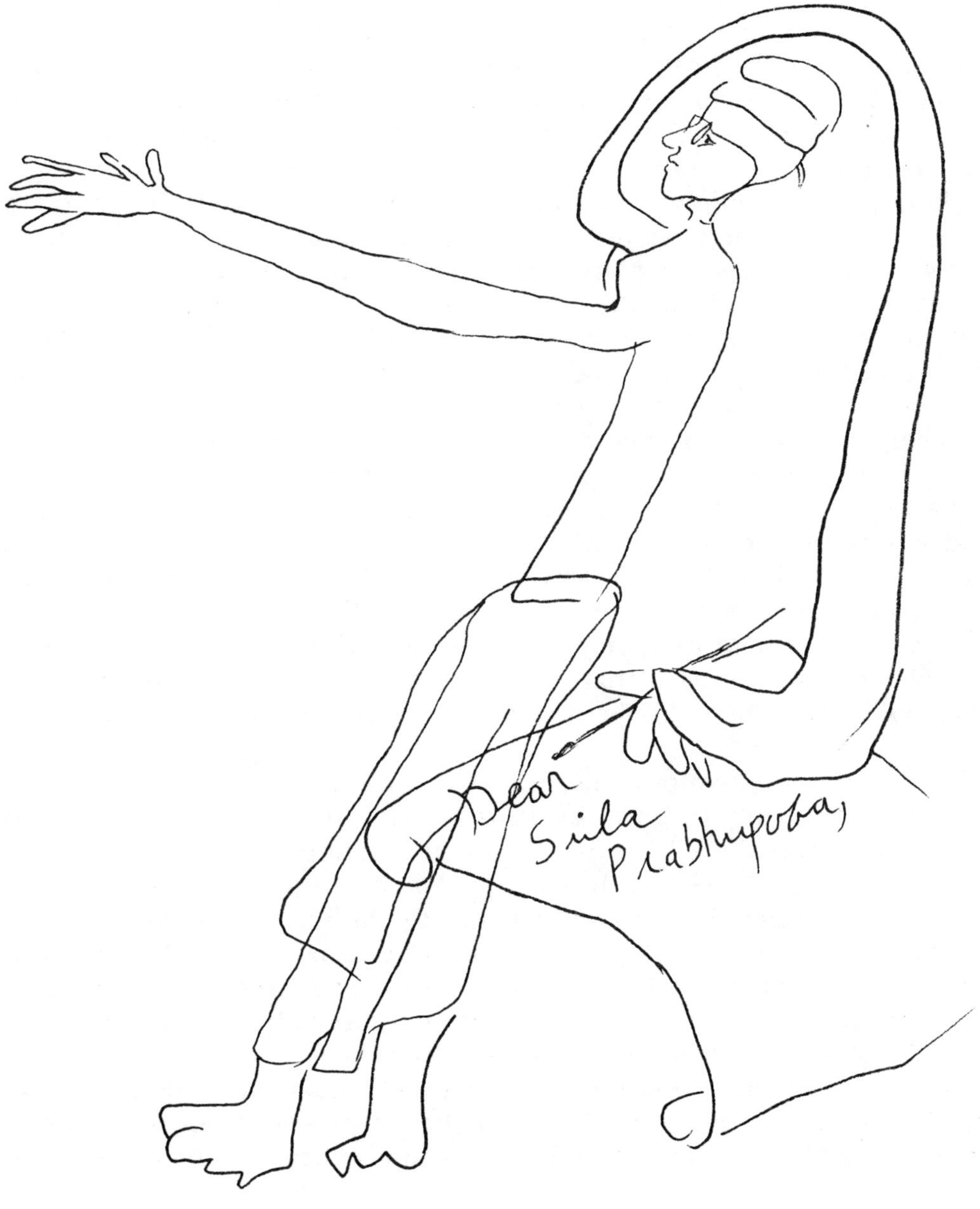

Prabhupāda and the devotees chanting Hare Kṛṣṇa kīrtana

Everything we are destined to experience must come to pass. When you go to the theater, the usher hands you a program. The program tells you what will happen during each act of the play, what time intermission will be, how long it will last, and the rules of the theater. There are also train programs and bus schedules, calendars, and daytimers. Time is gradually accounted for and passes away. As Lord Kṛṣṇa says in the *Bhagavad-gītā,* we were unmanifest, now we're manifest, and soon we will be unmanifest again. Why lament over this little change?

Madhu and I follow schedules. We were scheduled to travel to Rāḍha-deśa, and here we are. I wanted mail to be waiting for me here and it is. Sometimes our plans are thwarted, but generally, we are following the program that will take us to the time of death.

If we are moving toward death, shouldn't we be concerned about the quality of our lives? Quality is connected to death because our state of living culminates in the state of our dying. It reminds me of Salinger's character, Buddy, asking, "Are all your stars out?"

We want quality. We want deep involvement in our own lives. Once, Puṣṭa-kṛṣṇa asked Prabhupāda, "What does it mean that Lord Caitanya said His name would be known in every town and village and that ISKCON is fulfilling it? Will ISKCON fulfill it? Does it mean there will be a temple in every town and village or just that the *saṅkīrtana* party will have gone there and they can check it off on their list, 'We went to this town, we went to that town'?" I forget exactly what Prabhupāda said. "Oh," he said, "why every town and village? Every door to door."

Puṣṭa-kṛṣṇa's question contains a question, "How literally do we take these things?" To go to every town and village—does it mean to physically travel there? Does it mean more simply to touch people's hearts? How many people's hearts? And what does *that* mean?

Similarly, I thought we would come to Rāḍha-deśa and we did. I thought the mail would greet us and it did. Is something more supposed to happen? Was I supposed to *do* something that I didn't? Was I supposed to notice something that I missed? Did I fail to notice *everything*? Did I fail to notice the essence?

I led *maṅgala-ārati* this morning—I didn't make any mistakes, except I missed a word during the Nṛsiṁha prayers, but nobody noticed much. Basically I did everything I was supposed to do. Someone taped it and we got a pretty decent recording. But did I miss the whole thing? Was there something internal that I missed? This is what I want to know.

Prabhupāda and the devotees chanting Hare Kṛṣṇa kīrtana

I want to follow this idea some more because it's on my mind a lot. I seem to want to just get through. Like right now I'm trying to write and publish books and I don't want to be stopped. There's an idea in the back of my mind that somehow I might be stopped. The GBC might stop me, ISKCON might stop me, criticism might stop me. But if I don't get stopped, is that the success of my life? Nobody noticed me, I snuck through, I did things I wanted to do—published poetry books and this book and that book. The essence of these things is all right, but why the anxiety?

A materialist experiences this kind of anxiety in the extreme. He aspires to possess millions of dollars, so he makes it. So what? He meets a beautiful girl and has sex. So what? He eats and drinks. So what? How far can you go with that? Elvis Presley killed himself by taking so many over-the-counter drugs that his body just stopped functioning. I remember reading a newspaper article about it. It said he died of self-indulgence. What an idea! To die of self-indulgence! He just ate and ate and drank and drank and drugged and drugged himself and sang and tried to become famous and lost his fame and tried to get it back and got fat—and then he died at forty. But what was his life all about? It's over and he's gone and he'll never exist in that form again. He's not in a position now to enjoy the fame he now has. People are worshipping him, but where is he? He's not here to enjoy any of it. He's not there in the Graceland museum where his motorcycle sits behind a glass case. He's not here to see the tears people shed when they look at that motorcycle. He's probably living out in a doghouse in Chattanooga or Memphis. Who's to say?

Life is passing by so quickly. My father used to say, "Stop to smell the flowers along the way. Take time to stop and smell the flowers." That's a little wisdom my father tried to live by. He tried to slow down. He was a hard-working *karmī*, but maybe somewhere along the line he also saw the uselessness of all the sweating and the straining.

I also remember the title of his book about the history of the New York fire department: *As You Pass By.* I don't think my father pondered the meaning of that title exactly, but that book meant something to him. That book described how the fire department had evolved over the years from horse-drawn carts to big fire engines. I don't know what the author's intention was in naming his book that, but it gave an idea of how all things must pass. Our "programs" will inevitably be fulfilled.

Do you think they won't? What if the star actor doesn't appear? Then the program has to change. You get to the theater only to find out that Hamlet is being played by John Smithers. Who the heck is John Smithers? You went there to see Richard Burton. So it appears that the program has changed, but it hasn't, really. The real program is what your life means, not the details of what passes through it.

For myself, perhaps I think I'm being clever, sneaking through. I avoid this, I avoid that. No one called my name and made me stand up and recite, I didn't have to write the physics exam. I wasn't the one picked for special military dirty work. I wasn't the one who had to go into the flaming building to save the kids. (Or maybe I was the one.) But what is really happening?

Okay, enough of that. Today is Lord Nṛsiṁha's appearance day and I think the tendency is when you have a busy schedule to not stop and smell the flowers, to not stop and actually worship Kṛṣṇa. Worship is internal. Kṛṣṇa is internal.

There are so many things on my mind that I don't know which bullet to discharge first, so I'll talk faster. I just wrote a book called *My Relationship With Lord Kṛṣṇa.* One of the points I discussed was why I was talking about myself instead of speaking straight *kṛṣṇa-kathā.* Isn't Kṛṣṇa the center? I discussed that point in different ways. That felt good. You can read it if you want to know what I said.

Today I'll tell pastimes about Lord Nṛsiṁhadeva. We've all heard them a hundred times. Still, we can invest our speaking and hearing with feeling. That's what I mean about adding quality to your personal programming. Hiraṇyakaśipu had a long-standing hatred of Lord Viṣṇu, stemming at least from the time his brother was killed. Hiraṇyakaśipu swore that he would kill Lord Viṣṇu. That enmity was so strong that Hiraṇyakaśipu went to the forest to perform severe austerities. We'll tell the whole story.

Yesterday the mail arrived. I spent some time staring into the bundles it was divided into, trying to respond and satisfy people. I'm back to thinking more delicate thoughts, which I can't do when I'm operating under the crush of too many things to do.

Prabhupāda and the devotees chanting Hare Kṛṣṇa kīrtana

On the day I received *sannyāsa* and we were walking on the beach with Prabhupāda, I remember walking past people with our *daṇḍas.*

Someone called out, "Are you going fishing?" I remember thinking, "Yeah, we're fishing for souls."

Prabhupāda and his disciples reminded me of the image of Christ and his disciples. Christ said, "I am a fisher of souls." We were going to be preachers. We were all new *sannyāsīs*. We thought now we were going to get a lot less to eat, which didn't turn out to be the case. Hṛdayānanda Mahārāja and I went door to door to collect *dakṣiṇā* for awhile and we gave Prabhupāda everything we collected in an envelope. We were as excited as little kids to be going door to door and offering the results of our preaching to Prabhupāda.

The ladies in Los Angeles were in awe of us when we became *sannyāsīs* and they treated us with kindness and honor. Prabhupāda, you were so kind and daring to give young men the *sannyāsa* order, binding them to an entire life of strict celibacy. Thank you. You said it was fifty percent of our liberation.

Prabhupāda and the devotees chanting Hare Kṛṣṇa kīrtana

This morning Prahlādānanda Mahārāja asked me, "How are you?"

"I'm all right."

"I'm all right too." Then we both laughed. The body can't be all right. "Well, actually, we're just practicing until death."

Prahlādānanda Mahārāja is good at quoting *śāstra*. I used to think it was silly when people did that, as if they are incapable of being real people. But now I appreciate it. After all, what else is there to say?

When he made his philosophical point this morning, I batted something back at him. "Yes, the miseries are good for us because they help us to remember Kṛṣṇa. That's the real point, isn't it?"

Devotees are always giving friendly reminders, even at the end. Death is such a stark truth.

"When I dwell on death," I said, "I think, 'Wait a minute, I'm still living now.'" Prahlāda Mahārāja went to the school children and said that they should practice Kṛṣṇa consciousness while the body is still stout and strong and not embarrassed by dwindling. That was spoken to young boys, but it applies to us because we're still alive. I'm still relatively stout and strong, at least in spirit. I can write, I can talk, I want to think about what I can do for Kṛṣṇa. Prabhupāda was like that too, not dwelling on death but dwelling on life and trying to be Kṛṣṇa conscious. I mean, he was Kṛṣṇa conscious, but trying to save people.

Prabhupāda and the devotees chanting Hare Kṛṣṇa kīrtana

Here's some news: I'm going to turn Prabhupāda over to Bhadraṅga dāsa here at Rāḍha-deśa because his arm got broken a second time. I will have to start worshipping a picture of the *mūrti*. Right now I'm planning to do it as soon as possible, but I know I'll be sorry later when Prabhupāda is not there and I can no longer massage him.

Still, I feel a little relief at giving up the duties. They take time to perform and I don't always have a lot of that. Anyway, it seems sensible to turn him over because it's just getting too wild—his arm broken twice in one month and Prabhupāda having to sit on a corner of my desk in the van. The *mūrti* should be better cared for.

Time is fleeing, time is fleeing. I like the image of the rabbit in *Alice in Wonderland* running down the rabbit hole: "I'm late, I'm late for a very important date." Alice didn't think twice about seeing a rabbit talking, although she had never seen one talk before, but when he took a watch out of his waistcoat pocket, she thought that was quite amazing. He looked at it and hurried along, talking out loud to himself, "I'm really late." He went down into the rabbit hole and she went right down after him. Later she saw him running ahead, "Oh, oh, I'm late! I have to hurry!"

Lewis Carroll doesn't spell it out, but this is a symbol of time running out and then being faced with death. He just leaves us with this eternal rabbit running to his appointment with which to compare ourselves. We map out our days, sometimes by the minute, but the real thing is time itself. Time is coming to kill everyone.

Not yet, we're not ready yet. With this time I have, let me use it to write something better. Let me use it to develop my Kṛṣṇa consciousness. That's the proper use of time.

O Lord Nṛsiṁhadeva, please protect us from the demons. Today is Your appearance day and the day Prabhupāda gave me *sannyāsa*.

I'm tired. How will I stay awake? How will I stay alive to give my lecture? I don't want to sleep, so I hope that You, Kṛṣṇa, will be able—You are able—to let me be Your devotee and jibber-jabber forever some kind of Kṛṣṇa conscious service to Your Lordship.

The birds are chirping and another day has begun. I am already underway, running, flashing through my daily activities. Someone named Bhakta Slofko is getting initiated today. There's going to be a meeting about the Prabhupāda Centennial and how they are going to conduct it in Benelux, then the initiation, then a lecture, then a feast at 2:00. Oh, yes, there's going to be a feast at 2:00. Do you know what that means? I'll be able to eat for about fifteen minutes. That's all. Then it will be over. Please don't think of me as a spoil-sport. I'm just talking.

32

Prabhupāda and the devotees chanting Hare Kṛṣṇa kīrtana

Haribol. I'm broadcasting today from the back of the van, which is parked in a woodsy section at Rāḍha-deśa, Belgium. I feel good today, feeling how Kṛṣṇa is kind and rewards all desires. You have to be blind not to see His hand in things. I see it in my own life in terms of my writing and publishing ambitions. I can write in an experimental way, express myself, and achieve art along with spiritual vision. Before I met Prabhupāda, I never dreamed I would be able to write of the Absolute Truth, and in the beginning of my career in Kṛṣṇa consciousness, I didn't imagine I could write with art. But over the years, these two things have started to come together for me. Kṛṣṇa carries what we lack and preserves what we have.

We have to be careful not to ask to become something devoid of spiritual realization, whether an artist, a narcissist, a temple president, a GBC man, a *sannyāsī,* someone women look up to, someone men look up to. Really, we have to ask for love of God. I don't think I've been asking for that yet, at least not in the central way. Like Nārada said to Vyāsa, "Yes, you have written about Kṛṣṇa as a matter of course. In the *Mahābhārata,* He appears and He may be mentioned as Bhagavān, the Supreme Person, but you haven't *concentrated* on His activities. This is the cause of your lamentation."

As a matter of course, we say and act and think that Kṛṣṇa is the center of our lives and that we want to achieve love of Kṛṣṇa, but we don't yet make it the burning, single desire: *govinda-viraheṇa me,* the universe is empty without You. And we don't preach in Prabhupāda's mood, with that compassion and drive to bring others to Kṛṣṇa.

Yesterday, some devotees gave me a photo of Prabhupāda as a gift. It was the anniversary of my *sannyāsa* initiation, so these devotees were congratulating me that I have been a *sannyāsī* for twenty-two years. It was a fairly large blowup of a color photo of Prabhupāda sitting in a rocking chair. He's looking to one side, not directly at you, but he looks heavy in a grand sense. I was looking at the picture with Madhu and I said, "Yes, if he turns and looks at you, he'll be able to look right through you and ask, 'Who are you as a spirit soul? Who are you?'" And, "What are you doing to serve Kṛṣṇa?" He could always make us feel accountable. But that was just a minor emotion compared to the relief we felt that there was such a person as Prabhupāda who was in contact with Kṛṣṇa and who could make us accountable to Him. That's why I like this picture. It carries that mood.

I have another picture (which is going to be my worshipable deity now that I no longer have the *mūrti*). It's smaller. Prabhupāda is sitting in a chair—it's actually a *vyāsāsana*, but it's run-down and simple, the one they had in Bombay in 1974. He's leaning back on the bolster with his feet on the mat. It's a very good picture of his feet. But the way he's leaning back, it's not like he's ready to give a lecture or receive worship. It's more like he has just collapsed. He has no shirt on and his right hand is in his bead bag. His mouth is turned down. He's not looking into the camera, but he's thoughtful, self-absorbed, maybe not pleased, but grave, so you're not sure. I take it that he's estimating my worship: "What are you up to? What are you doing?" He would like me to do more. It's a wonderful picture, and he looks wonderful in it.

I can't even describe the emotions that I feel when I look at it or that Prabhupāda seems to be projecting. How I wish I could have more appreciation for him.

When I went to the temple this morning for *maṅgala-ārati*, there was a sign on the door telling us we couldn't go in immediately because Prabhupāda was being dressed. The men chanted in one room and the women in another until Prabhupāda's *pūjārī* finally let us in. I was the first one in. The *pūjārī* was quite a young man, and I thought, "You're very fortunate." I rang the bell and went up and bowed to Prabhupāda.

Now that I no longer have my own Prabhupāda *mūrti*, I wanted to capitalize on the presence of this *mūrti*. I touched his feet and then all the others started bowing down. So many young people. And you know how it is when you're all offering obeisances, devotees bow down and form a row into the middle of the temple room. The GBC passed a resolution this year defining the founder-*ācārya* in some solid terms. One of them was that everyone should worship Prabhupāda every day. I thought, "Here it is, all these youngsters worshipping Prabhupāda, and they're all fortunate. I'm fortunate too."

(All this that I'm saying is part of my initial comment that I'm feeling good.) After *maṅgala-ārati*, the temple president made announcements. I could hear birds singing outside and I thought, "It's almost the end of May. This is the best time of year. We're all so fortunate. What more could you ask? Birds are singing, it's *brahma-muhūrta*, you're in a Hare Kṛṣṇa temple, you have devotees in America dedicated to typing, editing, and producing your books, Kṛṣṇa is giving you facility to write, and you still have health and life duration. It's just wonderful." I don't want to miss the opportunity to acknowledge it here.

Prabhupāda and the devotees chanting Hare Kṛṣṇa kīrtana

This morning I was thinking about that story Simic tells about the flute player in the pit. That image meant something to me because at that time and still, I was trying to write without thinking how to please the audience. I just wanted to express myself to Prabhupāda and Kṛṣṇa and cry out to them. You don't want to say that you're alone without them, but perhaps you're not sure that they're there, and that's also a factor. You can't tell me the flute player doesn't wonder whether the gods are really there listening to him. His playing and dying have to be based on the hope and faith that the gods are there. Otherwise, it's meaningless. But the song might also contain moments of doubt. No one is interested in a Pyrrhic victory, where you achieve a state of pure expression but it doesn't mean a damned thing because nobody benefits or even listens. A Pyrrhic victory means you achieve perfection, but you lose everything. What good is that? Therefore, God has to hear it and it has to be for Him.

But who's this anthropologist creeping out of the woods? That's my dilemma. I want to cry out to God from the privacy of my soul, but I also want an anthropologist to be hidden and recording it. That's because ultimately, I want to share it.

Think of all the world's great flute players. Herbie Mann, the white man who made the very popular album called "The Common Ground." It was good. The title signified that his primitive improvisations could become the common ground between Africa and jazz and all the world's cultures. He was definitely performance oriented, wasn't he? And the others too—the classical flute players. Mozart composed flute music for an audience. There's Kṛṣṇa, of course, but that's different. He's in His own category. He's not alone, trying to please God. He's trying to please Himself by calling the *gopīs* with His flute song. I'm not Kṛṣṇa and my writing isn't the same as Kṛṣṇa's flute music. My playing is not like Herbie Mann's either. I'm playing to please Kṛṣṇa, so I have to shake off trying to be a jazz man or a flute man or a writer man.

I'm back to liking that image of playing alone and sharing it later. One could say you can't do that. You play alone for God and then you die. Who's that anthropologist creeping out of the bushes with his tape recorder? He's an intruder. Why doesn't God strike him dead?

We hear about things like that—that someone intruding on confidential religious rituals is suddenly stricken dead. For example, a lot of the people who broke into the Egyptian tombs died mysterious deaths. But what if the anthropologist isn't stricken dead?

Well, he can play his recording, but God will remove the sacred essence, the part that was pleasing to Him, and what remains will be hollow. Is that true? Maybe God will allow that sacred essence to be shared. We don't always know God's purpose. "Let this man think he's alone, playing for My pleasure, and let this other man secretly record it and share it with the world."

The point is that the man in the pit shouldn't know about the anthropologist if he's going to keep his art pure, and that's what I have been working on with myself in trying to balance writing with publishing. I told you how I lost my innocence after I recorded *Entering the Life of Prayer*. I made the recording unself-consciously—I didn't plan to turn it into a book. That's part of that book's appeal. A reader can almost surreptitiously share my experience as I walked alone and talked to myself about prayer. But immediately after that, I took walks with the tape recorder and *planned* to do a second volume. Part of the idea was that I would listen to it later and it would help me in my own prayer, but the other part was that it would be beneficial for others to hear this also. But who can pray in public like that? I kept thinking of Jesus' statement that when you pray, you should go into your closet. I couldn't do any more on *Entering the Life of Prayer*. Even in the mood of trying to pray publicly as preaching, I couldn't get past the loss of privacy and innocence.

So that's my problem. My type of preaching means being alone and developing my Kṛṣṇa consciousness in private, but at the same time, sharing it with others. It requires a kind of split personality to pull it off. You can't say that I'm a phony or a cheat for trying to do this; this is how I do it. But it requires rigor and that I make certain policies with myself. I have to follow a strict dedication so that it doesn't become cheap. You might trick yourself and you might even trick the audience, but you're not going to trick Kṛṣṇa in any case. I'm going forward on the assumption that it can be done.

There are other forms of expression I could take up where I would be more aware of my audience. They're right there—I can look at them and I can use them for communication—but there should be a time and a place for playing the flute at the bottom of the pit only for Kṛṣṇa. It means I have to go all the way.

Prabhupāda and the devotees chanting Hare Kṛṣṇa kīrtana

The other image I think about is the image of the curtain being up. There's one entry in a book of writer's meditations that says the curtain is already up. Whatever you're doing, this is it, this is your life. It's not just a rehearsal. Just keep writing and be aware that this is your best offering. You're not going to get another chance later. In youth, we tend to think that what we're doing is not for keeps. When we grow up, we think it is for keeps. Later we find out that it was always for keeps. There's no point waiting to live life to its fullest until later. No, this is it right now. Do you want to be a writer? Then write. And what you write, that's your work.

Anyway, I was thinking of this meditation not in terms of writing, but in terms of what I was saying earlier on this show—Kṛṣṇa is right here and He is reciprocating with us. We should pause and thank Him. It has to do with living in the present moment of our Kṛṣṇa consciousness.

Why can't we live in the moment more? We're afraid because it means gaining more access to what we are actually feeling. If we open ourselves more to the moment, then when there are terrible moments, we won't blanket them. That means we'll really suffer. We'll feel our pain. That's the problem, though, isn't it? If we cover up the painful feelings, we'll also have to cover up some of the good ones, and with all that covering up, we'll lose track of ourselves.

And that's the point. If we have to live in the present, we will have to live in Kṛṣṇa's shelter. Kṛṣṇa is our protector. When we live in Him, then even painful feelings become a source of turning toward Him.

So I say the curtain is up and the show has already begun. You're living right now. What are you going to do?

Of course, another fear may be that our experience is so small that it has no value. It's easier to think that our experience will be more momentous in the future, when we're better at what we're doing or better at what we're trying to be. But this is what it is. You came to the human form of life, you met the pure devotee, and you spaced out during the *āratis* and couldn't come close to Kṛṣṇa. You made mistakes. What can be done? Don't worry about it. Keep living and trying to surrender to Kṛṣṇa.

Prabhupāda and the devotees chanting Hare Kṛṣṇa kīrtana

Another point: clear the mind from clutter. Or use clutter as energy to disentangle ourselves from superficiality.

We're really helpless. We're so bewildered. We can't think clearly. When we get a chance to speak, we only speak of the clutter. I have been thinking how to clear my mind of all this.

That's what I mean by using clutter as energy to disentangle myself from clutter. You grab hold of the first piece of clutter that passes through your mind and talk about it. Maybe it will lead you somewhere else and maybe it won't, but by listing off all the things that are floating on the top of your consciousness, you can look at them as a superficial totality. It's not reality, but by facing it, you can sometimes dig below it and find out what's under the clutter.

Real life is to be with Kṛṣṇa in the spiritual world. Is that abstract?

I'm running out of time. I just heard the van door slide open. That means breakfast. It's fascinating trying to be in the pit. I'd like these radio shows to be from the pit (and from the pit of my stomach too), and I would like them to hit you in the solar plexus, in the heart.

33

Prabhupāda and the devotees chanting Hare Kṛṣṇa kīrtana

Hare Kṛṣṇa. I'm in the mood to talk about Śrīla Prabhupāda and about replenishing and depleting. I made a note to myself: "Need to read Prabhupāda's books." You know, in Vṛndāvana I made a resolution to try to come back to him more. I started out with a good resolve to read through the *Bhāgavatam* and to do various other things. It's still going on, but unless I'm careful, it could fall apart. One of the limbs of my return was to worship a Prabhupāda *mūrti*. That's been stopped. Another limb was the reading itself, but when I'm in a temple, it's hard to find the time. Therefore, I want to be careful that my resolve doesn't erode.

We have a principle in this movement that the more you give out in Kṛṣṇa consciousness, the more you get back. Usually, we translate that concept into preaching. I believe in that, but I also believe that you have to manage your giving out in such a way that it becomes true for you and not just a dogmatic statement. You have to look at yourself and see if you are drained by preaching. Then you have to see how to give out Kṛṣṇa consciousness more purely so that you can get something back.

Sometimes I picture preaching to be like water in a well. When you pump out a lot of water, you may have to wait for some time—at least this is true for the kind of well I'm thinking of—for the water to fill up again. When it fills up, you can pump out the gallons again. This is a crude example, but I'm basically trying to say that there's a quality to the giving out.

Last night I held a disciples' meeting. After the formal meeting was over, the devotees were taking *prasādam* and I continued to speak. I felt I had to carry the moment by speaking, and also that I should reciprocate with what they wanted to hear from me. I spoke about a couple of pictures of Prabhupāda. I was actually rehashing, for their pleasure, things that I had already said or thought. I was using words like "lion" and "heavy" in describing how Prabhupāda looked in the pictures. It was a nice exchange, but when I returned to the van and looked at those pictures, I couldn't relate to them anymore. I know it was because I had spoken so much and overdone it. I lost the internal delicacy by which I was able to see something wonderful in the pictures.

That's what I mean by the quality of giving out. I wasn't sharing with them for any other reason than that I wanted to have a personal exchange. By doing so, however, I stepped on my personal feelings. Now I'm empty and I will have to wait until I'm filled up again. That's one reason why it's so important for me to go alone—so I can express everything I can in writing sessions, get in touch with what I have lost, and try to reclaim it.

Even to notice something such as that I'm not reading two hours a day. Or to begin to really pray to Śrīla Prabhupāda and to appreciate that he's giving me Kṛṣṇa. If you look at a picture of him, you'll realize you can be close to him in that way. This is a sensitive period for me, since I just gave up the *mūrti* worship. Now I have to connect with his picture. I have to go through the stages carefully.

When I go alone, I get my integrity back. Then I can give it out again at the next temple, at the next meeting or in writing or in letters. That's the process. When I speak, I try to give something that I have discovered and not just repeat the hackneyed and dogmatic words we've all heard before. I try to give some true appreciation that I recently received by Kṛṣṇa's mercy. Then I go away, try to increase my stock, and come and give it again. This is my experience, although some may say that it doesn't match up to the principle that Kṛṣṇa consciousness never suffers loss or diminution.

I say I am not in contradiction to that, but that there are ebbs and flows—rhythms—to our Kṛṣṇa conscious experiences and realizations. Prabhupāda also acknowledged that. He acknowledged it, I know, in terms of his own writing on the *Bhāgavatam.* Sometimes he would produce, then he needed to not produce, and then he would produce again. On occasion, he described these natural rhythms. There is a time to be quiet and a time to express yourself.

Prabhupāda and the devotees chanting Hare Kṛṣṇa kīrtana

I feel good about speaking on yesterday's show about the flute player in the pit. It's related to what I was just saying—that I need to go alone and play my flute for God's hearing. I haven't been put irretrievably into a pit to face death. It makes me think of Jesus Christ going into the desert for forty days to pray. When you go alone, part of your prayer is that you may return to society filled with Kṛṣṇa conscious realization and the other part of your prayer is that you can be with Kṛṣṇa in your closet. These images help me to understand how you can do both things at once—pray to Kṛṣṇa or express yourself to Him in the pit, and yet be interested in others' welfare. If Kṛṣṇa desires, He can use you as an instrument in that way.

So much for that theme. It has been exciting here at the temple, not only because of the temple activities, but because I received my mail. I haven't read the letters yet, but in the package were different manuscripts of mine that I have to proofread. I always find correcting and seeing my writing going through the stages of production exciting.

I got a message yesterday from the editor, discussing writing sessions and how she sees them. She said she understood that although I speak about myself in the sessions, I'm not just an autobiographical writer. That's a fact. When I look at autobiographies, they never represent what I'm trying to do in my own writing. They record what someone did in 1942, then in 1942 and a half, then in 1943. The main subject of an autobiography is a person's own life. My real purpose is to express Kṛṣṇa consciousness.

Anyway, I don't feel so much like talking about it right now, so I'll tell you what happened in this morning's *Śrīmad-Bhāgavatam* class. The verse discussed how wonderful it is that Kṛṣṇa makes Himself subordinate to His devotees, and how when He does that, He becomes dear to them.

When I was preparing for class, it struck me that we really should talk about this other entity, the Supreme Lord, this other-than-me, other-than-the-human-race. Prabhupāda talks about our self-absorption in *Message of Godhead.* "At present we are concerned primarily with two things: one, ourselves, and the other, the place where we live" (*Message of Godhead* Introduction, p. 1). Certainly this is a lot of the subject matter of my writing sessions. It's the natural way I start to speak, also, on the radio show. I say, "What made me happy? What moved me? And where am I?" I start to describe the place.

"We are concerned with two objects, everything that is related to our gross and subtle bodies and the world at large with all its paraphernalia. But there are others above us, the transcendentalists, who are concerned not only with their bodies and minds and the world at large, but also with the transcendental subject which is above the mind and body and the world at large" (*Message of Godhead,* Introduction, p. 1).

The hard-core materialist balks at this restriction. He doesn't think there is anything else. I sometimes tell about an acquaintance of mine on the Lower East Side—he wasn't one of my close friends—but he was really in the hip, drug-art-expression mood. He had a wife who painted abstract globs on canvas. Somehow or other, although my close friends didn't come to the storefront, he did. I remember introducing him to an axiom of our faith, that there's a spiritual reality, Brahman, from which everything comes. He didn't say so much, but his body language made his opinion of what I had said clear. "What are you trying to say? Hey man, what *is* Brahman?"

We '60s people thought we were sensitive barometers of the truth. We had our own code of truthfulness and we didn't appreciate anyone foisting anything on us, especially if we perceived he was being phony or cheating or ego-tripping. Anyway, this man obviously didn't want to get contaminated by my so-called artificial imposition on his mind. I went ahead anyway. I knew where he was at, but I no longer accepted his code of truth. Everybody had their own code.

That code—it's strange that we were so anti-establishment, yet we concurred so completely with the atheistic view of the scientists. We accepted Freud, Darwin, and Marx, and we were products of the intellectual culture. Atheism was our religion. We would never accept the concept of a descending process.

I notice that when I again come around to Kṛṣṇa, He is unfortunately secondary to these other concerns for me, like the self and the world. Therefore, there are people—and this is one of the most important proofs of God's existence—who are not concerned just with the self and the world at large, but with the Absolute Truth. These transcendentalists—saints, philosophers, reformers, messengers of God—appear in various places of the world at various times. They render transcendental service to the Absolute Truth and to humanity by preaching the message of the transcendental world. This is getting in touch with Kṛṣṇa.

I have a right to do that, a need to do that, and if it's awkward sometimes, then everything is awkward except the few things you can flow with. I get up at 12 A.M., so I get tired by *maṅgala-ārati* time. This morning I was really drowsy, so I had to jerk myself awake to get through the morning. Sometimes you just have to put your foot on the gas and command yourself to pick up speed. You don't have to float helplessly in the modes of material nature. "Oh, I'm tired. I guess that means I should fall asleep right now." Or worse, "I'm attracted to that girl. Let me follow up on how she makes me feel." That's animal life.

Similarly, I notice, "Oh, someone mentioned Kṛṣṇa, but Kṛṣṇa's not central to me. There's Kṛṣṇa again, the Other." I say "the other," but I think of Him with a capital O. There's the Other again—other than me, other than the world. He's the source of the world. There's that person, Kṛṣṇa, who likes to be subordinate to His devotees.

I want to pass over my lack of spontaneity and start to hear anyway, let the medicine work. Take to the healing process.

Yesterday, I went to see the doctor here, Vānamālī, a famous ISKCON Hungarian doctor. He has all these gadgets to diagnose and to treat a patient, to vacuum out the toxins from his body. He gave me a moxa thing in the navel, which is a bunch of burning herbs to create digestion. He also has acupuncture machines. He's there to revive the near-dead and to try and get them going again. It made me think that just as you have to do certain things to stimulate the body, you also have to do things to stimulate the spirit. You have to open the books and study. You have to accept the guru's discipline. Then you will develop a taste for hearing and chanting. That's *vaidhi-bhakti.* I have to do it.

Prabhupāda and the devotees chanting Hare Kṛṣṇa kīrtana

I think because of the temple schedule and my mood right now, I'm not going to talk for a full half hour. I'll stop here and say good-bye. But we did unearth an important point, and that is that talking about Kṛṣṇa has the most value. In order to talk about Kṛṣṇa, you have to be hearing from the *paramparā.* Keep that in mind. I know when I free-write, the first subject is always myself, but then I just jump over a mental creek and decide that the subject of the next paragraph is going to be Kṛṣṇa. Even if it comes out wooden or mechanical, I say it anyway. I don't wait for corresponding emotions.

We're going through thick and thin, with this *abhijñāta,* this unknown person, this dearmost friend, Kṛṣṇa. Devotional service simply means waking up and turning to Kṛṣṇa. Then you have the ideal union or coexistence of the individual self, the world, and the Supreme.

Prabhupāda and the devotees chanting Hare Kṛṣṇa kīrtana

34

Prabhupāda and the devotees chanting Hare Kṛṣṇa kīrtana

Well, I told myself this morning that I don't have time to do a radio show, but then I walked into the van and said, "Go ahead. Just get on the air." And what will I talk about? I had a couple of things in mind, and both of them seem too sensitive.

One is a nice thing. I'm thinking of doing a project called *Japa Walks, Japa Talks* when and if we get to Wicklow again and I can take walks.

The other thing is about something that came up in the mail. Some years ago, I reinitiated someone I knew at the time I shouldn't reinitiate. After the initiation, she had so much trouble with marriage and divorce and following the rules, violence, abandoned kids—so many troubles. I just got a letter from her. She says she's a born-again Christian. The reason she wrote was to tell me that Christ is the only one who came back from the dead. She says that's why I should accept him.

What a strange argument—that since Christ was the only one who came back from the dead, I should accept him. She told me that even Kṛṣṇa didn't do that, and that's proved by the *Śrīmad-Bhāgavatam.* That's really absurd because the *Śrīmad-Bhāgavatam* tells us that Kṛṣṇa is the origin of everything. *Janmādy asya yato* and *kṛṣṇas tu bhagavān svayam.* He's eternal truth; everything comes from Him. However, He winds up His pastimes in this world. If it appears to some that He died, that's not the point. The point is that He goes to the spiritual world and that He is eternal. It is certainly an extraordinary yogic feat that Jesus Christ came back to this world a few days after he died, but he's not the only one who has ever done this. Even the demon guru, Śukrācārya, brought so many demons back to life by dipping them in a pool of nectar. Everyone who died in the battle between Rāma and Rāvaṇa also got back their lives. The Christians place so much emphasis on the fact that Christ came back from the dead. It's a flimsy argument.

Why should it be turned into an argument at all? They make his deathlessness the proof of his ultimate prowess, but it's not. His ultimate prowess is in his saintliness and his love of God, tolerance, forgiveness, and doctrines. Any accomplished *yogī* can come back from the dead.

Anyway, that was in the mail.

Prabhupāda and the devotees chanting Hare Kṛṣṇa kīrtana

The *kīrtana* record I play in the background is coming toward its end. It's a little artificial of me to play such small segments because Prabhupāda has been gradually building up and is near his crescendo. For me to jump into that rapid tempo almost sounds frenetic. Prabhupāda always came to that stage gradually.

I have been feeling flashes of good feeling lately. Here in Belgium, I have been seeing a doctor. I've had three sessions with him so far. Each time I lay down on the bed, I think of telling him that I feel happy. I have a bubbling up of happiness inside of me. I was almost going to add, "I don't know if this is to do with my *vāta* constitution, but I am happy at this time of my life with my creative writing activities."

It was funny how he asked me after the first session how I felt and whether I felt any different. It made me laugh, actually, that he thought that after a little therapy, I was going to feel different. But I wanted to tell him that despite my maladies, I am happy. In general, this happiness is coming from Kṛṣṇa consciousness. It's not a theoretical happiness, but something bubbling on the perceptive level. It takes the form of wanting to do things, such as wanting to get back to writing and the happiness of books that are going to be published. It comes from inner life, from opportunities to write and preach (Madhu phoned the temple president in the Czech Republic and he was eager to receive us).

Part of it, I think, is the stimulation of living in a temple and being involved. It's happiness, but when you push past a certain point, it becomes stress. I think that instead of being alone, to be around different devotees, to see the Deities, to be paying one's dues, to not be getting headaches, and to be able to perform, gives you inner confidence and appreciation for life, both in its social aspect and in getting away from it.

Now I'm seeing an exotic Āyurvedic doctor. After that, I'll hurry back to the van, and the very fact that we are living in our van and disciples are helping us to do our service there makes me happy. Someone will bring hot water, then there'll be a nice lunch. Then there'll be this, then there'll be that. This kind of operation.

Now we want to ask the question, "Are these little waves of happiness illusory bubbles? Something temporary?" Maybe, and maybe also it's because I'm really plugged into the social, institutional life and there's a lot of stimulation. I remember when I lived with this stimulation all the time. It was a combination of stress and preaching exhilaration. I would push myself beyond my capacity, and then the reward would be a kind of passion that made me feel that the more exciting the activities I could perform, the more surrendered to Prabhupāda I would feel. That would spur me on to take yet another phone call and hold yet another meeting, to be engaged in keeping the movement going. I rewarded myself in this way because otherwise, I felt like a donkey being beaten.

The life I lead now doesn't have that kind of stimulation. It's quiet. You know, when you're too quiet, you can become dull or morose (or you may appear to be), but I overcome that when I'm writing. I also feel happy in this more quiet mood. Rather than stress, I sometimes feel the aloneness and quiet are too quiet and I get restless. I'm just analyzing here, aloud, these different moods.

Now getting back to what I'm feeling here at Rāḍha-deśa, this bubbling underneath. I get the feeling that I don't have time to write it down, I don't have time to write anything, but one would think it would be nice if I could—just as I could not tell the doctor, and I don't even tell Madhu—I would like to be able to describe it somewhere in writing. I'm afraid, though, that it's a kind of effervescence that's being wasted; it's just bubbling over and I can't put it to any use. I only hope that this energy will be there to be used at the right time so that others can benefit from it with me.

Sometimes I think it has to do with my having some health right now. I don't feel physically miserable. I have some reserve of strength and some endurance. Is this what is causing me joy? If this is pain, if this is suffering, if this is old age, well, it's really not so bad.

Of course, if the source of the happiness is physical, then it may disappear. Then I'll feel real misery and be stripped bare of whatever reserve I have left.

Another question is, who is the *ātmā* who is feeling this bubbling happiness? The body? The mind? The soul? I don't seem to be able to claim that it's really the pure soul, so I talk about this effervescence as positive stimulation. Will it stand the test of time? At death, it may be put aside as irrelevant, just a little toy, or it may be an indication of the soul's presence along with the confidence that even if my body is torn asunder, the self flows on. It's flowing without ceasing and without dying. I hope that this is what I'm in touch with, the eternal nature which feels good because whether you know it or not, you're part and parcel of eternal, joyful, unconquerable, deathless Kṛṣṇa. Hare Kṛṣṇa.

So that's a little appendix I wanted to add to our radio show. Okay, folks, it's afternoon and tomorrow we're on the road again. I don't know when we'll be able to do our broadcast, but I hope it will be before too long.

35

Prabhupāda and the devotees chanting Hare Kṛṣṇa kīrtana

Good afternoon. We're broadcasting from the back of the van at our parking spot next to the Medolago temple.

I just wrote a little bit in my travel diary on the theme that I have an inner life. It was a little bit sarcastic and strained, like a delicate prince who has piles and is telling about his pains.

(This is going to be a free-form radio show. As I look out the back window, I see a *brahmacārī* with a piece of bread. He's extending it, trying to entice a cow to come and take it. But the cow is content with her grass and isn't showing any interest. The *brahmacārī* just noticed that I'm watching him, so he's giving up the pursuit.)

The theme of what I wrote in the travel diary was that I have an inner life and I wish I could pursue it more on my own. People don't understand that when I interact with them, but I'll try to satisfy them. It might be nice if there were a world in which you could give your actual self to people instead of their making you feel that they're demanding you and pulling you and trying to get from you things that aren't really your essence and which only give you a headache or make you feel dissatisfied with them. This is the nature of this imperfect world, and you shouldn't come to this world if you want satisfying, loving relationships. That need should be directed toward Kṛṣṇa.

If we're both thinking of ourselves as the one who should be pleased, then we'll both feel frustration. "My dear subjects, my dear worshippers, you don't know how to please me. You're not going about it very well in your attempts because you don't know my actual nature. Maybe I can have a meeting with my subjects in this world and tell them who I actually am so they can better please me, since I know that's their desire."

If that's what you're trying to get through to people, then of course you'll be frustrated. And that's because people *aren't* your subjects and it's not their purpose in life to please you. They offer you amenities and facilities as part of their dealings with you, but it's not their constitutional nature to please you. Understand?

I'm being a little sarcastic with myself, but I do know that my need for inner life is real to me. Inner life means truthfulness; it means getting in touch with who I really am and offering that to Kṛṣṇa. It doesn't mean worrying about how others are treating me. Otherwise, we'd all be going around nursing our hurts and never thinking of Kṛṣṇa. Instead of being a little illusioned lord running around crossing interests with other little illusioned lords, we should try to see things philosophically and free ourselves from illusion. Then we can be magnanimous and help others become free of their own illusions.

Prabhupāda and the devotees chanting Hare Kṛṣṇa kīrtana

I wanted to mention something about autobiography. My writing is especially autobiographical nowadays as we travel. I write about what it was like to stop in a parking lot in Switzerland and how I feel taking rest at night, what it's like to start off in the morning, and so on. But I tell myself and others that I only use autobiography to express the truths of life itself. What can I possibly mean by that? It's a lot of literary talk. That doesn't mean it's bosh, because I am a literary person.

Some may say that literature is a cushion you try to put between yourself and life—life is naked and it rubs against you. There's no artistic expression to it. Life is life. When you try to make a cushion, you become a writer or an artist.

That, of course, is a nonwriter's view. A writer can't help but be a writer, and an honest writer tries not to make writing a cushion between himself and life, a way to gain unfair leverage over others. Writing for a writer is an inevitable expression and outpouring which he gives back to life. It's true that writers have said a lot about writing and have praised writing. Some have also condemned it and made cynical remarks about it. They have created so many imaginative worlds in the name of art and writing for other people to look at. There's a lot that's gone wrong in writing, and writers are often wrong, just as in religion. You have all kinds of crazy people practicing religion and doing cruel things in the name of religion. Writing is a big field.

I'm writing as a way to cope with life, but simultaneously as a way to contribute to people's lives by giving them something interesting to read. As a writer, I'm trying to commit myself to staying with true feelings and then sharing them with others. People don't usually examine their feelings so closely. They go through life superficially. Some people do, at least. To share the attempt to live more truly, closer to the actual feelings we have, is a social contribution. I am a social scribe.

Prabhupāda and the devotees chanting Hare Kṛṣṇa kīrtana

I told you about that cow who wouldn't take the piece of bread. Now she has gone on eating and summer has arrived. This is Memorial Day weekend in America. The spring Institute is on at Gītā-nāgarī. This cow reminds me of those Gītā-nāgarī cows—Brown Swiss. She has a white snout and she's twitching her ears to drive away flies. I don't think the flies have started so much yet, but that's what summer will bring. The dandelions are almost all gone now, but the poppies are still here.

Traveling in summer is very different from traveling in winter or early spring. People tend to stay up later and undress more. There is a predominant mood of enjoyment. We also lose our privacy at the campgrounds.

There's the loud steel on steel shutting of the van. Inner life within the van—what do you want, little man? A world of your own where people come and serve you and you write exquisite poems and slide them out under your cell door? You pray—you actually do pray to Kṛṣṇa—"Please deliver us all from this material world sooner or later."

I remember Thomas Merton saying that when you go alone, you're not turning your back on humanity, you're praying for all people. I could never relate to that, but I thought of it the other day and realized there may be a stage where you feel like that. It's not just idealism. We have our Vaiṣṇava examples. Advaita Ācārya prayed for Lord Caitanya to descend and save the world because only He could do it.

It's part of that often expressed ideal that I seek, the cycles of going alone and coming back, and when I do come back, having something to offer. I tend to spend my time writing, so what I come back with is something in writing. I don't come back with a new message, not even a new project that I've become fired up about and that I want to rope others into doing with me. I don't feel that I'm better than others when I come back. Sometimes I even feel a little depleted, more in touch with my spiritual poverty.

Prabhupāda and the devotees chanting Hare Kṛṣṇa kīrtana

In addition to the two Brown Swiss cows, there's a black and white one. I don't find cows so attractive. Prabhupāda says they're not such beautiful animals. You have to look at them in a certain way, I suppose, to appreciate them. Anyway, the cowherd man has come. It's 4:00. He called them once by their names, and like children, they all perked up and came running. There's over a dozen of them—fat, squat cows who can't move so fast.

Even though they're not very beautiful with their saggy front necks, their dirty haunches covered with flies, and their twisted horns, they are endearing the way they have run after their cowherd friend and the way they're producing milk. They're so big. Kṛṣṇa loves them. They're so dependent and docile that they come just when they hear their names called. The fact that he's a Kṛṣṇa conscious cowherd boy and that he calls them in such a gentle way makes it all a pleasant scene.

Prabhupāda and the devotees chanting Hare Kṛṣṇa kīrtana

Someone says he's sorry to hear I still get headaches and he tells me about all these different, crazy doctors (or not so crazy doctors) whom I can run and see. There's one who just by talking to her on the phone, will be able to tell me exactly what's wrong with me and cure me. Another man—you send him your name and he'll cure you through the ether. I say, "Well, okay, no expense connected with that. Tell him who you are and he'll take care of you." But what hope do I really have?

Then I told someone, "Yeah, I saw so-and-so and he's giving me acupuncture treatments."

"Oh, acupuncture. Didn't Prabhupāda say that was demoniac? I hate to see you being stuck with needles." They always put down whatever attempt you are making and then usually suggest something even more far-out or quack-like. One person's authoritative medical practitioner is another person's quack. Among the devotees, almost all the allopathic practitioners are considered quacks. Most devotees go in for alternative healing. But among those alternative methods, there is such a wide variety of following. What's the use anyway? But we keep trying.

Those cows are grazing peacefully in their lower consciousness, although they're tormented by flies. We delicate-bodied princes with piles make our thin, complaining whine. Where is the hero to sing the songs of mankind, leading them on to Kṛṣṇa?

36

Haribol. I'm speaking from the back of the van from our little radio studio. We're parked in a campground. Campgrounds are called *campaggio* in Italian. We're in a village called San Benedito, which is not far from Brescia. The van is a little hot, but I'm going to speak anyway.

SDG singing and clapping:

hare kṛṣṇa hare kṛṣṇa, kṛṣṇa kṛṣṇa hare hare
hare rāma hare rāma, rāma rāma hare hare

Sweating it out on the pavement of the downtown street, you know, that pale gray cement with divided lines you stand on with your two legs, with a bedraggled group of men, women standing separately, public wondering why the women are separated, but that's how we do it. They're banging away, clashing away on the *karatālas* and drums in the deep canyons of the city, with the sharp echo off the sharp buildings. Right in the midst of it where all the people are going back and forth in their suits and dresses, and now that it's summer, they're taking off some of those clothes, but still passionately rushing back and forth—slaves. And the devotees, so odd, clashing with the scene, singing their "gypsy rhythms," adding color to the downtown life (or, depending on how you see it, being a nuisance).

SDG singing and clapping:

hare kṛṣṇa hare kṛṣṇa, kṛṣṇa kṛṣṇa hare hare
hare rāma hare rāma, rāma rāma hare hare

The young men and the older men, all with strong bodies, sweat dripping, but probably not getting headaches, singing and pounding. Some of them are fearful, but at least one or two are fearless when the boppers bop down the street showing disdain for the devotees and wanting to show some of it. Or worse, the crazy or violent plunging into the scene or looking like they would like to. Who knows their minds, anyway? I don't. But the streets are full of threat. Still, these one or two devotees are fearless, and even the fearful ones hang in there because Prabhupāda wants them to be there and to chant.

Ladies as good as men. They're performing their own austerities with their frailer bodies and sweet simplicity.

What about taste? They're getting a taste to one degree or another, chanting Hare Kṛṣṇa in their hearts and minds and giving it out. There's taste in that.

The chanters go ten minutes, twenty minutes, thirty minutes. Different things happen. A million images bombard the eyes. Then the devotees walk on and stand somewhere else, then walk on, singing, aching, leading and responding, tolerating, changing the rhythm, serving.

My dear friends, we have gathered here today to talk about the merits of Kṛṣṇa consciousness, especially for those who are not so much able to do what they want one way or another. This is a message of sincere hope by which I say to you, let us read the *śāstras* and enjoy and follow what Śrīla Prabhupāda has written. Now you may say that the sound of my voice has something hollow in it. You may think I am making a formal, rhetorical presentation. Not only my voice, but my message seems that of someone pretending to be more spiritual than he actually is, who is pretending to have a hold on things more than he actually does. Who the hell is he to tell you where to find solace?

But, folks, I have to tell you that I am also paying my dues because I'm talking with a pain behind my eye. Of course, I shouldn't risk personal inconvenience, so I think I'm going to end this show earlier than usual. Neither should I tell you the price tag I have to pay in order to give you this gift.

Folks, the real thing is that you ought to read Prabhupāda's books and you ought to chant Hare Kṛṣṇa. You ought to work hard and stop being a nonsense and don't be envious and don't be a Māyāvādī and all that.

As a sample of what I mean when I say read Prabhupāda's books, you could consider *The Nectar of Instruction.* This book is good for neophytes. It takes them all the way to the advanced stages of Kṛṣṇa consciousness. For example, Text Five advises us to mentally honor the devotee who chants the holy name of Kṛṣṇa. And it tells us also how to deal with four kinds of persons, from the Supreme Lord to the devotee friends, to the innocent, to the *asuras.* Then there's Text Six, and that gives us the very important information about not seeing the body of a pure devotee as material. If you think he looks unattractive, don't find fault with him for that. Don't criticize. This text has a very heavy last paragraph where Prabhupāda defends his own position. Whatever Prabhupāda says is perfect, but that doesn't mean we should judge his Godbrothers exactly the way he does. Why can't Śrīla Prabhupāda speak his heart sometimes? It seems in this purport that he's disappointed that his Godbrothers don't appreciate his work. Therefore, he says that he is empowered—he must be empowered. How else could he have spread the Kṛṣṇa consciousness movement? Prabhupāda is entitled to speak like this because he saved the world.

Text Seven is an all-time favorite. It's about the jaundiced patient.

Let's go back to Text Five. At the end of the purport, Prabhupāda says you should accept an *uttama-adhikārī* as a spiritual master. This has been reasoned and interpreted by Vīrabahu Prabhu in a way that allows us non-*uttama-adhikārīs* to also be spiritual masters. You can read his book, *The Guru and What Prabhupāda Said.* I don't remember everything he wrote right now, but I remember feeling satisfied by it. He spoke about the emergency of the times and he balanced this statement with other statements Prabhupāda made indicating that he did want his disciples to become spiritual masters. Prabhupāda didn't exclude us just because we weren't *uttama-adhikārīs.*

You could also say that this Verse Five statement makes us aware that we have to refer our disciples to the *uttama-adhikārī* line of *paramparā.* Still, aside from all debate, it says a *madhyama-adhikārī* or a neophyte on the intermediate platform can accept disciples, but the disciples should be on the same platform and it should be understood that they cannot advance very well to the ultimate goal of life under his insufficient guidance.

I'm not going to comment on it, but that phrase is ringing in my mind, "insufficient guidance." One reason we can't talk about it is that we've got these extremists who jump on these things.

I think I should stop now because it's getting hot in here. I'm not feeling so well. Thank you very much.

37

SDG singing and clapping:

> *hare kṛṣṇa hare kṛṣṇa, kṛṣṇa kṛṣṇa hare hare*
> *hare rāma hare rāma, rāma rāma hare hare*

Good morning. It's definitely summer now.

The other day I saw myself in the mirror and saw that I was dressed in my full *sannyāsī* uniform—all saffron. Of course, I always dress in these clothes, but during the colder months, I usually have a gray or brown sweater on, and often I'm wearing a gray coat and a hat, things that make it a little less than the pure uniform. When I suddenly saw my image in the mirror, and my freshly shaved head, I felt proud and happy to be an authorized ISKCON *sannyāsī*. It's an honor and one that I pray to keep.

This got me to thinking about other uniforms I have worn. They are a shame to me. For example, I remember feeling ashamed whenever I publicly wore my sailor uniform. That's because usually people imagine a sailor to be a "jar-head," a stupid guy who is almost always drunk. I wasn't that kind of sailor, so it embarrassed me. I was a college graduate, an English major, a poet.

That's the only other uniform, I suppose. Oh, I remember an episode about a baseball uniform too. I must have been fourteen or fifteen years old. The local police sponsored a league in our area and I went to the try-outs.

In those years, I was quite small. On the day of the try-outs, I made a mistake in the infield—maybe let the ball go through my legs or something. I could never quite face a hard ground ball coming my way. I was always afraid I would get hit in the face. They let me be on the team, but they told me I wouldn't get to play much. I had mixed feelings about that.

Anyway, that league wasn't very well organized. Sometimes the coaches didn't even show up. I was always punctual. If they said something was going to happen, I believed it.

One night, they told us we would practice and then go over to a sports store and get our uniforms. That was really exciting. I wanted that uniform so much. In those days, baseball players wore slightly baggy pants. All my major league heroes dressed like that. Getting that uniform would make up even for the fact that I couldn't play.

After the practice, one boy after another was given his uniform. I waited and waited until the coach finally turned to me and said, "We don't have a uniform for you. However, I can find pieces of a uniform here that you can use." Then he gave me some hand-me-down gray baseball pants (the rest of the team had white) and a different kind of shirt than the rest of the team.

I was hurt and humiliated in front of the other boys, but I did my best not to show it. I don't remember that they teased me. They were all so absorbed in their own uniforms that they didn't pay attention to my rejection.

I went home and told my parents. "Look what they gave me." My father thought if we bleached the pants they would turn white and look like everybody else's, but it didn't work. They were ragged and couldn't take much bleaching. I attended a few games in that uniform and sat on the bench.

Then I found out in advance that one of the players was not going to be able to attend the next game. It occurred to me that maybe I could borrow his uniform for the game. He agreed. I was so grateful. While I was walking home, I imagined how I would look in the uniform. Then I put it on. That day, at least, I wore the uniform and traveled to the game. I wanted everyone to see me dressed as a regular player, if only for one day.

I didn't play that well and the pitcher yelled at me. I was only put in at the end of the game because our team was so far ahead, but I made a mistake and they all got worried that they would lose their big lead. In the end, we won the game.

I've thought about this story from time to time, but I never told it because I couldn't see a Kṛṣṇa conscious purport to relate it to. It occurred to me, though, that now, I wear a prestigious uniform. Of course, it depends on what group you're in. To college intellectuals, a kid's baseball uniform doesn't mean much. Similarly, to materialists, the uniform of a Hare Kṛṣṇa *sannyāsī* has no meaning.

I feel toward the *sannyāsa* uniform as I did toward the baseball uniform. I may sometimes take it for granted, or even be shy when I'm wearing it in certain company, but at heart, I'm proud of it.

I prefer it to any other religious uniform, even a monk's uniform, such as the classical Franciscan dress. We see many Franciscans here in Italy. They look quite tailored in their brown cloth hoods and rope belts. I prefer the lightweight, pleasantly colored dress of the Vaiṣṇava *sannyāsī*. This is almost like poetic justice for the humiliation I felt from being denied the baseball uniform or being forced to wear that navy blue jar-head suit. I hope I can always keep the *sannyāsa* honor, the duties of *sannyāsa*, and finally give even that up for the spiritual body and the spiritual dress most pleasing to Kṛṣṇa, whatever that is.

SDG singing and clapping:

hare kṛṣṇa hare kṛṣṇa, kṛṣṇa kṛṣṇa hare hare
hare rāma hare rāma, rāma rāma hare hare

A footnote to the uniform story: Prabhupāda gave me this *sannyāsa* uniform. He didn't say, "Satsvarūpa, I have been watching you try out and have decided you can be a part of this team, but you won't be a regular player. Is that all right?" He never said that. He saw me for what I was with all my strengths and weaknesses, but he acknowledged that I was sincere. He accepted whatever small thing I could do as service. I thrived on his acceptance. When it was time to give me titles and uniforms, a *brāhmaṇa* thread, a spiritual name, a *sannyāsa* robe and *daṇḍa,* he didn't say, "You're a Westerner. You're not qualified." He gave me everything—not only me, but others like me. This is the difference between Prabhupāda and the stingy materialists. Prabhupāda gave us everything, but he also asked us to give up our false claims.

Thank you, Śrīla Prabhupāda, for being the best coach of this team, for always being attentive. You didn't schedule games and then not show up. Your intelligence was strong and you always thought out your winning strategy. You gave us honorable positions and asked us to fill them to our best ability. All glories to Śrīla Prabhupāda.

SDG singing and clapping:

hare kṛṣṇa hare kṛṣṇa, kṛṣṇa kṛṣṇa hare hare
hare rāma hare rāma, rāma rāma hare hare

Today's radio show, by the way, is being broadcast from the back of the van. We're still in San Benedito. The noise you hear in the background is a friendly noise. It's the sound of a motorcycle mixed with the sound of someone mowing the lawn. We can think of Kṛṣṇa regardless. Please surround yourself with Kṛṣṇa consciousness on all sides.

We're spending a few days here in this campground and then we will be back on the road, this time to the Eastern European countries—the Czech Republic and Poland. We're not the most adventurous of travelers, but we get around.

(The lawn-mowing machine is getting so close that it's kicking pebbles up against the van. I can even see the guy. I have to close the door here. Okay. Now we're in our little world, barely protected from the outside.)

The Italians are friendly, though. I don't mind being in my uniform in front of them. I really want to stop feeling any kind of shyness or shame when I am dressed like this. Let people laugh if they will, but I don't want to give up ever being seen as a devotee of Kṛṣṇa.

We were on television in New York one time. David Susskind asked why we dressed like this. He asked, "What if somebody is going to work and he's reading the *Chicago Tribune.* Suddenly he looks up and sees you. What's the point?" I said, "What's he looking at in the *Chicago Tribune*? He's wrapped up in the illusion of the material world and he's forgetting God. If he sees us, he will think about Kṛṣṇa and Kṛṣṇa is God. Whether he likes the devotees or not, whether he believes that Kṛṣṇa is God or not, our uniform will still remind him of God. Besides that, even thinking of Kṛṣṇa's name has absolute value." I said something like that and I do believe that.

38

SDG singing and clapping:

hare kṛṣṇa hare kṛṣṇa, kṛṣṇa kṛṣṇa hare hare
hare rāma hare rāma, rāma rāma hare hare

I was just reading a *Śrīmad-Bhāgavatam* lecture by Prabhupāda in Vṛndāvana, 1972. It was on the verse:

naṣṭa-prāyeṣv abhadreṣu
nityaṁ bhāgavata-sevayā
bhagavaty uttama-śloke
bhaktir bhavati naiṣṭhikī.

Prabhupāda was talking about the Bank American card and how people work so hard to maintain *anarthas.* He was explaining the word "*anartha*" and how hearing the *Bhāgavatam* removes *anarthas. Anarthas* are things that are unnecessary. He included in that much of what we consider civilized life—consumerism and heavy sense gratification. If we take to Kṛṣṇa consciousness, sense gratification and its resultant entanglements get removed. He went over the four prohibited activities and how a devotee stops them—illicit sex, intoxication, etc.

He was doing a bit of transcendental boasting, you could say, that his followers have achieved this freedom from sense gratification. I had two quick impressions. One was that it was true about me. As he said, as soon as I took to Kṛṣṇa consciousness, I gave up intoxication and illicit sex.

That's as significant a confirmation I can make as a devotee for myself and for preaching to others. Let's not forget that in this age where there is sometimes doubt whether Prabhupāda's boasts about his disciples are true and whether the Kṛṣṇa consciousness movement is measuring up to the optimistic vision he had for it. I'm an example.

The other thing I thought about was when Prabhupāda was speaking about *anarthas,* I realized that so many devotees have left the Kṛṣṇa consciousness movement. Our movement is no longer unified the way it was when Prabhupāda was physically present. It's no longer growing like wildfire. Still, we have to go on. Times have changed.

There are new difficulties, but we have to prove ourselves sincere devotees of Śrīla Prabhupāda.

On this tape, Prabhupāda said that even if all our habits aren't immediately removed—they may come back by accident—we're still devotees because of our conviction in Kṛṣṇa consciousness. *Api cet sudarācāro.* Then he said that if we deliberately commit sinful activity, we're not devotees.

Anarthas are cleared by regularly hearing *Śrīmad-Bhāgavatam.* Although someone may say, "But Kṛṣṇa is not personally here speaking the *Bhāgavatam,*" Prabhupāda answered that doubt. He said we can hear from Kṛṣṇa's words and Kṛṣṇa's representatives. Kṛṣṇa's words are absolute when they are repeated in *paramparā—nityaṁ bhāgavata-sevayā.* They'll remove the dirty things from the heart.

And what are those dirty things? They are sense gratification and the desire for sense gratification. Those things force us to take birth after birth. They can be washed away, "reduced almost to nil." The devotee continues on the safe path, hearing and chanting and giving up sinful activities until he's ready to go back to Godhead. If he falls away from the path, Kṛṣṇa will insure that he can sometime again take up the path of Kṛṣṇa consciousness at some time.

SDG singing and clapping:

> *hare kṛṣṇa hare kṛṣṇa, kṛṣṇa kṛṣṇa hare hare*
> *hare rāma hare rāma, rāma rāma hare hare*

How am I doing? I ask myself that while I chant Hare Kṛṣṇa. Maybe a devotee is supposed to be what I am. Maybe it's rare that a person can get more taste in Kṛṣṇa consciousness. But why does Prabhupāda speak of an advanced state if we're not meant to attain it? Where does Prabhupāda expect us to be at now? Usually, whenever devotees tried to explain to Prabhupāda that their chanting was inattentive, he would console them. He told them to go on chanting anyway and not to be inattentive. *Utsāhān niscayād dhairyāt*—be patient, enthusiastic, and have confidence. Don't get depressed. That's how Prabhupāda encouraged us.

That makes me think that I'm backward, that I really should be doing a lot better, and that I'm a slow student. Prabhupāda encourages me anyway. His encouragement doesn't mean that I'm doing all right. Maybe I'm not doing all right, but there's no other recourse except to go on.

We have faith that the spiritual master accepts us as we are. We are who we are. If we can't make some quantum leap forward right away, then what can an encourager say to us except to tell us to stick to the process?

But is there no other alternative but to go on with our slovenly mental habits while chanting? With the bare sixteen minimum and while each round is going on, we think only of the count. The round is only a kind of muzak piped in as a background hymn to our actual thoughts. No, that's not what the verse says. It says *harer nāma harer nāma harer nāma,* in the age of Kali, there's no other way but to chant and to chant and to chant. There is an alternative to our bad habits and it's up to us to pray for it.

But I can't pray. Did I ever pray? Was I praying in the Pyrennes that time? Something was going on. I want those prayers.

When did I begin to be interested in prayer? I was doing some reading in Christian books about prayer. I ended up speaking with a devotee who had read something I had written mentioning one of the Christian saints. We spoke on the phone and he was preaching about the Christian saints who teach prayer and how we also have prayer in our *sampradāya.* He told me how he made his own prayer formulas—what the Christians call "ejaculatory prayers." In that type of prayer, you cry out in the midst of all your other activities: "O God, please help me!" Or for Christians, the famous Jesus prayer, "Jesus Christ, please have mercy on me, a sinner."

This devotee also talked about humility. I don't remember the details, but he was enthusiastic about what he was saying and I was willing to be open and hear from him. I changed the habits of my inner life, but since that time, I have become more careful about being influenced by others in developing inner prayer. We don't want to become affected by someone's fad or to become faddish ourselves. I'm admitting the fad roots of my prayer period.

I was trying to practice prayer, especially when I went to Ireland. I would get up early—12:30 or 1 A.M.—and in addition to my *japa* and reading, I tried to pray for half-hour periods. I would recite different things I had written on cards or prayer formulas such as, "Dear Śrīla Prabhupāda, I cannot pray. Please help me to pray. Please give me attraction to Rādhā and Kṛṣṇa."

A lot of it had to do with saying things in my own words, not just in Sanskrit or in the written words of the *śāstra.* "Please Prabhupāda, help me to be a devotee. I do not have a taste for the holy name. I'm dry, but you can drown me in nectar. Please give me your love. Please give me the strength to chant," and so on.

There were two main things to concentrate on while chanting Hare Kṛṣṇa. One was gratitude and the other was to call out of my own need—sometimes thanking Kṛṣṇa for the wonderful gift of the holy name and sometimes calling out to Him, "Please, give me the nectar of the holy name. I need it." I was trying to develop perpetual prayer. Later, I took walks and began to speak what later became *Entering the Life of Prayer.*

At various times of the day, I would bow down and say different prayers. I was excited about it and I shared it with Madhu. At first he resisted because he had strong feelings against the Catholic Church and their politics. Soon he gave in and expressed attraction to the Church's saints. Then we shared this kind of prayer life. I recorded all this in *Entering the Life of Prayer.*

Now I'll tell you how it ended. That book was published and it created a controversy. It was even discussed at the GBC meeting. Some people wondered why I was reading Christian saints and why I wasn't just reading our own *ācāryas*. I wasn't there to discuss it with them, but some of the GBC men in Vṛndāvana interviewed the devotee with whom I had been discussing all this, since he was mentioned in my book.

Later, I phoned that devotee and asked what had happened. He said he had changed his whole outlook and was no longer interested in Christian saints. He said as a result of reading *Caitanya-caritāmṛta* and seeing the *gopīs'* love for Kṛṣṇa, he saw that these *gopīs* are far greater than any of the Christian saints. Most Christian saints only address God in His majestic aspect.

Then he told me that he didn't care for my book, *Entering the Life of Prayer.* He thought it was premature. I should have waited until I had actually experienced mystical prayer before I wrote anything on it. He said the result would be to set back any movement within ISKCON for prayer by someone who admittedly hasn't attained a state of prayer.

That devotee also told me that I shouldn't write anymore. He said it would be an act of humility on my part if I stopped writing and publishing. He suggested I pray and serve with humility and not take advantage of disciples. I tried that for about six months—I didn't write. Then slowly, slowly, I allowed a self within me to speak back. "Why can't I write? Why is it considered not humble? I want to write, even if I'm not yet pure. I want to distribute it." I had been completely ready to dismantle Gītā-nāgarī Press, but with some encouragement from another devotee, I decided against that and began to write again.

I'm telling you this not just as autobiography, but to remind myself that I actually want to go forward now in prayer, especially while chanting Hare Kṛṣṇa. At this point, prayer means controlling the mind when I chant. When my mind wanders off, it makes me almost angry. Why can't I stay attentive to the holy name? Then, "Kṛṣṇa, please help me!" I say it with emotion. "Kṛṣṇa, my life is running out. I can't chant nicely. Maybe I am keeping pace with my contemporaries. Maybe we're *all* like this. Maybe I can't expect so much more than this. Should I just accept it?"

But it's not good. Prabhupāda says that if your mind goes elsewhere when you chant, it's not good. It's an offense and you shouldn't be offensive in chanting. We know that if you do nice service aside from your *japa*—your preaching, managing, or whatever you do in ISKCON, then Kṛṣṇa will reward you when you chant. But I can't seem to do much more than that. Therefore, I have to beg Kṛṣṇa for His mercy.

Unfortunately, I don't ask Kṛṣṇa with such seriousness. It would seem that crying out to Kṛṣṇa to help us constitutes prayer. Still, when I go to pray like that, there's a block. This block may have to do with the fact that I went through a fad period. Or perhaps it's because my introduction to prayer came through *The Way of the Pilgrim* and the *Philokalia.* I don't want to get into all that again. I want to find prayer in our own *sampradāya.* There is prayer in Kṛṣṇa consciousness. I have these mental grooves that make me think that if I'm interested in prayer, it means I graft on the Christian saints. I don't want to do that. I can have a natural life of prayer. There are Vedic prayers and there's personal prayer. Everything I learned about prayer life is valid, even without the Christian influence.

Anyway, I said this much, and it's good to at least note all this. But I also recognize that I don't care enough to make an intense effort. I don't give a damn. There's a part of me that's like that, that just doesn't care.

I do believe in the chanting process. It's a real part of my life. I like to chant, but as far as digging out *anarthas* and working to improve myself, I don't seem to want to work. It's hard work. And here's another problem. I get headaches if I work too hard, if I stress myself too early in the morning. The morning is such a peaceful, quiet time. I can't seem to turn it into a real work session. I'm not a young *brahmacārī* that I can shake my neck and head and pace back and forth when I'm chanting. I can't do it. The inner work is like that too. Maybe that's a kind of uncaring.

I remember confessing that part of myself that doesn't care to Prabhupāda when he said I wasn't careful in dealing with his correspondence. When he pointed it out to me, I cried. "I'm sorry I don't care more." Prabhupāda and Lord Kṛṣṇa are kind. They let you take to Kṛṣṇa consciousness even when it's not deeply internalized. They let you keep going, coasting. You can perform Kṛṣṇa consciousness without care and breeze along. Why is it that some part of us doesn't want to go deeper? Are we trying to avoid the stress of whipping the mind with a broom and a shoe? We don't want to make a bloody mess.

Is it even required?

Anyway, I've used up my time. I hate to leave this unresolved, but I'm going to stop anyway. At least we've discussed it and I hope we won't forget it. Don't give up your protest that you don't care. Look into yourself and get over whatever is blocking you in approaching Kṛṣṇa. Kṛṣṇa will help you. How He'll do that remains to be seen.

SDG singing and clapping:

hare kṛṣṇa hare kṛṣṇa, kṛṣṇa kṛṣṇa hare hare
hare rāma hare rāma, rāma rāma hare hare

39

I come to you, spotted and checkered and continuing and not pure yet, but gradually I will attain purity.

naṣṭa-prāyeṣv abhadreṣu
nityaṁ bhāgavata-sevayā
bhagavaty uttama-śloke
bhaktir bhavati naiṣṭhikī

If we were completely free from *anarthas,* then we would be liberated. It's not unusual that a preacher is still working on *anarthas,* but we shouldn't think he's not a devotee. He is resolved to serve Kṛṣṇa. That's what defines him as a *sādhu.*

All right, he's a *sādhu,* but is he a spiritual master? The debate can continue, but I'm in not in the mood to continue it.

What mood *am* I in? I'm in the mood where you come from being scrunched in the back of Dīna's car while we wait for the dentist to show up. Although I can't talk to him, he smiles in a humble way and renders us such nice service. Who are we to accept his service? Beggars. We accept free dental work, free doctor work, free whatever anyone will give us. We're all serving Kṛṣṇa, trying to become purified.

You have to be satisfied by your activities, but you have to have activities. You can't just sit and meditate. Then if you're satisfied with your Kṛṣṇa conscious activities, you'll continue them. Otherwise, you'll give them up. There are so many maxims and truths in Kṛṣṇa consciousness. I'm repeating some of them here, stringing them together, and calling it a radio show. I'm calling it a radio show because I'm broadcasting. Everyone is running around in their cars and their motorbikes, going to work, or here in the campground, enjoying in one way or another. Everyone has a plan. Even the birds have activities. We have our plan to try and serve Kṛṣṇa by apparently quiet methods, by reading these books. I'm in a mood because I didn't read so well just now. It was hard to pay attention. I'm tired, I guess, from the car rattling into Brescia and back. But before that, I got in three good hours of *bhajana,* first getting up to write, then to read. That was good reading. Then to chant. That's all I know.

SDG singing and clapping:

śrī-kṛṣṇa-caitanya prabhu nityānanda
śrī advaita gadādhara śrīvāsādi gaura-bhakta-vṛndā

hare kṛṣṇa hare kṛṣṇa, kṛṣṇa kṛṣṇa hare hare
hare rāma hare rāma, rāma rāma hare hare

Later in the day, I'll take another turn at these different activities I do—writing sessions, reading *Śrīmad-Bhāgavatam,* and so on, but I think, "Oh, well, it will be more of the same, my uphill attempt. It may not be so glorious." But don't think like that. Any little bit I can add to my stock of service has value. My dissatisfaction is going to add up to blazing Kṛṣṇa consciousness, so I keep bringing straw and twigs to keep the fire going, even though in itself, it won't bring *kṛṣṇa-prema.* When I have to die in so many years from now—ho, ho, ho, so many years?—I won't be at that topmost stage. Oh, alas, what did I expect? At least I would like to die with the hope of finding the desire for pure devotional service in my heart.

For those who are neophytes in yoga, work is said to be the means. For those who are advanced, cessation of work is said to be the means. What does that mean?

Prabhupāda said that it's not by knowledge, but by love that Kṛṣṇa reveals Himself to you. No one in the material world can know everything about Kṛṣṇa. *Bhagavad-gītā* is Kṛṣṇa's book. He is talking in every verse, even if He's speaking something preliminary.

mattaḥ parataraṁ nānyat
kiñcid asti dhanañjaya
mayi sarvam idaṁ protaṁ
sūtre maṇi-gaṇā iva.

Let Kṛṣṇa speak for Himself. The devotees want to hear Him.

We drag our heels. We're already in a hole. Don't dig us in any deeper.

No one wants to dig us in deeper, they want to get us out. Therefore, talk about Kṛṣṇa, *kṛṣṇa-kathā.* He's *uttama-śloka.* He's not *niraka.* He's not no-activities. He has wonderful activities. We cling to the resilient cord of Prabhupāda's books which connects us to the *paramparā.* "Please, Prabhupāda, pick me. Please empower me to speak about Kṛṣṇa." Prabhupāda answers, "What more do you need? Everything is there. Just go ahead."

Kṛṣṇa has many activities. He is the supreme and strong Godhead, the mystic source of everything. I want to know Kṛṣṇa, that self-sufficient philosopher who has been awarding everyone's desires since time immemorial. Think of Him as the one who is the greatest, the oldest, who is always a person, who is smaller than the smallest, bigger than the biggest. Those words describe Him, but not completely. These words are mystic prayers of reverence. I need those. They're reverent, but they're also loving. We remember that the person we're revering is actually full of play and love.

Listen to that campground talk. I'm sorry folks, I don't have a cork-lined studio. At least you can see I'm really in the world and I'm not such a recluse that I've gone to a golden mountain to hide out.

When we can't think of anything to talk about, when our intellectual faculties are exhausted, we can chant. Chanting isn't discursive. It doesn't require following a pattern of thought sequences, a narration, a story. It's pure repetition: Hare Kṛṣṇa Hare Kṛṣṇa, Kṛṣṇa Kṛṣṇa Hare Hare/ Hare Rāma Hare Rāma, Rāma Rāma Hare Hare. The only way to do it is to place your mind at the lotus feet of Kṛṣṇa. That's what it means to be like a lamp in a windless place.

SDG singing and clapping:

hare kṛṣṇa hare kṛṣṇa, kṛṣṇa kṛṣṇa hare hare
hare rāma hare rāma, rāma rāma hare hare

Prabhupāda said that we have achieved all the goals of yoga without going through the intermediate steps. He has taken us right to the heart of it. *Man-manā bhava mad-bhakto.* It reminds me of Durvāsā Muni. He's an example of someone who could do everything but think of Kṛṣṇa. He was a very powerful *yogī.* Still, when he went up against Mahārāja Ambarīṣa, whom Prabhupāda called an ordinary king compared to Durvāsā, he was defeated. Mahārāja Ambarīṣa wasn't a mystic *yogī,* and he didn't have anywhere near the power that Durvāsā had, but he could think of Kṛṣṇa. *Sa vai manaḥ kṛṣṇa-padāravindayor.* As soon as he started to think about Kṛṣṇa, he began to speak about his Vaikuṇṭha Lord: *vacāṁsi vaikuṇṭha-guṇānuvarṇane.* He engaged all his senses in the Lord's service. That means he was not an ordinary person—he had the Lord's great mercy.

If we could just get beyond keeping Kṛṣṇa in a book and instead fill our minds with Kṛṣṇa. We reach that platform by constant association with Kṛṣṇa, like the iron rod in the fire. Gradually, by our application of Kṛṣṇa conscious activities, we'll be molded into shape. Prabhupāda says, "Mold your life in such a way that you will only be able to think of Kṛṣṇa."

Kṛṣṇa gives us the muscles to overcome resistance to Kṛṣṇa consciousness. When we overcome resistance, attraction begins.

Have faith. By the activities given to us by the spiritual master, we'll reach the supreme goal. Faith is chastity. It's not that we are faithful toward everything—faithful toward Kṛṣṇa, faithful toward the demigods, faithful toward our own powers. Our faith should be the faith a wife shows toward her husband. She is not faithful toward all men. That's not *śraddhā*. I want Prabhupāda-*śraddhā*.

SDG singing and clapping:

śrī-kṛṣṇa-caitanya prabhu nityānanda
śrī advaita gadādhara śrīvāsādi gaura-bhakta-vṛndā

hare kṛṣṇa hare kṛṣṇa, kṛṣṇa kṛṣṇa hare hare
hare rāma hare rāma, rāma rāma hare hare

What has it really been like on my European tour this year? April and May have slipped through my fingers. It's already June. This year has gone by so quickly. So what?

So what? The "so whats" are the details of what I'm trying to do in serving Kṛṣṇa. Ultimately, Kṛṣṇa wants to see my sincerity. Nothing else really matters. Nothing lasts anyway. In the end, all we're left with is our sincerity. In the meantime, I'm left to work out the "so whats" in the context of my limited self.

I once read a poem by Yevteshenko. He said that in Russia, people used to be afraid. Now there's not much fear. Then he said that there are things people should fear. We should fear becoming indifferent to people who are suffering. We should fear the debasing of ideas by untruths. We should fear exalting ourselves with those untruths. "The desperate fear of not being fearless on canvas or drafting board, but as I write these lines and I am in too great a haste at times, I write with only the single fear of not writing with all my power."

That's the poet's fear. I can transpose that into Kṛṣṇa conscious terms: within the limited context of the back of this van, I have the *dharma* of being a Kṛṣṇa conscious writer. And to take that a step beyond *my* life, every one of us should use all our power to perform our chosen or appointed services. We should *all* be afraid of being half-hearted.

SDG singing and clapping:

> *hare kṛṣṇa hare kṛṣṇa, kṛṣṇa kṛṣṇa hare hare*
> *hare rāma hare rāma, rāma rāma hare hare*

When you feel like you have nothing to say, it doesn't make you sad, but it does produce thoughtfulness. Who are you? What are you doing with your life?

I seem to chew at the same piece for awhile, the same thought, and then it moves on. Lately, I've been thinking about one thing, and it tends to come out most when I am quiet.

It's a kind of dissatisfaction, actually. Whenever it comes out, I look at it and wonder where it comes from. Then I remind myself that I have the tendency to be chronically dissatisfied. Remember the old days in the 1970s when I had a sprawling zone in the Midwest, U.S.A.? I thought I was too bogged down by temple visits and institutional life. I was a *sannyāsī* and wanted to go preaching to the non-devotees. I got involved with a traveling party. Then I thought I might be neglecting my duties in the temple. Neither temple life nor traveling made me satisfied. Then Prabhupāda pulled me out of both and I became his traveling secretary. Then I became dissatisfied with that. Then I started the library party. I thought I was really doing something that was recognizable as preaching in ISKCON, but eventually I became dissatisfied with that too. My Godbrothers were managing temples and having so many GBC meetings while I was out preaching. Maybe I should be doing that too.

It seems like there is no way to satisfy me. Now I'm a writer, which has been my heart's desire. I'd probably be sad if it were taken away from me. I have to keep that dissatisfaction in check and be thankful for what I have and what I am.

My quietness is not an empty quietness, but every day I'm producing more writing—humbly, obscurely, doing what I can. I feel sorrow too, though, and that's something that runs deeper. It's a lack of Kṛṣṇa consciousness. I don't know what to do with my sorrow, whether to go deeper with it and try to become more sorrowful or whether to see it as an obstacle and give it up.

I once advised someone to have a kind of inner mournfulness about his lack of Kṛṣṇa consciousness. You can't just forget about the fact that you're not making quick advancement and then go on in a cheery way. According to the *Śrīmad-Bhāgavatam,* your heart is steel-framed if you don't feel emotion when you chant. You can't forget it, but how can you keep dragging it out and looking at it all day long?

I've accepted the fact that I've fallen short. I have come, by Prabhupāda's grace, a long way in this lifetime, from a desperate, drug-addicted hippie, to a happy and productive worker in ISKCON.

Still, falling short is falling short. It could be said that I'm not doing so badly, considering where I came from. On the other hand, I could be a better preacher, a better fighter in the *saṅkīrtana* mission. I could be more willing to sacrifice my time and my life for my spiritual master. Prabhupāda says, "Live with the devotees, even if it's a little inconvenient. Tolerate the bodily pains. Fight the obstacles of the nondevotees." But all of these things disturb me and I can't do it all the time. Others also have their shortcomings, and human nature is such that I use that fact to justify my own weaknesses. What kind of logic is that?

"My dear Lord Kṛṣṇa, my dear Śrīla Prabhupāda, I know I am fallen. Please help me. Please take me to the next life in Kṛṣṇa consciousness. I want to serve you."

These are some of the things that have been going on in my mind. It's quiet today, and cold, considering it's June. It rained all through the night and into this morning. I'm sensitive to weather. When it's overcast, it leaves me aware of unexplored quietness. The themes of my life are there and they're going along, for better or for worse. I'm plugged in, functioning, but quiet. I have nothing else to do but to go on with my duties. I'm on the right path, but my path is slow.

Part of my quietness is patience. Because of the quiet day, I don't feel my writing went so brilliantly, although I haven't forgotten that this is my way. Anyway, shake off the dissatisfaction. Get rid of any destructiveness in your mood. Those are leftovers from the past, that hopelessness.

I'm past that. I'm not going to destroy my progress, the great hopes I have, the carefully protected and maintained *bhakti-latā* which is slowly growing up to the spiritual world.

SDG singing and clapping:

hare kṛṣṇa hare kṛṣṇa, kṛṣṇa kṛṣṇa hare hare
hare rāma hare rāma, rāma rāma hare hare

Besides us, what is there? There is God and all the other living entities. That's a lot of "other," isn't it? We're so tiny? Why do we think we're so important? It's a terrible sickness, a bloated, selfish lunacy—the lunacy that brought us into this material world in the first place. False ego and the demonic attitude.

But we're not demons and we know that selfhood is important too. What is that selfhood? That we're the eternal servants of Kṛṣṇa. To realize this takes self-awareness. Therefore, we have to cultivate selfhood through self-examination.

Beyond self-awareness, we should also be aware of Kṛṣṇa. Kṛṣṇa talks to us directly in the *śāstra.* Sometimes He discusses and describes His pastimes, and sometimes He explains to us the precariousness of our situation. Right now, I'm reading Nārada Muni's teachings to King Prācīnabarhi. Nārada didn't teach the king much about the nature of the spiritual world, nor did he describe Kṛṣṇa's name, form, and pastimes. First he had to cut down the king's jungle of *karma-kāṇḍiya* by showing him how time steals away the life of a sense gratifier and how karma punishes ignorance.

I had a good reading session this morning. I'm reading while asking the question, "What is there besides me?" Of course, I know that that otherness is the major reality. There's something not quite right with self-absorption, but neither is it easy to simply toss it aside. We are who we are and it's natural to include that in our speech. Then we make the leap to Kṛṣṇa.

I saw how easily that works one time when I was practicing a writing technique called "webbing." "Webbing" means that you draw a circle in the middle of your page, write a word in the circle, then draw lines out from that word and make more bubbles. In each bubble, you write a word that has come to mind from the last word. That word in turn prompts you to think of another word, and so it goes. Lines and bubbles radiate out and a web is created. When you get it all done, something is supposed to click and you discover where all this was leading you to.

I've used this technique with limited success, but I mention it now because when I create a web like that, I often see that there's no real and direct concentration of Kṛṣṇa consciousness. Then I find a space on the page, and without anything connected to it, draw a circle and write "Kṛṣṇa." I follow that with a Kṛṣṇa conscious web. I want to talk about Kṛṣṇa. He is beautiful. He is Śyāmasundara.

cintāmaṇi-prakara-sadmasu kalpa-vṛkṣa-
lakṣāvṛteṣu surabhīr abhipālayantam
lakṣmī-sahasra-śata-sambhrama-sevyamānaṁ
govindam ādi-puruṣaṁ tam ahaṁ bhajāmi

advaitam acyutam anādim ananta-rūpam
ādyaṁ purāṇa-puruṣaṁ nava-yauvanaṁ ca
vedeṣu durlabham adurlabham ātma-bhaktau
govindam ādi-puruṣaṁ tam ahaṁ bhajāmi

premāñjana-cchurita-bhakti-vilocanena
santaḥ sadaiva hṛdayeṣu vilokayanti
yaṁ śyāmasundaram acintya-guṇa-svarūpaṁ
govindam ādi-puruṣaṁ tam ahaṁ bhajāmi

What better way to think of Kṛṣṇa than to recite prayers and verses? Kṛṣṇa is one without a second. He never falls down. He's unlimited. He is the cause of all causes. He doesn't have a father and mother, although He chooses some devotees to take those roles in His pastimes. He is eternal. He has inconceivable potencies. Therefore, we offer Him our obeisances. He is our protector, maintainer, and friend.

Kṛṣṇa is always young. He's difficult to know through the *śāstras*, but that doesn't mean we can't know Him. People sometimes think words are material and God is beyond them, but words can be used spiritually. When Kṛṣṇa uses them to reveal Himself, He says *tat śṛṇu*, just hear from Me. I am like this. "There is no truth greater than Me. Everything is depending on Me as pearls are strung on a thread." There is nothing greater than Kṛṣṇa.

How beautiful is He? Those whose eyes are anointed with the salve of love see Kṛṣṇa in their heart of hearts as Śyāmasundara—the beautiful, blackish boy. Kṛṣṇa is present in His name.

nāma cintāmaṇiḥ kṛṣṇaś
caitanya-rasa-vigrahaḥ
pūrṇaḥ śuddho nitya-mukto
'bhinnatvān nāma-nāminoḥ

Kṛṣṇa's name is full of nectar. It's perfect. It's *cintāmaṇi*. It can give us anything we desire. If we want liberation, the holy name can grant it. If we want love of God, the holy name can grant it. If we want only inattentive chanting, the holy name can grant that too. "O my Lord, You are so kind to put all Your transcendental energies into Your holy name . . . "

Kṛṣṇa is great and we are small. We are in a dangerous situation. What if we again enter the cycle of birth and death and take birth in a place like Bosnia or in the middle of some African revolution, or worse?

What is the solution?

īhā yasya harer dāsye
karmaṇā manasā girā
nikhilāsv apy avasthāsu
jīvan-muktaḥ sa ucyate

Become a liberated *jīva* even in this world. Become Kṛṣṇa conscious. There is no fear for one who is Kṛṣṇa conscious. And further, serve your guru. That's the real secret. Viśvanātha Cakravartī said, "As the life air is the very essence of our existence and survival—without it we die—so for the disciple, the order of the guru is his life charge. He would rather die than disobey the order of his guru."

40

SDG singing and clapping:

> *hare kṛṣṇa hare kṛṣṇa, kṛṣṇa kṛṣṇa hare hare*
> *hare rāma hare rāma, rāma rāma hare hare*

If you who listen to this don't like it when I speak about writing and expression in Kṛṣṇa consciousness, or about theories of art in Kṛṣṇa consciousness, then you aren't going to like this show. That's what I'm going to speak about.

These things are real to me. I don't want to sound pompous: "I will now discuss the Kṛṣṇa conscious theory of aesthetics. Few devotees have discussed this in the past as it refers to the modern idiom." So don't think I'm being pompous. I just have to work these things out.

I wrote a book in Ireland called *My Relationship With Lord Kṛṣṇa.* When I get it typed, I'll see whether I want to do more on it. While I was writing it, I thought it would be a big book and that I wouldn't be able to complete it quickly. Then I became anxious to complete it anyway, to get it out of the way.

I want to say something about that book. There were two approaches. One was to look within myself and ask, "What is my relationship with God, Kṛṣṇa?" I was willing to go with that for a while, but then I stopped short and asked myself questions like, "Well, who am I to talk about this? I should just repeat what the *śāstras* say." The *śāstras* are full of definitions of my relationship with Lord Kṛṣṇa. How else can I imagine it? *Jīvera 'svarūpa' haya—kṛṣṇera 'nitya-dāsa.' Nityo nityānāṁ cetanaś cetanānām, eko bahūnāṁ yo vidadhāti kāmān.* I am the eternal servant of Kṛṣṇa, a spirit soul, a person, eternally dependent on the Supreme Person. Or, as Prabhupāda once said, Kṛṣṇa is the bread supplier and we're the bread eaters.

Kṛṣṇa also tells me about the nature of my relationship with Him when He speaks to Arjuna in the *Bhagavad-gītā:* "You are My very dear friend." *Mamaivāṁśo jīva-loke, jīva-bhūtaḥ sanātanaḥ.* "All the *jīvas* are My eternal, fragmental parts." In this way, I have learned to define my relationship with Him.

I was going for something other than that—not other than that, but a more personal expression of it. I felt it was important to define the relationship in personal terms and in that way, to understand why Kṛṣṇa is putting a covering between us. I know I'm still impure, still envious, but to speak my heart to Kṛṣṇa in prayer seemed important to me at the time. Of course, the discussion had to be based on *śāstra.* That's where I get the understanding that I have a relationship at all. Anyway, I hoped in a therapeutic way to gain something by writing it down.

I can hear the challenges people will raise, though. A conservative devotee might say, "Expressing your relationship with Kṛṣṇa in your own words is not valid because it's not *paramparā.* You should only repeat the descriptions given in *śāstra.* That is the only way we can know about Kṛṣṇa or our relationship with Him."

Okay, but then what are the things I am talking about? Perhaps they are the babbling of a spiritual infant who is attempting to improve that śāstrically-defined relationship by calling out to Kṛṣṇa. A fallen soul should lament the distance between himself and Kṛṣṇa. He knows why the distance is there, but he prays to Kṛṣṇa, "Kṛṣṇa, please make an arrangement. You are all-intelligent. Make some arrangement whereby I can come to You."

I don't have so much more to say about the writing in that particular book. I hope I can do more on it. Right now, it's only about a hundred pages. It's done as directed free-writing.

Another thing I want to talk about is how to deal with my pre-Kṛṣṇa conscious impressions in this body. By the way, I read in Nārada Muni's descriptions of dreams where he clearly says—and Prabhupāda elaborates on it in the purport—that dreams are impressions of past life experiences. There are so many dream models and theories by psychologists these days. There are those who very much value dreams. Many psychologists these days are following Jungian models and they define dreams according to archetypal understandings. They say all human beings have certain images and that when we dream of them, they have basically the same meaning for each of us.

Other dream theorists resist this idea. They say (or I am writing it in our Kṛṣṇa conscious language) that we dream in a more personal way based on our own karma and individuality.

Nārada Muni's dream treatise, and Prabhupāda's elaboration on it, make several points. Prabhupāda says that dream images are often a combination of things we have not experienced in this lifetime. We put them together from a mix of impressions left over from previous lives. There's even a statement in 4.29.67 that we can't really experience anything now in a dream or thought that we didn't already experience in one bodily form or another.

This is a revolutionary dream theory. I don't know what it means exactly. If you have a dream now, what do you make of it?

I find these things intriguing, but it makes it more difficult to do any kind of dream work because if you have to deal with your past life feeding information into your present dreams, how are you going to know how to use them for self-improvement? If, for example, I dream of murdering someone, does that mean I was a murderer in my past life? I can't speculate on that. I don't know why certain dreams keep coming up for me.

I often employ my dreams in writing. I regard them as part of the creative process. They tell better stories than I can when I'm conscious. Because I'm a writer (as my service), *therefore,* I'm interested in my dreams. It's too much effort and seems to be a deviation when I do full-time "dream work." But from time to time, I write one in a writing session. I feel them and think about them—we all do that.

Of course, the other recurring description of dreams is that they are unreal. The dream state is a standard analogy in transcendental discussions for unreality. It is temporary, and whatever you see in your dream doesn't really exist. Similarly, the analogy continues: when you wake up and come into your physical consciousness and identity again, that is also a temporary dream that will soon vanish. The self remains aloof, whether in the dream state or in so-called wakefulness.

But none of this is my point. My point is that pre-Kṛṣṇa conscious life comes up in dreams and it comes out in writing. I don't necessarily culture it, but the kind of "freefall" I try to attain in writing sometimes approaches the dream state. Then all kinds of things come out. I can't censor them if I want to keep the writing flow going.

Okay, so they come out. I let them come out and then I deal with them. What I really want to say to myself and to my readers is that we should all be aware that my present intention is to let these things come and make their brief appearances. I am not interested in giving long, autobiographical accounts of my past—it's just too saturated with *māyā*. But brief accounts. It's my life and it's meaningful to me. These memories come up in certain contexts and I learn from them. Or if I don't learn from them, I release them, I confess them in such a way that it produces a healing and wholeness. I try to see whether they can fit into my Kṛṣṇa consciousness. I get them off my chest in a way that has meaning; I'm not just talking about them because they came to mind. I don't want to indulge myself, but in the creative process, you have to follow something, an intuition or heart's desire.

Some of the poems I wrote in the "Wind In The Chimney" series of *Writing In Gratitude* worked that way. I wrote them on big sheets of newsprint with colored pens while sitting on the floor in a cold room. I can think of one in particular that worked like that for me, even though it is a memory from after I met Prabhupāda.

After taking a walk with Madhu, I came back and wrote a poem. This memory came out: in Tucson one time, I was standing on the street distributing books. A storekeeper came out of his store, grabbed my *daṇḍa*, and broke it over my head. That memory came out in the small space of a poem and more or less said, "While on the walk this morning, I was trying to think of how I can increase my surrender to Kṛṣṇa. Who am I? Then this memory came up and I was able to look at it again. I remembered the hurt I felt at the time. There it is and that's it. Now I understand, as that poem ended, that I'm very, very lucky to have been taken in by Śrīla Prabhupāda." That feeling of great fortune came as I remembered what I have escaped from in this lifetime. It was a memory, that's all. It was a healing experience.

These things come out for me in little interjections or digressions. As I said, I speak about this at the risk of sounding pompous. But damn it, my consciousness, my life is that of an artist with the problem of how to use my resources, my life history, and my self to express the human experience of trying to surrender to Kṛṣṇa. For me, the danger is not philosophical deviation, but subtle deviation. I mean, I have to be careful not to give more importance to the expression of surrender than to surrender itself. When I surrender, then I will have something to express.

I remember reading in Mark Van Doren's introduction to Thomas Merton's poems that Merton couldn't have been a monk except as a writer. They went together for him. His spiritual advisors shouldn't look at that as deviation, and they didn't. His first confessor in Gethsemane told him to write, even though Merton thought his writing was based on false ego. His confessor encouraged him to write and help other people by publishing his books.

I beg Kṛṣṇa for protection in this work. I don't want to become contaminated by false ego. I remember reading about the life of the *haiku* poet, Basho. At the end of his life, he very much regretted that all he could think of was how to write a poem about the experience of dying and that that had precedence over his concern for his soul's welfare. He regretted that he had missed the opportunity to practice spiritual life and had instead chosen the life of a poet. Such a conflict is possible because poetry can become fixed on worldly images and temporary states of consciousness. Those are the tools a poet uses to create sharp and tangible images.

You can imagine, I'm sure, how a poet could become caught up in writing a poem describing his own approaching death. He wants to capture the human state just at the time of death as he's calling out to God, and for realism, he might want to choose an image that represents the soul's attachments to the world and to evoke emotion. The image would have to be perfect. He might choose a bird calling at the moment he died or something like that. He would be so fixed in choosing the words and images that the poem itself would represent the poet's foolishness. As Prabhupāda says, the poet would fall into the category of the man who tells his family, "Now my dear sons, please manage the property estates, take care of my wife, and please invest my money in this way after I am gone." He's still making adjustments in this world. "Please see that my name is commemorated by donations to a worthy cause and build a statue, if possible, in my honor. Always perpetuate my name and honor in this way." Ridiculous.

Better to write up until the end as the *ācāryas* have done—creating transcendental literature—and then just stop. They were already living in the spiritual world while in this world, and death only took them from here to there. That's why I'm always hoping to be able to write in a more purified way as soon as possible.

So it's a dilemma, but also a challenge. Capturing human experience doesn't have to be pompous or pretentious if I don't allow it to become so. I pray that Kṛṣṇa will teach me this art and how to perform it properly. I'm not a person of great talents or great scholarship; I'm not a conscientious craftsman or a great devotee. I do have an urge to write about Kṛṣṇa conscious life and to glorify Prabhupāda and Kṛṣṇa in ways that would nourish the devotees. After all, we all have to have *some* service. Therefore, please let me express sincerity and suffer austerity in this service.

SDG singing and clapping:

hare kṛṣṇa hare kṛṣṇa, kṛṣṇa kṛṣṇa hare hare
hare rāma hare rāma, rāma rāma hare hare

Okay, time is running out.

I am planning to embark on a series of poems about Prabhupāda with the idea that it's an exercise. I hope it will develop into something nice.

This is something more than artistic theories in the creation of art and literature. Damn literature and sometimes damn communication —just try to express yourself.

41

SDG singing and clapping:

hare kṛṣṇa hare kṛṣṇa, kṛṣṇa kṛṣṇa hare hare
hare rāma hare rāma, rāma rāma hare hare

Haribol. I thought of speaking about something Prabhupāda said in a lecture. He was speaking on a verse about how you have to rise above the modes of nature to practice Kṛṣṇa consciousness. Then he said that in his presentation of Kṛṣṇa consciousness, he didn't make any compromises, but just taught what the *śāstras* say. If people don't like it, they can go elsewhere, but he can't compromise. He is so strong in his faithful presentation, and aware that people's whimsical natures may not be satisfied. Still, he wasn't prepared to pander.

Of course, Prabhupāda's uncompromising nature is much of what attracted us to him. It's not that everyone who came to spiritual life was a perfect connoisseur of spiritual topics or such a penetrating truth-seeker that he couldn't be cheated. But Prabhupāda made us feel safe. Prabhupāda himself said that many of us came to him out of sentimentality. Of course, that was still good, but if we didn't become serious, we would fall away. His uncompromising nature helped us to become serious and to get past whatever sentimental reasons made us seek him out in the first place.

Then Prabhupāda said that to practice spiritual life, you have to rise above the modes, especially the modes of ignorance and passion. Again, he was uncompromising. He said we wouldn't be able to talk about spiritual life until we rose above those two modes. How can we practice spiritual life and at the same time, cultivate lust and greed? Therefore he told his students from the beginning that we had to give up illicit sex, intoxication, meat-eating, and gambling.

I recently heard Prabhupāda speaking with a representative of the Rosicrucian society in Paris. I say "speaking with," but it was more like Prabhupāda was piercing everything he said with his demanding logic. On the point of giving up sinful activities, the Rosicrucian said that they don't have any rules or regulations forbidding members to engage in any activity. He said that the Rosicrucians have been intelligent in not insisting on a pure life, because if you insist, a person will leave. His conviction was that after practicing the meditations and steps in their order, a person would naturally give up sinful activity. At no point would they demand or even check up on how their followers were doing in their attempts to find purity.

Prabhupāda demands that we rise above the modes. He doesn't compromise on this point. Prabhupāda's presentation covers everything. It's so scientific and deep, and he holds the process out, just waiting for someone to take it up seriously. Prabhupāda gave us the process of *śravaṇaṁ kīrtanam. Śṛṇvatāṁ sva-kathāḥ kṛṣṇaḥ*, or *ceto-darpaṇa-mārjanam*—chanting and hearing about Kṛṣṇa will clean our hearts. That is Prabhupāda's proposal.

SDG singing and clapping:

hare kṛṣṇa hare kṛṣṇa, kṛṣṇa kṛṣṇa hare hare
hare rāma hare rāma, rāma rāma hare hare

I read a statement lately by a BTG editor in response to a devotee who had written in. The editor wrote, "The problem I find in your essay is that you don't stick to one point, but you wander from point to point. Even if you make your essays short, there's no harm in that, but you should bring up one point and then lead the reader by the hand, step by step. If you don't do that—if he doesn't know where he is at every moment under your guidance, then he'll tend to get confused and lose interest."

On the one hand, I agree with this point of view, but when I think about it more deeply, I don't. The person he wrote to didn't agree with it either. He said, "I'm forty-nine years old and I've been through what I've been through. I have my way, my nature of presenting something, and I can't change it. That's the way I speak. I like to speak on different things."

The editor drew an image of the reader as a rather childlike person who needs the writer to hold his hand and take him through his points. I find that condescending. There are confused readers as much as there are confused writers. Still, most people don't see themselves as confused or lost or childish. Most people don't want to be led. They prefer to be inspired to follow. My own feeling is to trust that the reader has an active intelligence and can follow if he feels something is worth following.

A preacher wants to communicate, but he wants to do it as humanly as possible. Prabhupāda was uncompromising; he didn't care whether people's superficial interests were satisfied or not. He spoke the truth, what was good for people, and what would actually delight them in their constitutional nature. And he wasn't bored with his own presentation. He was always enthusiastic in his preaching. You can hear it in the early tapes. Prabhupāda would be speaking enthusiastically and philosophically, and then suddenly pause as if seeing the blank faces of his audience, "Oh, of course, this is a very dry subject. People will think we are talking about God and it is so much philosophy." Then he would chuckle, realizing that for a New York crowd to gather and not hear music or something more immediately sensational or controversial or attractive to the lower modes of nature was unusual. He couldn't expect to be too popular.

He chuckled and he realized it, but he went forward anyway with his *kīrtana* and his preaching. He did it because that's what Kṛṣṇa wanted. He wasn't interested in pleasing the crowd. He wrote that in one letter: "The *kīrtana* is not to please a crowd. The lecture is for Kṛṣṇa and for some sincere persons. No matter if nobody comes, you speak to the walls. We are *kṛṣṇa dāsa*, we are *guru dāsa*."

I'm not trying to put my type of presentation up against Prabhupāda's, but I want to keep these principles in mind. At the same time, I have to speak in my own voice.

Even my concerns are different from Prabhupāda's. (Oh, how can you say that? How can they be different?) I'm the son and he's the father. I am concerned to see his mission a success and to please him, and I am concerned with my own heart. Prabhupāda doesn't have to worry about removing *anarthas* from his heart. That's my problem, though. Prabhupāda is the founder-*ācārya* of the whole movement. Although I serve within the movement, I am not its leader. It would be madness to think that. "Don't be a slouch. You have to go all-out for Prabhupāda. You should take on the whole movement's concerns. That's what Prabhupāda wants"—taken to the extreme, would I say I am the founder-*ācārya*? Or if not the founder-*ācārya*, then the leading disciple? "I know all the answers. I have the capacity to absorb the sinful reactions of countless followers. Therefore, they should accept me as their leader."

No, I have different concerns. I simply pray that my concerns will be dovetailed in Kṛṣṇa's service and accepted by Śrīla Prabhupāda. I don't want to be caught holding up a limp banner, "Well, I'm not Śrīla Prabhupāda, you know."

SDG singing and clapping:

> *hare kṛṣṇa hare kṛṣṇa, kṛṣṇa kṛṣṇa hare hare*
> *hare rāma hare rāma, rāma rāma hare hare*

I don't have much more to say about that. I'm satisfied to see Kṛṣṇa in the pages of *Śrīmad-Bhāgavatam* and to be urged on to preach.

42

SDG singing and clapping:

hare kṛṣṇa hare kṛṣṇa, kṛṣṇa kṛṣṇa hare hare
hare rāma hare rāma, rāma rāma hare hare

Yesterday I gave myself permission and encouragement to tell *saṅkīrtana* stories on this radio show. These ones aren't going to be true, necessarily, but fantasies. Telling them reminds me of a poem I once read by a Vietnam veteran. In that poem, he spoke about being a prisoner in a pit and how his mind kept running through the plots of TV shows he had watched in the 1950s—"I Love Lucy," "Dragnet," and so on. I've heard of that before, how prisoners sometimes pass the time by exchanging movie plots. Those movies may have been boring and of no value in themselves, but in such a desperate situation, they might help two people keep their sanity.

Anyway, I'm not comparing myself to someone in such a desperate situation. I didn't give that example to draw a comparison between us, but to show you how it helps to borrow some of that desperation to build up the need to tell stories. Like Ali Baba and "A Thousand And One Nights." Ali Baba was supposed to be executed, but he managed to put off his execution by telling stories day after day. His executor liked the stories so much that the next night he would promise Ali Baba his life if he could tell another story.

Let me try one. This one happens to be true.

Once there was a little man named Duncan who lived in Dublin. He had trouble putting on his coat, he was so drunk. Anyway, he went out into the street and he was on the dole, which for you Americans, means on welfare. He spent his dole money on his rent and the rest in the pub. I'm not going to tell you too much more about him, but one day he was heading down the street and by the post office when a book distributor, a friendly fellow, came forward to meet him.

Suddenly, Duncan collapsed with what appeared to be a heart attack. A crowd gathered and the book distributor told everyone what had happened. Somebody even made a quip that maybe Duncan's collapse was the book distributor's fault. Finally, a policeman arrived on the scene and took charge. Duncan was not unconscious. He said he had a pain in his heart. Then someone called an ambulance. While they were waiting for it to arrive, the policeman decided to take Duncan to the hospital in his car.

At the hospital, the doctor diagnosed appendicitis and decided they should operate immediately. Another doctor, seeing Duncan's flushed condition, realized he was drunk and that he would have to sober up before they could operate.

Duncan was left alone in his hospital bed. In his half-conscious state, he fantasized himself drinking in the tavern with angels. As he "walked out of the tavern," he found himself wondering who the angels were. Were they his guardian angels? Or maybe they had come to punish him for all his sins. He had a guilt complex.

Then he saw himself walking past the book distributor and the book distributor offering him a book. He also relived the heart attack, but in his fantasy, he died. Horrible creatures pulled his soul to hell. More horrible creatures came. They grabbed him from either side and forced his mouth open while a third creature forced burning liquid down his throat.

Suddenly, an orderly came into his room and woke him from his dream. He had been screaming in his sleep. Duncan told him that he had had a nightmare in which he had gone to hell.

The orderlies and doctors weren't metaphysically minded. They assumed Duncan was drunk or crazy and decided to leave him alone. In fact, the doctor came by, looked him over, and said, "Duncan, you look all right to me. I think you should stop drinking so much, especially during the day. It could ruin you and send you to an early grave."

Duncan was still caught up in the meaning of his dream, so he took the doctor's advice seriously. "Thank you, doctor. I think the same myself." He dressed himself and left the hospital, leaving the bill to the Republic of Ireland. He felt like a new man, that he had seen death and what comes after and was sobered.

But there was some conflict in his mind. His dream showed him that there was a connection between his drinking and hell, but his church had never taught him of that connection. He decided to ask a priest about it and to tell him about his dream. The priest said, "My man, according to the Bible and according to the Church, drinking is not a sin, but gluttony. There is sin in excess. You should drink in moderation."

"That's what I thought," said Duncan. "That's what I thought."

He said his Our Fathers and Hail Marys as the priest requested and then went to the pub. He ordered a drink to calm himself. Duncan wasn't usually a dreamy person and wasn't given to spiritual visions. This was all quite new to him and he couldn't shake the impressions of the last few days.

After a few drinks, he realized he didn't know what moderation meant. Everyone in the pub had a different definition. One priest, who happened to be having a drink in the pub that day, said that moderation meant whatever a man could hold without losing his equilibrium. Otherwise, drink was a Christian tradition. Wine was even part of the Holy Mass.

Duncan didn't feel so bad after that. As he left the pub, he assured himself that he had been moderate that day because he still had his equilibrium. Then he saw the book distributor again, right in front of the post office. He immediately crossed the street to avoid him.

That's the end of chapter one.

Now for chapter two.

That night, Duncan had the same dream that he had had in the hospital.

He recognized the creatures as messengers of death. He screamed and woke up in a sweat with the landlady knocking on his door.

"I'm all right, it's nothing. Just a bad dream," he called out to her. But he wasn't all right. He had to save his soul, and that made him wonder whether the book distributor he had seen on the street at the moment of his collapse might have something to do with all this.

Now as far as Duncan knew, this fellow selling the books was a Hare Kṛṣṇa lad. Duncan didn't know much about the Hare Kṛṣṇas, except that they followed some kind of Eastern religion. Duncan was not a very educated fellow. He had seen *kīrtanas* on Saturdays when the devotees came into town and played their drums and cymbals. He thought they were nice, but he had never looked into it further than that.

Finally, on Thursday, Duncan got up his courage to go out and meet the book distributor. But he wasn't there. Then he remembered that there was a Hare Kṛṣṇa store on Dame Street—a store and a temple.

He found the place and went in. A young woman was selling incense and other imported items in the front of the store. He could hear a *kīrtana* going on in the back. He didn't want to go back there. After all, he was a Catholic. He didn't want religion. He just wanted to ask some questions. And he especially wanted to talk to that man.

"Oh, that's Prabhupāda dāsa. He's out there every Saturday."

"I'll have to wait a few more days." Duncan looked over at the book rack. There he saw a book called *Second Chance.* The cover was the scene from his dream. It was a picture of an old man lying in bed, obviously on the verge of death. Two horrible-looking creatures were ripping his soul out of his body. But in this picture, there were also two beautiful men who looked like they came from another world.

They had four arms. They seemed to be protecting the old man's soul from the horrible creatures. Duncan bought the book.

Duncan was worried that this might be a heathen doctrine, but in a simple way, he caught the drift of the story. Ajāmila, a great sinner (and also a drunkard), collapsed one day and was about to die. The Yamadūtas had come to take him to hell because he was so sinful, but because Ajāmila had called out the name of God, Nārāyaṇa, God's messengers had arrived just in time to save him.

On Saturday, he went and spoke to Prabhupāda dāsa on the street. Prabhupāda dāsa explained, in words that Duncan could understand, what was going on. They spoke for forty-five minutes. Prabhupāda dāsa willingly gave his time to Duncan and Duncan learned as much as he could absorb.

As I said, this is a true story and Duncan soon became a congregational member of the Hare Kṛṣṇa movement. He started chanting *japa* regularly and stopped drinking altogether.

I can't tell you why Duncan had intimations about his death and why that drew him so quickly to Kṛṣṇa consciousness. One thing I can say is that it appears that Duncan performed devotional service in a past life, so he again became the recipient of a devotee's mercy. The *Vedas* tell us that just by seeing a devotee of the Lord, one can get the Lord's mercy.

SDG singing and clapping:

> *hare kṛṣṇa hare kṛṣṇa, kṛṣṇa kṛṣṇa hare hare*
> *hare rāma hare rāma, rāma rāma hare hare*

Now, radio show fans, we're going to break camp. It shouldn't affect this show too much. This is the modern age. I don't need a two-hundred-foot radio tower and a cork-lined studio from which to broadcast my show. I need only a half hour of privacy and this little Sony dictaphone. I also need some presence of mind.

We're on our way through Austria next.

Hare Kṛṣṇa Hare Kṛṣṇa, Kṛṣṇa Kṛṣṇa Hare Hare/ Hare Rāma Hare Rāma, Rāma Rāma Hare Hare. Prabhupāda will travel, Rūpa Gosvāmī will travel, I will travel. Will we all go to the spiritual world? Yes, we can go to the spiritual world. Will Mālatī be there? Will Sarasvatī be there? Will Pradyumna be there? Well, we'll have to see. Will I be there? Well, we'll have to see. Prabhupāda said it can be an ISKCON in the spiritual world.

Someone may hear that and say, "Oh, no, an ISKCON! I don't want to go there. I'd rather go to hell than go to ISKCON."

No, Prabhupāda said there would be an ISKCON, but it would be a Vaikuṇṭha ISKCON, and devotees who are cent percent sincere will be able to go there. That means that ISKCON is Kṛṣṇaloka, is Vṛndāvana, with its cowherd boys and *gopīs*. That's the essence of ISKCON.

43

SDG singing and clapping:

hare kṛṣṇa hare kṛṣṇa, kṛṣṇa kṛṣṇa hare hare
hare rāma hare rāma, rāma rāma hare hare

Can a radio show be done at a P-stop in Austria while you're walking and the sun is coming up and there's two big, new jet trails as fresh as fresh baked bread? The sky is such a beautiful, whitish-gray today. Let's talk for awhile.

Any more *saṅkīrtana* stories?

What about the man who pulled into a P-stop in Austria of all places? He was driving a double trailer and he was traveling between Italy and Germany. He climbed out of his truck to urinate. Parked in front of his truck were two devotees in their van. They were on their way to join a traveling *saṅkīrtana* party in Eastern Europe. Their spiritual master was strong on book distribution, so they liked to take every opportunity to distribute books. They were both Italians, and in fact, one of them had recently gone into the Fascist headquarters.

As you may know, the Italian government is currently a right-wing coalition, which includes the radical Fascist party. They're somewhat respectable now. Anyway, this devotee went to their headquarters. The secretary received him pleasantly enough and he convinced her to buy a book for the equivalent of $40.

Then he asked if he could see the big man there.

"Oh, he's very busy."

"*Please* let me see him," he cajoled, and finally she let him in.

As soon as he saw him, the big man said, "Oh, Hare Kṛṣṇa," and he also took a book and gave a donation.

Now these devotees were quite spirited and ready to go anywhere. This incident had convinced them to not make distinctions based on a person's politics. Everyone can receive Kṛṣṇa's mercy.

Back to our trucker. The two devotees waited for him to finish and then they ran up to him and said, "Dear sir, please take this book." Of course, he didn't speak Italian and they spoke only broken German, but he understood enough to reach into his jeans pocket and take out a little money. One of the devotees ran back to the van and rummaged around until he found a German book.

As soon as the trucker touched the book, he broke spontaneously into song: "O my homeland, my homeland, green mountains and lakes, the dawn full of bird song and clouds filled with sunshine. This homeland of ours comes from the heart of God, who is the God of all gods and all lands. Our homeland is not here but in the kingdom of God, but from here we yearn and see God in our land." The devotees were impressed. Not knowing exactly what to say, they asked, "Would you like to hear our song?" Then they sang, *"Cintāmaṇi-prakara-sad-masu kalpa-vṛkṣa-, lakṣāvṛteṣu surabhīr abhipālayantam/ lakṣmī-sahasra-śata-sambhrama-sevyamānaṁ, govindam . . . "*

"That's a strange song. What's it about?"

"It's about our homeland. Just as your song tells of the kingdom of God, our song says that too, but it also describes the nature of the spiritual world. Whatever we see here is a reflection of the spiritual world. In God's kingdom, the ground is not made of pebbles set in tarmac, or even green grass like we have here, which unfortunately is growing on acid rain and is filled with condoms and candy wrappers. The ground in the spiritual world is made of gems. The grass is so beautiful that we can't even understand it. Everything about the spiritual world is inconceivable. The cows there give endless sweet milk that doesn't give you cholesterol, and they are never killed. Also, the Lord is served by many cowherd girls."

When they mentioned the cows, they realized that they had struck a nerve. This guy was carting cows.

"We're having such a nice exchange here, and yet you're about to commit a dastardly crime by helping to kill all these cows. Why do you do it?"

"Well, I don't like to do it, but I have to."

The meeting was getting quite sticky. How could the devotees propose that he not deliver the cows? And what if he agreed? He couldn't just let the cows loose and they would all live happily ever after, could he? Where would they all go? It's becoming too fantastic, isn't it?

Anyway, let's pretend the fantastic happens and he agrees to release the cows. The devotees actually talk him into changing directions and driving the cows to the Polish farm, New Śāntipura. They assure him he can deal with the legal repercussions later.

"I can't steal these cows! I'm not a thief. Okay, after this shipment, I'll quit. I can't change the whole world, but I'll change myself. But I can't just steal these cows. They're not mine!"

They talked back and forth while the sun rose brilliantly like a big pat of butter melting in a frying pan. The air was still cool, and this rough trucker's heart had somehow been changed so that he was actually considering the reckless path the devotees suggested. He jumped into his truck and started down the road.

What was he doing? After a mile, he pulled over and told them he had changed his mind. "I can't do it. I'll get in too much trouble. I have a family to take care of. They'll put me in jail. But what I will do is quit this business after this shipment. Then I'll move to your farm and help with the cows you have there."

A few weeks later this fellow and his family actually showed up at the farm. He's still there taking care of the cows.

SDG singing and clapping:

hare kṛṣṇa hare kṛṣṇa, kṛṣṇa kṛṣṇa hare hare
hare rāma hare rāma, rāma rāma hare hare

I stopped writing my travelogue. I don't know why. I don't want to say it was too external, but I wanted to get back to the more elemental writing I do in the writing sessions.

The sun is just coming up. Madhu is cooking what I call a "formula" breakfast—measured out to the ounce so we have no leftovers. I see a hawk hovering overhead. Our van looks all right. There's a sign here that says "Die Donau." I don't know what it means because I don't read German, but it reminds me that we have to die to the material world and live in Kṛṣṇa consciousness. Hare Kṛṣṇa Hare Kṛṣṇa, Kṛṣṇa Kṛṣṇa Hare Hare/ Hare Rāma Hare Rāma, Rāma Rāma Hare Hare.

It's so nice to be able to chant Hare Kṛṣṇa. I hope once we get going I won't get too sleepy. I've chanted seven rounds so far, so I have a lot to go. We should be at the Czech border in less than an hour, and hopefully we'll get over all right. In any case, chant and chant.

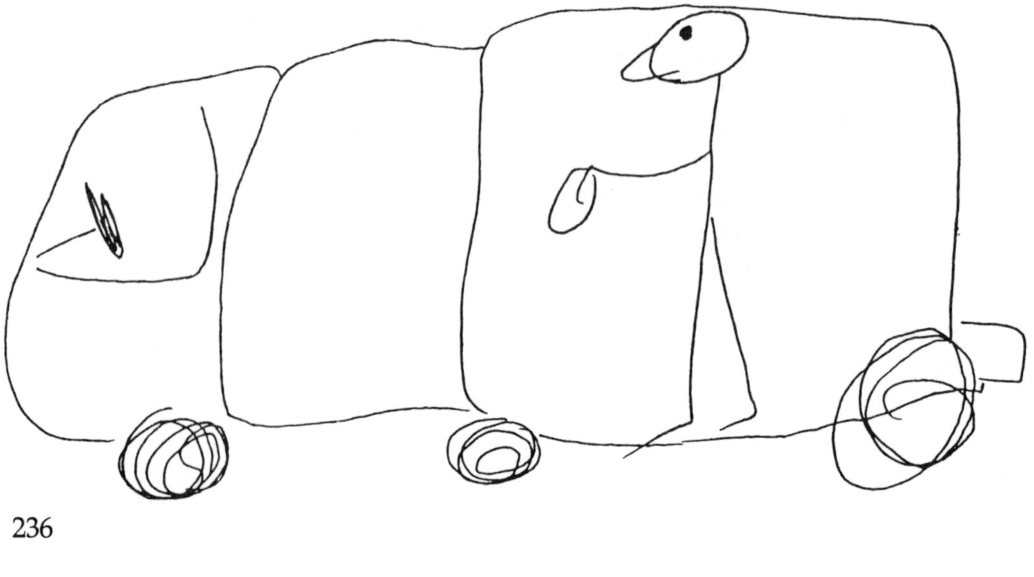

We were stopped at the Austrian border yesterday. We weren't expecting any problems, but we were still delayed. I had the beginnings of a headache. Madhu put his earphones on and I began to chant. I felt my reserve of patience was being called on. It's funny how when your reserves are called on, you feel like there's plenty of reserve left.

I remember feeling that once when I lived in Staten Island. I was in the Great Kills train station, and I think I was running down the stairs to catch the train. This feeling about my inner reserves came up. I don't think I was at any crisis point in my life, but I just felt the depth of my patience and endurance and knew that I had enough to get me through. It's like being informed offhand that you have a lot of money in the bank. What do you do but take stock of that information and go on with your life?

It's good to subject yourself to conditions which remind you of death, like being lost or in pain. They make you strong. I remember Dr. Sarma telling me that I should learn to endure chilliness. It's good for the body—better than always insulating yourself and staying indoors.

Travel does that to you. It's a little bit like being lost when you are always moving among strangers, even in the ISKCON temples. The insecurity I feel helps me to depend more on Kṛṣṇa.

Last night I woke up a few times and wondered where I was. "Oh yeah, I'm at a P-stop." I heard the traffic and I imagined some rough Austrian neo-Nazis breaking into the van and stealing from us. It could happen, you know. I chanted fervently when I thought about it: Hare Kṛṣṇa Hare Kṛṣṇa, Kṛṣṇa Kṛṣṇa Hare Hare/ Hare Rāma Hare Rāma, Rāma Rāma Hare Hare. That rush, that flow of chanting when you really mean it, came to me for a while. That's the kind of thing I'll be able to call on later.

It's time to go now. Madhu is almost ready to serve breakfast. He likes to have breakfast on time, so I have to be back at the van on time. Please accept this radio show. It's been done by a cellular, cryptographic air message and delivered through the ether. Today's broadcasting studio was in the midst of jet trails and sunshine, and the message was carried through telephone poles and the roots of trees and the tips of grasses. The *autobahn* police monitored it, couldn't make it out, and allowed it to go through. It's available to you wherever you are—in your car, your home, even if you are sitting between two rocks broadcasting in your own studio of familiar places. Hare Kṛṣṇa.

44

SDG singing and clapping:

hare kṛṣṇa hare kṛṣṇa, kṛṣṇa kṛṣṇa hare hare
hare rāma hare rāma, rāma rāma hare hare

Today's show is being broadcast overlooking the sharp valleys and hills of Poland on a cold June day. So many wild flowers—the stalks and puffballs of gone dandelions, bright yellow buttercups, all kinds of wild cabbage and flowering things that I don't know the names of. On our way up here, we saw quite a few varieties of milkweed too. Such a wonderful place, not just because it's so beautiful, but because there's a devotee community here.

I haven't gone around to see the agriculture and cows yet—we just arrived last night—but I met with the devotees. They held a reception for me, as they do for every senior devotee who visits here. I thanked them and told them that actually, the ceremony of washing the feet means the *sādhu's* feet are dirty from walking on the road. My feet weren't dirty because we drove here in our van, but I felt cleansed by the ceremony from having witnessed all the licentious advertisements while traveling, after being stopped by four different borders, traveling through cities and past factories—I was sufficiently covered with road dirt that their ceremony sanctified me.

Most of the devotees here are young—a new generation. They're still fresh and enthusiastic. Of course, I don't want to be cynical and say that we were all like this when we were young. They'll get cynical too when they're older. But maybe they won't, especially if they learn from the previous generation's mistakes. Isn't that the best way to benefit from mistakes, that others can see them and try not to commit them themselves? I hope so.

We just gathered and sang before their large brass Pañca-tattva deities. We worshipped Lord Kṛṣṇa the way Lord Caitanya wants us to worship Him, by chanting the holy names. We sang the *tulasī* songs around a healthy, green *tulasī* plant, then one devotee recited and we each responded to the *"Śikṣāṣṭakam."* Soon, I'll be giving the *Bhāgavatam* class. They're discussing Nārada Muni's teachings about dreams at the end of the chapter about King Bhariṣat.

Aside from dreams, the topic of the class is how transmigration is brought about by the shape of the mind and its desires. We should be urgent in our Kṛṣṇa conscious practices. If we don't focus our minds on Kṛṣṇa, then they will be focused on things that bind us to the material world. Better we repeat the *mahā-mantra* than repeat the experience of *saṁsāra.*

SDG singing and clapping:

> *hare kṛṣṇa hare kṛṣṇa, kṛṣṇa kṛṣṇa hare hare*
> *hare rāma hare rāma, rāma rāma hare hare*

O Kṛṣṇa, O Kṛṣṇa O Kṛṣṇa, O Rādhā O Rādhā, O Rādhā, O Kṛṣṇa O Kṛṣṇa O Kṛṣṇa. They are dancing with Their arms upraised—Lord Caitanya, Nityānanda, and Gadādhara. Those three. Advaita and Śrīvāsa have their palms folded in prayer.

I'm really quite tired. It was a cold night and I didn't sleep well. Perhaps I should only do a short show. I remember when I was growing up, there was a fifteen-minute radio show called "Vivaldi Revival." The announcer was super-enthusiastic about Vivaldi's music. He used the word "super" a lot, even before it became popular. Everything was super-excellent. Vivaldi, of course, is a high-spirited composer. I still remember all those violins playing in unison in the orchestra. This announcer was obviously cultured, but he had all the zeal of a sportscaster. "This is a great piece!" Everything was "great" and "super," and he "loved" Vivaldi. It was infectious, even though it only lasted fifteen minutes.

I don't have so much enthusiasm today, but maybe I can get myself going for another fifteen minutes.

SDG sings Vivaldi

I think that's from Vivaldi's "The Four Seasons." How I love four seasons. I always say that to people and it's true. I do love them, especially when I'm in some part of the world and I can see the distinctions between them. But it looks like my days are over, at least for now, and I'm glad they are, of staying in one place all year round. The joy of carefully observing the gradual changes of the seasons and weather and plant life and birds and sky has to be given up with that, though. You can't watch it so sensitively when you're always traveling, sometimes in the tropics, sometimes in Europe, sometimes in America. You lose the sense of time and natural movement.

The nice thing you gain from travel is that you realize you don't only belong to one family, but to the whole ISKCON family, and not just impersonally, but intimately. In my case, travel means the freedom to stop and go at my own pace, and time to write my scratchy, sketchy, playful, personal, *paramparā* writing sessions, which are part of the larger work of my whole life. The rest of the time I spend lecturing and reading. It's a good life. I wouldn't trade it to be in charge of any zone or even nestled in any secret hideaway in the country (although that is tempting too). As long as our brakes hold out and the engine turns over, the chassis is in place and the driver keeps driving, I'll keep moving.

I'll end this show here. Hare Kṛṣṇa.

45

SDG singing and clapping:

> *hare kṛṣṇa hare kṛṣṇa, kṛṣṇa kṛṣṇa hare hare*
> *hare rāma hare rāma, rāma rāma hare hare*

Milkweeds, buttercups, dandelions, weeds whose names I don't know, hello. I see you stretching like a sea out the back window. I also see a stripped-bare telephone pole. It looks like any telephone pole you might see in Iowa or Anyplace, America, standing straight and tall. It's supported by a cable to make it stronger. Then it's been given its load of wires to carry, just like we are.

The wind—of course, you can't see it—but I see it moving through June leaves. It's mid-June, but cool up here in the Polish mountains.

I'm keeping that heater on because the noise it makes helps me feel more private. I'm sharing the van with Madhu. Although he'll hear the show later, I somehow have to speak it alone now. Every time I come here to do this show, I'm starting from scratch. I'm not playing the top twenty hit records and interspersing them with commercials. Nothing is cued on this show. As a matter of fact, my radio show isn't even charted.

It would be nice to tell some more fantastic *saṅkīrtana* stories, but you really have to be daring and carefree and playful, it seems, and more than that, not afraid of failure or embarrassed by the very nature of your imagination.

What's so embarrassing, you ask? It's embarrassing to say, "Here is my creativity. Here is my art," and then all you end up with is a little story. Nothing so unusual, nothing so fantastic really, but you put it forward in the world to stand beside the greatest stories ever told.

Let me try anyway.

Bhakta Joe, his wife, and five of his friends left the farm to go into town. They were going to hold a parade and a puppet show.

"Oh, my heart is breaking," said Bhakta Joe. "I just can't do it again. I just don't have the enthusiasm."

"Well," said his wife, Bhaktin Agnes, "you'd better find the enthusiasm, and as your wife, I suppose I should supply it to you because we've come all this way. We've worked hard to collect money, people have donated for our van, and you've dragged us all out here. One of our friends built the cart and another one trained the oxen. Another got the dioramas together. The local mayor has given us permission and we've already cooked all the *prasādam*. How can you decide you can't even do it one more time now? What about your duty?"

"Oh, Mā," said Bhakta Joe, "that was a pretty good speech. I guess you're right."

Joe put aside his lackluster feelings and went down the mountain with his wife and friends and the van and the cart and the trained oxen. He knew it was true; until he got things going, nothing ever got going.

Everything went smoothly in town. The police were friendly and waiting as they hitched up the oxen and started on the parade. Bhaktin Agnes went in front, handing out *prasādam*, and they all chanted Hare Kṛṣṇa.

Then Joe felt his lack of enthusiasm again. The voice in his mind said, "I'm going to quit, I'm going to quit." It was becoming an ache and it filled him with a sense of defeat. He also recognized the honesty of the voice. Still, how could he respond to it? He had no choice but to keep going.

Gradually, the voice died down and then rose up again, coming and going in waves of strength and defeat. It was just something he was going to have to deal with today, just like someone else might be dealing with indigestion. He simply had to tolerate the waves of discontent. "The *Bhagavad-gītā* says we have to tolerate," he thought. "I can't always be operating under full enthusiasm."

Joe was seeing the day's events from a distance. Some curious teenagers approached him. People aren't so sophisticated in these countries, and they are still able to walk up to other people and ask questions. The kids were probably attracted by the oxen, but you can imagine how interesting it must have been for a Polish teenager to suddenly come face to face with Hare Kṛṣṇa devotees.

Joe showed them the dioramas and sold a few books, still fighting the waves of his loss of enthusiasm. He wondered if his spiritual master, who is a disciple of Prabhupāda, ever got these feelings. Maybe it was something he could ask him. But no, it probably wasn't proper to ask your spiritual master if he ever loses heart when he's doing his service.

Still, his spiritual master was a down-to-earth person. He seemed honest and open to questions. Maybe he could ask. His spiritual master just happened to be visiting the farm where Joe lived.

A few hours later, they wrapped up their program after having done the puppet show for the three hundred and third time. The crowd loved it, as they always did, especially the special effects. (They always flashed the lights and let out a puff of smoke when Rāma shoots

Rāvaṇa.) The other part the people always liked is when Hanumān fights the demons. Instead of a puppet doing the fighting, Joe himself popped up from under the stage wearing a rubber gorilla mask and big rubber claws. The crowd always liked that part and Joe always got a charge out of that. He liked to see the crowd happy. But today he thought, "I'm so far away from actual Kṛṣṇa consciousness with my rough-hewn ways."

By late afternoon, they started back up the hill. The going was difficult because of the weight of the paraphernalia and the oxen. The oxen were tolerant, making no comment, and for all we know, not feeling those waves of defeat that Joe was feeling.

When they reached the farm, one of his Godbrothers asked Bhakta Joe to please bring water to where his spiritual master was staying. Joe brought it, and although he knew his spiritual master didn't like impromptu talks of any depth or length—he liked to prepare himself for things—Joe sprung his problem on him in an indirect way.

His spiritual master asked him, "How did it go in town?"

"It went well, but sometimes I don't feel so enthusiastic, even though we're doing a good program. What is that, when we don't feel enthusiastic?"

"Lack of enthusiasm for our service may have different causes. Perhaps familiarity has bred contempt. Maybe it's a sign that something is wrong with our chanting or hearing or thinking in Kṛṣṇa consciousness. Of course, we can't wait to operate on the purest enthusiastic platform—we have to do our duty regardless—but if it keeps coming up, you'll have to examine it and do the needful so your *utsāha* doesn't fall apart. Everything depends on *utsāha.*"

Joe asked, "Do you ever feel that lack of enthusiasm?"

"Yes, sometimes. For example, there are some services that I like to do more than others. These things come and go like waves, but we tolerate them and just go on with faith that Kṛṣṇa will be pleased with us and award us steadier feelings. If He doesn't, then we keep tolerating it for Kṛṣṇa. It's just another austerity to prove we care, that we'll do our service no matter what, and that we're not serving because we want to feel bliss."

These words made sense to Joe. It made him feel good to know that his spiritual master understood this problem but was handling it in a better way than Joe had today. "It's something to tolerate."

Joe thanked his spiritual master-to-be for these words and went home a little more enthusiastic. He went to feed the oxen and to see how the devotees in his group were doing. He felt fresh attachment and camaraderie for the devotees who were traveling with him. Their banner read, "Padayātrā: March For Peace And Spiritual Enlightenment From Belfast To Moscow." Yes, it was a good thing to walk and to perform this service in so many places. Many people have said that they like it. "I shouldn't be ungrateful or Kṛṣṇa may take this service away."

Joe showered and went to *sundara-ārati.* He prayed before the Pañca-tattva deities, "Please give me a drop of enthusiasm to serve the holy names and let me never begrudge Kṛṣṇa conscious service. Let me serve You under any condition. But I'm sorry, Lord, that sometimes You have this sour puss for a servant of the servant. Please disregard me dragging my heels. It's just the way I walk. Actually, my heart is light and I do like to serve You. I wish to serve You always. Thank You."

His spiritual master then sat down on the *āsana* to give *Bhagavad-gītā* class. He glanced over at Bhakta Joe. He was glowing with an air of intensity borne out of his austerities on the road with his Padayātrā crew and his strong desire to do a very basic program of *harināma-saṅkīrtana.* His spiritual master admired Bhakta Joe. His answering Joe's question had strengthened his own resolve to go on with his own service of speaking from *Bhagavad-gītā* from such an unrealized position. They pushed on—everyone did—with mutual respect. Another day on *saṅkīrtana* over.

SDG singing and clapping:

> *hare kṛṣṇa hare kṛṣṇa, kṛṣṇa kṛṣṇa hare hare*
> *hare rāma hare rāma, rāma rāma hare hare*

A little kid comes down from his bedroom into the kitchen where his mother is sitting. Let's say that she's pulling strings out of the string beans. "What are you looking so happy about?" she asks.

"I just told another story."

"That's nice. It's nice that you have something creative to do that makes you happy."

"Yeah, it really makes you feel good when you tell them. And you know, it's for Kṛṣṇa. I'm doing them for Kṛṣṇa."

"Oh," his mother says, "you are so fortunate to be able to serve Kṛṣṇa. I wish I could serve Kṛṣṇa."

"Oh, you are serving Kṛṣṇa, Mom. Just by stringing those string beans that are going to be offered to Kṛṣṇa. You just have to realize it, and that's what makes it enlivening."

That's what makes it enlivening.

Yes, if we're feeling lackluster or queasy, we may have to talk about that. That's okay. Better that it's out in the open than that we live a hype of not-always-there enthusiasm. But don't forget the little boy who comes down from his room feeling happy. His happiness makes him restless, so he paces back and forth in front of his mother. That mother is *bhakti* and that boy is the spirit soul who is willing to serve and who has been used by the spiritual energy.

As to whether his story is "any good," i.e., has any literary value, that's a different thing. That's something for critics and people like that to mess around with. We're talking about devotional service. We're talking about serving Śrīla Prabhupāda from the heart without caring about the results, and about doing it again and again. We're talking about the inner nature of service and prayer and how it can manifest in somewhat unusual ways, like stories and scribblings and writing sessions. We're talking about that energy that never runs out because it's eternal and it's not false, and the happiness that comes from that. When we feel the spiritual energy, our guts make us push on, even when our minds hang back. And we thank Kṛṣṇa for the transformation . . .

46

SDG singing and clapping:

> *hare kṛṣṇa hare kṛṣṇa, kṛṣṇa kṛṣṇa hare hare*
> *hare rāma hare rāma, rāma rāma hare hare*

I'm in Prague, Czech Republic. I rarely visit here. Franz Kafka lived here. This is not an imaginary Prague where Franz Kafka is buried in a cemetery in the old part of the city, where the architecture is specific to Eastern Europe, and where the ghosts of past Nazi occupations and persecutions still hover. For me, Prague is the inside of this van, which we have parked on this quiet suburban street across the lawn from the rented house they call their temple. The house is unpainted and made from cement, but it's modern in the European style.

It's Pāṇḍava Ekādaśī today. Most of the devotees are out on *saṅkīrtana,* but they'll be back in a couple of hours, and then I will give a class. All the devotees here are young and they all religiously attend the ISKCON *guru-pūjā,* which occurs fifteen minutes before the Prabhupāda *pūjā.* The pictures of their gurus are all lined up and they chant to them, for sure they chant. That's what a visit to Prague is like for me. They look to me as an old Prabhupāda disciple and they listen to my classes. They are all respectful because they respect my Godbrothers and their surrender to Śrīla Prabhupāda's movement and books.

I have been thinking about being in the West. Why is it this year that I want to stay in the West and preach, and not become contaminated by the West, rather than go to Vṛndāvana? Preaching means reaching out to all the non-Vrajavāsīs. The actual Vrajavāsīs already know that Kṛṣṇa is everything. That's *all* they know. They already have their conceptions of Kṛṣṇa and there's not much that we can give to them. Therefore, to preach we have to go elsewhere.

ISKCON is Lord Caitanya's merciful movement to give people Kṛṣṇa consciousness. There are so many people joining our movement—very slowly—and we have to learn to increase it. I like to think that my attempts at experimental writing, and my attempt to also prepare myself and to practice honesty, are all in the context of being a devotee in the Western countries. I am not a Vrajavāsī. I'm a material product. I'm a spirit soul, of course, but I have to face my conditioning. My surrender to Kṛṣṇa involves this surrender, this overcoming of the modes of nature. That's part of my song of triumph.

Of course, I could overcome my conditioning in Vṛndāvana, but I can also do it in the West. There are two ISKCON sayings and both have their specific applications: "Wherever you are, that's Vṛndāvana," and, "You can take the boy out of New York, but you can't take New York out of the boy." If I'm in Vṛndāvana, I have no other way to express myself but through my New Yorkness. I try to see myself as pure spirit soul, as a disciple of Prabhupāda, and as a devotee of Kṛṣṇa, but it occurred to me that my present state is not exactly the spiritual world in Goloka, but neither is it the material world.

Hmm, let me try to say that better. It is the spiritual world, but the spiritual world as brought here in Prabhupāda's movement. We're part of this spiritual history, and that is our identity. This is who we are. It is our *siddha-svarūpa* to be humble devotees of Śrīla Prabhupāda and to try to please him by preaching.

I'm happy and satisfied to roam around in the van, do radio shows, write, and yes, lecture in the temples. I know I don't do so much, but at least I do something and I'm grateful.

SDG singing and clapping:

hare kṛṣṇa hare kṛṣṇa, kṛṣṇa kṛṣṇa hare hare
hare rāma hare rāma, rāma rāma hare hare

It's 5:20. At 6:30 I have to give the lecture. Tonight we'll cover *Bhagavad-gītā* 14.21. I have everything prepared for it. If anything, I'm too prepared and not prepared enough to surrender or to give them my realization. Still, I have some good quotes, quotes that I care about. It's a Bhaktivedanta Swami Prabhupāda students' class and I'm a scholar of what he says. It will be beneficial for those who hear and I'll be grateful to be able to speak.

What about prayer? "My dear Lord Kṛṣṇa, although I cannot pray to You directly, I wish You to not be so far away. I don't want to have to fight to get to You. But if I do have to fight because of my Western conditioning, then give me the strength to wield the weapon and do it well."

My dear Lord Kṛṣṇa, I want to be aware that You are the real person. You are everywhere and everything. You're so great and powerful, and yet You're my friend. I want to understand You in Śrīla Prabhupāda's unique expressions in his books. That means reading the books and not concocting who You are. Kṛṣṇa, You say that when You appear, all imaginative iconography is defeated. Just as in a court of law, if some witness is missing, people may speculate, "Where is he? Is he alive?" But if he comes into the court, their speculation is finished. Imaginative iconography is defeated by the actual appearance of the Lord.

I like Prabhupāda's language in giving us the *Śrīmad-Bhāgavatam* purports. I want to stay tuned to them. In short, I want Kṛṣṇa to be my friend. Kṛṣṇa *is* my friend, but I want to know Him as real and true. Why can't He be like that for me? That's what I ask, that's what I pray. And if that means less eating, mating, sleeping, and defending, or less self-absorption, or whatever, then I pray to Kṛṣṇa to direct me to whatever is necessary so that He is more centered in my life. That is my prayer.

SDG singing and clapping:

> *hare kṛṣṇa hare kṛṣṇa, kṛṣṇa kṛṣṇa hare hare*
> *hare rāma hare rāma, rāma rāma hare hare*

I have a dozen burners going on my stove. Of course, it's not my stove, it's Kṛṣṇa's stove. He gave it to me to use in His service. There are so many projects in the pots now and I'm grateful that there are. Would you like to hear about some of them?

Seminar with disciples, radio show, reading Prabhupāda's books, hearing his tapes, walks, prayer, and especially these writing projects —writing sessions, stories, poems, book-type projects, then things I have already done that are just being published. I look forward to all these maturing and developing. That's my service.

I have written in another place, but it's worth stating it here too, that Prabhupāda defines liberation and describes the preacher as a liberated person. I am drawn to his statement because I see it as something I can use to prove to myself that my kind of writing and trying to find breakthrough genres and honest forms of writing are actually a preacher's meditation. If I practice them completely, they are a kind of liberation. Here's the statement:

"A devotee doesn't care whether he's going to be reborn or not. He's simply satisfied with the Lord's service in any condition. That is real *mukti. Īhā yasya harer dāsye,* a person who always desires to serve Kṛṣṇa is interested in ways to convince people that there is a Supreme Personality of Godhead and that the Supreme Personality of Godhead is Kṛṣṇa. That is his ambition. It doesn't matter whether he's in heaven or hell. This is called *uttamaśloka-lālasaḥ" (Bhāg.* 5.14.43). Especially this sentence: "He is interested in ways to convince people that there is a Supreme Personality of Godhead." He's so absorbed in this that that's more important to him than going back to Godhead.

I think like that, that I have to write better, do more writing sessions, even if when I first write, I have to write through my infatuation with words and the self and whatever dirty things come out. I keep going and hope that the result will be useful in preaching. People will read it in one form or another and they're going to appreciate that it's real and helpful to them in Kṛṣṇa consciousness. If I can meditate like that—how to bring people to Kṛṣṇa . . .

You may say, "How is your writing about yourself going to bring them to Kṛṣṇa? This is just going to bring them to you and your problems." I don't agree. I'm improving the writing and Kṛṣṇa will help me. It's striving. It's a devotee's life. I'm just writing what Prabhupāda has given us and my attempt to practice it. I have that confidence that the more I work at this writing service and this life, the more I'll be able to remain in a liberated mentality. How exactly it comes out, how it gets polished, how it gets prepared, how many people it reaches—I can't worry about all that. I just have to make the sincere effort and not be concerned. I know the connection has to be there between self-expression and Kṛṣṇa consciousness. I'm not looking for Natalie Goldberg's writing heaven. The connection has to be there that this writing is for preaching.

SDG singing and clapping:

hare kṛṣṇa hare kṛṣṇa, kṛṣṇa kṛṣṇa hare hare
hare rāma hare rāma, rāma rāma hare hare

Now I have done a radio show in Prague. It didn't have weathered gargoyles in it, or Franz Kafka's tortured genius and his thwarted, sex-starved, searing honesty. It didn't even have that Prague of old buses and trolley cars and black smoke and clouds and cold weather and dirty buildings and Communist commissars and queues to get food and boots and metal and America-in-the-'50s rock 'n' roll. It didn't mention that people here smoke American cigarettes and walk down cobblestone streets, or that the opera house has classical gilded figures out front, or that people tend to gather around the outdoor fountains. They look like they're straight out of the 1950s and '60s and I love them for that. It looks so much nicer than the modern American look. Not that Prague, but the Prague of this suburb and house where the devotees put flowers on the steps leading into the temple and where the inside is full of shoes and the language is strange. But you know it's ISKCON. Devotees give you garlands and you sit down and chant, "*Nama oṁ . . .*" They know all the tunes and all the words and how to play the *karatālas* to the one-two-three beat. They pray to their Deities, Nimāi-Navadvīpa-candra, in the Czech language, that the Lord should help them do *saṅkīrtana.* They are really *saṅkīrtana*-conscious because this is a zone where that's emphasized. I'm taking advantage of it, getting in there and speaking. I'm in this Prague where I am accepted and where I am going to speak again tonight. This is where I spoke this radio show.

I expressed that I want to pray to Kṛṣṇa and that I'm grateful for the writing ability He's given me. I told you how I have a dozen burners on my stove. Even if it gets hot in the kitchen, I'll stay in there and beg Kṛṣṇa to give me time to write in that liberated state where I care about giving people Kṛṣṇa consciousness. I want to be attracted to Kṛṣṇa myself—to Kṛṣṇa, Kṛṣṇa, in madness, so I can chant Hare Kṛṣṇa in the morning.

We've been in this Prague only a day. Tomorrow we leave. We're going back to the Czech farm. I like to drive there in the morning just as the sun is rising. It reminds me of going from Calcutta to Māyāpur and stopping in the mango grove. When we get to the farm, we'll park the van, get the books in order, find out what verse they are on in the *Bhāgavatam* class, and prepare a lecture.

47

SDG singing and clapping:

> *hare kṛṣṇa hare kṛṣṇa, kṛṣṇa kṛṣṇa hare hare*
> *hare rāma hare rāma, rāma rāma hare hare*

Haribol. I haven't done a radio show in quite awhile, since Prague, over a week ago. Since this show is being broadcast from a different place, let me start by telling you where we are.

I'm broadcasting from the back of the van as usual, so in that sense, it's the same place with the yellow curtains I can barely see through and the blond, varnished, wooden desk and the wall of the van with its laminated pictures. I still have that picture of Prabhupāda sitting on his rocking chair with one shoe off and his bare foot pointing. Then *paramparā* pictures—Pañca-tattva, Rādhā-Śyāmasundara. Looking up, I have Prabhupāda's books to the right, and his tapes. Behind me, my bunk. This world is the same.

But we're in Switzerland at a P-stop. When I say P-stop, that means parking. You see the big P signs on the highway. They usually come up within five hundred meters after that. They're the most transient places. People often stop for no more than thirty seconds, although sometimes they stay longer. We usually stay overnight in them, which few people do. It's not recommended.

But right now, two big tour buses have stopped, so there's quite a commotion as the senior citizens get out to use the bathroom and stretch their legs. This particular P-stop is a little better than most we've been in. There's a telephone here and a little lake with ducks swimming in it.

Anyway, the people are spread out all over the grounds. When we first arrived, no one was here at all. Madhu has been driving all day, except when we took a lunch break. It's now 5:55 P.M. That means he drove for almost twelve hours straight. He was looking forward to winding down by the lake and chanting *japa.* I didn't trust the solitude down there. It looked too quiet to last for long. Within minutes of his going down to the water, these maxi-buses arrived and Madhu's solitude by the lake was shattered.

We're on our way to France. Of course, I'm reporting all this in my travel diary.

SDG singing and clapping:

hare kṛṣṇa hare kṛṣṇa, kṛṣṇa kṛṣṇa hare hare
hare rāma hare rāma, rāma rāma hare hare

Did you ever share a really small space with a few flies? Why do they prefer to land on any exposed skin they can find? It tickles and it's hard to tolerate. These little living entities, little spirit souls, are bothersome. Prabhupāda used to marvel at how nature constructed them (and God behind nature with His *acintya-śakti*). They are pilots of their own body-planes. They do have *śakti*, that's for sure—the way they land on your body and you can't catch them in your hands. You can't scare them away either. No matter how many times you chase them, they keep returning to torment you. They can disrupt a peaceful situation.

I could, of course, murder them. I could just get in a passion and swat them with a big cloth. Sometimes I tell them to watch out, but of course, they don't understand. They're brave in their primitive, low consciousness. I tried opening the back of the van to shoo them out, at the risk, of course, of letting other flies in. I got one out, but the others are still here. I know when I take rest in an hour or two they will torment me and make it hard to sleep.

Sorry to be talking about flies. Let's see if I can elevate the situation.

The best thing I did today was read in Hari Śauri's *Transcendental Diary* while we drove. That was certainly nice, and I hope to read more of it tonight. I'm reading about Prabhupāda's arrival in Māyāpur in 1976. It's full of philosophy and Prabhupāda's presence and demanding ways. He demands of himself and he demands our surrender to Kṛṣṇa. You can't be lackadaisical while reading it. You have to keep asking yourself, "How am I doing? How am I going to serve Kṛṣṇa?" In that sense, it's demanding, but it's a little bit lighter reading on a day like today when it's harder to read *Śrīmad-Bhāgavatam.* It's a nice companion to have.

SDG singing and clapping:

hare kṛṣṇa hare kṛṣṇa, kṛṣṇa kṛṣṇa hare hare
hare rāma hare rāma, rāma rāma hare hare

I read some good things in Hari Śauri Prabhu's book. One was Prabhupāda's defense of the name "Rādhā-Pārtha-sarathi." Then he was in Māyāpur, walking around. He saw the six rooms of weavers. He said some envious people might criticize, "Oh, this is temple and they are weaving? They are not worshipping? Yet others may accuse us of being parasites. But in *Bhagavad-gītā* Kṛṣṇa says *sva-karmaṇā tam abhyarcya, siddhiṁ vindati mānavaḥ.* Whatever a person knows, he can work in that way and get perfection, provided he is Kṛṣṇa conscious. Because they are preparing the cloth for the devotees and not for business, they are therefore serving Kṛṣṇa."

I also read that peas are a non-Ekādaśī food and shouldn't be served on Ekādaśī. Prabhupāda said when he heard that Yamunā dāsī was living apart—at least he wrote to her—that they should live humbly, not attempt to start any large program. "In *bhakti* there is no grotesque program. A humble program is better. We are doing all these grotesque programs to allure the masses. My Guru Mahārāja used to say that no one hears from a person coming from a humble, simple life. You remain always very humble."

Both things are there: the preacher has to do something bombastic to attract people, and he has to remain humble. The big program is for preaching, but it is not a necessary ingredient of Kṛṣṇa consciousness. I underlined that.

Then he spoke about *vaidhi-bhakti.* Tuṣṭa Kṛṣṇa wrote him with some implied criticism of ISKCON's pressure to do book distribution. Prabhupāda said, "So far devotees being hesitant to distribute books on a kind of pressure, sometimes pressure is required, especially when one is not so advanced. Of course, it has to be applied properly. Otherwise, there may be some bad taste. But spontaneous service can only be expected from advanced devotees. It is *vaidhi-bhakti. Vaidhi* means must. Sometimes devotees are promised a plate of *mahā-prasādam* for the biggest distributor. Actually, one should try to serve Kṛṣṇa to his or her full capacity without thought of reward. Service itself is the reward. But this takes time to actually realize, and until that platform is achieved, some pressure or inducement is required."

I wrote that down, I guess, for both reasons: to remind myself that pressure is not always a negative thing, and to show that Prabhupāda acknowledged that his devotees could also operate in the spirit of accepting their own service as their reward. I'm doing what I want to do, not what someone is pressuring me to do. Hṛdayānanda Mahārāja is also doing what he wants to do, but what he wants to do is glorious. He wants to become a recognized Sanskrit scholar, to glorify Prabhupāda's *Bhāgavatam* as the best translation, and to make so many points for the *bhakti* point camp. I want to do something like that too. Neither of us are doing it because we are being forced.

Prabhupāda also says that there's jealousy in the world, and disagreement and misunderstanding . . .

SDG singing and clapping:

> *hare kṛṣṇa hare kṛṣṇa, kṛṣṇa kṛṣṇa hare hare*
> *hare rāma hare rāma, rāma rāma hare hare*

48

SDG singing and clapping:

hare kṛṣṇa hare kṛṣṇa, kṛṣṇa kṛṣṇa hare hare
hare rāma hare rāma, rāma rāma hare hare

I'm sitting in the dark where I can't see the big Disney poster showing the birth of Bambi on the wall. I've seen it before, so I can still picture it in my mind. We're taking a break from our travels on our way to New Māyāpur, and we have rented a lodge for a few days.

That poster is such a sentimental scene. Bambi is born in the melting snow of spring with all the cuddly little animals in attendance, as if it were the birth of the Messiah in the manger. All over the poster, the Disney cartoonist has painted big drops of sparkling light. It catches the effect of melting snow, but it's also meant to give a supernatural aura to the moment. What nonsense.

Coincidentally, I have just been reading about Bharata Mahārāja and his affection for a fawn. Prabhupāda gives stern warnings that we should never think we are so advanced that we can abandon the rules and regulations.

As I said, I'm sitting in the dark. I have closed all the shutters and turned off the light to discourage the mosquitoes. A few drops of sunlight are squeezing through the closed shutters. It's almost 5:30 P.M., but the sun is still quite strong.

Dear Lord Kṛṣṇa, thank You for letting me write today, and thank You for letting me be peaceful. I don't want to get dissuaded from my spiritual practices like Mahārāja Bharata was swayed from his. My dear Lord Kṛṣṇa, please protect me. If such an advanced devotee as Mahārāja Bharata could fall into an animal body, then what about me? Mahārāja Bharata was experiencing *sāttvika-bhāva* and had achieved complete spiritual identification as the servant of the Supreme Lord. Still, he came down to affection for a beast. That can happen to me too. Therefore, I pray for Your protection.

SDG singing and clapping:

hare kṛṣṇa hare kṛṣṇa, kṛṣṇa kṛṣṇa hare hare
hare rāma hare rāma, rāma rāma hare hare

I'm sorry that I don't have the Prabhupāda *mūrti* anymore. I miss him. Prabhupāda told the four of us when we took *sannyāsa* that Lord Caitanya didn't travel with a Deity. He always had His beads and His *daṇḍa.* Chanting the holy name is the real worship. Still, it was nice having Prabhupāda with me in the *mūrti.*

This room is bigger than I am accustomed to after living in the van for so long. I have made a nice altar here. It's nice to be able to walk around the altar when I chant. I'm taking advantage of the early morning coolness to chant as well as I can. I can't say I am really concentrating, but I like to chant and I look forward to doing it again tomorrow morning. I usually light votive candles on the altar and that keeps the Pañca-tattva and Prabhupāda on the edge of my consciousness.

Prabhupāda said it's not enough to go alone to a secluded place; one should distribute the chanting. I'm trying to do that, if only I could chant better myself.

I already listed all my woes in *Begging For the Nectar of the Holy Name.* One devotee said that that book was tough to read. She said it contained unremitting self-criticism. Then she said, "I was glad that you seemed to improve near the end and I also picked up my spirits in reading it." It would be nice to write a triumphant book, but maybe the real triumph is to always be honest and to never give up.

I certainly don't want to abandon the rules and regulations. It will also be a triumph if I can always stay in the ISKCON "forest." Where will I go in the end? Back to Godhead? Somewhere in this world? As long as it's with devotees. Hare Kṛṣṇa Hare Kṛṣṇa, Kṛṣṇa Kṛṣṇa Hare Hare/ Hare Rāma Hare Rāma, Rāma Rāma Hare Hare.

SDG singing and clapping:

hare kṛṣṇa hare kṛṣṇa, kṛṣṇa kṛṣṇa hare hare
hare rāma hare rāma, rāma rāma hare hare

I'm stopped up right now.

Boy, this radio show is supposed to be a place where I don't get stopped. What's the problem? I am unworthy.

If I rap about a Hare Kṛṣṇa community, that's bad business. I remember Śubhānanda writing an essay while he was a devotee, telling about our activities. He described the devotees chanting japa in the morning. He described what it would sound like to an outsider—all these different voices chanting. He said some of them gobble like turkeys, and then he used other words—squawk and burble. The *japa* sessions are a strange cacophony of sounds. In a kind of droll yet sympathetic way, he clued the outsider in to what a big *japa* session is like in a Hare Kṛṣṇa temple. Even the devotees found it humorous. I liked it at the time, but it wasn't long afterward that Śubhānanda again became Steve Gelberg, lover of Emerson, Whitman, and loose girls. Then he again wanted to be a writer and decided to write of his exit from the Hare Kṛṣṇa movement.

You'd better be careful with your waggish tongue and don't tease the devotees. Better that you tease yourself if you're in the mood to tease.

Okay, you shut my mouth. I can't play a trumpet, I can't play a saxophone, I can't play a violin because the strings are made of cat gut, I can't eat voraciously, I can't eat chocolate, so what can I do?

You can give up this body and the bodily concerns.

Oh, the powerful mind. I say that not in worship, but in recognition of this raging back and forth, *tyāga-bhoga*-muscled instrument which can be your best friend or your worst enemy. Lord Ṛṣabhadeva was so aware of the dangerous tendencies of the mind that he never trusted it. The question was asked why he didn't use his mind for *yoga-siddhis.* The answer is given that he didn't trust the mind. He thought if anything wonderful could come from his activities, it would be because Kṛṣṇa made it happen. It's better, he said, to always engage the mind in Kṛṣṇa's service.

Of course, Prabhupāda wants us to be safely ensconced in Kṛṣṇa consciousness, but at the same time to take risks and to be daring. We have to learn how to do that. He said that a *sannyāsī* could wear Western clothes to preach. He knew that his devotees were traveling and sleeping in vans and meeting nondevotees all day, which meant women too, in order to sell his books. He knew his devotees were straining to collect money to pay mortgages. He himself had accepted all kinds of unusual situations in order to preach, especially in the early days in New York City. But Kṛṣṇa always protected him and will always protect the devotees.

However, you have to have good concentration. You can't only pretend you are preaching while internally you are enjoying the "unusual situations." Bharata Mahārāja was feigning meditation near the end. Inside, he was really thinking about the deer. "Alas, the small deer, while playing with me and seeing me feigning meditation with closed eyes, would circumambulate me due to anger arising from love, and it would fearfully touch me with the points of its soft horns, which felt like drops of water" *(Bhāg.* 5.8.21). Instead of meditating on Vāsudeva, he was meditating on a deer.

Worship is useless if it is only the outer form of worship. Real Kṛṣṇa consciousness can't be feigned. That's what's so unfortunate about our chanting—we're only chanting the outer form of the holy name. We can pray, "Kṛṣṇa, please, please, *please*, let me chant. I don't like to chant, but I want to chant. I want to like to chant. I want to be encapsulated in the chanting, to take to it wholeheartedly like the pilgrim who searched out and found perpetual prayer."

A great prayer, even if I don't make it enough. Sometimes I try gadgets to help me increase my chanting—a stopwatch to time the first sixteen, to stand on my head, to light three candles, whatever it takes.

But none of the gadgets work forever. It didn't work for long when I used to hold a mirror up in front of my mouth and watch that I was saying all the words. The gadgets work for a while. We're always trying something.

So folks, I'm talking to you out there. You also have to improve. When I talk to myself, when I talk about myself, it's not just some solipsism. It's for you too. You ought to, I ought to, we all ought to improve our chanting. Then we'll see those sparkling, melting snow drops that Disney tries to paint, only we'll see the real thing. We'll see the sparkle in Kṛṣṇa's eye.

What do you mean, see the sparkle in Kṛṣṇa's eye?

See the sparkle at Kṛṣṇa's lotus feet then? Okay, maybe I shouldn't have said it. Maybe it was extravagant. But you know what I mean. Instead of seeing a Disney painting heralding the birth of Bambi, we'll see the sparkle of a world pervaded by sweetness and spiritual bliss. Because a devotee is happy. How is he happy? By chanting. *Evaṁ prasanna-manaso, bhagavad-bhakti-yogataḥ.* Yes, he's always happy because he chants Hare Kṛṣṇa. We'll feel some of that, and we'll feel some regret that we don't chant well. Now we just grind, grind, grind, like grinding wheat into flour. Grind, grind, grind, Hare Kṛṣṇa Hare Kṛṣṇa.

SDG singing and clapping:

> *hare kṛṣṇa hare kṛṣṇa, kṛṣṇa kṛṣṇa hare hare*
> *hare rāma hare rāma, rāma rāma hare hare*

Ladies and gentlemen, the remaining part of this radio show will be broadcast by a satellite located a few miles north of Boston and which is connected with the CNN radio broadcasting system. In case you don't know it, in former times there were more sophisticated methods of communication available. Sañjaya could see by mental "television" what was taking place on the distant Battlefield of Kurukṣetra.

There are possibilities for this radio show too. We're trying to broadcast heart to heart. All kinds of connections can take place when we're working on the heart level. My voice is not ordinary, either, because it is enriched with Kṛṣṇa consciousness.

One day on a morning walk, Prabhupāda was talking about Kṛṣṇa. Hṛdayānanda Mahārāja said, "Prabhupāda, it's so nice to hear you talk about Kṛṣṇa." There was a pause and Prabhupāda said, "Kṛṣṇa is nice whether I talk about Him or you talk about Him. Whether you take a sweet from my hand or someone else's hand, it's a sweet."

The sound vibration spoken and heard on Kṛṣṇa conscious topics can purify the person and the place and we should have faith in it. Moreover, we should make sure that our sound vibration is not *prajalpa*.

Did you know that Prabhupāda named the Deities Rādhā-Pārthasarathi and that one of his devotees asked, "Prabhupāda, how can these two names be together?"

Prabhupāda said, "Oh, on the Battlefield of Kurukṣetra, does that mean that Rādhā is out of Kṛṣṇa? *Hlādinī-śakti* is always within. It is not always manifest."

49

SDG singing and clapping:

hare kṛṣṇa hare kṛṣṇa, kṛṣṇa kṛṣṇa hare hare
hare rāma hare rāma, rāma rāma hare hare

The red light is on, signaling that we're on the air. This is the radio show (I don't have to say it so loudly). We're in a dark, cool room in South France, keeping away from the heat, but still trying to reach out to people and tell them about Kṛṣṇa because without Kṛṣṇa, everything is hellish. That's the natural state of the material world where people are in such illusion that they're not aware of this.

That's why Prabhupāda said Kṛṣṇa consciousness isn't a religion, it's a science. It's the most important thing in human society. Once you speak of religion, there will be so many opinions. Some will say it's worthless, others will say it's good. But even those who believe in religion have many strange ideas as to what it means. Prabhupāda spoke about science. Even the word science is sometimes pejorative. This science is not just another department of life. Kṛṣṇa consciousness is the great necessity of life. It's the answer to why we are here and why we are suffering.

It should at least be investigated by people who want to make life sane for themselves and others and who want to combat all the problems of life. They should understand the main points Kṛṣṇa consciousness teaches and find the real nature of the self. People don't have time. They're so wrapped up in the externals of living.

Of course, it's not that people can just gather a few details about being spirit soul and then concoct the rest. It takes time and attention to the *śāstras* to learn how to become Kṛṣṇa conscious. Otherwise, there is no way people can free themselves from suffering in this world.

They have to start with the understanding that the self is different from the body. Then they can progress to understanding the Supreme Self and our relationship with Him. We become happy by sacrifice to Him. The more they hear about Kṛṣṇa as Bhagavān, the more they will respect His opulences.

mattaḥ parataraṁ nanyat
kiñcid asti dhanañjaya

mayi sarvam idaṁ protaṁ
sūtre maṇi-gaṇā iva

This is our preaching message. It's good that so many young people, and now again older Prabhupāda disciples, are trying to spread this message in tactical ways, especially by distributing Prabhupāda's books. Book distribution has been compared to dropping bombs.

After the books have done their work in bringing people to Kṛṣṇa, more has to be done. If the demon in people surrenders and they come forward, we have to engage them according to the tenets of the books. It's not enough to destroy illusion; we must, as a movement, provide a place where they can carry out devotional service.

That's where I have my place in the preaching. I once lived with a *sannyāsī* Godbrother in Vṛndāvana. He said he sometimes felt that the devotees were becoming too much like preaching machines. I don't remember so much what he was emphasizing exactly, but it had to do with our learning to worship Kṛṣṇa with our feelings. My preaching is to help devotees who have already had their illusions destroyed to take the further steps in taking up a life of *sādhana* and prayer. None of us can wait until we become perfect before we preach, but we should continue to work on being perfect while we preach. *Āpani ācari' prabhu jīvera śikhāya.*

SDG singing and clapping:

hare kṛṣṇa hare kṛṣṇa, kṛṣṇa kṛṣṇa hare hare
hare rāma hare rāma, rāma rāma hare hare

So many controversies, so many less-than-important things going on in the mind. You'd rather be fixed in prayer. Prayer means to be aware that your life is ebbing and that the goal of it, Kṛṣṇa consciousness, has not been attained. It would be tragic to miss that goal. Human life is rare and has its own special quality. It's not that humans have better quality sex or eating or can live in better houses. Neither do humans have a spectacularly long life duration. The quality of human life is the ability to reason and to understand God.

But it's Kali-yuga, and our societies are filled with faithlessness and confusion. In the name of "humanism," people deride religion. In the name of "science" and "advancement," people call atheism honest.

We chant and beg for mercy: "Please let me be fixed in my Kṛṣṇa consciousness, my original, constitutional position. Nothing else matters." Prayer means getting down to core expression. We see that writers are sometimes concerned with how to shape their expression. Should they write a sonnet? Should they write a narrative? Should they write like this? Should they write like that? Don't bother with that. Just get down to honest, core expression. Throw off all artifice and get to the heart.

SDG singing and clapping:

> *hare kṛṣṇa hare kṛṣṇa, kṛṣṇa kṛṣṇa hare hare*
> *hare rāma hare rāma, rāma rāma hare hare*

So, folks, this radio show is a serious one and it's sponsored by earthquakes and earthworms and similar fuzzy things. But it's not really sponsored at all. It's sponsored by playfulness, bare toes in summer, truthfulness, which means that although you speak big, big words, you prefer to sit back, lean against pillows on a bed, and talk a radio show. Although the topic is serious, you can't take yourself too seriously because that's who you are. You like to take a break, you like to drink water, you like to taste *prasādam* (especially sweets), you like words and stories and poems and books. Not all your likes and dislikes are completely lined up with what is absolutely best for a devotee. In other words, you're a little flaky. At least you should let people know that.

Rādhā-Mādhava in Māyāpur, Rādhā-Mādhava in Belfast. Kṛṣṇa is not alone. He is with all these excellent devotees, performing His pastimes. It can't be comprehended, certainly not by ordinary people, and not even by ordinary devotees. Kṛṣṇa is so nice and He wants us to know Him in these features, but we have to qualify. We have to give up sin and speculation and the self-centered body-conscious-false-ego-madness where we think we're the enjoyer instead of Kṛṣṇa. We have a lot of work to do to scrub out all that dirt from our hearts.

Prabhupāda has given us a vision of Kṛṣṇa:

> *jaya rādhā-mādhava kuñja-bihārī*
> *gopī-jana-vallabha giri-vara-dhārī*
> *yaśodā-nandana, braja-jana-rañjana*
> *jamunā-tīra-vana-cārī*

Therefore, this radio show is brought to you by Vraja-jana-rañjana, by Gopī-jana-vallabha, by Gopīvallabha, Kṛṣṇa, Govinda, Śyāmasundara. This is the Kṛṣṇa of Vṛndāvana, the only place in the world where people chant, "*Jaya* Rādheeeeee-Śyāma."

Rādhe-Śyāma. Rādhe-Śyāma. Rādhe-Śyāma.

This radio show has been brought to you by the dust of Vṛndāvana and by Prabhupāda's books, which will take us from *A* to *Z* to the infinite stages and bring us back again to focus purport by purport. Even if we think we have read it all before, we may not have examined our own responses to how we are reading. There are always new things for us to contemplate. Here Prabhupāda says we should read *Śrīmad-Bhāgavatam* twenty-four hours a day. How am I responding to that? This is how we can keep our reading of *Śrīmad-Bhāgavatam* always fresh—don't just read, but respond.

And gratitude has to be a central part of our existence. We should be grateful for our Kṛṣṇa consciousness. And when we're really thankful, we'll want to offer ourselves at the feet of our benefactors, Prabhupāda and Kṛṣṇa.

50

SDG singing and clapping:

hare kṛṣṇa hare kṛṣṇa, kṛṣṇa kṛṣṇa hare hare
hare rāma hare rāma, rāma rāma hare hare

Hello out there. Hello. This is Lawrence, Kansas. Do you remember that movie all the devotees were watching eight or nine years ago? It was filled with horrible images. A man was radioing out from a nuclear bomb shelter on the day after the holocaust. "Hello out there. This is Lawrence, Kansas. Is anyone out there? Is anyone out there? Anyone at all?" He got no response.

I was just reading from Baladeva's book about therapeutic hypnosis. The book was written by a follower of Erickson, who is a well-known hypnotist. There was one reference in the book by one of Erickson's students. He said that when he first read Erickson's books, he thought Erickson was clever and manipulative. When he met him, however, he realized he was actually a more caring person than he had picked up in his writing. Later, he saw that he was gentle and influential.

There's an underlying assumption in hypnosis that the hypnotist is trying to manipulate someone else in order to help him gain access to his subconscious emotions and to resolve problems. I think that's true not only for hypnotists and their clients, but for almost any relationship between people.

For example, I'm a writer and a talker, and even when I'm alone and expressing myself to Kṛṣṇa, it seems I'm always trying to express, assert, and create some kind of influence on others. Even when I talk to Kṛṣṇa, I'm trying to influence Him to give me mercy. A prayer like "Gopīnātha" is so pure, yet it's a petition: "Gopīnātha, You are the most intelligent. Can You arrange some way to save me and bring me out of this low condition?"

To say that we are trying to influence each other is not bad, but I still don't always like to think about it. In my mind, it threatens pure expression. It seems that pure expression means freedom from trying to influence someone else. On the other hand, pure expression is not opposed to creating an influence. It's not that the whole purpose of pure expression is to speak without influence or to escape coherency; it is a purpose, however, just to escape "isms" and to flow toward being who you are.

Before a Kṛṣṇa conscious writer comes to the page, he or she has already made so many deliberate and conscious efforts to practice devotional service. He doesn't have to worry, then, that his expression will be Kṛṣṇa conscious. It doesn't take deliberation, but just being himself. When he gives up deliberation and comes down to the level of who he is, then he can approach pure expression. If there's any attempt to guide it, then it has to be steered toward Kṛṣṇa. Better he guide his speech toward Kṛṣṇa than reach into the void.

It can be compared to the choice each of us faces between living and dying. It's natural to choose life. It's only when death is inevitable that a person even considers accepting it—when he sees that it's being forced upon him.

Similarly, we want to make choosing Kṛṣṇa as natural as choosing life. We don't want to live a life where that choice is always forced, but we want it to become as natural and deep as breathing. Pure expression is as natural as breathing, as natural as falling asleep. We don't have to judge it as it comes out. An editor can do that later. But when pure Kṛṣṇa conscious expression becomes as natural as breathing, nothing is out of bounds.

As I'm talking about this, the image of an alligator of all things keeps coming to mind. I see its long snout floating on top of the river and see it looking around. Roaming around. This is free expression—I'm telling you what creatures appear in my mind.

I had another image, but it slipped my mind. It was something similar—oh, I remember—the whole of Jack's Pond frozen over. As kids, when the whole pond froze, we skated all over it. We weren't afraid to skate even in the middle, even though usually the ice was too thin there.

What does this mean? Does it fit into my discussion of free expression? I'm not sure. The meaning is not as important to me as the astounding fact that suddenly I saw Jack's Pond—the skating pond of my youth. But is there such a thing as being off-limits?

No, you can't be afraid. If you're hitting a limit, the ice will crack before you fall through and you will still have time to get away. I'm mostly talking about exploration, not insanity. The limits are set by what is favorable for Kṛṣṇa consciousness and what is not.

All right, we can call this a kind of selective or conditional roaming without a preset idea of forbidden areas or boundaries. The spirit of pure expression is to seek out and express the truth, but with intelligence and caution.

SDG singing and clapping:

hare kṛṣṇa hare kṛṣṇa, kṛṣṇa kṛṣṇa hare hare
hare rāma hare rāma, rāma rāma hare hare

I also read in the therapy book—it wasn't a major topic, but in passing—that people tend to fall into the habit of not discovering anything new and how they sometimes need to break out of that habit. That led me to think about the offenses in chanting. "If one's chanting is infested with offenses, then despite his endeavor to chant the holy name for many lifetimes, he will not get the *prayojana*, or goal of this chanting, which is *kṛṣṇa-prema*." We have to break the habits of inattention and fault-finding.

It's the same in writing. It's possible to get yourself into the same grooves, the same obsessions, and not be able to cut through them. There's no progress. Sometimes there's nothing you can do but repeat the pattern and that's part of your dedication. That's also part of the process, to accept that you can't break through right now, but you're still writing. A ferret finds a rabbits in its hole. The truth-seeker sometimes finds the truth and chases out the faults. It's good to keep trying to break through old habits.

Breaking patterns—of offensive chanting, of being stuck on the same theme, of asking the same old questions without asking the questions that should be asked now. Breaking through being afraid to explore areas that may be painful to look into and admitting they're not all clear. Being confused. And writing. A lot of faith in writing itself as a method of service.

Faith should not be in something material that we call writing, but faith that writing is a service, is spiritualized, can be spiritualized, and therefore we do that service.

These are some thoughts. I don't know what you would call these thoughts, but this is radio show number 50 and we're talking, trying to keep up with the flow.

How nice it is to see things clearly and to get a little bit closer to the prayer state. How nice it was this morning to talk about Kṛṣṇa. I complain about having to perform in the *Bhāgavatam* class, but at least the wonderful thing about it is that it must be a Kṛṣṇa conscious presentation. Nothing else is acceptable. As virtuous as the search is for Kṛṣṇa consciousness, there's certainly virtue in making the authorized presentation of the already researched and perfect truth and just using yourself as the servant to give the class. There are definite boundaries to what's acceptable in the *Bhāgavatam* class, and you can work within them to create the genre called the lecture. It's a challenge to prepare a lecture and then to give one. I'm pleased I was able to speak about Kṛṣṇa so much. They were on those wonderful verses about Kṛṣṇa leaving Hastināpura for Dvārakā, and how the ladies on the roofs spoke their hearts and pleased Kṛṣṇa. Today we began the first of ten verses in which they praise Kṛṣṇa. I advocated to the devotees (and to myself) that if we think of Kṛṣṇa and chant His names, all our problems will be solved—our community problems, our relationship problems, and our personal problems. I have that faith. The *Bhāgavatam* class demands that we believe it.

SDG singing and clapping:

> *hare kṛṣṇa hare kṛṣṇa, kṛṣṇa kṛṣṇa hare hare*
> *hare rāma hare rāma, rāma rāma hare hare*

Only a few more minutes left on this show. Everything is unexpected. Out the window, I see cows swishing and twitching their tails and ears to drive away flies. Cows all over the world do this. What is there to say about the tumult of human expression which rises higher and higher and breaks through the ozone? Kṛṣṇa hears it all—the wails and cries and grimaces and shouts of pleasure, the orgasmic exultation of the poor slobs and beasts, then the prayers and penitent cries—everything is rising up and Kṛṣṇa hears it all. Kṛṣṇa is kind.

51

SDG singing and clapping:

hare kṛṣṇa hare kṛṣṇa, kṛṣṇa kṛṣṇa hare hare
hare rāma hare rāma, rāma rāma hare hare

Haribol, ladies and gentlemen, children and broadcasters and birds and cows and dogs and grass that grows along the way. This is another radio show. This is not affiliated with Hare Kṛṣṇa Rural Life or Padayātrā, with the Centennial or book distribution. Still, I hope it will be acceptable to devotees no matter what project they work for.

I'm not speaking for many devotees, but I do hope my friends are listening in different places. I don't have to be the official representative of any particular department. I can speak to individuals in this Hare Kṛṣṇa movement.

SDG singing and clapping:

hare kṛṣṇa hare kṛṣṇa, kṛṣṇa kṛṣṇa hare hare
hare rāma hare rāma, rāma rāma hare hare

Would you like to know where I am? I'm in a cow shed which also serves as a tool shed and a farm storage shed in a devotee's backyard. In this shed, on the far left, there is a pile of wood for burning. There's also a shelf with different things on it, like paint cans and tools and boxes—I can't see them so well. There's a bird house and a pole, and a pile of hay, which is the home of the black cat whose name I forget. There's also an old-fashioned wooden sled with wooden runners and a big trunk and two plastic baby bassinets. Over on this side, I can see tools hanging on nail pegs—a rake, a shovel, an ax, a pitchfork, and clippers. There are bags of manure and compost on the floor.

This shed is made of cinder blocks cemented together and has a corrugated tin roof at a slant. It's like a shanty. The door tends to swing open in the breeze, but I've got it hooked by a chain. I can see the light gray Irish sky over the top.

I am sitting here fumbling, uttering, mumbling, trying to speak clearly. I wanted to speak like a person chained down or abandoned or like a man in a monk's cell hiding out in peaceful, blessed solitude. I wanted to wood-shed (that's musician's talk).

SDG singing and clapping:

hare kṛṣṇa hare kṛṣṇa, kṛṣṇa kṛṣṇa hare hare
hare rāma hare rāma, rāma rāma hare hare

On the one hand, I say it's a shame we have to justify our actions so much, but in Vedic society, that is required. The *kṣatriya* comes around and wants to know what you're doing and whether you're following the rules of your *varṇa* and *āśrama.*

"Well, I'm-I'm a *brāhmaṇa,* sir. I'm performing this *yajña* and chanting these Vedic mantras and I live on whatever is provided. I'm studying the *Vedas.* As for my behavior, you can ask the people around here or stay with me if you like." Somehow or other, the *brāhmaṇa* has to show that his activities are brahminical. Mahārāja Parīkṣit saw the misbehavior of the black person dressed as a king, Kali, and he said, "What are you doing dressed as a king but acting as a rascal? How dare you beat a cow and bull in my kingdom. This has never been done." He was ready to kill him.

We are accountable, but the *brāhmaṇa* is also not accountable provided he is following guru, *śāstra,* and *sādhu.* I mean, he shouldn't be stopped from what he is doing by some external controls. No one should tell him he should influence people on someone else's behalf or that he should take up activities that are contrary to his brahminical honesty and detachment. The *brāhmaṇa* has to be free to follow his conscience and his guru.

Brāhmaṇas like to be trusted. They don't like to be patronized or over-directed or controlled.

All right, so what's that got to do with this radio show?

All I'm saying is that you have to leave me alone to speak what comes while I'm sitting back and squinting at the white sky and waiting and praying, *kṛṣṇa kṛṣṇa kṛṣṇa he/ kṛṣṇa kṛṣṇa kṛṣṇa he.*

SDG singing and clapping:

hare kṛṣṇa hare kṛṣṇa, kṛṣṇa kṛṣṇa hare hare
hare rāma hare rāma, rāma rāma hare hare

Big flies and bees flying in and out of here. They're not embarrassed by their bodily condition. Prabhupāda says you don't have to go to school to learn how to eat, mate, sleep, and defend. He compares it to the children who approach him in the morning when he hands out sweets. They open their hands. No one taught them how to beg for food. Education is for culturing higher topics, and ultimately for culturing knowledge of God and the soul.

Kṛṣṇa teaches about the soul in the *Bhagavad-gītā.* That's real education. What does Kṛṣṇa say in the *Bhagavad-gītā,* especially when He talks about Himself ?

"Seeing Arjuna full of compassion, his mind depressed, his eyes full of tears, Madhusūdana, Kṛṣṇa, spoke the following words. The Supreme Personality of Godhead said: My dear Arjuna, how have these impurities come upon you? They are not at all befitting a man who knows the value of life. They do not lead to higher planets, but to infamy."

These are the verses, and what about the purports? Śrīla Prabhupāda says, "Material compassion, lamentation and tears are all signs of ignorance of the real self. Compassion for the eternal soul is self-realization. The word "Madhusūdana" is significant in this verse. Lord Kṛṣṇa killed the demon Madhu, and now Arjuna wanted Kṛṣṇa to kill the demon of misunderstanding that had overtaken him in the discharge of his duty."

Kṛṣṇa (and Kṛṣṇa's devotee) can give us real education. All other teachers and preachers are misdirected. Even honest talkers, friends, if they're ignorant of the soul, are misdirected. Such people can't have real compassion because they don't know who they are or who anyone else is. Whatever compassion they do feel is fragmental.

Bhagavad-gītā is there and I'm going to read it. I'm going to be cured of doubts and fogginess and the unwillingness to serve. I'm going to become attracted to Kṛṣṇa, the supreme person. Prabhupāda will help me fight off the demons. I simply have to hear from him. He is speaking for our benefit because we've been afflicted by demonic doubts, materialism, and atheism. Who can claim to be unaffected by these things in this age?

Prabhupāda will fight on our behalf, and we're going to become free sooner or later if we apply ourselves to his instructions.

52

SDG singing and clapping:

> *hare kṛṣṇa hare kṛṣṇa, kṛṣṇa kṛṣṇa hare hare*
> *hare rāma hare rāma, rāma rāma hare hare*
>
> *nama oṁ viṣṇu-pādāya kṛṣṇa-preṣṭhāya bhū-tale*
> *śrīmate bhaktivedānta-svāmin iti nāmine*
>
> *namas te sārasvate deve gaura-vāṇī-pracāriṇe*
> *nirviśeṣa-śūnyavādi-pāścātya-deśa-tāriṇe*

Beginning another radio show. It's been awhile since I did one. The last time I tried to do a radio show, I was attacked by swallows. I've given up trying to sit in the tool shed, and instead I'm in the backyard. Hopefully, the horse flies will leave me alone. I certainly won't be bothered by the big silent pines.

We should be Kṛṣṇa conscious, shouldn't we, even if it means closing our eyes to this nature, this waving, weed-swaying nature which entrances us. If we were here, speaking on a particular verse of *Śrīmad-Bhāgavatam* to a particular audience, that would be different. I remember in Dallas, it would get so hot in the summer that we would hold *Bhāgavatam* class outdoors. It was so cool at that early hour. That's a nice place to have a class.

I don't have any book with me. I also don't have any photographs of Prabhupāda with me. I just received a big batch of photos of myself with Śrīla Prabhupāda from the Archives. They sent me hundreds of pictures, many of them practically the same. For example, there's a whole series of photos of Prabhupāda in front of the Eiffel Tower, almost all alike. I'm in every picture, usually just a dot. There's even pictures of the devotees gathered in front on the lawn in Māyāpur. All you can see are many little heads. But there are other pictures in which Prabhupāda and I are exchanging glances—usually on morning walks as I asked questions or took the role of the Māyāvādīs or atheists. When I look at those pictures, I can see the love we shared.

It would be easy to make fun of myself while looking at these photographs. It's funny now to look at them and see how young I was in those days. There's no point in making fun, though. It's infinitely better than looking at pictures of myself standing by old girlfriends or even a wife when we were young. "Oh, here's the picture of when we went to Niagara Falls for our honeymoon. Remember when we stood behind the cardboard figures of the fat man and the fat woman? Now we are both fat." This is infinitely better than that.

If I had a *Bhāgavatam* out here, I would be able to read to you. You really have to pray when you have that book. The *Bhāgavatam* is for prayer. Whenever I read it, I like to pray for patience.

I am preparing to give classes to devotees at Inis Rath soon. One class will be on *Prabhupāda Meditations*. There's one section in *Prabhupāda Meditations* where I tell how I had to slow down to read the Swami. I was so hyped up in those days. I was even proud that I couldn't pay attention to books unless they were practically crazy. I liked to read things like William Burroughs' clipping words together from different magazines in *Nova Express*—it made almost no sense at all. And I read other books like that which were "hip" and reached out for some higher perception.

Anyway, in *Prabhupāda Meditations*, I told how I was willing to slow down and read the *Bhāgavatam*. There was something strong and appealing in what the Swami was saying, and he had his own uncompromising use of language—with all its typing and grammatical mistakes. He was talking about transcendental loving service to the "Lard." I slowed down to read.

The other day when I first looked through that section of *Prabhupāda Meditations*, I knew I wanted to speak on it, but I couldn't think of why. Now it occurs to me that my slowing down for the Swami is not just an interesting story of how a hippie came to Kṛṣṇa consciousness in the 1960s; it's something I still have to do. I have to enter a prayer state to read *Śrīmad-Bhāgavatam*. I don't take drugs anymore, nor am I involved in a high speed life. Perhaps the words "slow down" are not completely applicable today, but I still have to fend off the feeling that I've read it all before, the tendency to read and blank out rather than pray.

That's why reading has to be done in good consciousness if it's going to be meaningful and not just an exercise to later pat yourself on the back and say I read today. It's got some real purpose. That's why I read early in the morning and why I'm thinking about prayer lately.

What is prayer? I know what prayer is for me. It's to chant Hare Kṛṣṇa or to read the books with submission. Faithful hearing, *śraddhā*. Prayer means hearing as if you need to hear.

Mahārāja Parīkṣit said, "I am fasting even from water. someone else might be troubled if they did that, but I'm not troubled because I'm hearing all this nectar from you. These subjects seem newer. I'm becoming addicted to them."

nivṛtta-tarṣair upagīyamānād
bhavauṣadhāc chrotra-mano-'bhirāmāt
ka uttamaśloka-guṇānuvādāt
pumān virajyeta vinā paśughnāt

Who will not be eager to hear the messages that come in *paramparā* from his spiritual master? Those messages can cure all material diseases and they are appealing to all kinds of people, including those who are liberated, those who are trying to become liberated, and those who are sense gratifiers. Everyone will be attracted except the killer of the animals and the killer of the self.

The prayer state is not automatic. We have to cultivate it. It reminds me of the Christian practice of *lectio divina.* I also tried counting down and trying to relax before hearing. We tried that technique when I taught the *Kṛṣṇa* book course, although I haven't done it since. These days, I don't put any special labels on my reading preparation. I'm just mentioning it because it came to mind.

I can hear different sounds outside here. If you're out at the wrong time of day, you can hear the men rounding up their sheep and cattle. It's an unpleasant sound because I can't help thinking of their murderous intent. At this time of day, I mainly hear the buzzing of insects.

At this time of day, I can usually feel my own body. I mean, I'm more conscious of its workings. I can feel it quietly waiting, pulsating, wanting me to take it to a Kṛṣṇa conscious state. I don't think this is a fanciful dream. The body gets accustomed to the mental and psychic state of the person. By this time of day, my body has already slept and eaten, and although it will have to do those things again in due course, it is presently not distracting me. My body is ready to receive the chanting of the holy name and pastimes of Kṛṣṇa.

My dear self, I did not bring a book out here for this show, nor did I bring any pictures, but I do have my impressions of Kṛṣṇa consciousness with me. My body is in its offstage, more private and relaxed mood, and it wants to be Kṛṣṇa conscious.

Kṛṣṇa is in our hearts. He is our best friend. "What do you want?" He asks.

Svāmin kṛtārtho 'smi varaṁ na yāce: "I don't want material things, I just want to serve You."

Kṛṣṇa says, as He said to Dhruva, "I know you want something else, don't you?" Kardama Muni wanted a wife. "You have this desire, Kardama, and you are My devotee. Here, take the best wife, this beautiful princess, Devahūti. Have children by her. Be happy. Come to Me in the end."

"And you, Dhruva, you came to Me with the great determination to get a kingdom greater than your grandfather's. Take the pole star." Dhruva regretted that desire. He realized he should have asked for pure devotional service. "I came looking for pieces of broken glass and instead I found a great jewel."

Are we like that? Kṛṣṇa is in the heart. He sees our desires. Are we begging Him for ashes? Are we like the old woman who asked to have the bundle put back on her back? Kṛṣṇa fulfilled her desire.

So many self-satires, expressions of falling short, limits on all sides, but aspirations too, that somehow we can pray to Kṛṣṇa. Please, Lord, I'm sorry. Again I have missed the opportunity to serve You birth after birth. Let this be my last life. Let me give up my foolishness and sense gratification and simply let me serve You.

itthaṁ satāṁ brahma-sukhānubhūtyā
dāsyaṁ gatānāṁ para-daivatena
māyāśritānāṁ nara-dārakeṇa
sākaṁ vijahruḥ kṛta-puṇya-puñjāḥ

53

SDG singing and clapping:

> *hare kṛṣṇa hare kṛṣṇa, kṛṣṇa kṛṣṇa hare hare*
> *hare rāma hare rāma, rāma rāma hare hare*

Haribol. I would like to continue where I left off yesterday, although I can't just pick it up again. I can hardly remember what I was doing yesterday at this time. I do remember I was rambling. I tried describing the surroundings in the backyard, being honest with what was on my mind, but hoping to enter a Kṛṣṇa conscious state. I remember quoting at the end:

> *itthaṁ satāṁ brahma-sukhānubhūtyā*
> *dāsyaṁ gatānāṁ para-daivatena*
> *māyāśritānāṁ nara-dārakeṇa*
> *sākaṁ vijahruḥ kṛta-puṇya-puñjāḥ*

The cowherd boys play with Kṛṣṇa after accumulating heaps of pious activities.

I don't remember the context of all that. Perhaps I was reminding myself that there are pure devotees of Kṛṣṇa who serve Him without material motivations. Although the *Bhāgavatam* instructs us through the examples of Ajāmila and even Dhruva Mahārāja, who began their service imperfectly and then later came to the pure standard, there are also examples of unalloyed service to Kṛṣṇa.

I was also praying to pray, or talking about wanting to pray, to have the kind of inner life where you really care about Kṛṣṇa as a person and always think about Him. *Man-manā bhava mad-bhakto, mad-yājī māṁ namaskuru.* By chanting Hare Kṛṣṇa, you can think of Kṛṣṇa. You can go back to Kṛṣṇa in the spiritual world. That's the goal of this movement. I was thinking of these things and feeling the desire to move in that direction.

Kṛṣṇa consciousness is simple: chant Hare Kṛṣṇa, give up material desires, engage in Kṛṣṇa's service according to your propensity and under the guru's order, and engage the senses in Kṛṣṇa service—*hṛṣīkena hṛṣīkeśa-sevanaṁ bhaktir ucyate.* Then you'll achieve perfection and go back to Godhead. So simple?

Māyā-devī is not easily impressed and Kṛṣṇa is not cheap.

nāhaṁ prakāśaḥ sarvasya
yoga-māyā-samāvṛtaḥ
mūḍho 'yaṁ nābhijānāti
loko mām ajam avyayam

"I am never manifest to the foolish and unintelligent. For them I am covered by My internal potency, and therefore they do not know that I am unborn and infallible."

Kṛṣṇa is not cheap. Even His mercy is not cheap. He doesn't easily bestow attraction to Himself until we decide that we no longer want to be attracted to the material world.

Let's look at that *nāhaṁ prakāśaḥ* verse: "I am never manifest to the foolish and unintelligent." Am I foolish? Not me. And I'm certainly not unintelligent. Kṛṣṇa must be talking about the nondevotees —the *karmīs* and *jñānīs* and mystic *yogīs*. I'm a *bhakta.* "For them, I am covered by My internal potency and therefore they do not know that I am unborn and infallible."

In the purport, Prabhupāda talks about why Kṛṣṇa isn't manifest to everyone. For example, there were only a few people who could understand Kṛṣṇa when He was present on the earth. Although we could blame the nondevotees' lack of intelligence, Kṛṣṇa says in this verse that He covers Himself from them.

> It may be argued that since Kṛṣṇa was present on this earth and was visible to everyone, then why isn't He manifest to everyone now? But actually He was not manifest to everyone. When Kṛṣṇa was present there were only a few people who could understand Him to be the Supreme Personality of Godhead. . . . He was not revealed to the nondevotees and the common man. . . . He was manifest only to His devotees as the reservoir of all pleasure. But to others, to unintelligent nondevotees, He was covered by His internal potency.
>
> In the prayers of Kuntī . . . it is said that the Lord is covered by the curtain of *yoga-māyā* and thus ordinary people cannot understand Him. This *yoga-māyā* curtain is also confirmed in the *Īśopaniṣad* (mantra 15), in which the devotee prays:
>
> "O my Lord, You are the maintainer of the entire universe, and devotional service to You is the highest religious principle. Therefore, I pray that You will also maintain me. Your transcendental form is covered by the *yoga-māyā*. The *brahmajyoti* is the covering of the internal potency. May You kindly remove this glowing effulgence that impedes my seeing Your *sac-cid-ānanda-vigraha*, Your eternal form of bliss and knowledge."

Again, it's the Māyāvādīs who can't see Kṛṣṇa. I don't want to be one of them. Kṛṣṇa, please remove Your *yoga-māyā* covering. Out of millions and millions of men, some try to become perfect, and out of thousands of such perfected men, hardly one can understand You in truth. Back to our question: is Kṛṣṇa consciousness simple? All it means is giving up material desires, working under the guru's instructions, and controlling your senses.

Because I'm speaking about this, I'm going to create a context here. It's not a digression. I'm talking in the backyard. I hear bumblebees, see the gentle weeds, and Madhu is sawing away in the front yard. He's ripping out the old interior of our van and building a new one. He has asked for help from a devotee in these parts who is not strictly following the regulative principles. This devotee is an expert carpenter and he has a good heart, and therefore we call him a devotee.

I'm thinking of that devotee and how he's not following. He can't control his senses. He has a kind of hippie whimsy which manifests itself in the form of long hair, a beard, an earring, things like that that are not conducive to Vaiṣṇavism. By not following the rules and regulations, he has gotten himself entangled with women and intoxication. This is how he's damaging his own progress.

It's easy for me to see how he's deluded. It's easy for him to see it too, but it's not easy for him to stop his sense gratification. By contrast, I control in myself the types of desires that are causing him problems. He frankly can't give them up because he still finds them enjoyable. Although he has tried to live like a monk, it didn't work for him.

Many people have romantic ideas about what it means to live simply and austerely. They imagine themselves wandering homeless, begging at people's doors, and chanting all day long. But they can't do it. They get lonely or they don't have enough taste for *sādhana.*

We can all see the problem, and it's pitiful, but there doesn't seem to be anything any of us can do about it when we run into it in ourselves. Conditioned souls work on the pleasure principle. Whatever gives us satisfaction, whether spiritual or material, is the activity we will naturally pursue. We are no different than the moth flying into the fire.

I say I have control over the desires that bother our carpenter, but I am afflicted by different obstacles. It's the same thing, actually. I can't sustain intensive *sādhana.* I'm not becoming overwhelmingly attracted to Kṛṣṇa. Why? Because I'm still working on my subtle attachments and identifications.

What do I enjoy? I say I want to chant intensely, but because I can't seem to do it, I take pleasure in walking in the countryside, in peace, in being away from crowds. I enjoy—not only enjoy, but become absorbed in—self-exploration, self-expression, and the art of writing. Some of these things are distractions, some of them are preliminary work that lead to Kṛṣṇa consciousness, and I know there's a difference between them and the stage of really loving Kṛṣṇa, of feeling the whole world vacant without Him.

All kinds of people like us are left to say from time to time, "If Kṛṣṇa would only reveal Himself. If the *śuddha-sattva* would only come down to me. If only Kṛṣṇa would make me intoxicated with the holy name." Then someone else may say to us, "If you'd give up your foolishness, then you could practice Kṛṣṇa consciousness unimpeded." And so it goes.

SDG singing and clapping:

> *hare kṛṣṇa hare kṛṣṇa, kṛṣṇa kṛṣṇa hare hare*
> *hare rāma hare rāma, rāma rāma hare hare*

Preaching is very important for persons on the beginning and intermediate stages. We are kept busy by it and it captures Kṛṣṇa's attention. It seems we have two types of devotees in this movement. There's the devotee who is not so involved with the preaching spirit and who is trying to reach Kṛṣṇa by chanting and hearing, but he has difficulty occupying himself fully in it. Then there's the other type of devotee who chants his prescribed rounds and follows all the rules and programs. He doesn't fully taste the *sādhana* practices, but he does like to preach.

The *Bhagavad-gītā* tells us that the guru's representative, even if he's a neophyte devotee who preaches and has compassion for his fellow humans, is very, very dear to Kṛṣṇa. His activities are attracting Kṛṣṇa to Him.

"For one who explains the supreme secret to the devotees, pure devotional service is guaranteed, and at the end he will come back to Me.

"There is no servant in this world more dear to Me than he, nor will there ever be one more dear."

Prabhupāda didn't write a purport to that verse. I don't need to add one here.

SDG singing and clapping:

> *hare kṛṣṇa hare kṛṣṇa, kṛṣṇa kṛṣṇa hare hare*
> *hare rāma hare rāma, rāma rāma hare hare*

(The sheep are baaa-ing in the hills. Foolish creatures. I guess I was doing the same until I had lunch. Now I'm satisfied for another day.)

O Lord of the universe, O soul of the universe, please save me from the *brahmāstra* which is coming toward me fast, Uttarā prayed. Queen Kuntī prayed, O Lord, You appear like an actor who is covered by His costume. You appear to be like somebody's nephew in this world, somebody's cousin, somebody's son, but You are the Supreme Personality of Godhead. You are all-pervading by Your energies. You are invisible to the nondevotee, but those who are fortunate understand Your true position and they render You service through Your pure devotees. O Lord of the universe, O soul of the universe, let my affection for You flow like the Ganges to the sea without obstruction, without being deviated to anyone else. Sever my tie of affection to the Vṛṣṇis and the Pāṇḍavas. Please let me be Your devotee.

Working on the lower platform, not availing ourselves of the most forceful methods of purification, still we protest, "Kṛṣṇa, I love You." Or, "Kṛṣṇa, I want to love You. Kṛṣṇa, please descend." Then what?

"As all surrender unto Me, I reward them accordingly. Everyone follows My path in all respects." Why are you keeping this elephant goad if you have sold the elephant of your material attachments? Why are you keeping these rocks if you want to cross the ocean? Why don't you surrender?

54

SDG singing and clapping:

hare kṛṣṇa hare kṛṣṇa, kṛṣṇa kṛṣṇa hare hare
hare rāma hare rāma, rāma rāma hare hare

Haribol. I was talking to a friend today and something he said stuck in my mind. Let me get to my point as quickly as possible. I want to speak to these devotees about the importance of chanting and hearing. I usually speak on that subject, and there are many *Bhāgavatam* verses I could choose to back up my points. I have been thinking of speaking on the verse:

dharmaḥ svanuṣṭhitaḥ puṁsāṁ
viṣvaksena-kathāsu yaḥ
notpādayed yadi ratiṁ
śrama eva hi kevalam

"The occupational activities a man performs according to his own position are only so much useless labor if they do not provoke attraction for the message of the Personality of Godhead" *(Bhāg.* 1.2.8).

Before I push or suggest or advise them that they should take the time to chant and read, I thought I should know how much time they actually had in their schedules. I didn't want to be unsympathetic, because then they would think I didn't understand their life circumstances. After all, I don't have a job like they do.

When I asked my friend, he said, "This is not the problem. You can go ahead and blast us. It's just a lack of desire to chant and hear."

Then by way of complimenting me or by way of explaining himself and the difference between us, he said, "I see the way you come here and follow a schedule. I see you out early in the morning taking your walk. I saw you the other day sitting down in the garden reading and writing. You devote so much time to hearing and chanting. You spend long periods of time by yourself. To me . . ." Then he hesitated. He knew what he wanted to say, but he was afraid to say it. Then he laughed, "Well, it's almost like being in prison." Then he went on to something else.

Since he moved on to another topic, we didn't talk about his comment. Now I'm thinking about it. On the one hand, I took it as a compliment. He was indicating that I had some taste for my *sādhana* and that he didn't. When you have a taste for chanting and hearing, you don't feel like you're in prison. I thought to myself, "Well, I'm trying to *develop* a taste. I may not have a deep taste for hearing and chanting, but I do have a taste for trying to develop one."

I want to take his remark personally for a minute. One response I had in myself: "Well, if this is true about me, that means I have a monk's nature. Why don't I get into this even more? Why don't I start reading about those monks who spent all their time alone, like the monks in the *Philokalia*, who lived in their cells while they practiced a rigorous inner prayer life?" Of course, those monks have a different discipline than the Gauḍīya Vaiṣṇava *sannyāsīs*, so it's not that I particularly relate to their way. My point is that his comment attracted me to think of going deeper into "prison."

I actually hadn't thought of this difference between us so much before, but his comment made me realize that this is something specific about my nature. It's not a matter of it being more Kṛṣṇa conscious or less Kṛṣṇa conscious, it's just my nature. It could stem from frustration at not being able to get along with people, or from a genuine attraction for the cultivation of things that get cultivated in solitude.

But is it "just my nature"? How, then, can I push the devotees in this direction if it's opposed to their natures? Why don't I just become a solitary monk and leave them to their own lifestyles? They don't like to be alone—not that I tell them they have to practice their *sādhana* alone. They can chant and hear together.

Being alone right now means going into this radio studio. There's no engineer hanging around, and no audience, yet I speak to whoever is listening. "Hello? Is there anyone out there? Anyone at all? This is Satsvarūpa. This is Satsvarūpa. Is there anyone out there? Anyone at all?"

I don't want to hear a crackling on the line and a voice, "Hello, hello, hello Satsvarūpa. I heard your call. Now, my question is . . . " Then I have a talk show on my hands with commercials every five minutes.

Yes, I live in a heavenly prison, a self-imposed cell. Do Vaiṣṇavas like solitude? I thought Vaiṣṇavas like to be with other Vaiṣṇavas in the *kīrtana* rumba back and forth. They like the *saṅga*. "Hey, *haribol, haribol*!" They like to sit in rows at *prasādam* and sing *śarīra abidyā-jāl*. I like to be there too, but not all the time.

To all those listening who also like to be in "prison," keep up the good work, and you know what I mean.

SDG singing and clapping:

hare kṛṣṇa hare kṛṣṇa, kṛṣṇa kṛṣṇa hare hare
hare rāma hare rāma, rāma rāma hare hare

yac-cakṣur eṣa savitā sakala-grahāṇāṁ
rājā samasta-sura-mūrtir aśeṣa-tejāḥ
yasyājñayā brahmati sambhṛta-kāla-cakro
govindam ādi-puruṣaṁ tam ahaṁ bhajāmi

It's nice when you read things in Prabhupāda's books that stir you to action. I read a purport where Prabhupāda says Kṛṣṇa gives only a hint of His abode, Goloka Vṛndāvana, in the *Bhagavad-gītā.* Vivid details are described in the *Brahma-saṁhitā.* I thought, "That's a real recommendation for *Brahma-saṁhitā.*" I don't happen to have that book with me as we travel, but I decided to try and get a copy.

He also said something about the hellish planets and how if you kill insects, you go to a hellish planet. If you kill anything, you will have to suffer. It made me think of the moths that fly into my votive candle when I chant *japa* in the morning. After I read that, I decided to stop using candles that so obviously attract the moths.

When we respond to Prabhupāda's instructions, it keeps us in touch with Prabhupāda and from gathering dust on ourselves. We also dust off our *sādhana* by hearing from him regularly.

Another example of an instruction that moved me to act: "Only persons who constantly engage in welfare activities for other living entities can reach the Vaikuṇṭha planets" *(Bhāg.* 4.12.36). Statements like that are deep. You can't always immediately run out and do something about them because they require developing a quality in your character. Prabhupāda makes it clear, however, that you need to be compassionate toward others. It's not enough simply to practice Kṛṣṇa consciousness in "prison."

There were other things that I read that now stick in my mind and spur me to action:

In the *Bhagavad-gītā,* Prabhupāda said something about how Kṛṣṇa speaks in the *Bhagavad-gītā,* and that therefore, the devotees want to use the *Bhagavad-gītā* in their preaching. That gave me conviction about wanting to hear Kṛṣṇa speak in the *Bhagavad-gītā* and to take it more earnestly in my life.

When we study Prabhupāda's books, it becomes obvious that we have to control the amount of time we spend in things other than Prabhupāda's books. I mean, specifically in nondevotee literature and association. Their atheistic or materialistic association is bound to affect us in an adverse way. We don't always want to have to fight for our faith, whether internally or externally. We are more interested in relishing Kṛṣṇa consciousness.

For example, the *Brahma-saṁhitā* says: "Let me worship the Supreme Personality of Godhead, Govinda, [Kṛṣṇa], who is the original person and under whose order the sun, which is the king of all planets, is assuming immense power and heat. The sun represents the eye of the Lord and traverses its orbit in obedience to His order."

"The sun is the king of the planets, and the sun god (at present of the name Vivasvān) rules the sun planet, which is controlling all other planets by supplying heat and light."

This radio show is meant to give faithful devotees another place they can go to receive Kṛṣṇa consciousness, a place where the existence of the sun god is already accepted and established. This space is for devotees.

I don't want to say that nondevotees cannot enter here, but this space is claimed for Kṛṣṇa. This is a non-smoking zone. Anyone is welcome, but they have to follow our rules to be admitted.

The sun god is rotating under the order of Kṛṣṇa and Kṛṣṇa originally made Vivasvān his first disciple to understand the science of *Bhagavad-gītā.* "The *Gītā* is not, therefore, a speculative treatise for the insignificant mundane scholar but is a standard book of knowledge coming down from time immemorial."

śrī-bhagavān uvāca:
imaṁ vivasvate yogaṁ
proktavān aham avyayam
vivasvān manave prāha
manur ikṣvākave 'bravīt

"The Personality of Godhead, Lord Śrī Kṛṣṇa, said: I instructed this imperishable science of yoga to the sun-god, Vivasvān, and Vivasvān instructed it to Manu, the father of mankind, and Manu in turn instructed it to Ikṣvāku."

Prabhupāda said that this is the history of the *Bhagavad-gītā* coming down from a remote time. It was taught to the rest of the world by the kings—they are supposed to teach of the eternal relationship with the Supreme Personality of Godhead to their subjects.

Prabhupāda said that religion is not a nominal or sectarian practice. People can practice different religions, he said, implying that we don't object. It's not that everyone has to call God "Kṛṣṇa" and if they don't, we'll fight with them. The point is to follow religious principles, not just nominally acknowledge them.

Hearing this, I felt enlivened at what you could call the liberal side of things, to see God in other religions. There is no such thing as a true religion devoid of God consciousness. Although I thought of this as a liberal stance, I realized that most religions don't teach who God is. What kind of religionist is it who worships God without knowing who He is? It's like being an American citizen and not even knowing the name of the President. I think he quoted *sa vai puṁsāṁ:* "The supreme occupation *(dharma)* for all humanity is that by which men can attain loving devotional service unto the transcendent Lord. Such devotional service must be unmotivated and uninterrupted to completely satisfy the self" *(Bhāg.* 1.2.6).

Real religion, the most developed religion, is Kṛṣṇa consciousness.

SDG singing and clapping:

hare kṛṣṇa hare kṛṣṇa, kṛṣṇa kṛṣṇa hare hare
hare rāma hare rāma, rāma rāma hare hare

I'm broadcasting today from the *tulasī* house. I came in here because it's too windy outside. However, now I realize that it's too warm in here.

Dear friends, dear fellow parts and parcels of Kṛṣṇa, we are gathered here today to observe the presence of *tulasī-devī.* Let us pray. Dear Kṛṣṇa in everyone's heart, we bow down to You. Dear *caitya-guru* in everyone's heart, thank You for sending us Śrīla Prabhupāda, the outer manifestation of *caitya-guru.* Dear Lord Kṛṣṇa, we speak these words with such a lack of knowledge and sincerity that it becomes almost a mockery, but we don't want to give up our praying. We have heard that even Lord Brahmā and Ananta-śeṣa cannot praise You adequately according to Your infinite qualities. We should not stop our attempts even though they are imperfect. We also know that prayers that are not backed up by *sādhana* are less effective and that Kṛṣṇa conscious behavior includes preaching. We feel inadequate, therefore, by our activities, to claim to speak to You in prayer. But You have said it is all right that even if we cannot praise You adequately, we may attempt to do so, because one who wants to get out of this material world praises Kṛṣṇa. *Man-manā bhava mad-bhakto, mad-yājī māṁ namaskuru/ mām evaiṣyasi . . .* he thinks of Kṛṣṇa and he goes to Kṛṣṇa.

We pray in that way more and more, not giving up the attempt, being with people to tell them about Kṛṣṇa and then going alone again to be with Kṛṣṇa so that we can quiet the noise and hear Kṛṣṇa. We want to distinguish all the clutter of our inner life—the voices and influences and false priorities and unnecessary anxieties—and see our death-bound condition.

My dear Lord Kṛṣṇa, although we cannot pray nicely, we ask You to accept our humble obeisances, our parrot-like words.

śrī-kṛṣṇa-caitanya prabhu nityānanda
śrī-advaita gadādhara śrīvāsādi-gaura-bhakta-vṛnda

Please let us go to Navadvīpa-Māyāpur for a pilgrimage.

śrī-kṛṣṇa-caitanya prabhu nityānanda
śrī-advaita gadādhara śrīvāsādi-gaura-bhakta-vṛnda

We like to play and make prayers as a child might, imitating the priest's voice, the *brāhmaṇa's* voice, using sonorous tones. Maybe it's play-acting, but it's not so bad. We're lucky we don't still want to be Batman.

55

SDG singing and clapping:

hare kṛṣṇa hare kṛṣṇa, kṛṣṇa kṛṣṇa hare hare
hare rāma hare rāma, rāma rāma hare hare

Haribol. This is a radio show. It's being broadcast from a *tulasī* house in the backyard. Please don't find fault with us. You are all very advanced people. Please hear from us the philosophy of Lord Caitanya. The horse's head nods and nods as he pulls the load. The school student's head nods and nods as he falls asleep during the teacher's lecture. The teacher sees the student and sarcastically inserts into his lecture a remark about people who sleep during class. Life is meant for awakening, and he accompanies his remark with a look in the direction of the errant student.

Wake up, wake up sleeping soul. How long will you sleep in the lap of the witch called Māyā? "Sleep knits the raveled sleeve of care of the weary traveler." In other words, while he's unconscious in sleep, sleep mends his weariness, or so goes the metaphor. Sleep mends our lives, which tend to become so strung out. How long can we go without feeling the need of a new start?

Did you know that at the end of Brahmā's day, he falls asleep and all the *jīvas* are plunged into annihilation? When he awakens the next day, they are "reborn." At the end of his life, then everything in the cosmos gets wound up into Viṣṇu in a kind of sleep. More than sleep—inactivity. Only when Viṣṇu decides to give the *jîvas* another chance does He order creation. Then everything and everyone comes into being again.

Sleep is a profound metaphor. That may sound cheap, as if some people think a literary example is not life. But we're not interested in a removed, abstract level of reality. Metaphors are not meant for abstraction, but for clarifying reality. That's particularly true of this metaphor about sleep. That's the big metaphysical question, isn't it? What happens after we die? Are we annihilated, which is so frightening we can't face it? It is equally frightening to contemplate that everything we're doing is accounted for. Everything has been witnessed and judged. Based on our activities in this life, we will have to go to a next life at death.

The *śāstras* give us information of these facts beyond our own experience, but we cannot experience the truth of the *śāstras* until we die.

Even then, our perspective is not God's perspective, but the perspective of a tiny *jīva.*

One may say that those who haven't flown in a plane have no experience of what flying is. I would add that those who have flown in a plane have only a limited experience of flight. What happens? You arrive at the airport, then board the plane. Maybe you fall asleep during the first few hours of the journey. Then you eat and read a magazine. Five hours later, you land. What has that experience got to do with flying? The captain of the plane has an entirely different perspective on what the flight meant. We are each limited by our own consciousness.

All of us share the experience of sleeping and waking again. We also share the experience of dreams, although our dreams are individual and according to our individual karmas.

Dreaming is another profound metaphor which explains the unreality of our temporary, physical existence. A dream appears real—it's filled with pain and pleasure and emotion and forms and relationships and activities and ego—but it is washed away when we awaken. According to the *Vedas,* our waking life is little better than our dreaming life because we do not recognize our actual constitutional natures. Prabhupāda says the only difference is that waking life is a long, twelve-hour dream while the sleeping dream may only last half an hour. We think it's real, but it has the same insubstantiality. We are such stuff as dreams are made of and our little life is rounded with sleep.

This is who we are and what we have to suffer through. We experience intense attachment *(rāga)* to and identification with the material objects in our lives. At death, we're forced to let go of them. A devotee's interest is to voluntarily give up material attachment while still living and then to become attached to Kṛṣṇa. We don't have to let go of Kṛṣṇa at the time of death. Instead, we go to Him.

When we think of the master plan of our lives, we imagine the many chapters—the sufficient old age, the autumn season of our lives mellowing us, the recognition we will finally receive for our achievements, the respect people will feel for us at the end. We plan a dignified passage. Our preferred script is not necessarily the one coming to us through our karma. The Boy Scouts' motto is, "Be Prepared." The only way to be prepared for death is to practice being attached to Kṛṣṇa and detached from this world. *Ante nārāyaṇa smṛtiḥ.* Whatever your life has been, think of Kṛṣṇa at the end and you'll be successful.

That's what the wind is saying in the pine trees. You wanted to know what it was. Get ready. Turn to Kṛṣṇa. Turn your face away even a little from your attachments and entanglements—wife, children, house, garden, all things that are dear to you, and from the duties which may not be dear to you but seem real now—mortgage, car, physical therapy. You will have to leave it all. And beyond these things, detach yourself from the minutiae and trivia which are accompanying you through this life, floating through your memory and dreams, sometimes just below the surface and sometimes fully visible. Those will also be destroyed at the time of death. We are eternal, but a lot of what we think of as "me and my world" is not eternal. Therefore, the *Vedas* call it a dream. It will be annihilated in the end.

How painful death is. Fortunate people can live in a $300,000 house made of bricks, with a nice expanse of lawn and three cars parked in the driveway. Imagine the good fortune of those living in a suburb like Potomac, Maryland. But death has no boundaries. They leave their lives sometimes unceremoniously by heart attack, or even ignominiously at the hands of a thug who throws them down on the street while he makes off with a few credit cards. One way or another, we all have to leave.

Kṛṣṇa consciousness helps us face this truth. Bit by bit, we gain conviction about the eternality of the soul and then act accordingly to make a better next life. People need this information so that they can stop acting like animals. Anyone who does not achieve success at the time of death is a fool. Life means more than eating whatever tastes good or having sex thousands of times and with dozens of people and then sleeping when you're not trying to defend it all and dying like a cat or a dog.

SDG singing and clapping:

hare kṛṣṇa hare kṛṣṇa, kṛṣṇa kṛṣṇa hare hare
hare rāma hare rāma, rāma rāma hare hare

C stands for centigrade, *F* for Fahrenheit. Take your choice in *tulasī's* house and read by one standard or another. But the effect is the same: when it's hot, it's hot. When it's cold, it's cold.

We were talking yesterday on the radio show about being alone. A similar point is being quiet. It's hard to find quietness in the modern world. Even if you're alone, there's always some machine vibrating somewhere. Quietness doesn't only mean the absence of sound vibration; it means peace. There are sounds which are conducive to peace—the wind, birds chirping, natural sounds. There are other sounds, though—the sound of Kṛṣṇa's flute, the *vīṇā*, the sound of the sincerely spoken benediction, "May Kṛṣṇa bless you," the sound of God's names.

SDG singing and clapping:

hare kṛṣṇa hare kṛṣṇa, kṛṣṇa kṛṣṇa hare hare
hare rāma hare rāma, rāma rāma hare hare

Jaya rādhā-mādhava, kuñja-bihārī. Prabhupāda chanting in the Los Angeles temple, while the chorus of two or three hundred Americans swelled. Only a few years before, those Americans had never even heard of Kṛṣṇa. Now they seemed like Vaikuṇṭha angels to Prabhupāda—the men with shaved heads and the women in *sarīs*, all of them clean and bright-faced, devotees of Kṛṣṇa. All of them responding: *jaya rādhā-mādhava, kuñja-bihārī. Gopī-jana-vallabha giri-vara-dhārī.* The men playing the *mṛdaṅgas* the way Prabhupāda taught them, getting better with practice, and *karatālas* keeping time. *Yaśodā-nandana braja-jana-rañjana. Yaśodā-nandana braja-jana-rañjana.* Prabhupāda keeping his eyes closed, seeing Rādhā and Mādhava in the *kuñjas.* He is the Lord and She is His dearmost devotee. Kṛṣṇa, who lifts Govardhana Hill, whom all the *gopīs* love, Yaśodā's darling, is wandering on the banks of the Yamunā. *Yamunā-tire vana-cārī.* Prabhupāda opens his eyes and looks again to this world, to his happy, hopeful, neophyte children. He looks at them with such compassion and hope, and in retrospect, perhaps we can now see a little poignancy in his gaze. He knows that their karma for sense gratification will catch up to them again and he feels sorry about that. Still, he extends himself as much as he can, giving them the strength of Vedic knowledge and inspiration and encouragement to continue.

Prabhupāda didn't just close his eyes and stay with his vision of Goloka Vṛndāvana, just as he didn't stay in Vṛndāvana. He came to the West and went from place to place, absorbed in preaching Kṛṣṇa consciousness. Wake up, wake up sleeping souls! Don't be plunged into this sleep again. Come to Kṛṣṇa consciousness. Chant *Jaya rādhā-mādhava.*

Prabhupāda taught us two things: material detachment and attachment to Kṛṣṇa. He taught us that we couldn't just learn about Kṛṣṇa and then not do anything about it. *Mahātmānas tu māṁ pārtha, daivīṁ prakṛtim āśritāḥ/ bhajanty ananya-manaso*—always engage in serving Kṛṣṇa. *Satataṁ kīrtayanto māṁ*—always chant Hare Kṛṣṇa.

I wish to always be active in the service of my spiritual master, Śrīla Prabhupāda. Let us offer our respectful obeisances unto the lotus feet of such a spiritual master, who has poured nectarean rain on us to relieve us from the fire of repeated birth and death, who is ecstatic in his preaching and chanting, who teaches us how to worship in the temple, who gives us *kṛṣṇa-prasādam,* who has an intimate relationship with Rādhā and Kṛṣṇa in Goloka Vṛndāvana, and who is acknowledged by all the great authorities as the direct representative of Kṛṣṇa. By pleasing him, Kṛṣṇa is pleased. If you do not follow, if you do not please the spiritual master, you cannot have any place in Kṛṣṇa's service. All glories to Śrīla Prabhupāda.

So, that's the end of our radio show for today. One squeaky-voiced attempt to remind us all of this wonderful opportunity. Stay in Kṛṣṇa consciousness one way or another—by reading the books, by associating with devotees, by attending devotional festivals, and by being absorbed in service. Don't become discouraged by whatever obstacles you meet. They are part of the process. Kick out *māyā.* She's not offering you anything you need. Stay with Kṛṣṇa. Simply pray for perpetual engagement in Kṛṣṇa's service. Kṛṣṇa will give it to you if you really want it.

56

SDG singing and clapping:

> *hare kṛṣṇa hare kṛṣṇa, kṛṣṇa kṛṣṇa hare hare*
> *hare rāma hare rāma, rāma rāma hare hare*

Haribol. It's Sunday and overcast. We have our portable studio out here at the end of the meadow in this backyard. We have a studio audience of flies, big ones that buzz around and don't particularly want to land on anybody, and a revolving water sprayer out in the garden. We also have the background music provided by the electric saw. Madhu's work partner has finally arrived. He's cutting big pieces of wood so Madhu can build a new interior in the van.

Sunday afternoon means that I spent the morning speaking the *Bhāgavatam* to the devotees. It was more than a formal presentation, and I used my intelligence as best I could to answer their questions. When you speak like that, you take the position of being the one with all the answers. I answered their questions, but I also wanted things to be realistic. I couldn't just give pat answers because their intelligent minds wouldn't be satisfied with that. Anyway, I gave what I could and I think they were satisfied.

After the program, I felt some exultation. Then that passed and I had lunch and a rest and here I am. This morning's experience made me think of a topic I would like to discuss. I wrote myself this note: "Discuss phenomenon of how talking of Kṛṣṇa consciousness doesn't deplete you. Yet in one sense it does, or it seems like it does." I always want to go alone after a lecture to replace what was depleted. What is it I want to say to myself to help myself recover after I've given all I could in a lecture to devotees?

I don't feel depleted right now, however, but there is a difference between giving out what you have and replenishing it. One could overdo any kind of analysis like this. The general feeling among devotees is that the more you give, the more you'll have. It works opposite to the principle that you have a certain amount of money. If you generously give that money away, you'll have nothing left. It's the same with food. Giving away Kṛṣṇa consciousness works on a different principle. As you give, it is instantly replenished and you are able to give more and more.

I think although I can accept that as generally true, it does seem that if you give and give without some kind of replenishing, you start to feel a strain. A liberated devotee can keep giving Kṛṣṇa because to "give" Kṛṣṇa, you don't steal from your own stock. You just dip into the eternal current, into the limitless ocean, and talk about Kṛṣṇa. There's no end to it. Rather, you feel like doing it more and more. We can see this phenomenon in the *Bhāgavatam* as Śukadeva Gosvāmī speaks and Mahārāja Parīkṣit hears.

It may be different for a tiny, not-yet-liberated *jīva*, especially if he's a counselor and he's always listening to other people's material problems. Sometimes he spends so much energy listening that he doesn't have enough mental peace and space to practice his own *sādhana*. He gets worn down. He may begin to feel lust again, or his tendency to be strict might slacken. He recognizes that the counseling is taking time from his personal practices, but he thinks, "What the hell, I've got to help these people." Then he becomes proud. People tell him he's wonderful and helpful—a touchstone—and he believes it. He thinks he's still immersed in *brahma-niṣṭhām*. Unfortunately, he's not, and his quiet moments of dissatisfaction prove that to him.

I'm sorry, I feel like I'm not talking from the heart. That's what happens to me when I feel the need to replenish myself. I start making speeches instead of talking from the heart. I lose my inner quietness. I become—what's that word, stentorian? I find myself projecting my voice even when I'm alone, and I take a lot of time to make a point while I try to hold my audience's attention. That, instead of some guy talking what he really feels as if he had nothing to lose and nothing to count. Whenever I get like that, it makes me want to take stock of myself and to build up my reserves.

I suppose one reason for this is that I have integrity. Out of the need to give yet another lecture, I don't want to start saying things I'm not practicing myself. Another reason is that I tend not to separate topics according to "private" and "public." I just want to go for what's true. I don't want to always meditate on how to please and satisfy an audience, or how to balance others' minds. If I speak too much renunciation, then the householders might object. If I speak too permissively, the very same householder devotee might object.

I don't always like to map out the territory for my listeners, assuring them that I'm aware of all the broader limits of the topic and that what I finally say about it is my well-considered opinion. The ability to always reassure an audience, the confidence and deftness to do it, requires a kind of aggressiveness which reminds me of an entertainer or a doctor, counselor, "strong" person, enlightener, teacher. The teacher is a good one, and spiritual master, guru, gurujī. He who holds others up.

I hope I don't sound sarcastic about all this. I don't mean to if I do. All I'm trying to say is that there is an area of the self that is private and needs expression, and when you cultivate that area, it's bound to have an effect on the public realm of expression too.

Enough said. I read some sketches of the early Church fathers, Christian monks. One of them was described as always trying to be in a place where he couldn't see others and they couldn't see him, even when there was a gathering of parishioners or a church meeting. It's helpful to one's spiritual life to get out of the limelight.

In our society, this is the position we usually give to women. We tell them they're not important, so they should stand in the back or we give them the worst seats. No one wants to see them. Although they're at a disadvantage, the women try to hear what's being said, and sometimes they feel excluded. This monk wanted that position. He wanted to cultivate his inner life without disturbance.

I know I say this at the risk of being misunderstood—mister understood and miss understood went to a party in the grotto where they prayed without worrying that it was cold and people would object and censor the matter.

SDG singing and clapping:

> *hare kṛṣṇa hare kṛṣṇa, kṛṣṇa kṛṣṇa hare hare*
> *hare rāma hare rāma, rāma rāma hare hare*

I wrote an author's note to this collection of radio shows, which are to be gathered together into a book. I'm satisfied that I expressed what I was trying to do—to preach Kṛṣṇa consciousness, to speak without the constraints of censors or critics, and to pray—all in the mode of a radio show.

O brave new age, O brave psychological attitude, O interesting speaker, tell us more.

Grass blades of grass, I used to pick you and play with you, placing you between my thumbs and making a shrill-sounding whistle. Green grass, you were the friend of a lonely boy who wanted to live close to the earth despite his secrets and the stuff he kept in his pockets. Boys are not angels.

This morning at the meeting, I saw Patri's boy. He's only three or four and his face was full of abrasions. He said he fell while speeding on his bicycle. It was shocking, like a strawberry mash, but he wasn't badly hurt.

After the talk, everyone came up for sweets. He was the first boy. He asked loudly, "Please give me a sweet," and then, "Thank you very much." All the ladies laughed. As I was going out the door, another boy, a little older than Patri's boy, came up to tell me that he also had scratches from riding his bike. I didn't see any scratches, but since having scratches seemed to be a good way to get attention, he made it clear that he had scratches too.

When we talk, when we write, sometimes we're saying that we have scratches too. I once read a book of writing meditations. The author said that what's interesting is not so much our smooth sailing, but our experience of suffering. So show me your wound stripes. For some of us, it's not a question of showing them, they're all over our faces. All we have to do is speak honestly. But without Kṛṣṇa, it's all useless.

This morning, I recited the verse where Kṛṣṇa says that without Kṛṣṇa consciousness, everything is a waste of time. Someone asked whether this included Kṛṣṇa conscious activities. He thought the *Bhagavad-gītā* says that anything we do is good. Maybe, but why be wishy-washy?

Please forgive me for taking so much time on this radio show to recover out loud. I guess since it's taken so long, you can see what I meant at the beginning of the show about being depleted. I want to express Kṛṣṇa consciousness. As a benediction, I want to have millions of ears to go on hearing Kṛṣṇa's message spoken by pure devotees. Those pure devotees pick up the saffron particles at the lotus feet of the Lord, and when they speak, spread them to others. I want to hear from those pure devotees.

In Chapter Thirteen of the Tenth Canto, Śukadeva Gosvāmī congratulates Mahārāja Parīkṣit on his enthusiasm to hear about Kṛṣṇa. He says that pure devotees are attached to hearing about Kṛṣṇa the way materialists are attached to hearing about sex. *Nivṛtta-tarṣair upagīyamānād.* One is advanced when he has the taste to go on hearing the apparently same *kṛṣṇa-kathā* and to get to know Kṛṣṇa. After all, isn't that why we hear about Kṛṣṇa, to get to know Him?

Don't feel hopeless because you don't yet have that taste. Be encouraged. Prabhupāda always encouraged us. He was so perfect that he simultaneously did two things: he let us feel good and happy to be devotees, and he kept us humble by reminding us how far we were from the actual goal. He never let us think we were Vaiṣṇavas, but he encouraged us to be the servants of the Vaiṣṇavas. It didn't take us any imagination to know that he was the Vaiṣṇava we should serve. Who could appreciate all of Prabhupāda's talents? His Godbrothers didn't know how he did it. He was so expert at keeping the Westerners encouraged with the right amount of balance. All glories to Śrīla Prabhupāda.

Whenever we heard Prabhupāda speak about Kṛṣṇa, Kṛṣṇa became real to us. That was the wonderful thing—it's still the wonderful thing. Prabhupāda makes God a person for us.

I want to recover my Kṛṣṇa consciousness, lost for eons. Please, Lord, let me be used by You to please You. I don't want my life to be useless labor. Let me climb into the ocean of Kṛṣṇa conscious nectar and swim there. Please allow me to continue chanting, not as a wishy-washy or nonsense person who likes to hear himself talk, but as Your devotee.

57

SDG singing and clapping:

hare kṛṣṇa hare kṛṣṇa, kṛṣṇa kṛṣṇa hare hare
hare rāma hare rāma, rāma rāma hare hare

Haribol. I'll try to be controlled and not just say anything that pops into my mind. I mean, not the immediate surface stuff. I'd rather make a real presentation.

Śrīla Prabhupāda is with us. This morning I heard a morning walk tape. Candanācārya was asking Prabhupāda, "You say in your books that Kṛṣṇa consciousness is easy, but determination is difficult." Prabhupāda replied that you gain determination through austerity. Our austerity is to follow the four rules and chant sixteen rounds—to follow our initiation vows. Prabhupāda said the difference between an animal and a human being is that an animal can't make a promise whereas a human being can. That's because an animal has no sense of honor. You feed it, you pet it, but it doesn't have any concept of gratitude and honor.

As far as I'm concerned, Prabhupāda's answer was right to the point. When you listen to tapes that are twenty years old, you have to wonder what devotees had in mind, even subconsciously, when they asked these kinds of questions. Prabhupāda was always pertinent in his answers, although devotees were sometimes put off by the fact that Prabhupāda either apparently didn't respond directly to their questions or seemed to be accusing them of deviation.

I remember how it was on those walks. We tried to engage our spiritual master in polite and meaningful conversation to clear up our philosophical points. Sometimes devotees even seemed to be interrogating Prabhupāda, especially if he perceived any contradiction in Prabhupāda's presentation on a certain point. "I detect some contradiction in what you have written in several different places, or it's not clear to me. You may not have understood, dear Gurujī, all the implications of what you said, so now I am asking you to make it clearer." Then the guru turns around and seems to almost accuse the disciple of not following, or of not wanting to follow, the principles.

On this tape, Candanācārya came back, "You say that determination comes from *tapasya,* but performing *tapasya* requires determination." He's implying that Prabhupāda hasn't fully answered the question.

Logically, you could say that Candanācārya's question was valid and that Prabhupāda would now have to explain the source of determination, but no, Prabhupāda hammered right on the same point: "You promised at initiation that you would follow. If you can't follow, why did you get initiated? Why did you promise? You are an animal. You are no better than an animal." Then he added, "You should not have gotten initiated. As in a court, the person swears on the Bible, on God, on God's honor, God's word, that I shall tell the whole truth. If he is found out to be lying, then that is punishable. In the same way, before the fire, before Viṣṇu, before the Vaiṣṇavas, you promised."

Prabhupāda goes on to make it clear that there's really no logical game involved here, no puzzle, and there's no use pleading that we didn't get what we needed to follow when we took initiation. Prabhupāda doesn't want to hear that. He knows that we promised and therefore we should have the strength to follow. The strength comes from our decency as human beings. Don't come later and ask how to follow something you have already promised to do.

That was one exchange on the walk. Prabhupāda had other disciples present. Svarūpa Dāmodara then asked about the function of the brain. Prabhupāda described the brain as a machine. Svarūpa Dāmodara said, "Yes, but such a machine! There are nine billion cells in the brain." Prabhupāda answered, "There may be so many billions. That is because you have been given a very good machine. You have been given that machine, but the soul is the body to work that machine or some other machine that you get."

Then the talk went on to some other topic before Svarūpa Dāmodara said, "Back to the brain." In this way, questions and answers were exchanged. These exchanges were invigorating for Prabhupāda and are invigorating for us to hear, but the hearers have to be careful not to be thrown off by externals and to try to hear deeply. Usually after hearing a lecture or a room conversation, I flip the tape and hear the other side right away. But I also realize that it's sometimes better to just stop and let what I have heard sink in.

SDG singing and clapping:

hare kṛṣṇa hare kṛṣṇa, kṛṣṇa kṛṣṇa hare hare
hare rāma hare rāma, rāma rāma hare hare

It has been raining here. Before I could come out to this picnic bench and table, I had to wipe off the water. Now the sun has come out and brought with it some slow-flying insects. They cling to you. Of course, if I were a killer, I could easily wipe them out. But I'm not. I have to tolerate.

I began reading *Bhagavad-gītā* verses aloud this morning, ones that I had previously picked out as Kṛṣṇa speaking to us. I finally started putting them on tape—that's the first stage—and thinking, "If I continue to play this even while we travel, then I'll get some idea of how to pray with them."

The first thing is to record them and then hear them. Get a little familiar with them and then in some cases, even memorize them. Then, I hope, starting to go out with them on my walks in the future. When I get time, not right now, not this month, not this day, not this retreat, but at a future one, I want to take them with me for prayer walks.

They're sawing wood for the van's new interior.

hare kṛṣṇa hare kṛṣṇa, kṛṣṇa kṛṣṇa hare hare
hare rāma hare rāma, rāma rāma hare hare
hare kṛṣṇa hare kṛṣṇa, kṛṣṇa kṛṣṇa hare hare
hare rāma hare rāma, rāma rāma hare hare

There seems to be a limit to what I am willing to reveal on these shows. After all, we're retrieving this sound vibration and I'm aware of that. I don't want anything I say to be held against me. I'm copping the Fifth Amendment.

Now the whole idea—telling you, not telling you—am I supposed to tell somebody something? Am I talking to somebody? Is my listener a big psychiatrist's ear? Is there something I'm supposed to do? An expectation I'm supposed to fulfill? I don't want it to be like that. I want to be alone and speak to people who want to hear. I'm not even imagining the people who may hear this and not like it. Otherwise, I'd have to stop these shows.

Which means that the radio shows haven't reached the level of commitment I feel for the writing sessions.

Hare Kṛṣṇa. I'm feeling gagged. Feeling not deeply unworthy myself, but feeling hung up with this expression, that you won't like it, it won't be good. Who has time to hear? Why should anybody have time to hear the meanderings of one Satsvarūpa dāsa? I'm sorry I ran into this. The voice is supposed to be a better warrior even than the pen in getting through these things.

Well, let's talk about Kṛṣṇa. Of course, I told you what I'm starting to do with the *Bhagavad-gītā*. I read the verses where Kṛṣṇa talks about the immortality of the soul. Just now, I opened the book right to a page that is central to the theme of Kṛṣṇa speaking directly to us. The verse is 4.4, where Arjuna asks: "The sun-god Vivasvān is senior by birth to You. How am I to understand that in the beginning You instructed this science to him?"

This verse is not Kṛṣṇa speaking, but it primes us to hear from Him. Arjuna is inviting Kṛṣṇa to speak by asking a doubtful question. In the purport, Prabhupāda talks about this great opportunity we have when Kṛṣṇa prepares to speak. Prabhupāda writes, " . . . Arjuna put this question before Kṛṣṇa so that He would describe Himself without being depicted by the demons, who always try to distort Him in a way understandable to the demons and their followers. It is necessary that everyone, for his own interest, know the science of Kṛṣṇa. Therefore, when Kṛṣṇa Himself speaks about Himself, it is auspicious for all the worlds."

While I was eating lunch today and listening to a tape, I began to think of taking what he said and repeating it. I even imagined the audience. Some years ago, I spoke at a Hindu conference. Today, I imagined I had another Hindu audience who were mainly interested in hearing about Hinduism. Prabhupāda defined the word "Hindu" as a misnomer. Actually, he was originally talking about demigod worship and how we may worship the demigods if we want Kṛṣṇa consciousness from them. We'll go to anyone, we'll go anywhere, if it will enhance our Kṛṣṇa consciousness. We're not really worshipping the demigod or the rich patron; we're begging on Kṛṣṇa's behalf.

He mentioned mothers. He used the word *amba.* Then he said that the name Bombay came from the word *"amba,"* because there's worship of a Kālī deity there. That's a misnomer—*amba* to Bombay based on the Britishers' mispronunciation—similarly, the word "Hindu" was coined because of a mispronunciation. The word "Hindu" doesn't exist in the *Vedas.*

I thought about what he was saying and imagined how I would present this teaching to an audience. I thought I wouldn't completely deny the meaning of the word "Hindu," but at least I could show that I was aware of its source and that they too should know that it's not a Vedic word. The real concept of what they want to celebrate and identify with is India's religion, which should not be something foisted upon them by the mispronunciation of outsiders. They should study and develop their own culture, *sanātana-dharma.* Then I could explain *that* term and its rich associations.

The living entity is *sanātana,* eternal. God is *sanātana,* eternal. The science of the relationship between the living entity and God is known as *sanātana-dharma.* The Lord's abode is called *sanātana-*

dhāma. Sanātana-dharma is not sectarian; it is the constitutional nature of all living beings.

Hindus usually like to think of their religion as being spread all over the world. On the other hand, they don't like to admit foreigners into their culture. They don't like to think that white men can quickly become Hindus. Some deny that it's possible at all. That's because they are absorbed in bodily consciousness. How can a preacher sidestep those feelings? He may have to be careful not to tear them apart, but instead present himself as unfortunate for not having taken birth in Bharata-varṣa.

Then I imagined myself speaking on the Fifth Canto verses about how fortunate it is to be born in Bharata-varṣa. That's a different angle and that does admit that someone who is born in India has the special privilege of inheriting the wisdom of the Vedic sages. But the word *Bharata-varṣa* can also be taken to mean the whole world. In either case, the wisdom of Bharata-varṣa is meant to be shared with the whole world because everyone is part and parcel of God. India is the land where Kṛṣṇa appeared. How glorious it is! Therefore, the Indians should be in the forefront of the Kṛṣṇa consciousness movement. We Westerners, who haven't heard about Kṛṣṇa from birth, can offer due respect to those who are born as Indians, but at the same time, who don't confine *sanātana-dharma* to small-minded bodily consciousness.

I was imagining all this when Madhu came in and asked me something about the size of the desk in the van and whether I had finished lunch so he could take the plate out. I spoke to him, but I continued to live in my imaginary lecture hall.

When Kṛṣṇa speaks for Himself, it's auspicious, and when the pure devotee, Prabhupāda, speaks, it's also auspicious. Hearing from Prabhupāda allows us to hear about Kṛṣṇa from the devotees instead of the demons.

". . . such explanations by Kṛṣṇa Himself may appear to be strange because the demons always study Kṛṣṇa from their own standpoint, but those who are devotees heartily welcome the statements of Kṛṣṇa when they are spoken by Kṛṣṇa Himself. The devotees will always worship such authoritative statements of Kṛṣṇa because they are always eager to know more and more about Him."

Then I went back to thinking about prayer. I don't want to concoct a prayer system, but I do want to be able to pray in a personal way, and in a way that frees me from ordinariness, mechanicalness, duty, memorization. I am looking for something more mystical in prayer, something that delves deeper than the intellect and actually enters the heart. I want to recognize Kṛṣṇa when He's speaking to me. I want to understand *how* He is speaking to me. I want to hear from Him.

And I want the *Bhagavad-gītā* to become my prayer book. I want to understand it fully. *Vāsudevaḥ sarvam iti, sa mahātmā su-durlabhaḥ. Vedaiś ca sarvair aham eva vedyo, vedānta-kṛd veda-vid eva cāham.* I want to have faith.

Speaking about Hinduism, the *Bhagavad-gītā* is not the book of the Hindus. Kṛṣṇa is not the God of the Hindus. He is not a myth. He is not a "Hindu god," as opposed to the "Christian God."

I want to see Kṛṣṇa beyond storybook paintings and children's coloring books, sentimental paintings, Indian movie actors playing Kṛṣṇa, and Kṛṣṇa's name being taken in vain. Kṛṣṇa, Kṛṣṇa, the real Kṛṣṇa, as He spoke Himself, as I can hear Him. This is Kṛṣṇa consciousness.

58

SDG singing and clapping:

hare kṛṣṇa hare kṛṣṇa, kṛṣṇa kṛṣṇa hare hare
hare rāma hare rāma, rāma rāma hare hare

Haribol. This radio show is being conducted outdoors at a picnic table in a backyard. It has been raining—it has stopped temporarily—and I had to wipe the water off the chair and the table before I could start. In the same way, I want to wipe off the fear and contradiction involved in trying to do this show while simultaneously speaking to myself and to an audience. I could talk about that contradiction, but I would rather just wipe it off and sit down and talk about Kṛṣṇa consciousness.

Talk about Kṛṣṇa consciousness. It seems the thing we want to do is to speak candidly from the heart. We want to serve Kṛṣṇa with genuine feeling and feel purified. Prabhupāda gave us the secret when he spoke about writing: a writer writes for his own purification first. That means that simply by speaking about Kṛṣṇa, who is all pure, the writer cleanses all impurities from his heart.

naṣṭa-prāyeṣv abhadreṣu
nityaṁ bhāgavata-sevayā
bhagavaty uttama-śloke
bhaktir bhavati naiṣṭhikī

Dirty things in his heart are removed.

śṛṇvatāṁ sva-kathāḥ kṛṣṇaḥ
puṇya-śravaṇa-kīrtanaḥ
hṛdy antaḥ stho hy abhadrāṇi
vidhunoti suhṛt satām

It's also said in the Second Canto that when the *Bhāgavatam* is spoken, the speaker, the hearer, and the place all become purified. These are auspicious topics. And, of course, the obvious extension of that is that since these topics are so auspicious and purifying, why not preach them widely? It doesn't matter whether we understand how the purification is taking place; we simply have to have faith that it does and repeat Kṛṣṇa's message without changing it.

Kṛṣṇa conscious purification is deep. Prabhupāda recognized that those who were coming for some superficial titillation would find the topics dry. Therefore, few are interested. He knew that hearing only the outer form of Kṛṣṇa consciousness is difficult—it sounds too much like theological talk. People are more accustomed to listening to things that attract their material senses—nice music, a speaker with good intonation, etc.—and they don't get that gratification when the speech is full of foreign words, talk of sin and God consciousness and morality. When a devotee starts to describe the misery of material life and how we are all entangled in it, it can seem remote. They fly away, unfortunately.

Devotees also experience the same problem. Sometimes the philosophy has too much technical terminology and it's usually all in Sanskrit. It's also sometimes hard to understand the wonder of what is being said. We have no direct experience of Kṛṣṇa. Or, we want a quicker access to the nectar, but it just can't be gained so quickly.

When we actually become serious, we'll accept the seriousness of our situation. Then we'll take any edification as valuable and begin to understand it as nectar. The whole process will become nectarean. It won't be dependent on whether there's a harmonium or cymbals or an electric bass in the *kīrtana*, but our attachment to Kṛṣṇa will be awakened by something more internal—something that has been covered over for many lifetimes and that we had given up hope of ever finding.

Any discussion is nectarean, even the most preliminary discourse on the nature of the soul. In the beginning, we need proof. Therefore, there are so many analogies and proofs. Once we become more advanced, we accept Kṛṣṇa's authority. Step by step, we go forward. It requires concentration, which unfortunately we have in limited amounts. Life is tense. Arjuna only had an hour to spare to hear Kṛṣṇa's discourse on the *Bhagavad-gītā*. Therefore, Kṛṣṇa got to the heart of the matter quickly:

sarva-dharmān parityajya
mām ekaṁ śaraṇaṁ vraja
ahaṁ tvāṁ sarva-pāpebhyo
mokṣayiṣyāmi mā śucaḥ

Lord Caitanya made this message even easier and more accessible: Kṛṣṇa has put all His transcendental energies into His holy name. Therefore, chant Hare Kṛṣṇa Hare Kṛṣṇa, Kṛṣṇa Kṛṣṇa Hare Hare/ Hare Rāma Hare Rāma, Rāma Rāma Hare Hare.

Let's get to the heart of the matter. We encounter Kṛṣṇa consciousness for a few tense moments in this life and if we don't take to it fully, we'll have to come back and try again.

If we're chanting Hare Kṛṣṇa properly, we'll be like the bee stuck in the lotus flower. Have you ever seen a bee stuck in a fragrant flower? He's intoxicated by the fragrance and the honey. He goes on tasting and gathering until he can't pull himself away from it. When will we land in the internal energy and understand what chanting is? The chanting is Kṛṣṇa. Kṛṣṇa is relief from confusion. Kṛṣṇa is the way back to Godhead. Kṛṣṇa is the love that we seek and have not been able to find life after life. He is the beauty, the satisfaction, and the real essence of life.

SDG singing and clapping:

hare kṛṣṇa hare kṛṣṇa, kṛṣṇa kṛṣṇa hare hare
hare rāma hare rāma, rāma rāma hare hare

I said in the beginning that this broadcast, no matter where it takes place, has an inner shape. You have to enter it as you would enter a cave or a bottle that is capped. You have to open it and get inside. Sometimes the initial work throws us off, or once inside we get restless due to our material desires. But have faith. Gradually, we'll learn how to always stay in the internal energy.

My time is running out, both on this radio show and for purification. Please make me a stronger person to serve You and serve others and taste the nectar of Kṛṣṇa consciousness. I want to get out of this material world even while living in it, all for Lord Caitanya's cause.

All glories to Prabhupāda. All glories to you, my listeners. May we be able to speak better next time and the time after that. May Kṛṣṇa appear in these words and these places in our hearts. Let us not take advantage of each other, but serve Kṛṣṇa together and not be afraid. Pray to Kṛṣṇa to chant His holy names with taste and affection.

SDG singing and clapping:

hare kṛṣṇa hare kṛṣṇa, kṛṣṇa kṛṣṇa hare hare
hare rāma hare rāma, rāma rāma hare hare

59

SDG singing and clapping:

> *hare kṛṣṇa hare kṛṣṇa, kṛṣṇa kṛṣṇa hare hare*
> *hare rāma hare rāma, rāma rāma hare hare*

On this show, I'll try to glorify Kṛṣṇa from the texts of the *śāstra.* I will also try to do more than repeat it mechanically. I want to have some feeling for what I am repeating.

People who have enthusiasm about what they are speaking can preach well. In mundane academic circles, they call it "scholarly enthusiasm." I remember the enthusiasm of some of my college teachers; those particular teachers had a genuine love for the poets and writers, or American history, or the mathematics they were teaching. Because of their dedication, the students both learned and became enthusiastic to understand the subject matter. The perfection of scholarly enthusiasm is a devotee's enthusiasm for and dedication to Kṛṣṇa conscious *śāstra*. That dedication is never mundane; it evolves into love of God.

Kṛṣṇa is a historical figure who appeared five thousand years ago. He spoke the *Bhagavad-gītā* near the end of His pastimes on this earth, and His other activities are described in various scriptures, especially in the Tenth Canto of the *Śrīmad-Bhāgavatam*. There it's described that Kṛṣṇa is not only a historical figure, but the Supreme Personality of Godhead. He's not a human being with mortal limits. Aside from the Tenth Canto, the *Śrīmad-Bhāgavatam* describes His different appearances in this world in His different forms. It also describes eternal Vaikuṇṭha and tells us that all these forms of God are expansions of Kṛṣṇa. *Ete cāṁśa-kalāḥ puṁsaḥ, kṛṣṇas tu bhagavān svayam.* Kṛṣṇa is the origin of all the incarnations.

For knowledge about God, we have to consult scripture. We cannot understand Him by what's called the "enlightenment consensus"—the opinion that reality is compromised of gross matter and three dimensional space. You won't find Him there—He's *adhokṣaja*. He's behind that. We have to learn that from the scriptures.

We get faith in the hearing process when we hear the pure devotee's explanations of the *śāstra*. If after hearing about Kṛṣṇa from the pure devotee, we reject this transcendental knowledge, then Kṛṣṇa says:

avajānanti māṁ mūḍhā
mānuṣīṁ tanum āśritam
paraṁ-bhāvam ajānanto
mama bhūta maheśvaram

na māṁ duṣkṛtino mūḍhāḥ
prapadyante narādhamāḥ
māyayāpahṛta-jñānā
āsuraṁ bhāvam āśritāḥ

There are strong words for people who don't accept Kṛṣṇa as the Supreme Personality of Godhead. "Fools deride Me when I appear in My human form. They don't know My transcendental nature as the Supreme Lord of all that be."

Prabhupāda says that there are impersonalists who say that Kṛṣṇa is a historical person and not God. They think the Absolute Truth is formless, but Kṛṣṇa appeared to have a human form. Prabhupāda says that although the personalist and the impersonalist will fight with one another perpetually, a perfect devotee in Kṛṣṇa consciousness knows that although Kṛṣṇa is the Supreme Personality, He is all-pervading. This is confirmed in the *Brahma-saṁhitā.* Although His personal abode is Goloka Vṛndāvana and He lives there eternally, by His different manifestations and plenary expansions, He is present everywhere in all parts of the material and spiritual creation.

SDG singing and clapping:

hare kṛṣṇa hare kṛṣṇa, kṛṣṇa kṛṣṇa hare hare
hare rāma hare rāma, rāma rāma hare hare

How am I doing? The answer to that question depends on who I ask. If I ask that question of a sympathetic devotee, he'll say, "You're doing okay. You look a little pale and your voice is a little monotonous, and I detect that you don't have complete conviction and enlivenment in what you're saying, but you're hanging in there and getting the philosophy right. You stayed with the *Bhagavad-gītā* and that's all I can ask. Even Prabhupāda said that his great credit was that he didn't try to change the message of *Bhagavad-gītā.* He just repeated it. I think you're doing all right." But if I ask that question of a nonsympathetic nondevotee, then watch out. I do like to ask that question, "How am I doing?" of myself, and I suppose that's all right.

I accepted *sannyāsa* from Prabhupāda for renunciation and preaching in 1972. Shortly after that, I wrote to Prabhupāda and admitted that I was not a bold preacher. Prabhupāda responded kindly: "Yes, I also in the beginning when I had to speak did not feel bold." That was a wonderful gift, that Prabhupāda made that personal disclosure to me. I could barely imagine a time when he wasn't bold, but I accepted his gift of his understanding my feelings of inadequacy.

Then he explained that I could become bold by practicing to speak Kṛṣṇa consciousness. "We are not cheating anybody." We're speaking on the authority of the Vedic knowledge and sages, so we *can* be bold. We're not going to hurt anybody. And we don't have to be bold on our own strength, but because we are representing the all-powerful Supreme Personality of Godhead, we can be as regal in our presentation as the king himself. He said of himself that he speaks boldly and no one can defeat him because he speaks only what his spiritual master and Kṛṣṇa have said.

Thus boldness becomes a symptom not of arrogance, but of humility. Humility is precious. Prabhupāda gave us the truth. Why should I be hesitant to present it?

I'm saying, therefore, that when I want to ask this question, "How am I doing?" I should be sure that I'm making a *paramparā* presentation and doing all right. But part of that "doing all right" is to go on and to not fumble. Fight for Kṛṣṇa against all forces within and without that want to prevent Kṛṣṇa consciousness from being accepted.

We can be confident that we're following the *paramparā* as long as we're not mixing in our own speculations or confusions. In a lot of what I present, you could say there is a mixture of straight texts and personal admissions. I find myself spending a considerable amount of time defending that. Not only do I do it, but I'm aware that it's controversial because there is little precedent in our *paramparā*. I break the ground for it, explain it, advocate it, justify it. It's a kind of obsession or need that I have. Well, the die is cast by now.

Part of why I make this kind of presentation is because I want my Kṛṣṇa conscious song to be a spontaneous one. I defend it more to blast through my own blocks than to convince others. Kṛṣṇa consciousness is usually presented according to time, place, and person. For the first time in history, people who are considered *mleccha-caṇḍālas*, who have been raised as meat-eaters, are taking to Kṛṣṇa consciousness. These people are becoming capable to present the Vedic knowledge in *paramparā*. They are preaching to the Western mindset. There's bound to be changes to how Kṛṣṇa consciousness has been presented since ancient times. We simply have to be skillful in order to do it faithfully.

What kind of changes? Well, we now have to address the relationship between Kṛṣṇa consciousness and Christianity, and Kṛṣṇa consciousness and Western science, and Kṛṣṇa consciousness and Western psychology. The *śāstras* have covered all areas of knowledge, but we may have to find new ways to apply them to the Western mindset.

In the West, of course, there is a relatively long-standing cultural development. Western culture is recent compared to Vedic culture, but people still have attachment for their literature and philosophy and theology. Kṛṣṇa consciousness is not one hundred percent opposed to everything in Western culture, so bridges can be built between them. Also, we can use the Western cultural forms to present Kṛṣṇa consciousness—novels, plays, poetry, art. Our contribution to modern Western culture is only beginning to develop. It takes some pioneer spirit to develop it further. There's got to be some daring, and it's inevitable that there will be what some devotees would call mixtures—what I prefer to call healthy hybrids. The Bhaktivedanta Institute scientists were almost all raised in Western culture; now they are turning and attacking their own science culture both by tearing at its arrogance and using its appeal to teach their own Vedic understanding. This is part of the intelligent spreading of Kṛṣṇa consciousness.

You know the example of the tree. The tree tells the woodsman that he can't chop him down unless he gets a handle for his ax. The woodsman then takes one of the tree's branches to make an ax handle and then cuts the tree down. We Westerners are the handles. Prabhupāda has fastened the Vedic, anti-materialistic philosophy to us and we're chopping down the tree.

In my case, if I can dismantle one person's false ego—namely, my own—and transform one dirty person into a devotee—namely, myself —and if I write about that process, then that is an artistic and useful addition to preaching in the West. It's a successful literary presentation and it's a successful life of surrender.

Even though I'm saying all this, I still feel apprehension every time I speak about this to ISKCON devotees. It's our tradition that everything should be done strictly according to *paramparā*. Nothing should be spoken that has not already been spoken. But Prabhupāda has also encouraged us to serve with our intelligence. He gave us the formula and the example, and we have to apply it, following in his footsteps, but with our own intelligence. The *Śrīmad-Bhāgavatam* purport says that devotees are always thinking of ways to present Kṛṣṇa consciousness in dynamic ways. Kṛṣṇa consciousness is itself dynamic. Nothing is stereotyped. We may invent methods of injecting Kṛṣṇa consciousness into the dull brains of Kali-yuga populations and thus serve in that way.

I would also like to say that although devotees accept this point when preaching to the nondevotee Westerners, they don't usually accept it when applied to preaching to devotees. Prabhupāda used to like us to print "how I came to Kṛṣṇa consciousness" stories in *Back To Godhead.* It's usually a dramatic story and it concentrates on a person's pre-Kṛṣṇa conscious state up until he became a devotee. The rest you fill in for yourself. Did he live happily ever after in ISKCON? Not likely. The further chapters are not usually so easily victorious. There is more than one struggle in the taking to Kṛṣṇa consciousness. There's "How I came to Kṛṣṇa consciousness" and "How I stayed in Kṛṣṇa consciousness." And we could add, "How I suffered in Kṛṣṇa consciousness," "How I thought I got rid of my *anarthas* after I left my girlfriend and college education behind, how the *anarthas* returned, how I persisted, how I made mistakes and deviated, how I came back to Kṛṣṇa consciousness and got Kṛṣṇa's and the devotees' mercy, how my history in ISKCON is checkered, but how I'm still hoping to surrender to Kṛṣṇa's lotus feet." That story is enduring and that's the story I'm interested in telling. That's why I'm defensive and why I dwell on this subject. Still, I would like to get over my defensiveness and get on with telling it.

This show is coming to an end—another backyard broadcast. Speaking loudly to the pines and to the white butterfly and to all the weeds that have stood alert and attentive—I thank you all. I don't mean to be joking about it, or if I joke, I share the joke with you. The joke's on me. You numerous living entities in your bodies, you know that Kṛṣṇa is the Lord. You don't have to defend it. He's your controller, birds sitting on posts. Have pity on us human beings. We tend to speculate and agonize. The joke's on me, the defender of the faith, who makes a big thing out of being a Westerner when actually we're all pure spirit souls.

Kṛṣṇa, I pray that You will deliver me from all this speckled ordinariness, down-fallenness, and let me sing boldly and without awkwardness, Hare Kṛṣṇa.

60

SDG singing and clapping:

hare kṛṣṇa hare kṛṣṇa, kṛṣṇa kṛṣṇa hare hare
hare rāma hare rāma, rāma rāma hare hare

What do you think about the difference between implicit and explicit Kṛṣṇa conscious expression? I remember reading something Thoreau wrote. He used to give lectures around his Massachusetts neighborhood. He made a little money at it, but not much because he wasn't in demand. Anyway, he made a comment about his own lecturing—I think he said this to an audience—that although they had come in because they were interested in the particular subject he was going to speak on, he was going to let them know that they were also going to get a dose of the speaker himself. I thought, "Yeah, that sounds like Thoreau and we're the better for it, that he gave himself in addition to information on the migration of the such-and-such duck."

I think it's natural that a speaker includes himself when he speaks. It's welcome. Devotees often think that it's all right for Thoreau to give us himself in his lectures, but somehow it's against the *paramparā* for devotees to give us themselves. It's true that the *Bhāgavatam* class is a particular forum. We expect to hear about Kṛṣṇa, the verse, and the Bhaktivedanta purport. I don't think it's so permissible to talk about ourselves while sitting on the speaker's *āsana*.

However, there are other forums where it's not so bad for a devotee to talk about himself. Or, perhaps I should be framing this as a rhetorical question: is it always a sign of false ego when a devotee talks about himself?

It seems a little artificial for people to say they're not interested in themselves and that therefore, when they communicate in earnest, they don't speak about themselves or that it is *māyā* if they do. At least we can see that neophyte devotees—and by that I don't mean a certain group of ISKCON devotees, I'm humbly referring to contemporaries the way Prabhupāda referred to us as conditioned souls and included himself—that devotees in our state want to know themselves. We can see this in how popular astrology and palm-reading are among devotees. These arts are part of Vedic civilization, but it is an indication of the devotees' need to know themselves in detail. Devotees also go to psychologists. It can also be said that part of the reason devotees get married is to have someone care about them. We all crave intimacy. Marriage provides a forum in which it's not considered *māyā* for another person to be interested in us as much as we are interested in ourselves.

Why do we suppress such self-expression, then? How can we say that nobody should reveal themselves or be interested in themselves or talk about themselves?

Anyway, I'm just venting some things that are on my mind.

When I am in a quiet mood, I often try to get in touch with myself intimately. I ask myself two questions: "What do you want to say?" and, "Kṛṣṇa, what do You want me to say?" To the first question, I go ahead and respond with whatever is on my mind. Then I turn to Kṛṣṇa in my heart. I have faith that Kṛṣṇa is in my heart, even if I don't perceive Him due to my lack of advancement. Still, He can speak through me and I can learn to listen to Him.

Self-realization depends on our purity and intelligence. *Teṣāṁ tv anta gataṁ pāpam, jñānaṁ puṇya-karmana . . . Dadāmi buddhi-yogaṁ taṁ, yena mām upayānti te.* Kṛṣṇa assures us that one engaged in His devotional service and who worships Him with love, will be given the intelligence by which to come to Him.

Very early in my relationship with Śrīla Prabhupāda, before I was initiated, I asked him a question on this point. "Swamijī, it seems to me that I can be many different persons. When I think of who I am, I think of a composite of different persons. The moods are like different persons I can be. I have heard that the best thing is to act to please Kṛṣṇa. My question is, how do I know which person in me or what kind of person Kṛṣṇa wants me to be?"

I have described this exchange in a couple of places. I condensed it in *haibun* form in the *haiku* book, *Under the Banyan Tree.* I said it was a complicated, mental question—too mental, and probably typical of a young, intellectual New Yorker. But it was a real question to me at the time. I kept thinking of all the selves within each of us that come out in different situations. Some help us survive privately and others help us to survive socially. I was aware of how I changed my nature to please different people.

Swamijī didn't answer the "mentalness" in my question, but he turned to some of the other people in the room and said, "This boy Steve is nice. He gives his money and he does typing. You also should do like this."

I wasn't the least bit disappointed with his response. After all, what was I seeking but love, encouragement, and exchange? He looked at me as I actually was in his eyes, who he wanted me to be—a simple servitor who gives plainly and practically what he has. He didn't see me as somebody so mental as to be ineffectual, so self-conscious as to not be able to serve.

This reminds me of something else. There's a line in a poem by Allen Ginsberg that refers to Bhaktivedanta Swami. You imagine Prabhupāda seeing Allen in London or in New York and Allen writing candidly about it afterward. "Swami Bhaktivedanta looks at me with a sad eye, at my impossible self-consciousness." Allen was aware that Prabhupāda saw his lack of surrender. Allen could not become a devotee of Kṛṣṇa. Prabhupāda was sad, compassionate. He saw that Allen was too much into himself and his own concoctions to surrender to Kṛṣṇa. Poets like Allen are too busy writing their own "song of God" to hear the message of *Bhagavad-gītā.* They don't have faith. They don't accept Kṛṣṇa's representative. As Allen summed it up, it was due to his self-consciousness. He could never get past his own false ego consciousness.

Prabhupāda looked at me differently. He saw a soul in the body of a young man, twenty-six years old, who lived in New York City. He saw my many impurities, but he also saw that by my actions, I had some sincerity. He praised that sincerity when he answered my question and I was satisfied.

I know I should say that that question has been answered for all time, but it hasn't, and Swamijī is not here in the same way to blast through a question like that—a question I'm crying out to have answered. After all, I wasn't asking that question so Prabhupāda would flatter me. I was crying out. I was trapped in my mirrored selves as I resorted to different kinds of selves and behaviors in order to get along in the world. Prabhupāda cut through that for me then. That's the benefit of having a guru right there. You put yourself on the line and he cracks or cuts the knot in your heart. He doesn't just work on the generic knot shared by all living entities, but very directly and personally works on your attachments and confusion. Now that Prabhupāda has disappeared, I feel the difference.

When I think of that question, I think also of a popular song. I don't remember the words exactly but it's something like this: "I can be good, I can be bad, I can be happy, I can be sad, it all depends on you." I can be any one of these things and not be particularly happy or sad, except relative to what you want, my dear. I will do what pleases you. As you act toward me, I respond toward you. I have no self per se, except for my relationship with you. I have no self except as you define it in our loving, living relationship, our demanding relationship. Kṛṣṇa consciousness means I am the eternal servant of Your lordship. What do you want me to do?

If we can sincerely ask that question, then Kṛṣṇa will tell us what He wants us to do. God told St. Francis, "Repair My Church." Lord Nityānanda told Kṛṣṇadāsa Kavirāja, "You did well today in the argument with your brother. Go to Vṛndāvana. There you will attain all things." Satyabhāmā told Rūpa Gosvāmī, "You are contemplating a drama you want to write in which the heroines will be Satyabhāmā and Rādhārāṇī. Rūpa, write two dramas, one for Satyabhāmā and one for Śrīmatī Rādhārāṇī."

I ask the question of myself, "What do you want to say?" Then I say, "My Lord, what do you want me to say?" Then what do I hear? Silence? Swamijī? What I now begin to speak is the best I can do and I hope it will take me forward.

SDG singing and clapping:

hare kṛṣṇa hare kṛṣṇa, kṛṣṇa kṛṣṇa hare hare
hare rāma hare rāma, rāma rāma hare hare

This radio show is coming to an end. It's a pretty day, gray, weeds growing unrestricted. Flies are buzzing around my water bottle. Madhu is working in the van several hundred feet away. Cows in the next yard, sheep too, but we're thinking of Kṛṣṇa, aren't we? Hare Kṛṣṇa is the sound vibration that saves us from being mundane and self-conscious, and from Prabhupāda being displeased with us.

Prabhupāda, please be pleased with me. Please accept my humble offering. Tell me what you want me to do so I can make a better offering. Give me the strength to surrender so my offering is not crooked or stunted. Please guide me. I am very fallen and in need of your help.

SDG singing and clapping:

hare kṛṣṇa hare kṛṣṇa, kṛṣṇa kṛṣṇa hare hare
hare rāma hare rāma, rāma rāma hare hare

Signing off from Brooklyn, Vṛndāvana, South India, material world, spiritual world . . .

Acknowledgments

I would like to thank the following disciples and friends who helped produce and print this book:

Baladeva Vidyābhūṣaṇa dāsa
Caitanya-dayā-devī dāsī
Guru-sevā-devī dāsī
Kaiśorī-devī dāsī
Kalki-devī dāsī
Keśīhanta dāsa
Lalita-mañjarī-devī dāsī
Lalitāmṛta-devī dāsī
Madana-mohana dāsa
Mādhava dāsa
Madhumaṅgala dāsa
Nārāyaṇa-kavaca dāsa
Prāṇadā-devī dāsī
Rukmavatī-devī dāsī
Yamunā-devī dāsī

Special thanks to Rādhā-Ramaṇa dāsa for his kind donation to print this book.